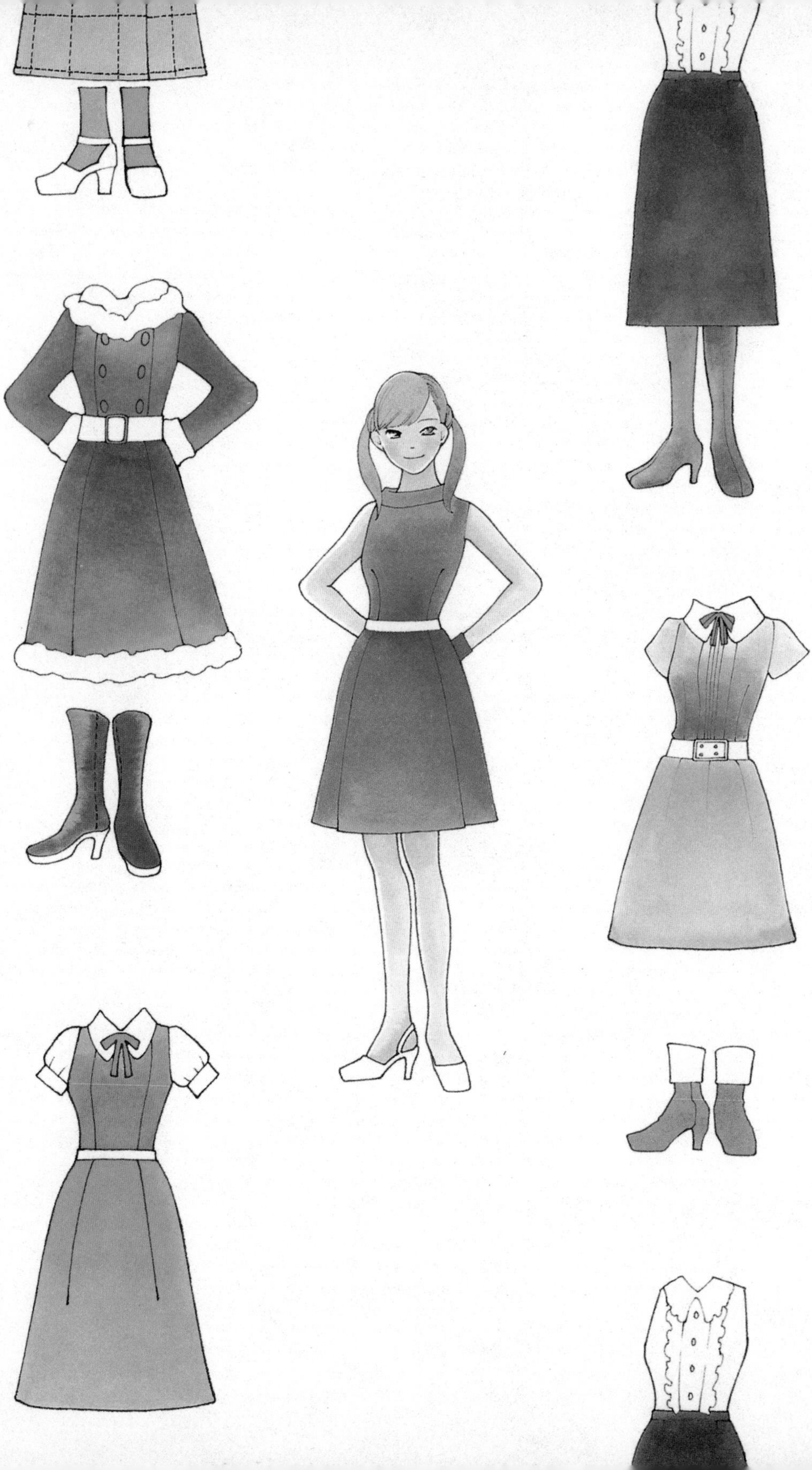

Fantagraphics Books, 7563 Lake City Way NE Seattle, Washington 98115 | Publishers: Gary Groth & Kim Thompson; Translation: Matt Thorn; Editorial Liaison: Gary Groth; Design: Alexa Koenings; Lettering: Paul Baresh, Kristen Bisson, Tom Graham, and Jack McKean; Production: Paul Baresh and Emory Liu; Associate Publisher: Eric Reynolds | Wandering Son Volume 4 copyright © 2005 Takako Shimura. All rights reserved. First published in Japan by ENTERBRAIN, INC., Tokyo. English translation rights arranged with ENTERBRAIN, INC. No part of this book (except small excerpts for review purposes) may be reproduced in any form or by any electronic or mechanical means without the written permission of the publisher. | To receive a free full-color catalog of comics, graphic novels, prose novels, and other fine works of artistry, call 1-800-657-1100, or visit Fantagraphics.com. | ISBN: 978-1-60699-605-8 | First Fantagraphics printing: February, 2013 | Printed in China

WANDERING SON

Volume Four

THE WANDERING SON BOARD GAME

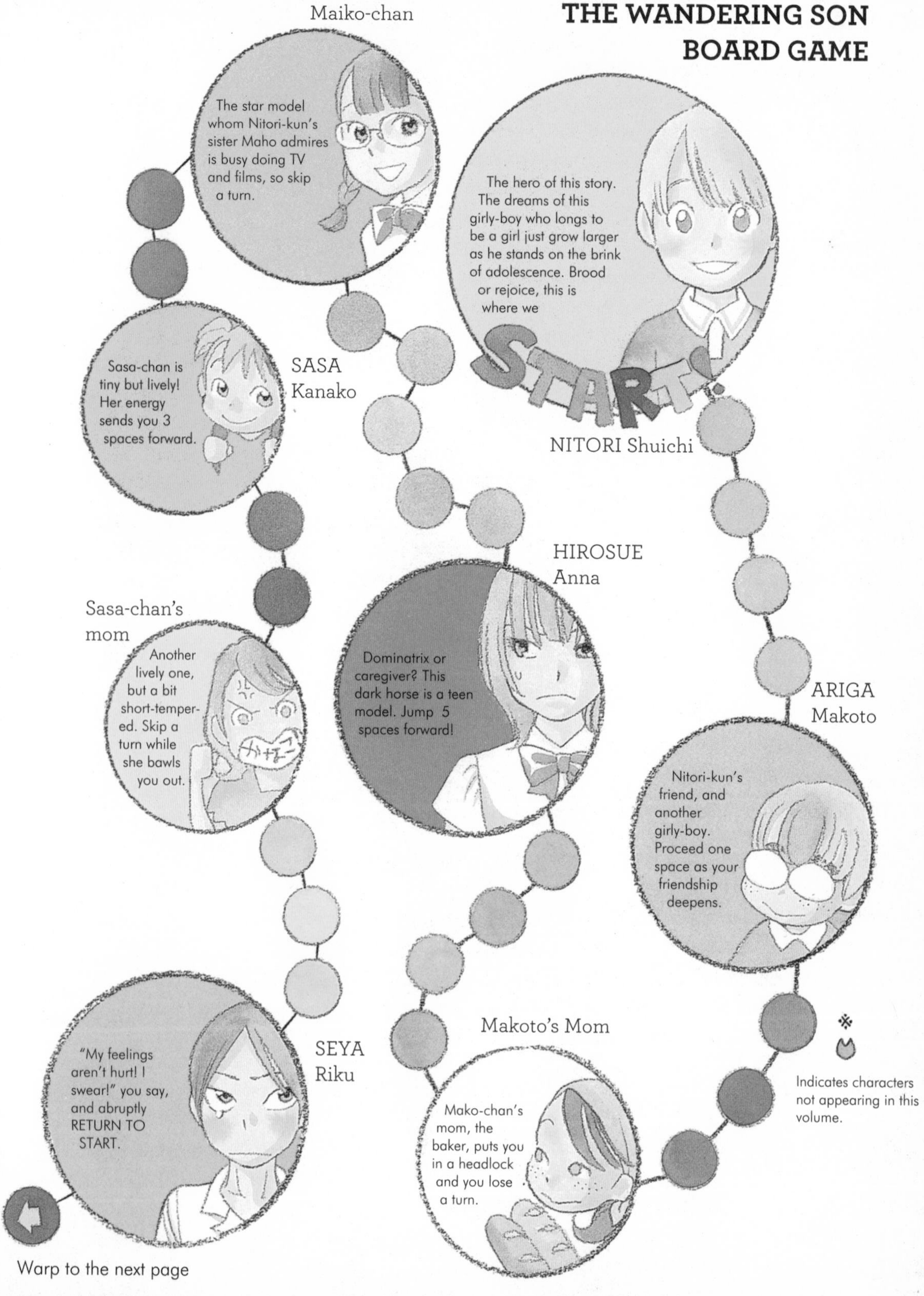
NITORI Shuichi
The hero of this story. The dreams of this girly-boy who longs to be a girl just grow larger as he stands on the brink of adolescence. Brood or rejoice, this is where we
START!
ARIGA Makoto
Nitori-kun's friend, and another girly-boy. Proceed one space as your friendship deepens.
Makoto's Mom
Mako-chan's mom, the baker, puts you in a headlock and you lose a turn.
HIROSUE Anna
Dominatrix or caregiver? This dark horse is a teen model. Jump 5 spaces forward!
Maiko-chan
The star model whom Nitori-kun's sister Maho admires is busy doing TV and films, so skip a turn.
SASA Kanako
Sasa-chan is tiny but lively! Her energy sends you 3 spaces forward.
Sasa-chan's mom
Another lively one, but a bit short-tempered. Skip a turn while she bawls you out.
SEYA Riku
"My feelings aren't hurt! I swear!" you say, and abruptly RETURN TO START.
Warp to the next page
※ Indicates characters not appearing in this volume.

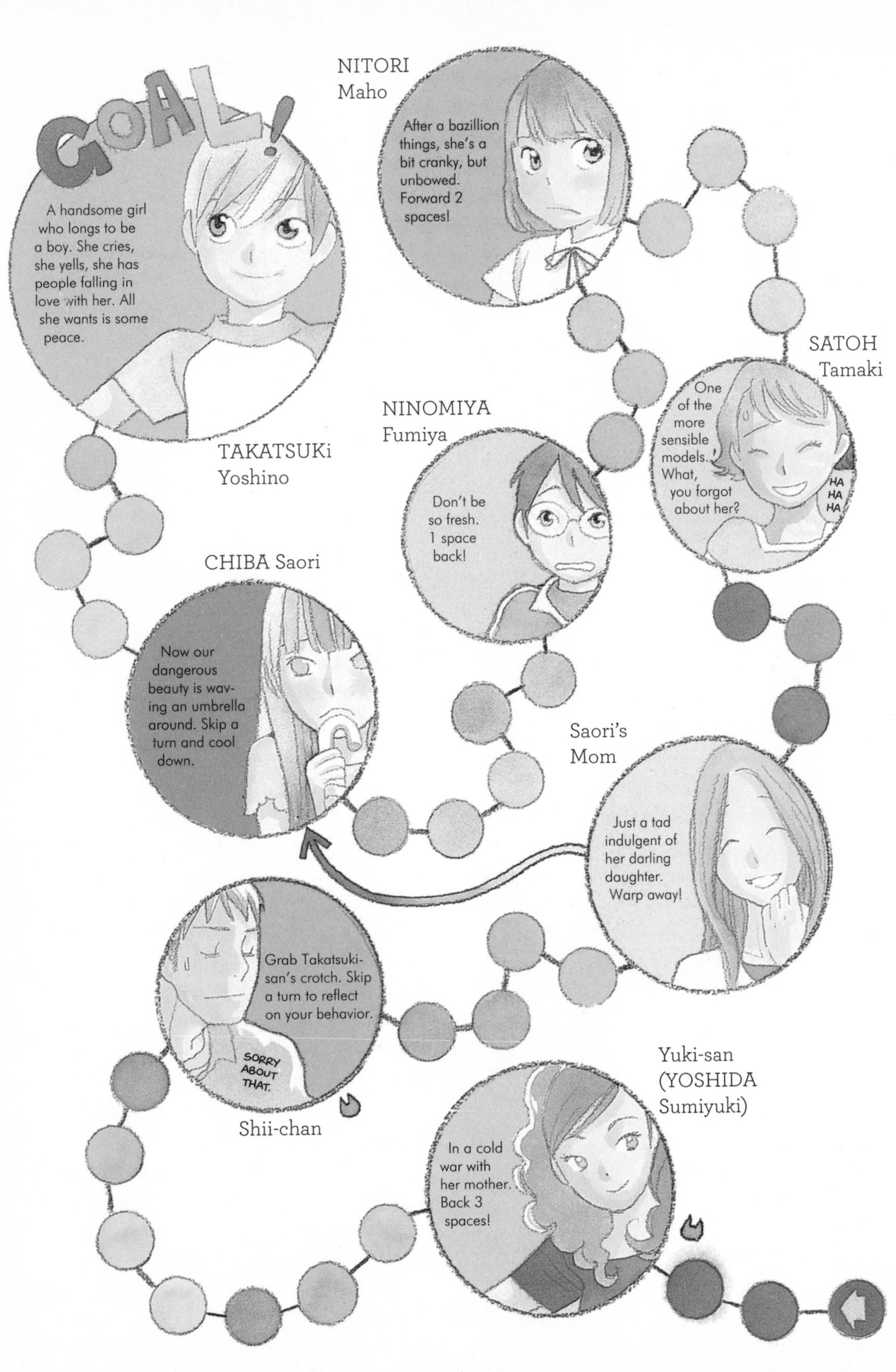
NITORI Maho
After a bazillion things, she's a bit cranky, but unbowed. Forward 2 spaces!
GOAL!
A handsome girl who longs to be a boy. She cries, she yells, she has people falling in love with her. All she wants is some peace.
TAKATSUKi Yoshino
SATOH Tamaki
One of the more sensible models. What, you forgot about her?
HA HA HA
NINOMIYA Fumiya
Don't be so fresh. 1 space back!
CHIBA Saori
Now our dangerous beauty is waving an umbrella around. Skip a turn and cool down.
Saori's Mom
Just a tad indulgent of her darling daughter. Warp away!
Grab Takatsuki-san's crotch. Skip a turn to reflect on your behavior.
SORRY ABOUT THAT.
Shii-chan
Yuki-san (YOSHIDA Sumiyuki)
In a cold war with her mother. Back 3 spaces!

CONTENTS

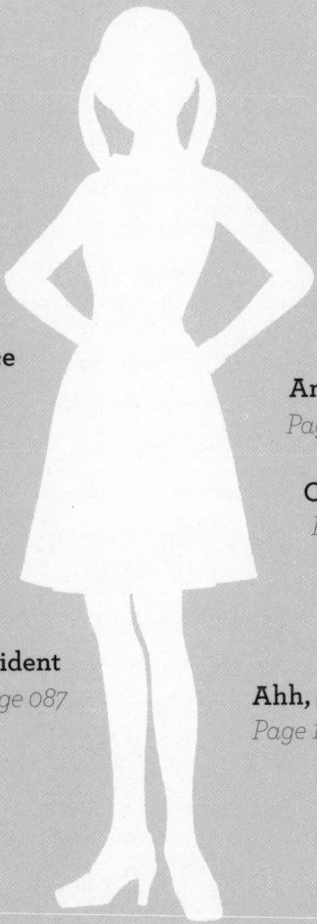

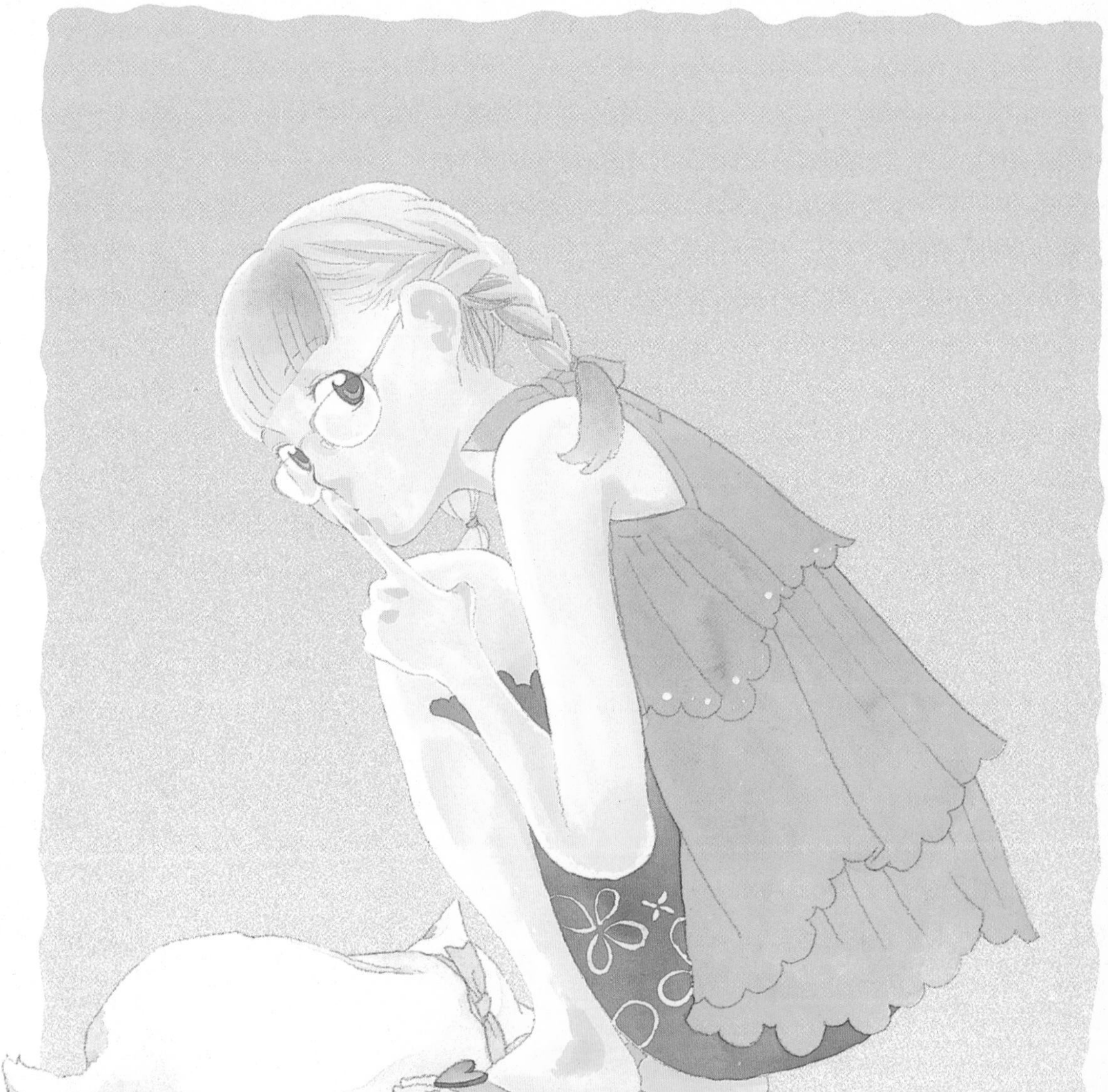

26

Big Sister's Romance

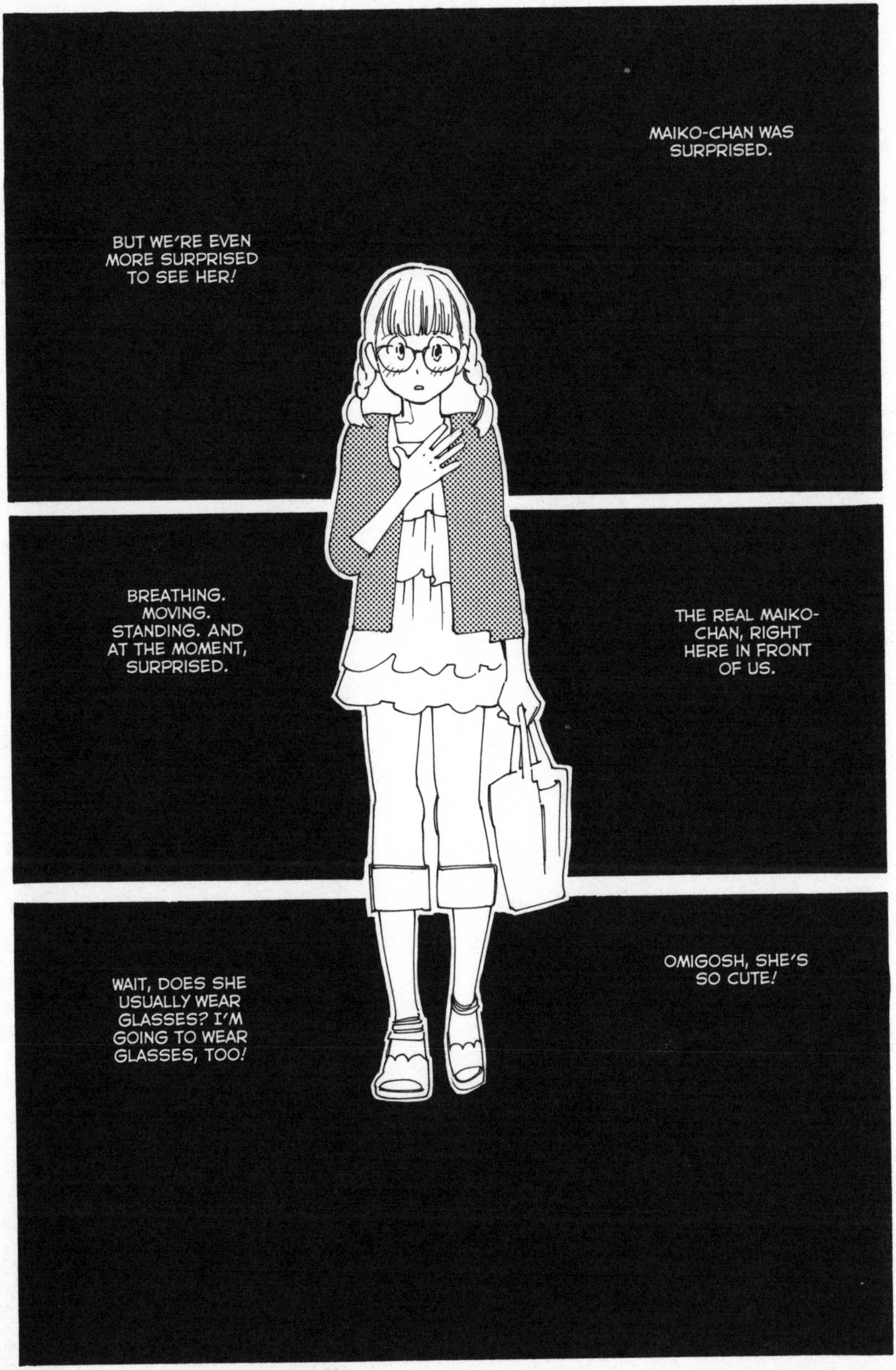
MAIKO-CHAN WAS SURPRISED.
BUT WE'RE EVEN MORE SURPRISED TO SEE HER!
THE REAL MAIKO-CHAN, RIGHT HERE IN FRONT OF US.
BREATHING. MOVING. STANDING. AND AT THE MOMENT, SURPRISED.
OMIGOSH, SHE'S SO CUTE!
WAIT, DOES SHE USUALLY WEAR GLASSES? I'M GOING TO WEAR GLASSES, TOO!

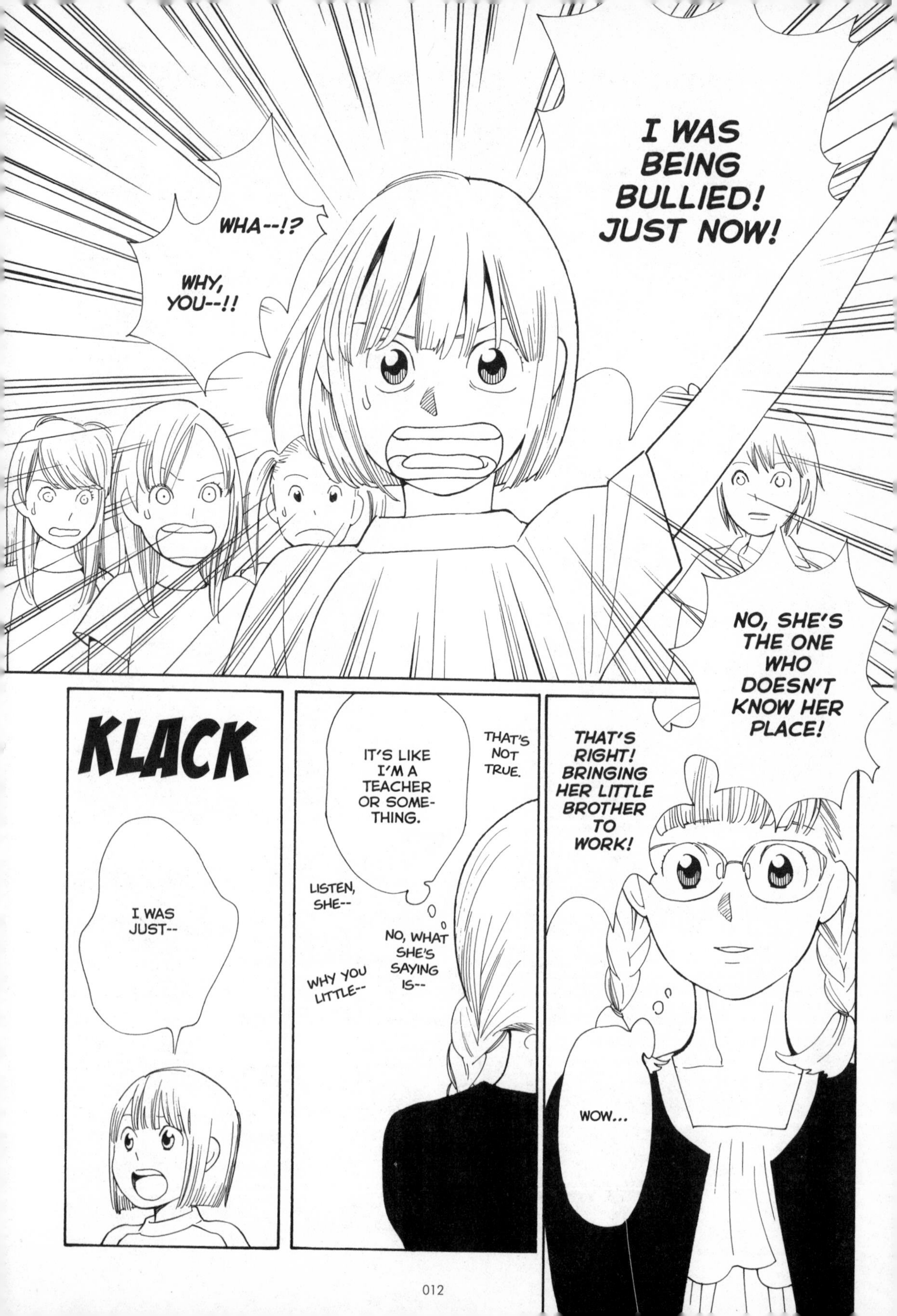
I WAS BEING BULLIED! JUST NOW!
WHA--!?
WHY, YOU--!!
NO, SHE'S THE ONE WHO DOESN'T KNOW HER PLACE!
THAT'S RIGHT! BRINGING HER LITTLE BROTHER TO WORK!
WOW...
THAT'S NOT TRUE.
IT'S LIKE I'M A TEACHER OR SOME-THING.
LISTEN, SHE--
NO, WHAT SHE'S SAYING IS--
WHY YOU LITTLE--
KLACK
I WAS JUST--

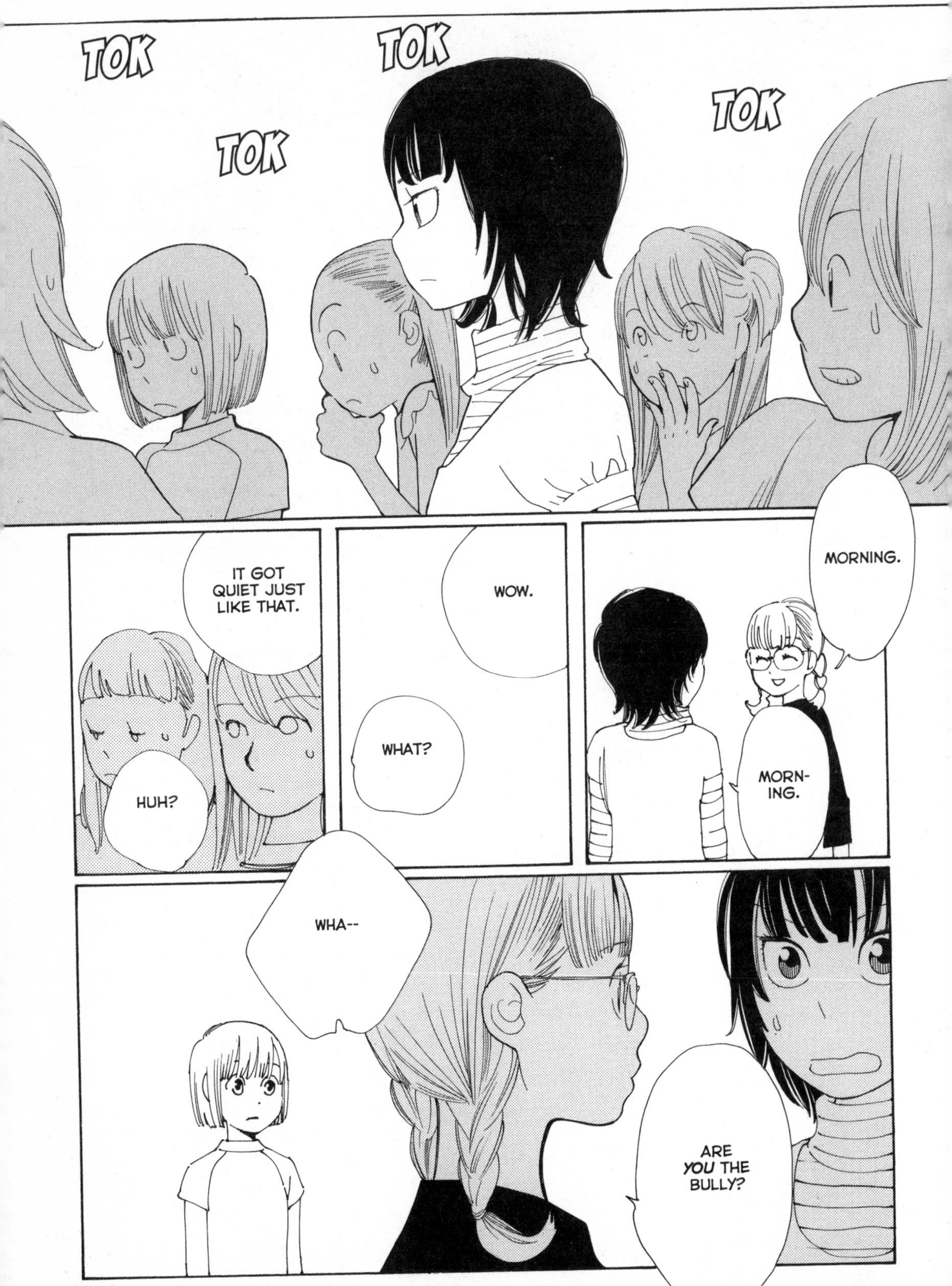
TOK
TOK
TOK
TOK
MORNING.
MORN-ING.
WOW.
WHAT?
IT GOT QUIET JUST LIKE THAT.
HUH?
ARE *YOU* THE BULLY?
WHA--

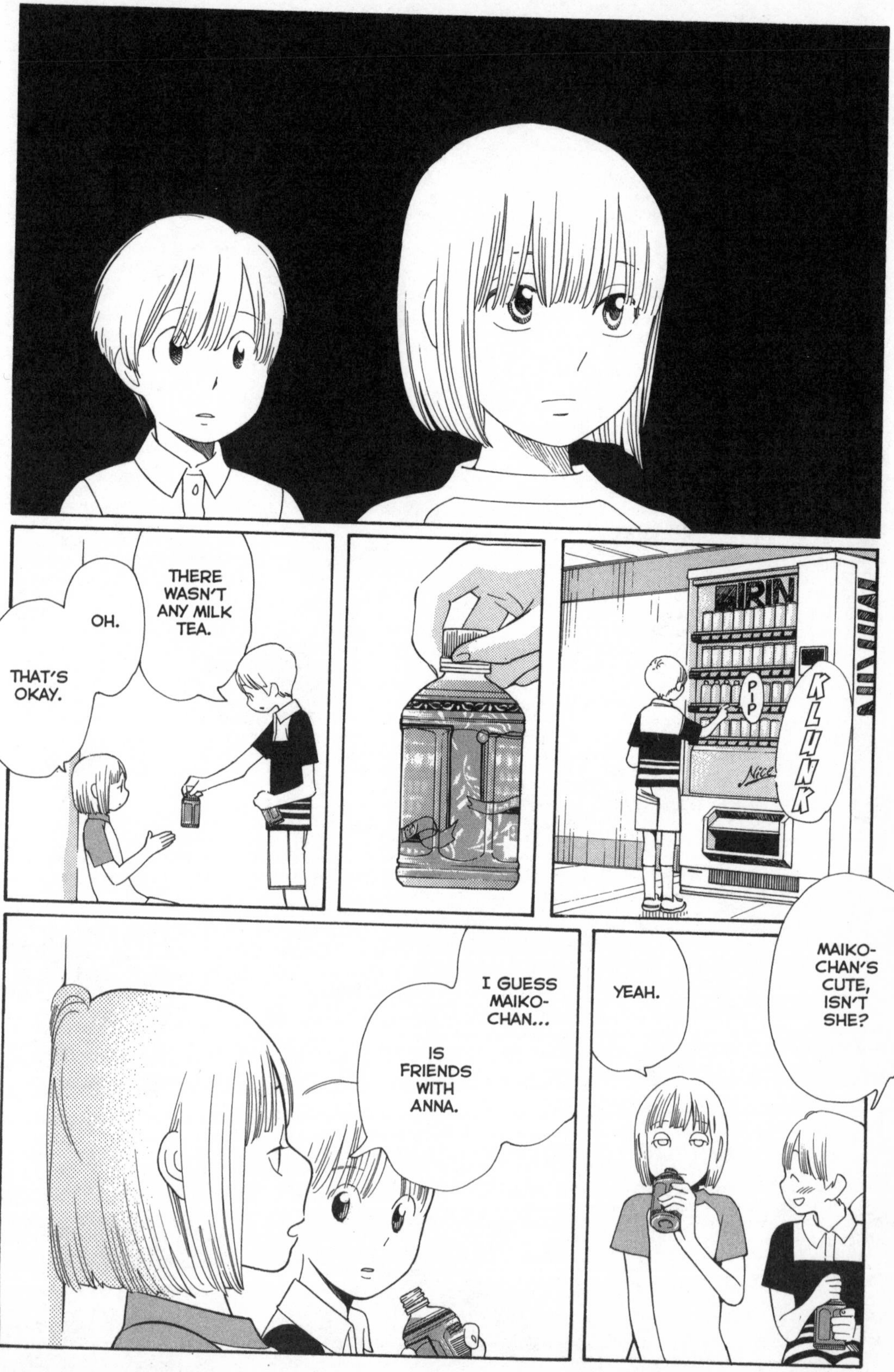
PIP
KLUNK
Nice
THERE WASN'T ANY MILK TEA.
OH.
THAT'S OKAY.
MAIKO-CHAN'S CUTE, ISN'T SHE?
YEAH.
I GUESS MAIKO-CHAN...
IS FRIENDS WITH ANNA.

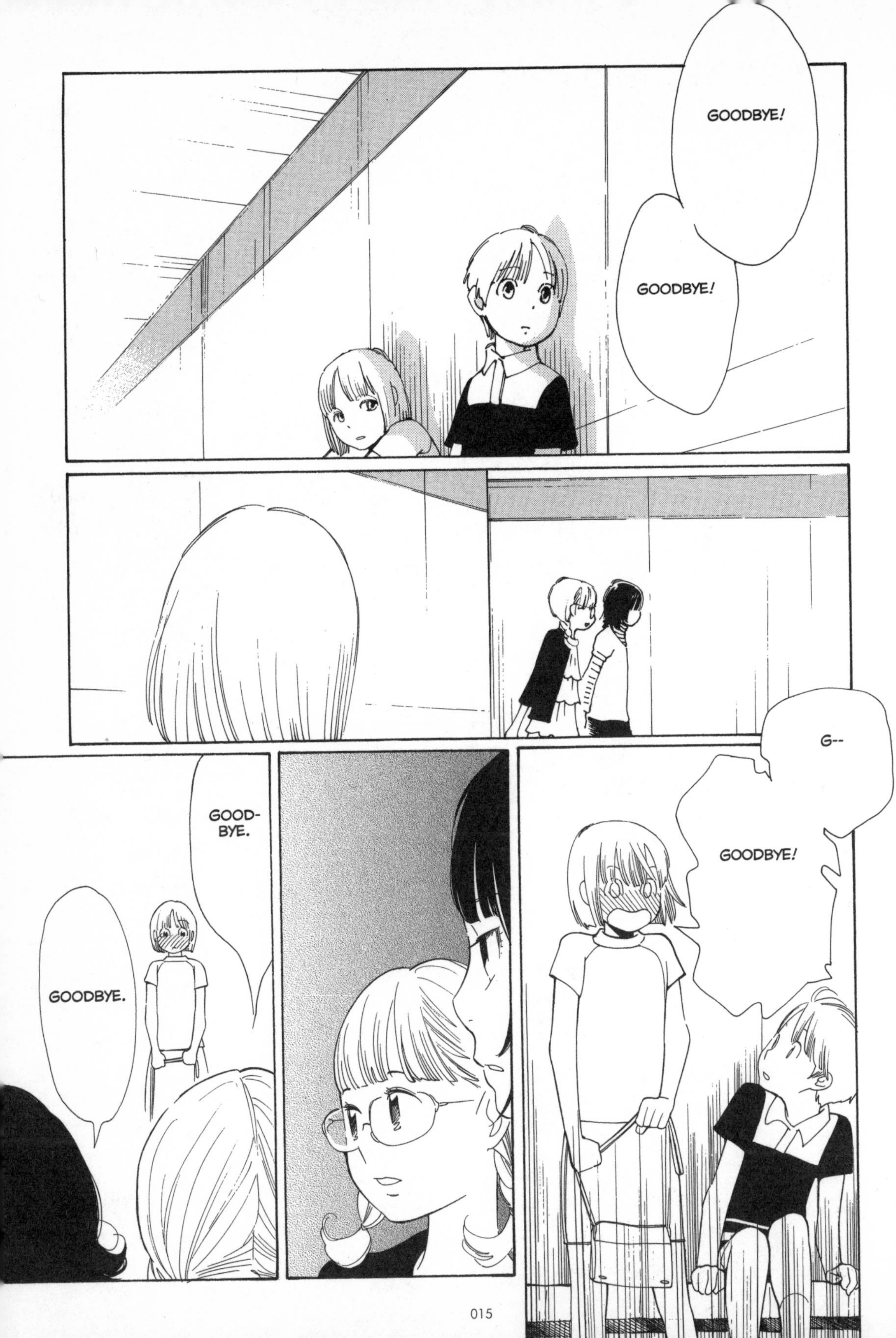
GOODBYE!
GOODBYE!
G--
GOODBYE!
GOOD-BYE.
GOODBYE.

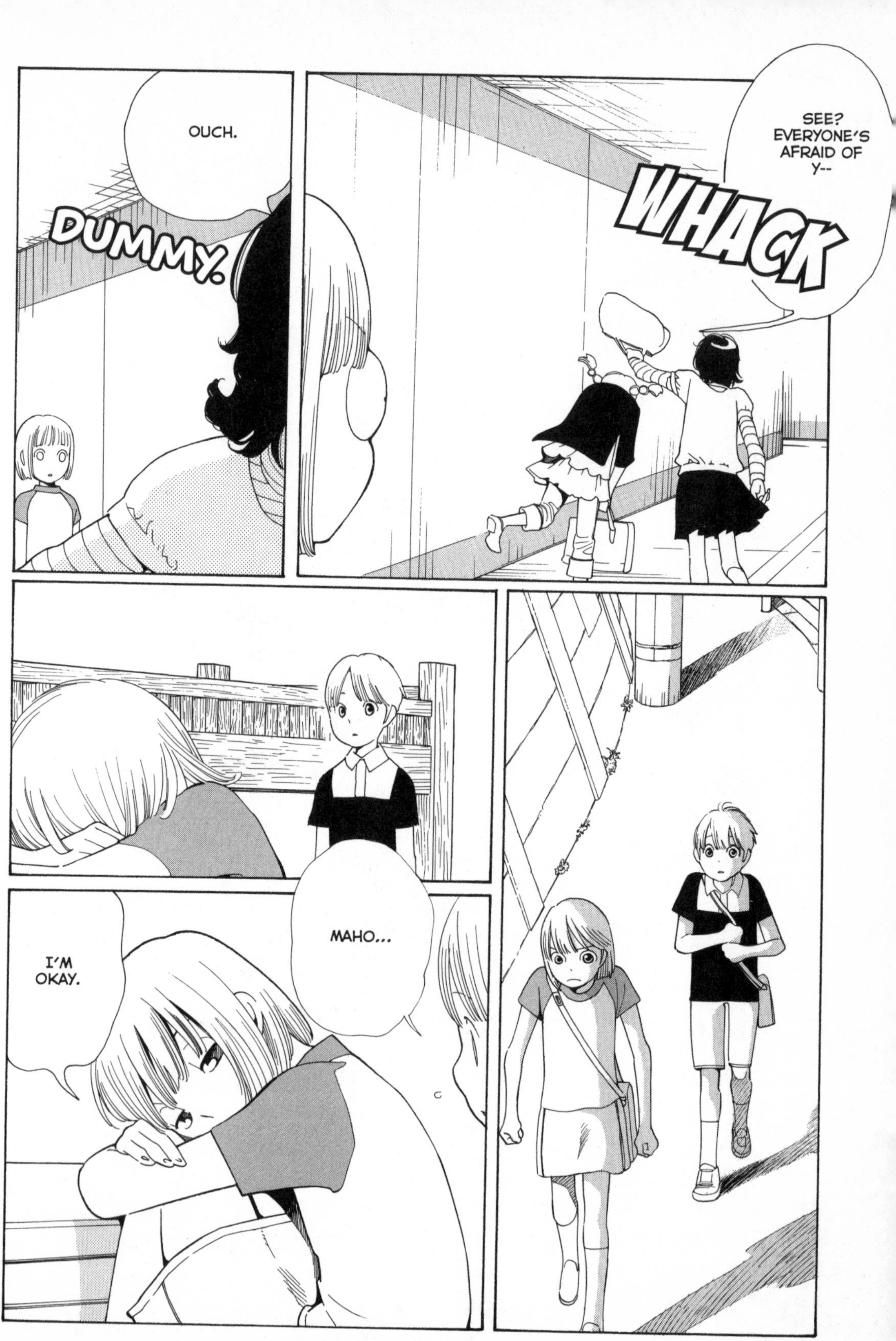
SEE? EVERYONE'S AFRAID OF Y--
WHACK
OUCH.
DUMMY.
MAHO...
I'M OKAY.

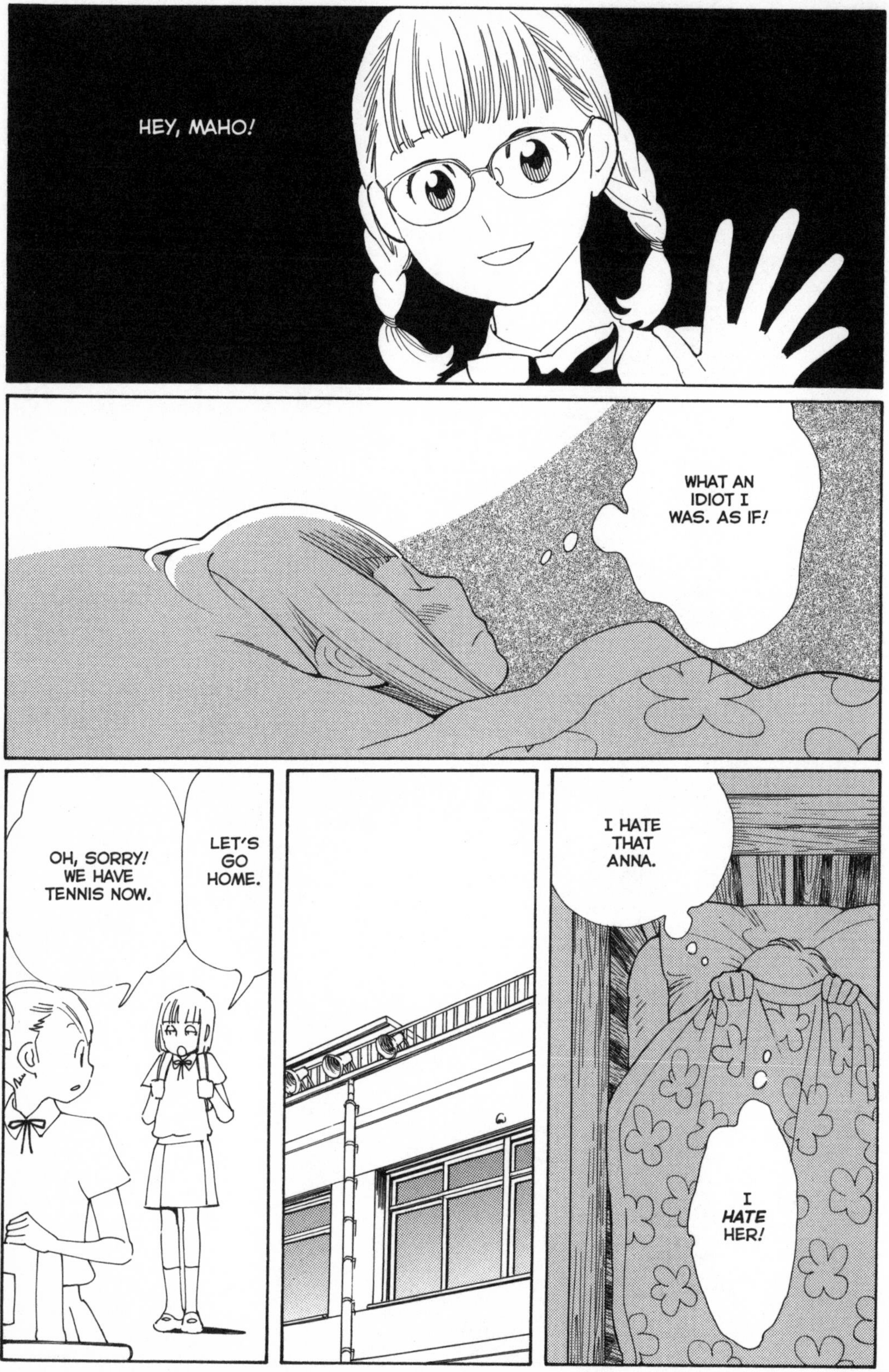
HEY, MAHO!
WHAT AN IDIOT I WAS. AS IF!
I HATE THAT ANNA.
I *HATE* HER!
LET'S GO HOME.
OH, SORRY! WE HAVE TENNIS NOW.

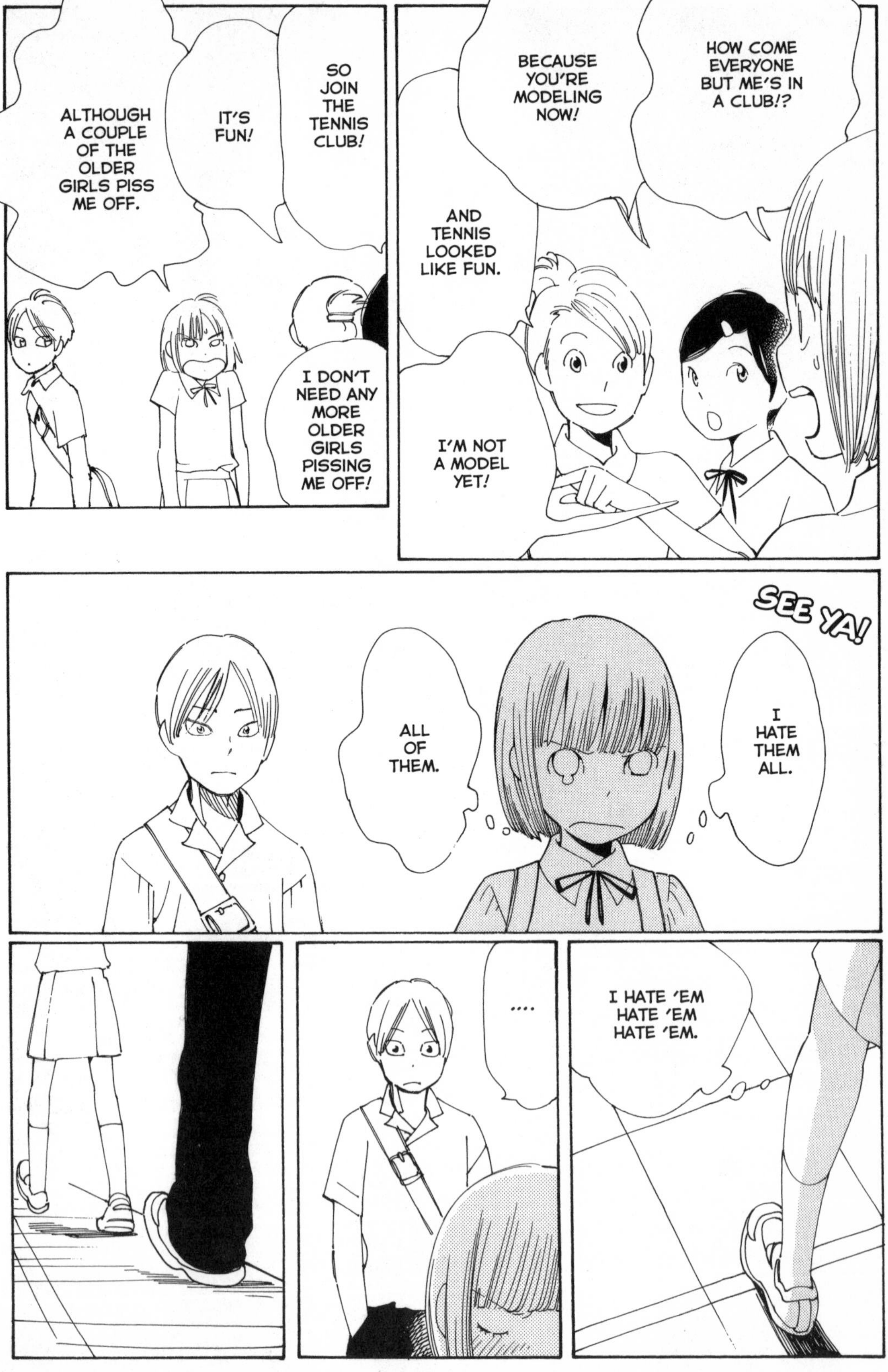
HOW COME EVERYONE BUT ME'S IN A CLUB!?
BECAUSE YOU'RE MODELING NOW!
AND TENNIS LOOKED LIKE FUN.
I'M NOT A MODEL YET!
SO JOIN THE TENNIS CLUB!
IT'S FUN!
ALTHOUGH A COUPLE OF THE OLDER GIRLS PISS ME OFF.
I DON'T NEED ANY MORE OLDER GIRLS PISSING ME OFF!
SEE YA!
I HATE THEM ALL.
ALL OF THEM.
I HATE 'EM HATE 'EM HATE 'EM.
....

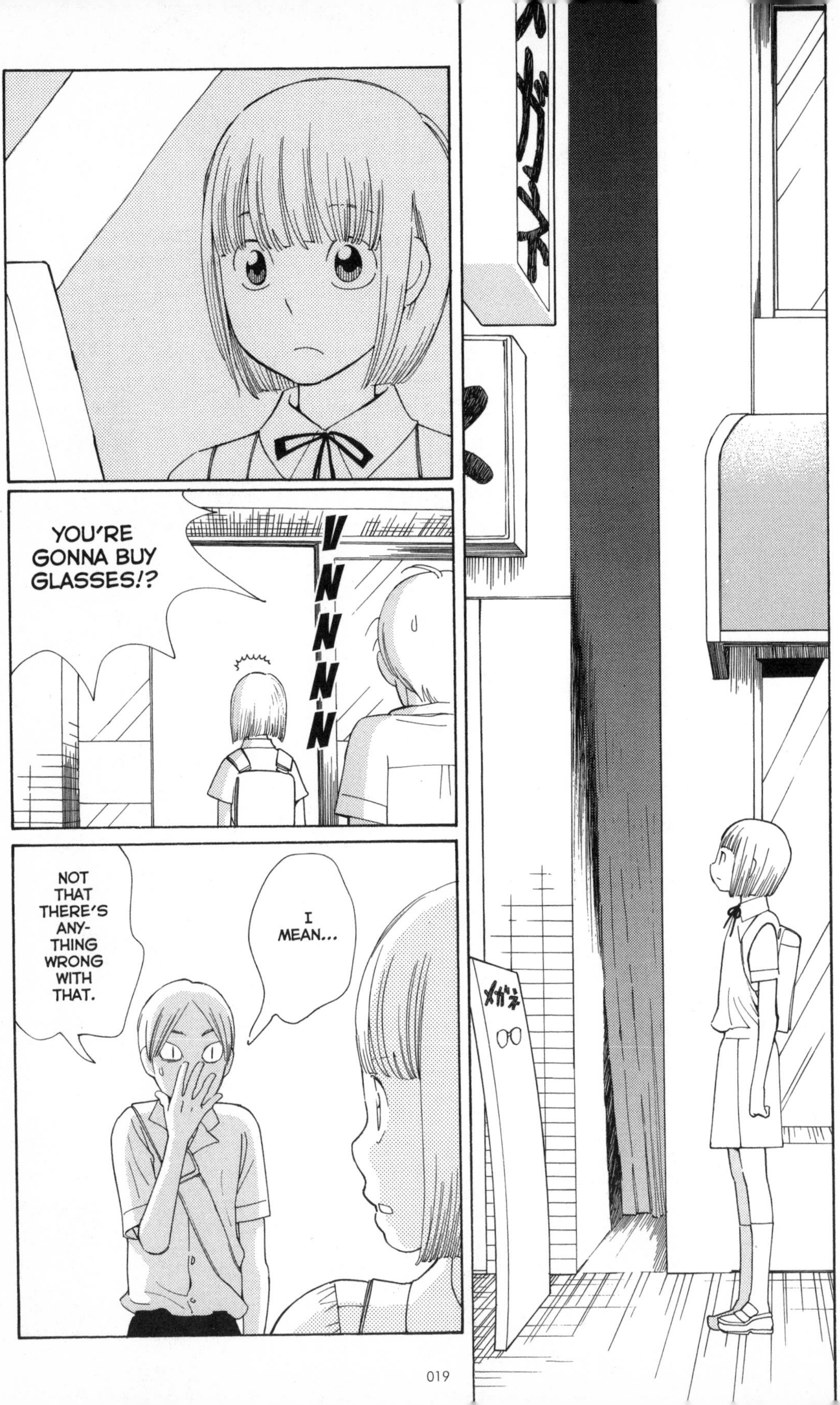
メガネ
YOU'RE GONNA BUY GLASSES!?
VNNNNN
I MEAN...
NOT THAT THERE'S ANYTHING WRONG WITH THAT.

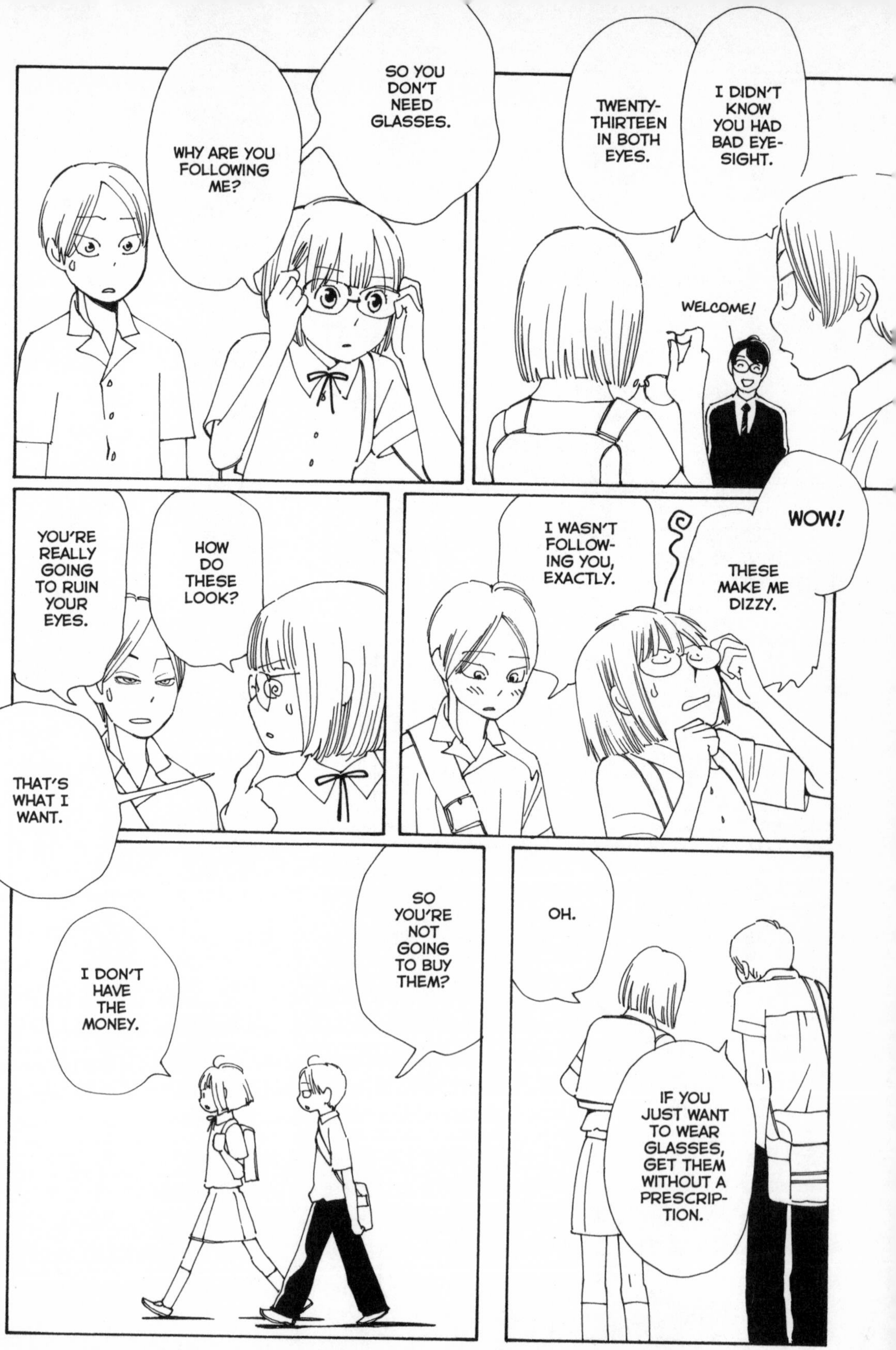
I DIDN'T KNOW YOU HAD BAD EYE-SIGHT.
TWENTY-THIRTEEN IN BOTH EYES.
WELCOME!
SO YOU DON'T NEED GLASSES.
WHY ARE YOU FOLLOWING ME?
WOW!
THESE MAKE ME DIZZY.
I WASN'T FOLLOWING YOU, EXACTLY.
HOW DO THESE LOOK?
YOU'RE REALLY GOING TO RUIN YOUR EYES.
THAT'S WHAT I WANT.
OH.
IF YOU JUST WANT TO WEAR GLASSES, GET THEM WITHOUT A PRESCRIPTION.
SO YOU'RE NOT GOING TO BUY THEM?
I DON'T HAVE THE MONEY.

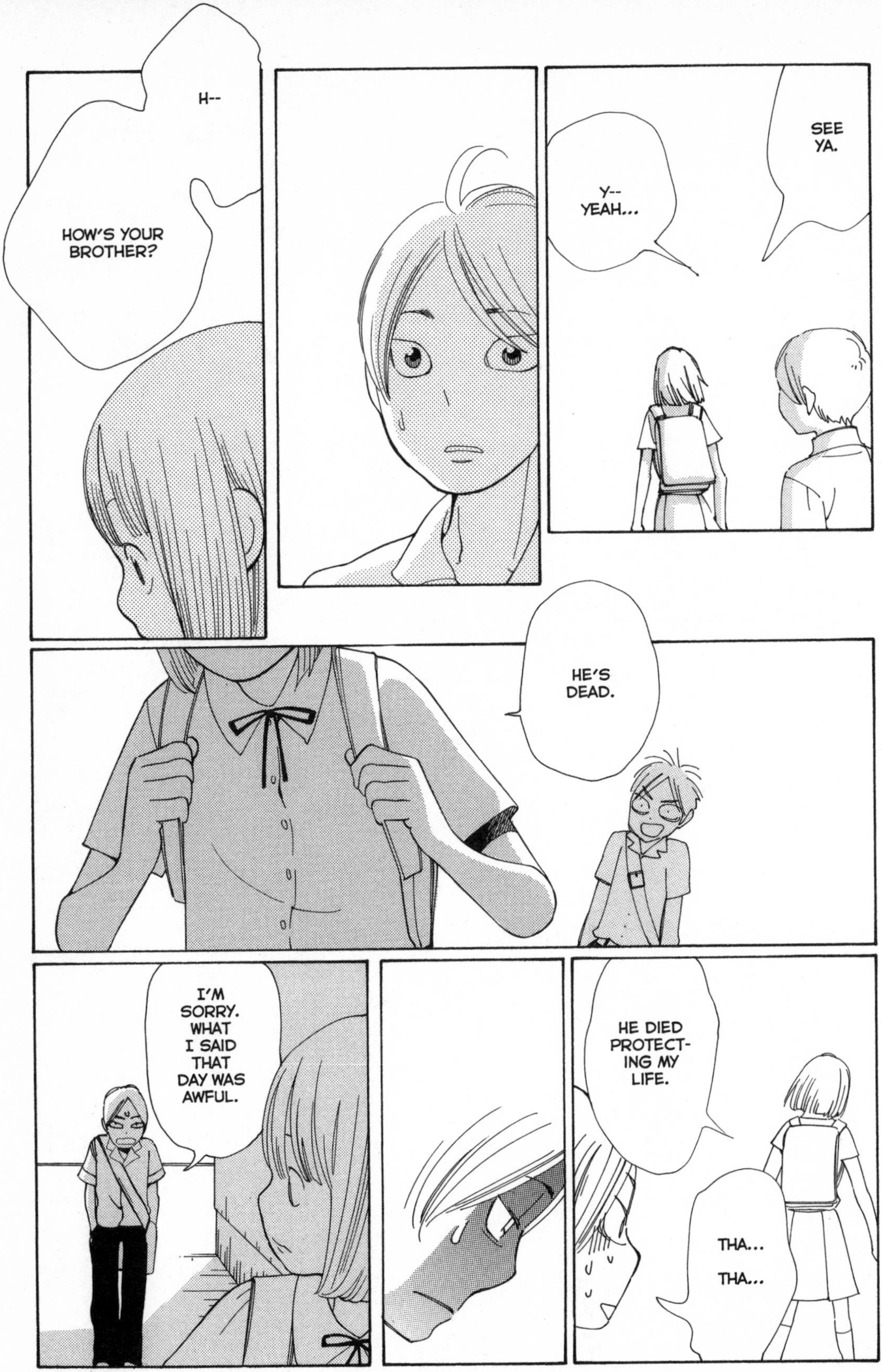
SEE YA.
Y-- YEAH...
H--
HOW'S YOUR BROTHER?
HE'S DEAD.
HE DIED PROTECT-ING MY LIFE.
THA...
THA...
I'M SORRY. WHAT I SAID THAT DAY WAS AWFUL.

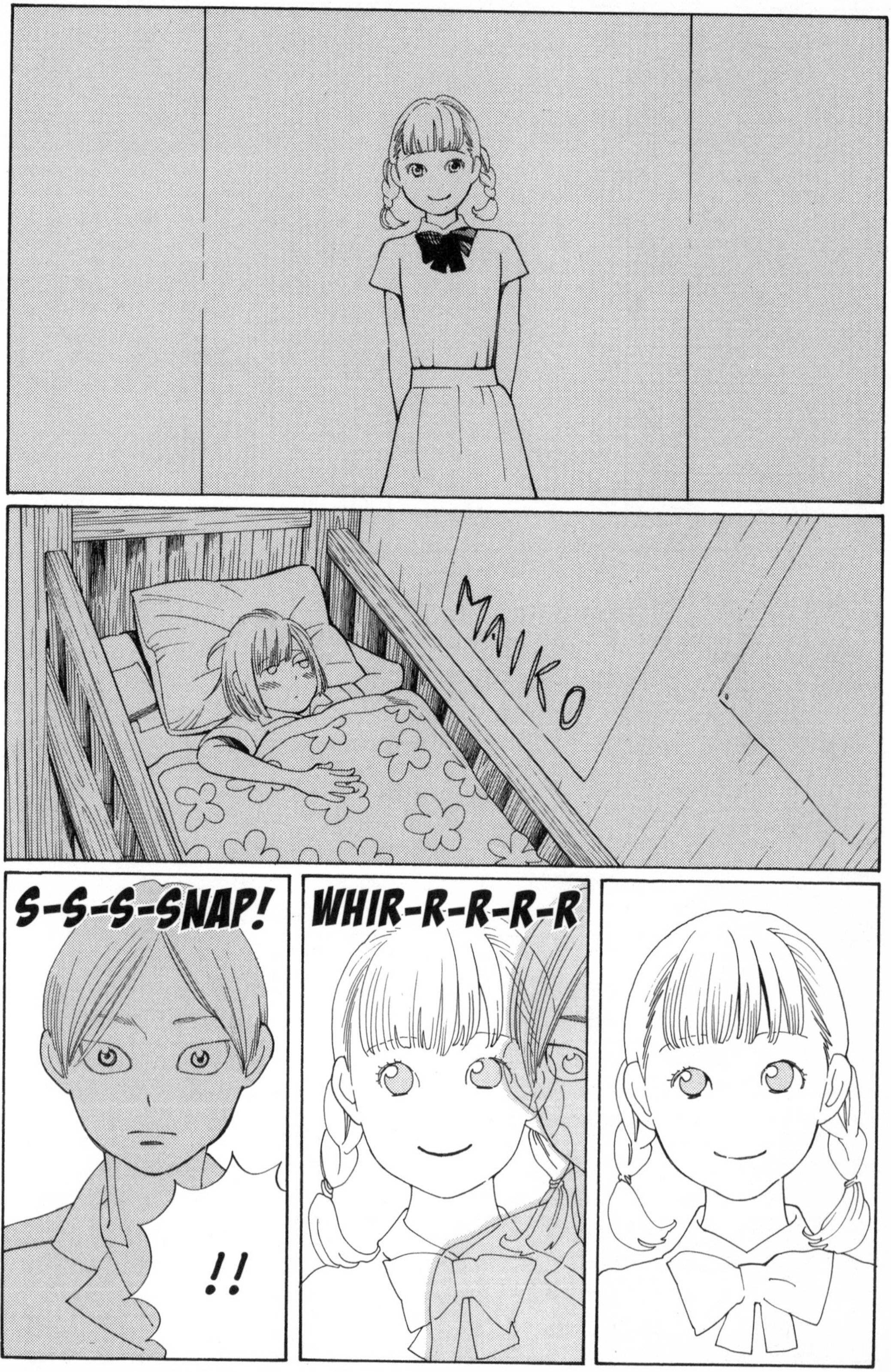
MAIKO
WHIR-R-R-R-R
S-S-S-SNAP!
!!

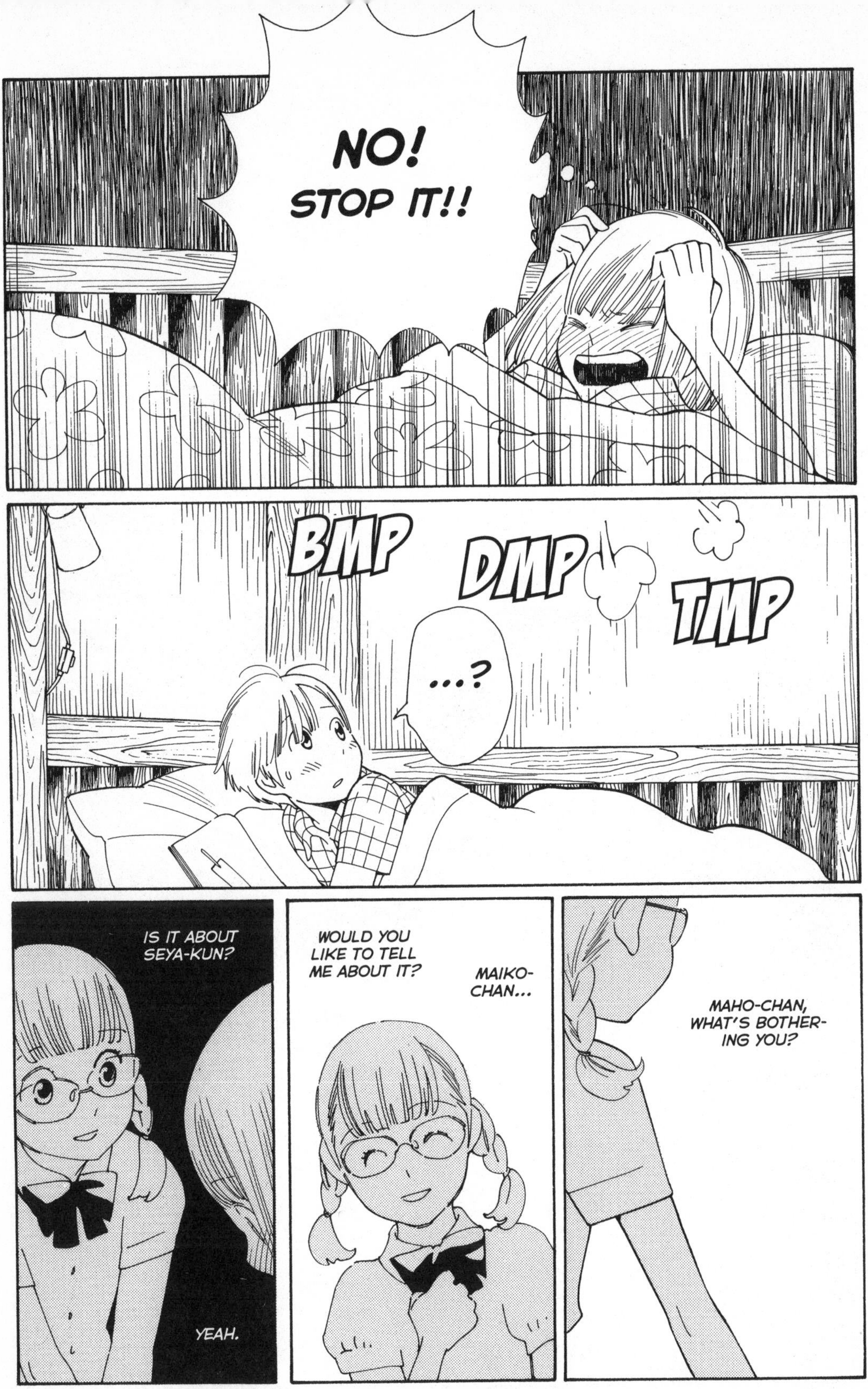
NO!
STOP IT!!
BMP
DMP
TMP
...?
MAHO-CHAN, WHAT'S BOTHER-ING YOU?
MAIKO-CHAN...
WOULD YOU LIKE TO TELL ME ABOUT IT?
IS IT ABOUT SEYA-KUN?
YEAH.

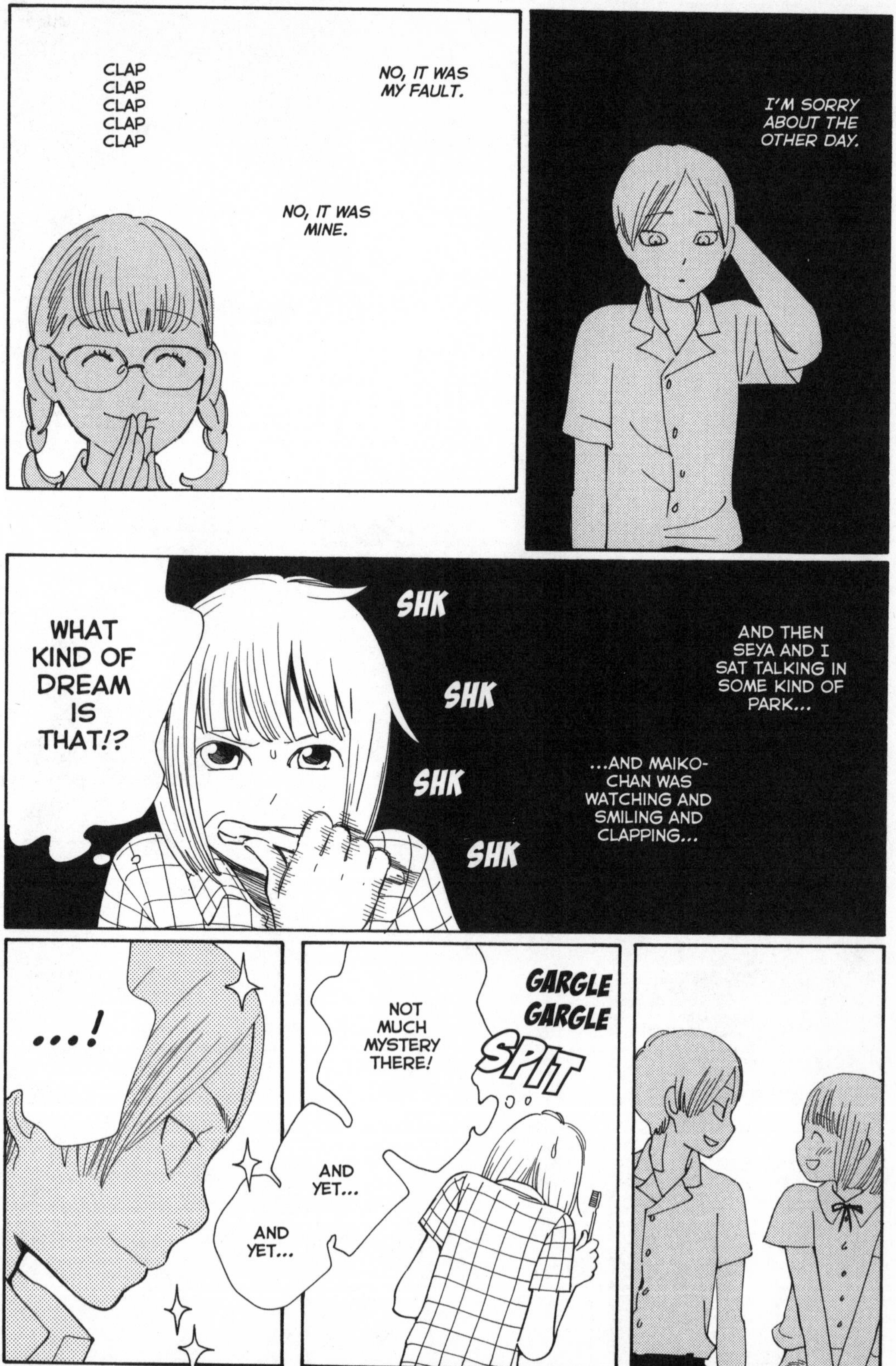
I'M SORRY ABOUT THE OTHER DAY.
NO, IT WAS MY FAULT.
CLAP CLAP CLAP CLAP CLAP
NO, IT WAS MINE.
AND THEN SEYA AND I SAT TALKING IN SOME KIND OF PARK...
...AND MAIKO-CHAN WAS WATCHING AND SMILING AND CLAPPING...
SHK
SHK
SHK
SHK
WHAT KIND OF DREAM IS THAT!?
GARGLE GARGLE
SPIT
NOT MUCH MYSTERY THERE!
AND YET...
AND YET...
...!

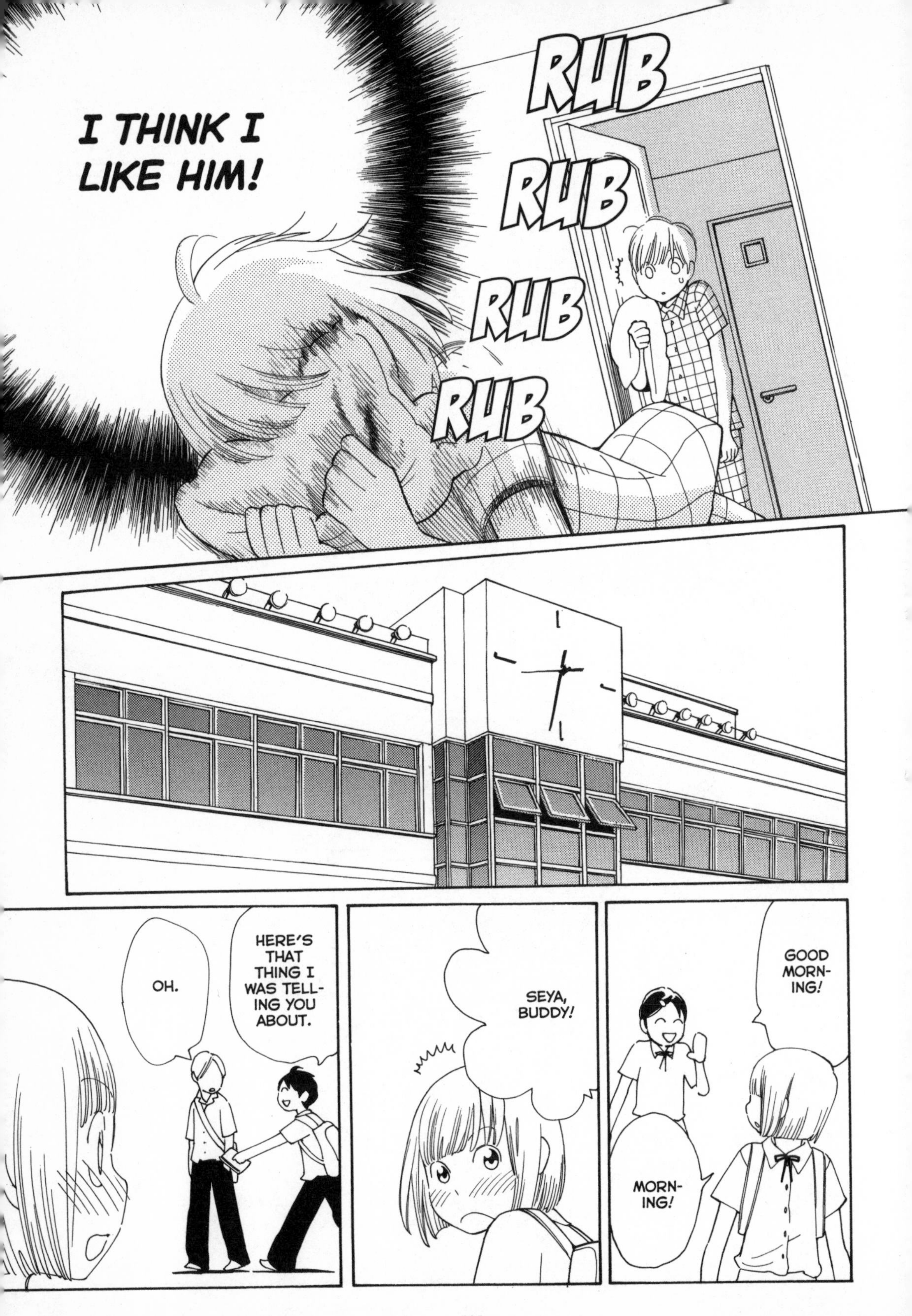
RUB
RUB
RUB
RUB
I THINK I LIKE HIM!
GOOD MORNING!
MORNING!
SEYA, BUDDY!
HERE'S THAT THING I WAS TELLING YOU ABOUT.
OH.

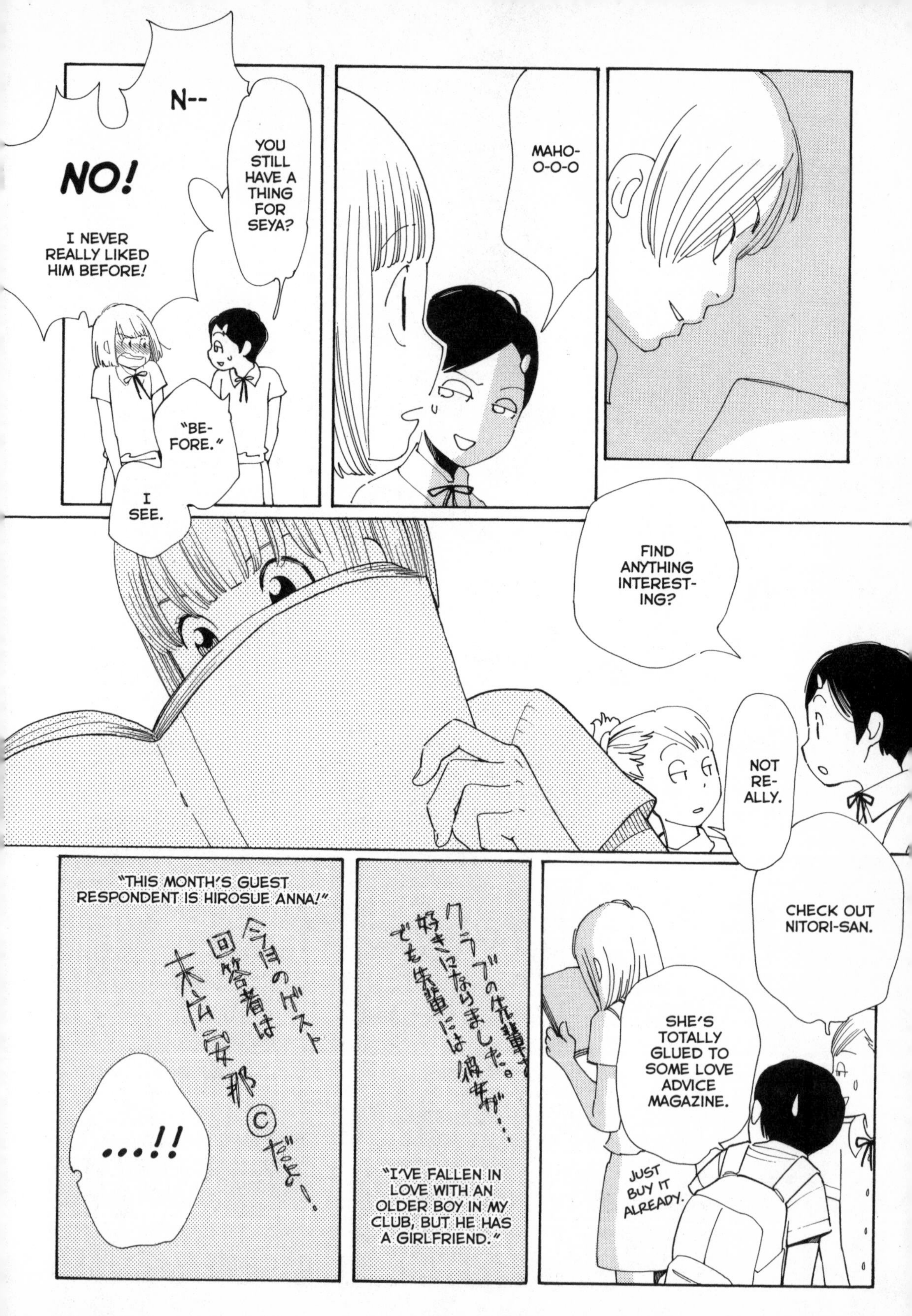
MAHO-O-O-O
YOU STILL HAVE A THING FOR SEYA?
N--
NO!
I NEVER REALLY LIKED HIM BEFORE!
"BE-FORE."
I SEE.
FIND ANYTHING INTEREST-ING?
NOT RE-ALLY.
CHECK OUT NITORI-SAN.
SHE'S TOTALLY GLUED TO SOME LOVE ADVICE MAGAZINE.
JUST BUY IT ALREADY.
クラブの先輩を好きになりました。でも先輩には彼女が…
"I'VE FALLEN IN LOVE WITH AN OLDER BOY IN MY CLUB, BUT HE HAS A GIRLFRIEND."
"THIS MONTH'S GUEST RESPONDENT IS HIROSUE ANNA!"
今月のゲスト回答者は末広安那ⓒだよ！
...!!

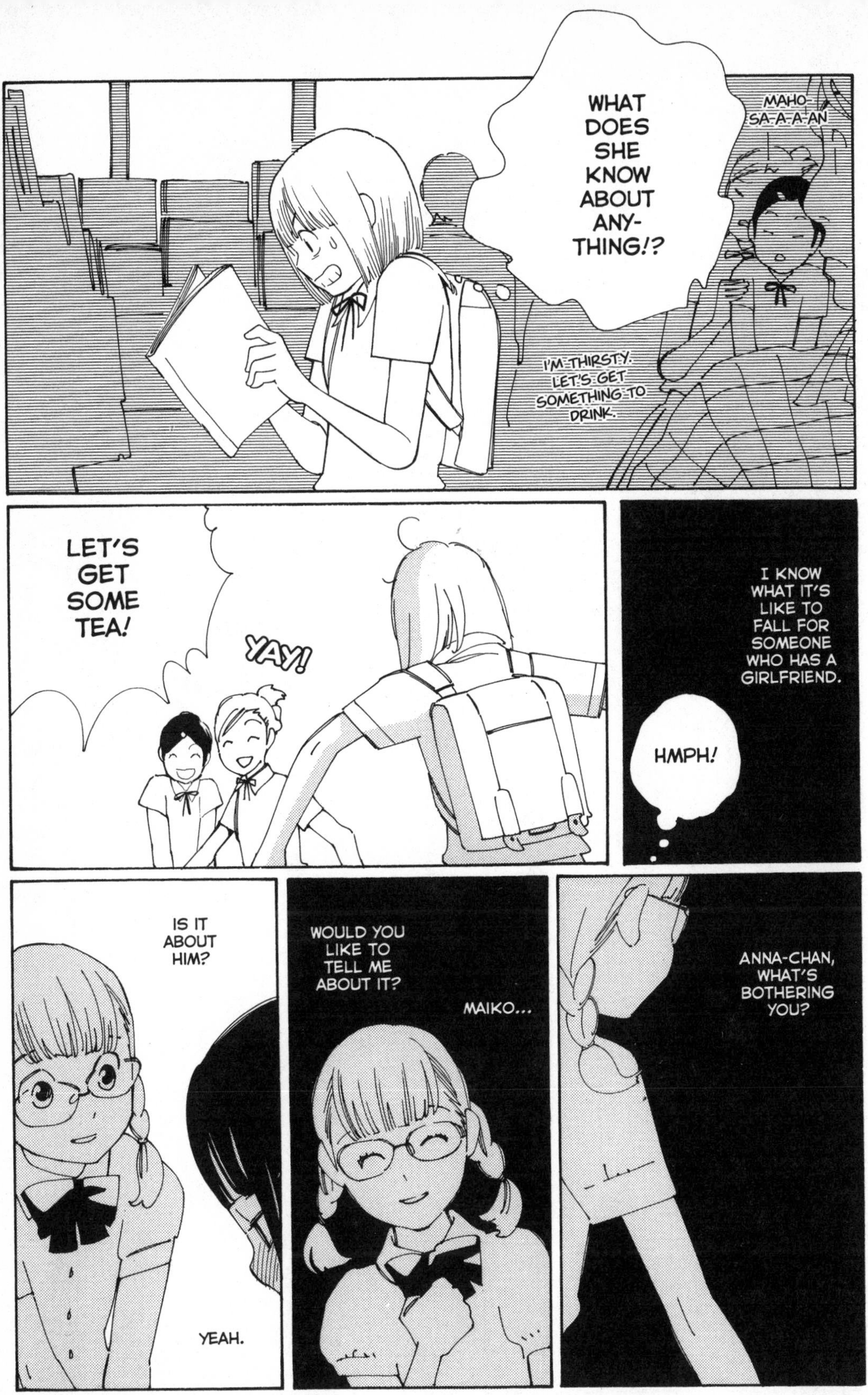
MAHO-SA-A-A-AN
WHAT DOES SHE KNOW ABOUT ANY-THING!?
I'M THIRSTY. LET'S GET SOMETHING TO DRINK.
I KNOW WHAT IT'S LIKE TO FALL FOR SOMEONE WHO HAS A GIRLFRIEND.
HMPH!
LET'S GET SOME TEA!
YAY!
ANNA-CHAN, WHAT'S BOTHERING YOU?
MAIKO...
WOULD YOU LIKE TO TELL ME ABOUT IT?
IS IT ABOUT HIM?
YEAH.

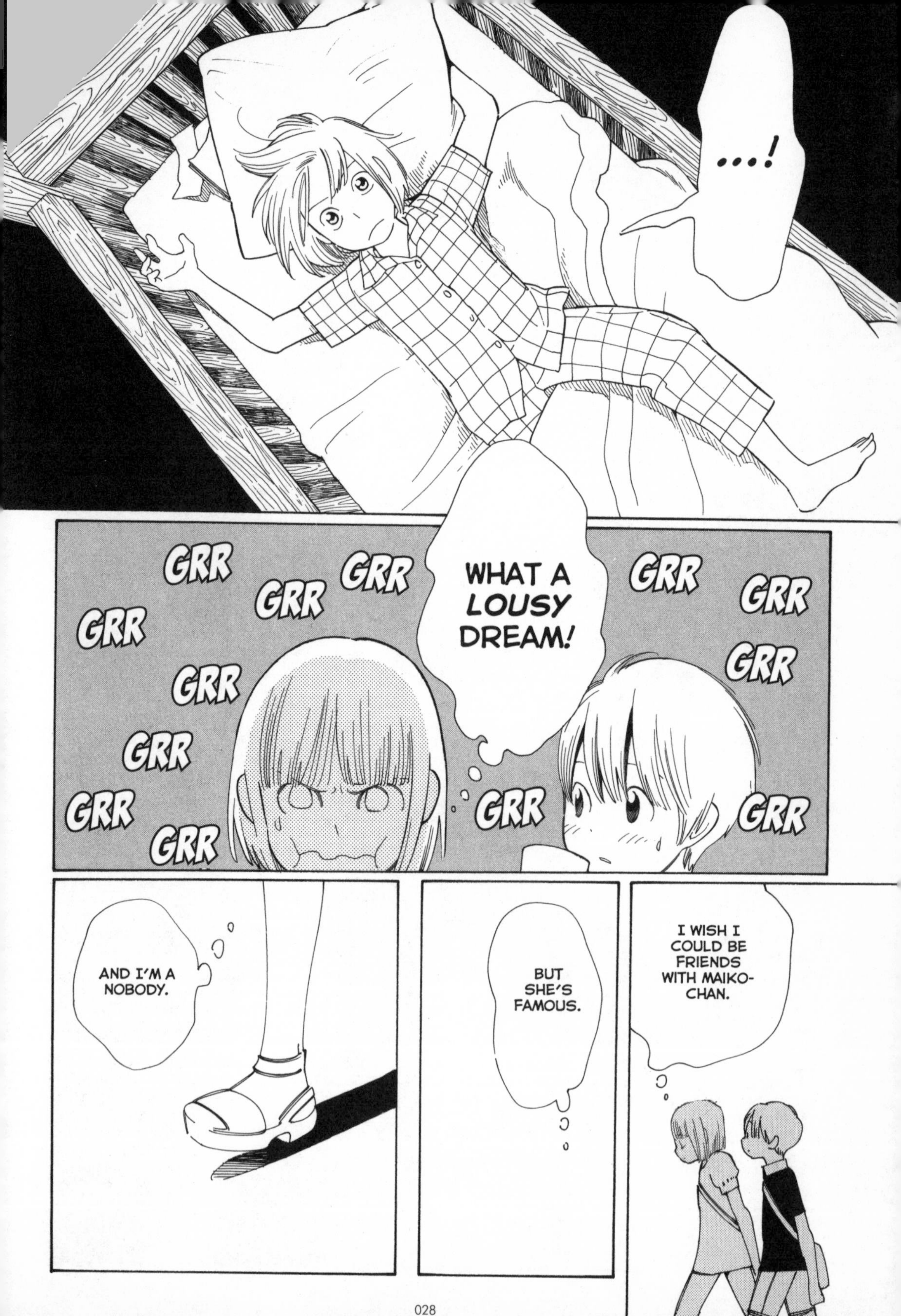
...!
GRR
GRR
GRR
GRR
WHAT A LOUSY DREAM!
GRR
GRR
GRR
GRR
GRR
GRR
GRR
GRR
GRR
I WISH I COULD BE FRIENDS WITH MAIKO-CHAN.
BUT SHE'S FAMOUS.
AND I'M A NOBODY.

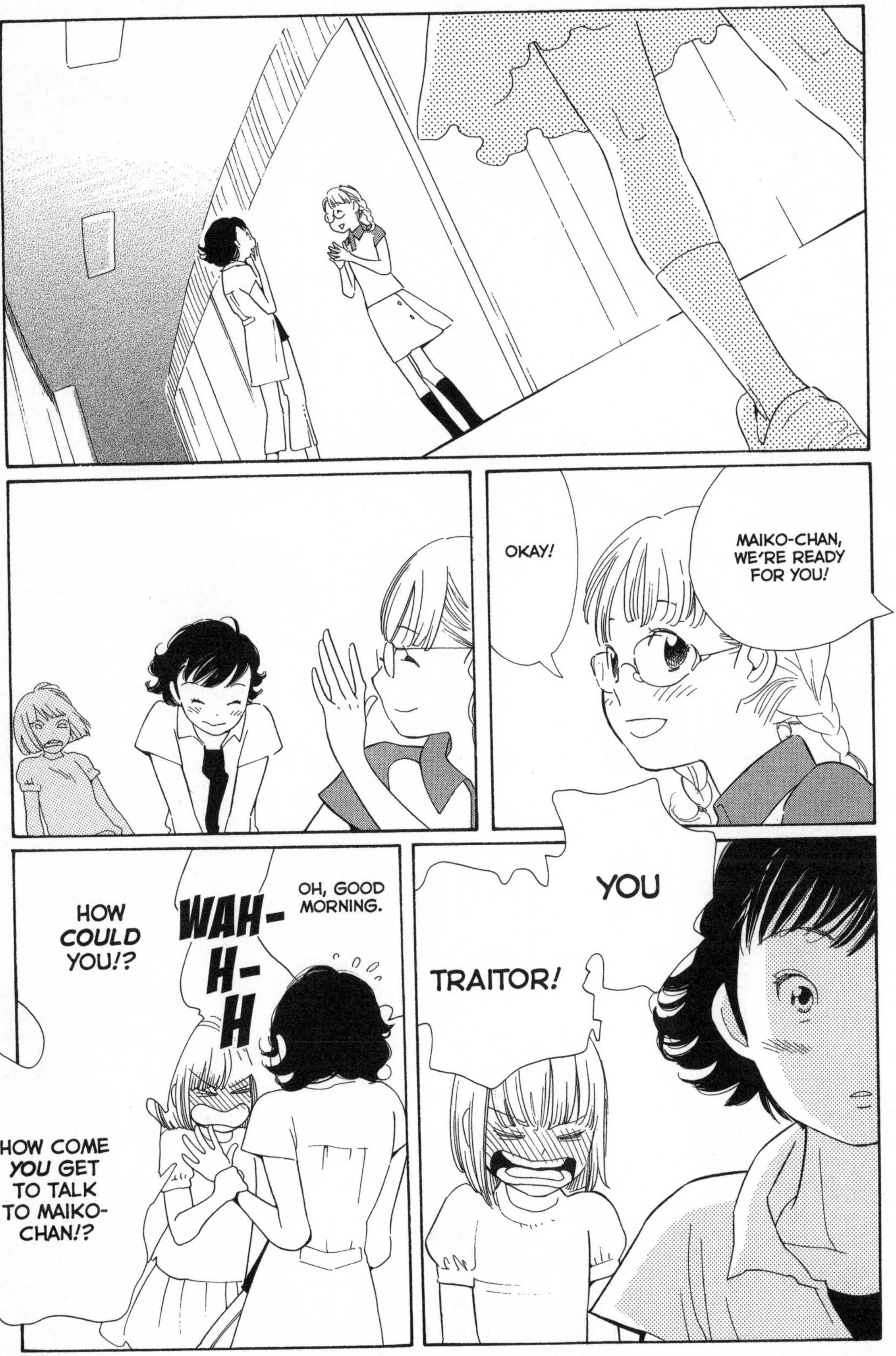
MAIKO-CHAN, WE'RE READY FOR YOU!
OKAY!
YOU TRAITOR!
OH, GOOD MORNING.
WAH-H-H
HOW COULD YOU!?
HOW COME YOU GET TO TALK TO MAIKO-CHAN!?

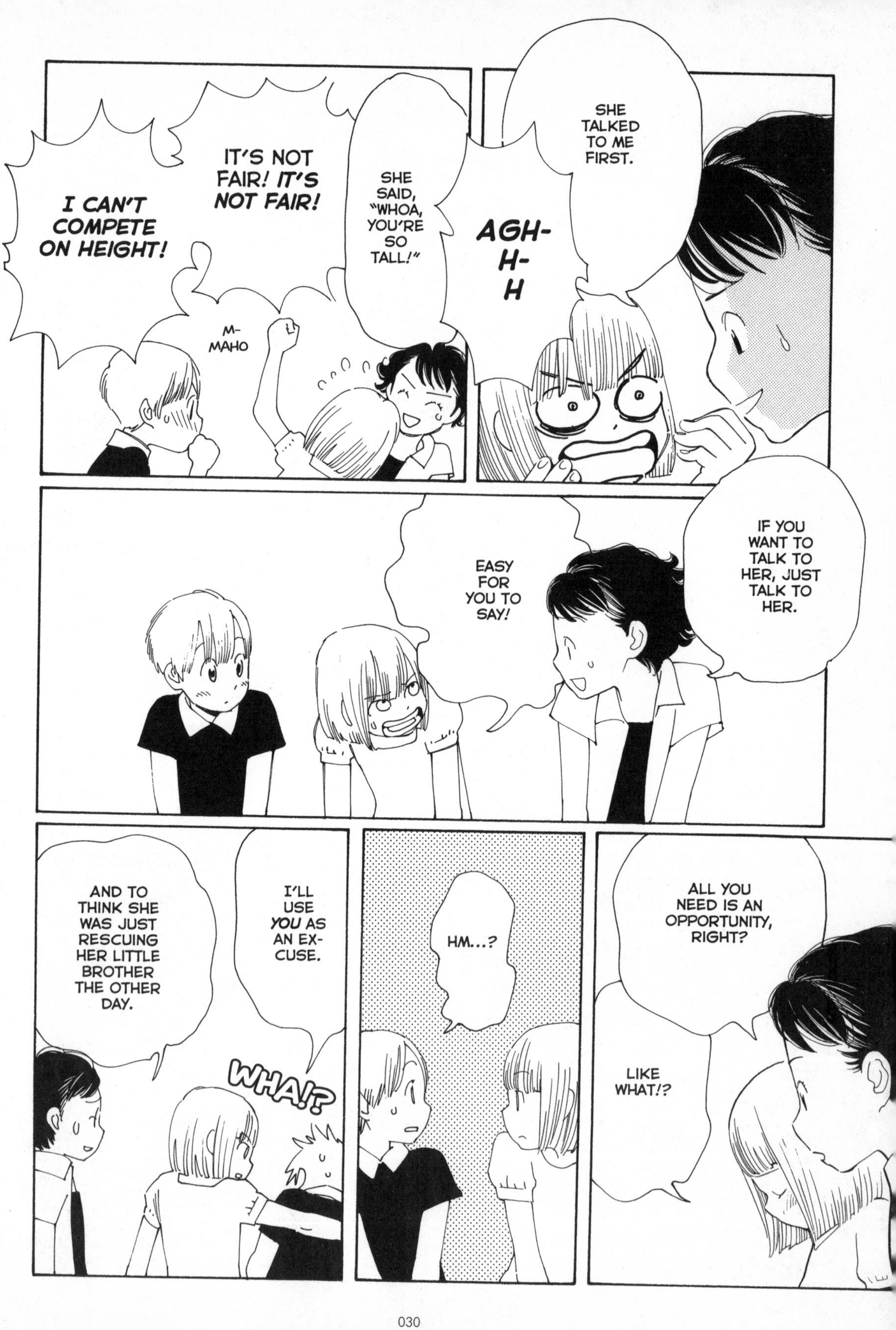
SHE TALKED TO ME FIRST.
AGH-H-H
SHE SAID, "WHOA, YOU'RE SO TALL!"
IT'S NOT FAIR! IT'S NOT FAIR!
I CAN'T COMPETE ON HEIGHT!
M-MAHO
IF YOU WANT TO TALK TO HER, JUST TALK TO HER.
EASY FOR YOU TO SAY!
ALL YOU NEED IS AN OPPORTUNITY, RIGHT?
LIKE WHAT!?
HM...?
I'LL USE YOU AS AN EX-CUSE.
AND TO THINK SHE WAS JUST RESCUING HER LITTLE BROTHER THE OTHER DAY.
WHA!?

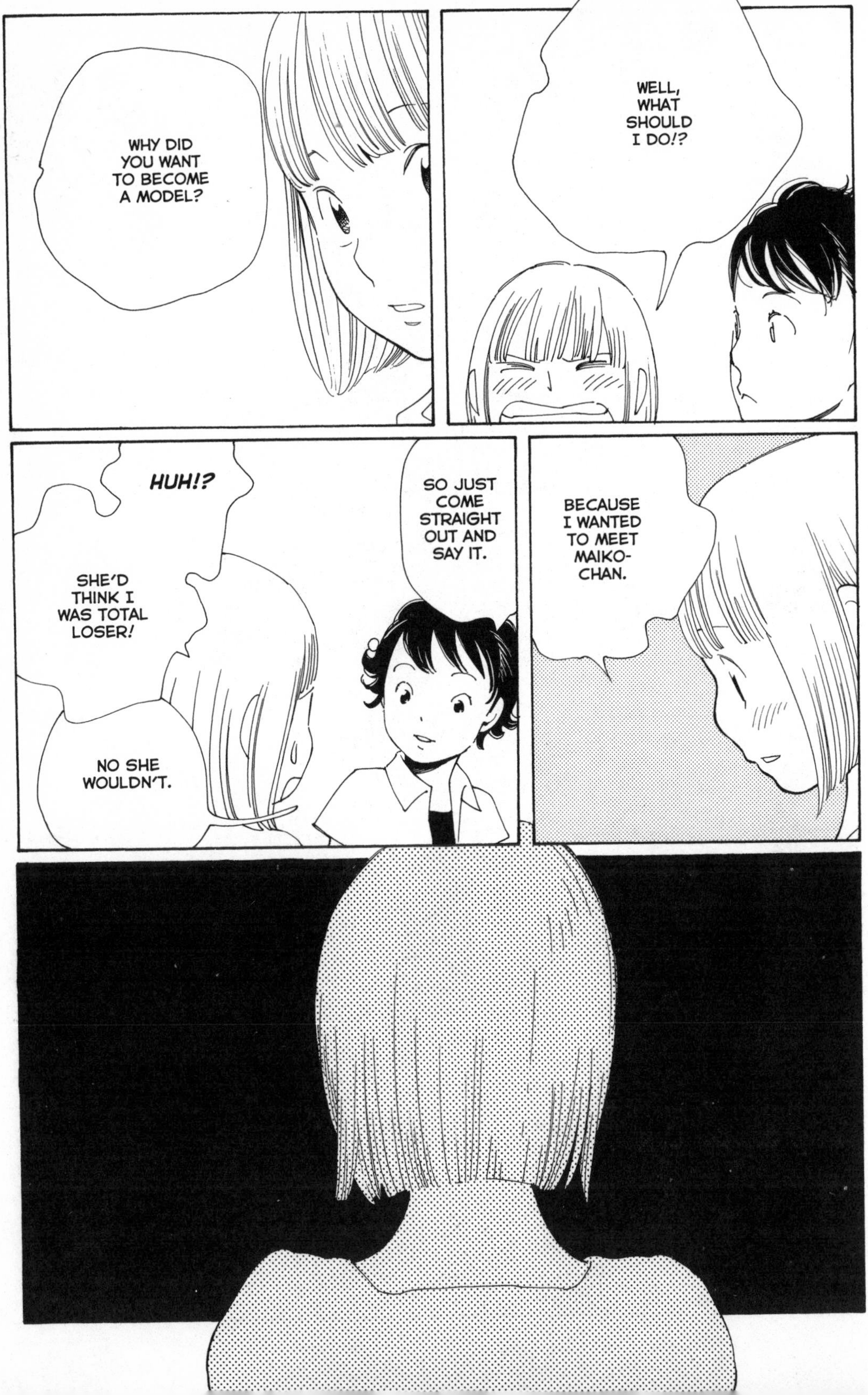
WELL, WHAT SHOULD I DO!?
WHY DID YOU WANT TO BECOME A MODEL?
BECAUSE I WANTED TO MEET MAIKO-CHAN.
SO JUST COME STRAIGHT OUT AND SAY IT.
HUH!?
SHE'D THINK I WAS TOTAL LOSER!
NO SHE WOULDN'T.

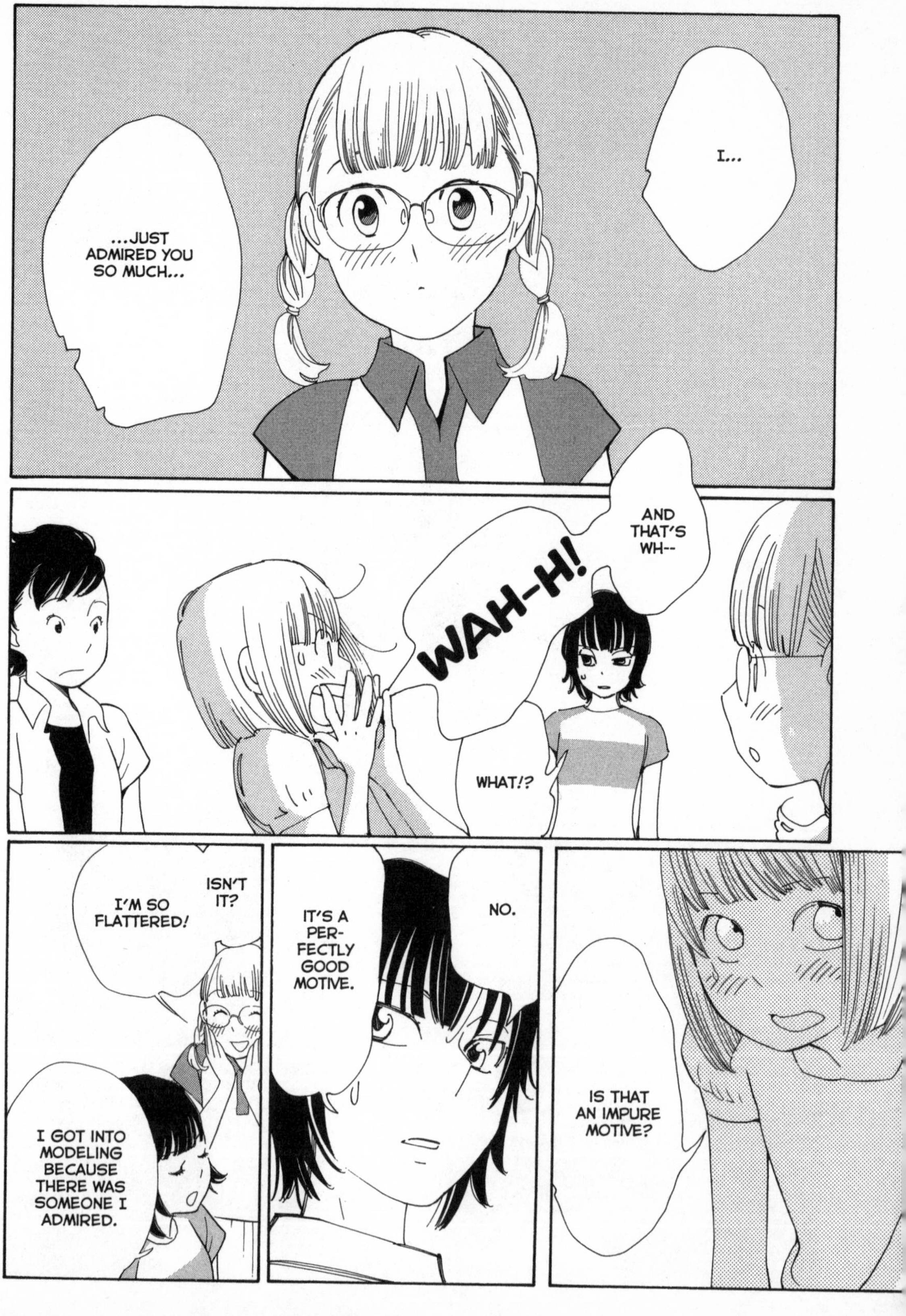
I...
...JUST ADMIRED YOU SO MUCH...
AND THAT'S WH--
WAH-H!
WHAT!?
IS THAT AN IMPURE MOTIVE?
NO.
IT'S A PER-FECTLY GOOD MOTIVE.
ISN'T IT?
I'M SO FLATTERED!
I GOT INTO MODELING BECAUSE THERE WAS SOMEONE I ADMIRED.

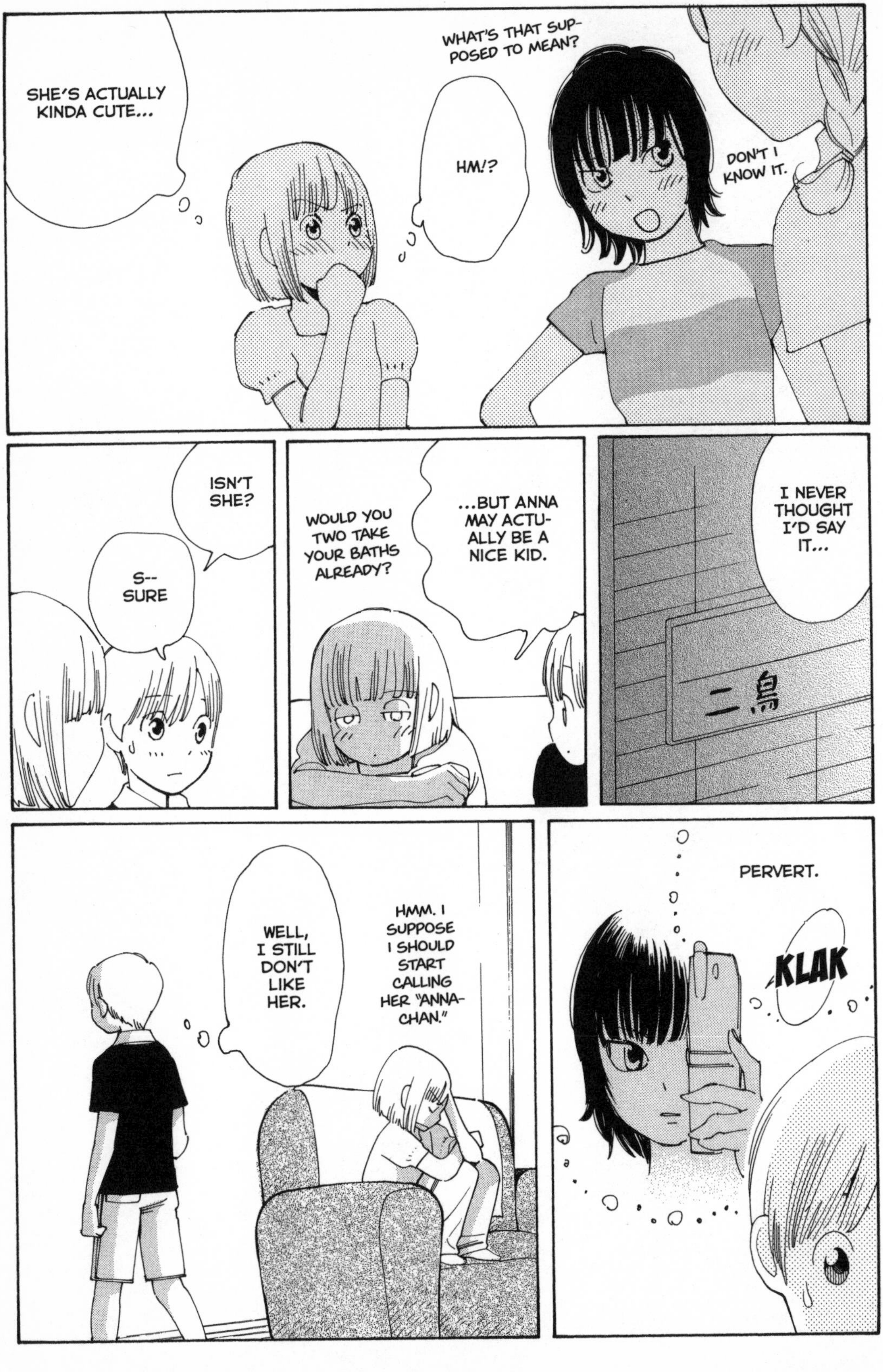
WHAT'S THAT SUPPOSED TO MEAN?
DON'T I KNOW IT.
HM!?
SHE'S ACTUALLY KINDA CUTE...
I NEVER THOUGHT I'D SAY IT...
二鳥
...BUT ANNA MAY ACTUALLY BE A NICE KID.
WOULD YOU TWO TAKE YOUR BATHS ALREADY?
ISN'T SHE?
S-- SURE
PERVERT.
KLAK
HMM. I SUPPOSE I SHOULD START CALLING HER "ANNA-CHAN."
WELL, I STILL DON'T LIKE HER.

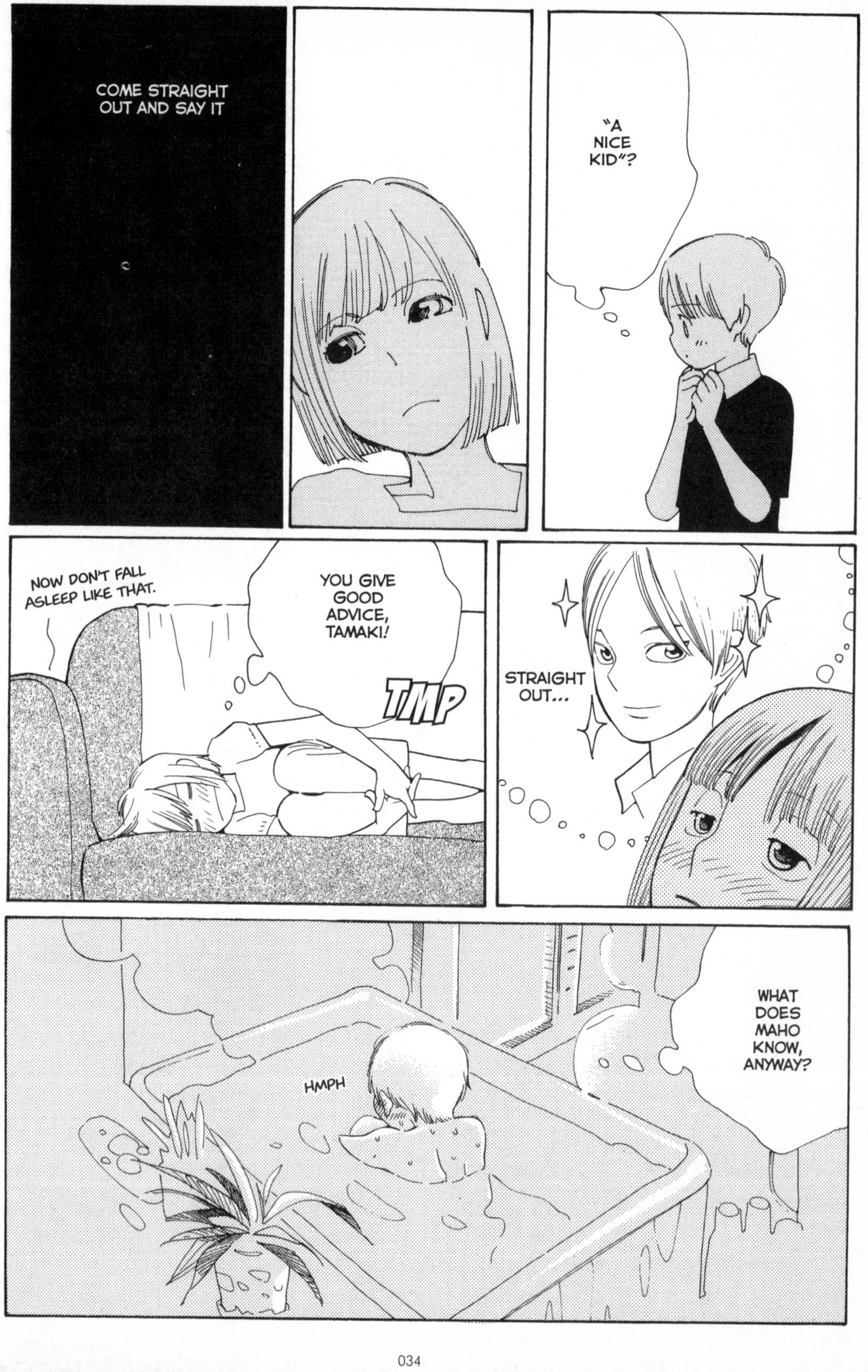
"A NICE KID"?
COME STRAIGHT OUT AND SAY IT
STRAIGHT OUT...
YOU GIVE GOOD ADVICE, TAMAKI!
NOW DON'T FALL ASLEEP LIKE THAT.
TMP
WHAT DOES MAHO KNOW, ANYWAY?
HMPH

27

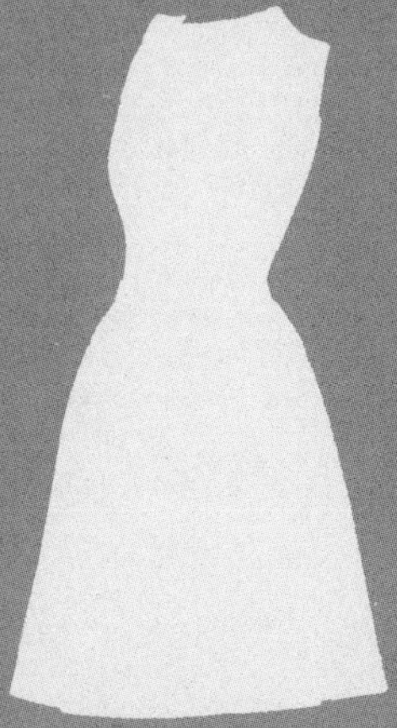

The Tragic Princess

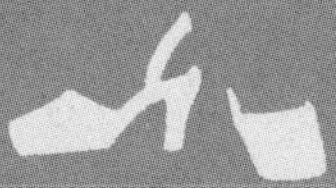

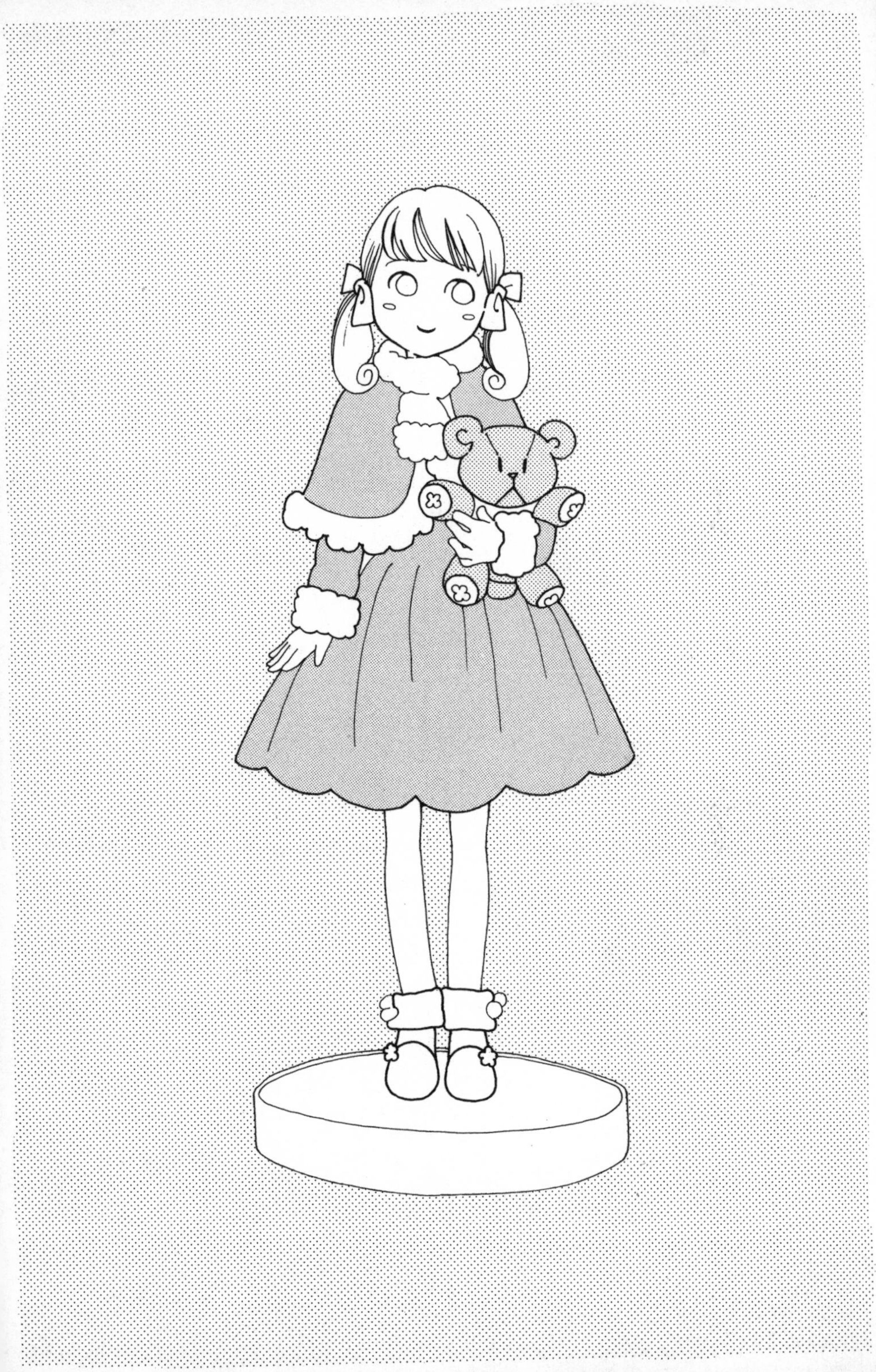

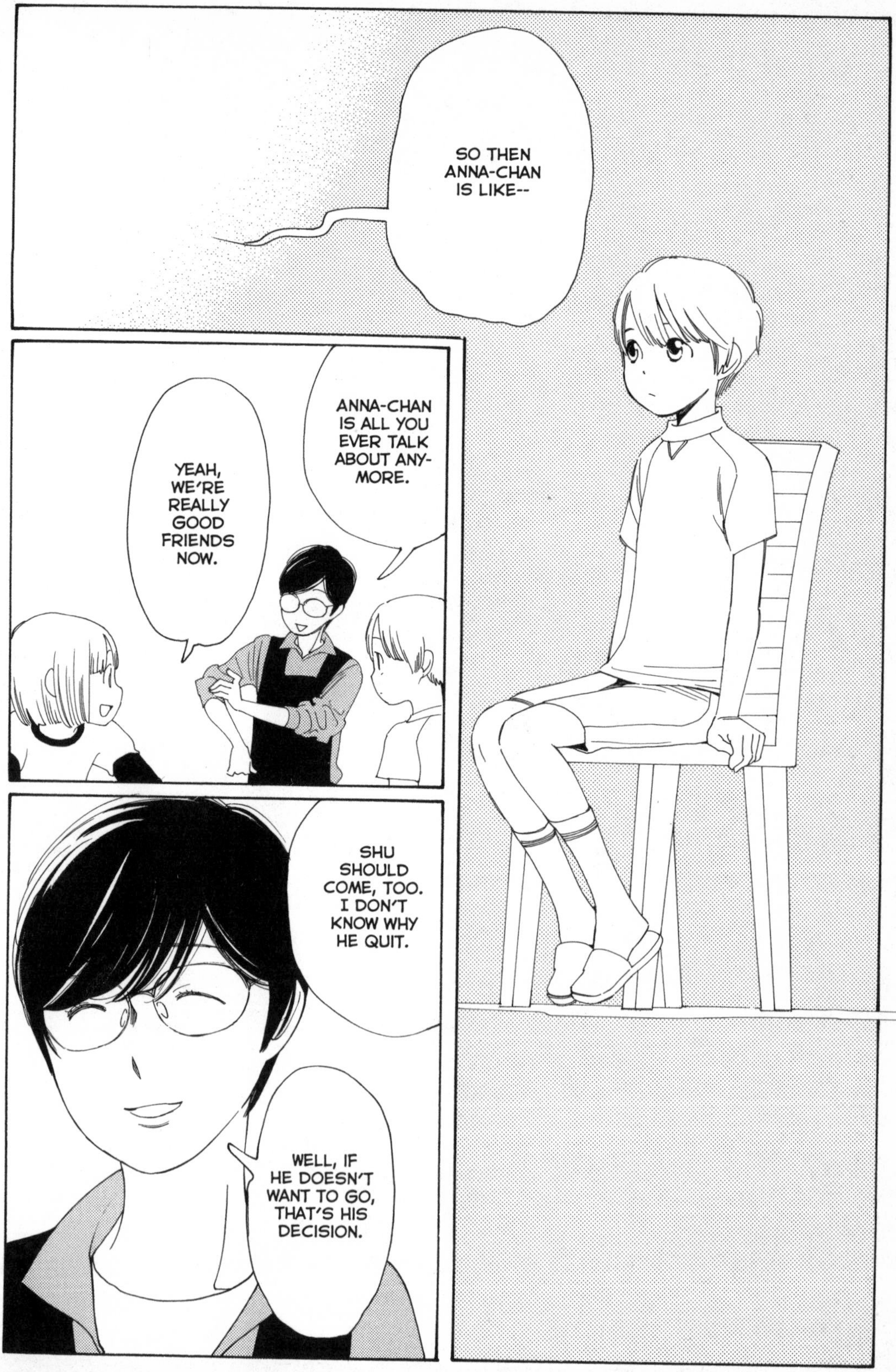
SO THEN ANNA-CHAN IS LIKE--
ANNA-CHAN IS ALL YOU EVER TALK ABOUT ANY-MORE.
YEAH, WE'RE REALLY GOOD FRIENDS NOW.
SHU SHOULD COME, TOO. I DON'T KNOW WHY HE QUIT.
WELL, IF HE DOESN'T WANT TO GO, THAT'S HIS DECISION.

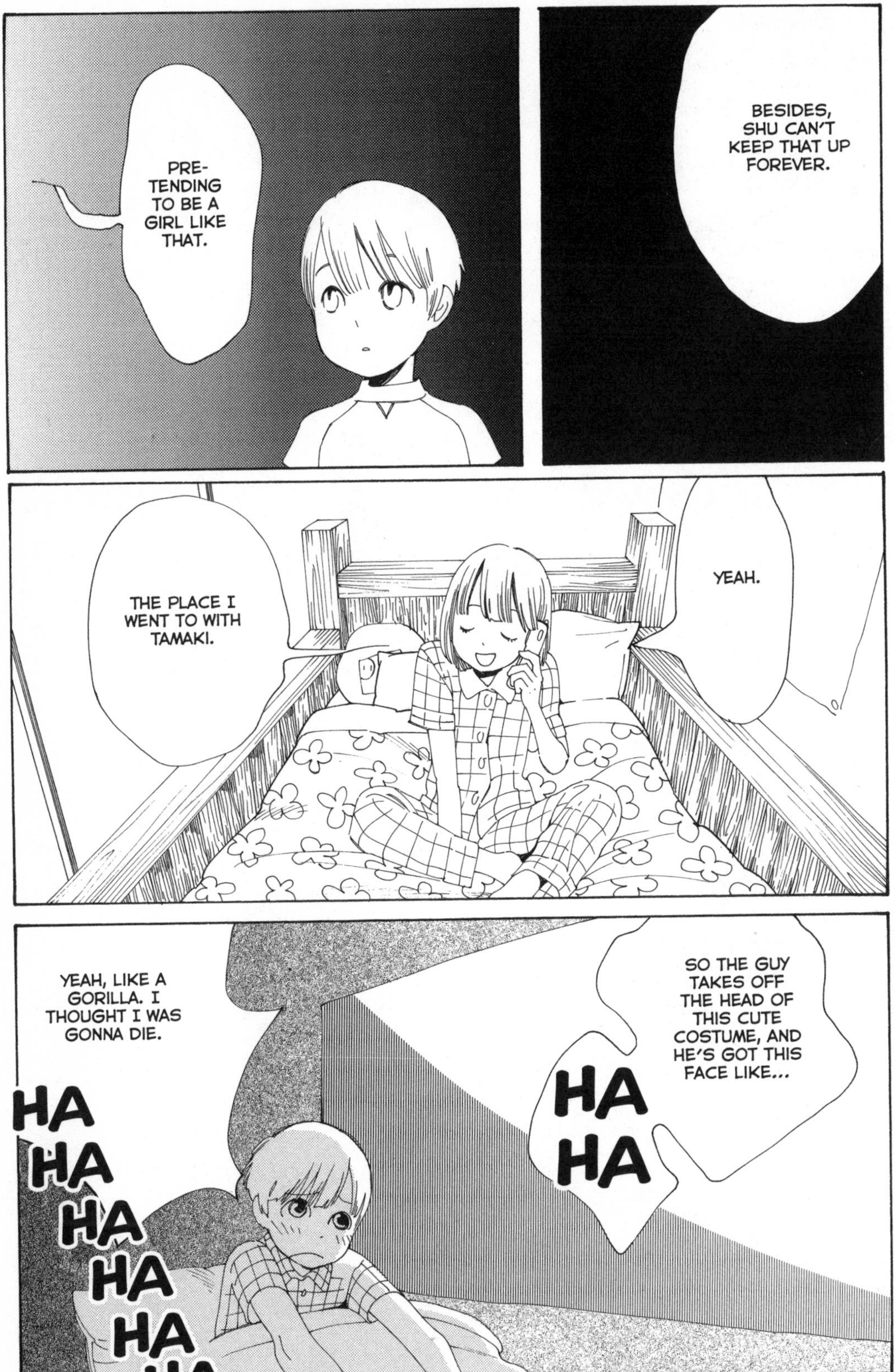
BESIDES, SHU CAN'T KEEP THAT UP FOREVER.
PRE-TENDING TO BE A GIRL LIKE THAT.
YEAH.
THE PLACE I WENT TO WITH TAMAKI.
SO THE GUY TAKES OFF THE HEAD OF THIS CUTE COSTUME, AND HE'S GOT THIS FACE LIKE...
HA HA
YEAH, LIKE A GORILLA. I THOUGHT I WAS GONNA DIE.
HA HA HA HA HA HA

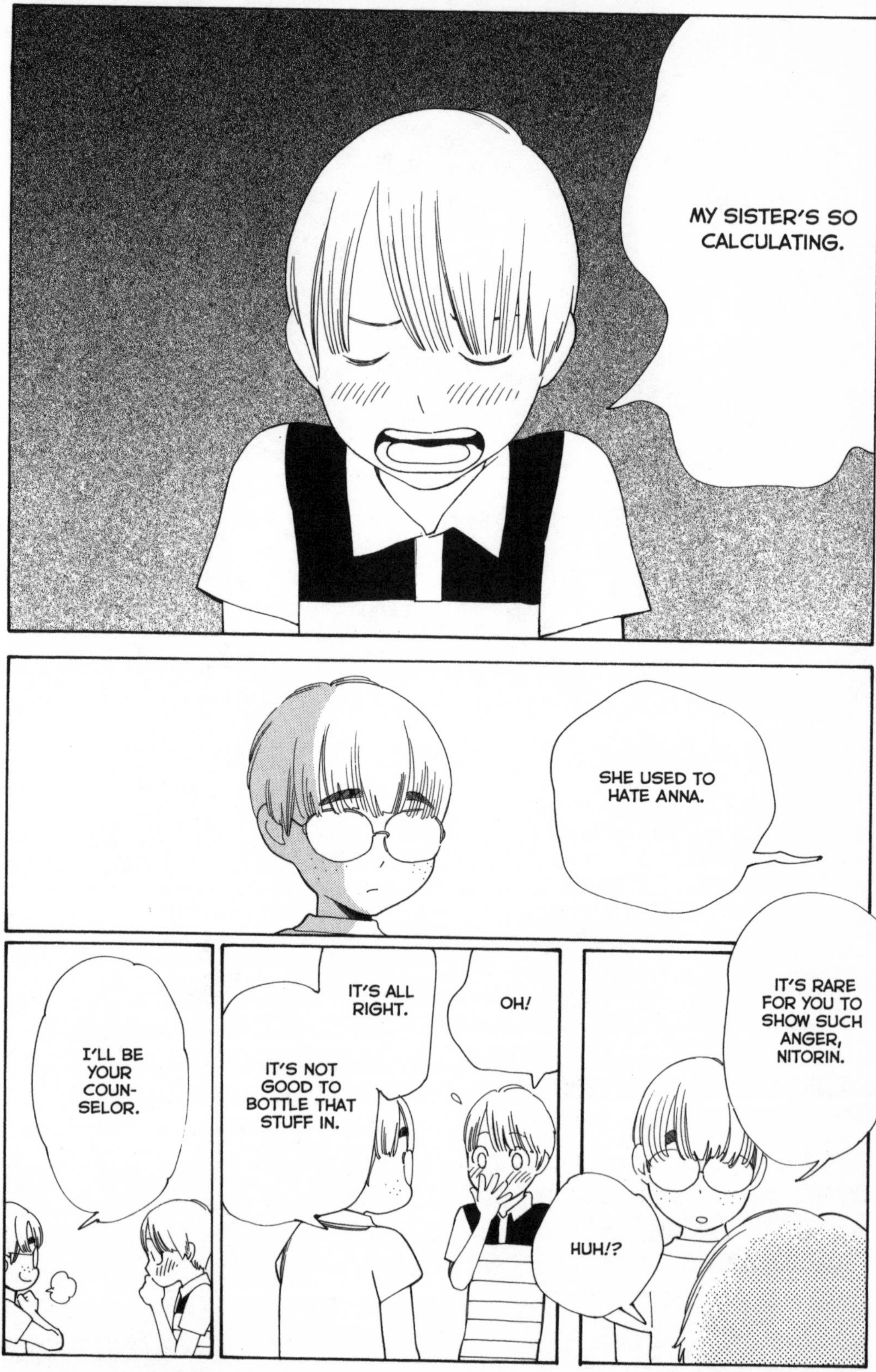
MY SISTER'S SO CALCULATING.
SHE USED TO HATE ANNA.
IT'S RARE FOR YOU TO SHOW SUCH ANGER, NITORIN.
HUH!?
OH!
IT'S ALL RIGHT.
IT'S NOT GOOD TO BOTTLE THAT STUFF IN.
I'LL BE YOUR COUN-SELOR.

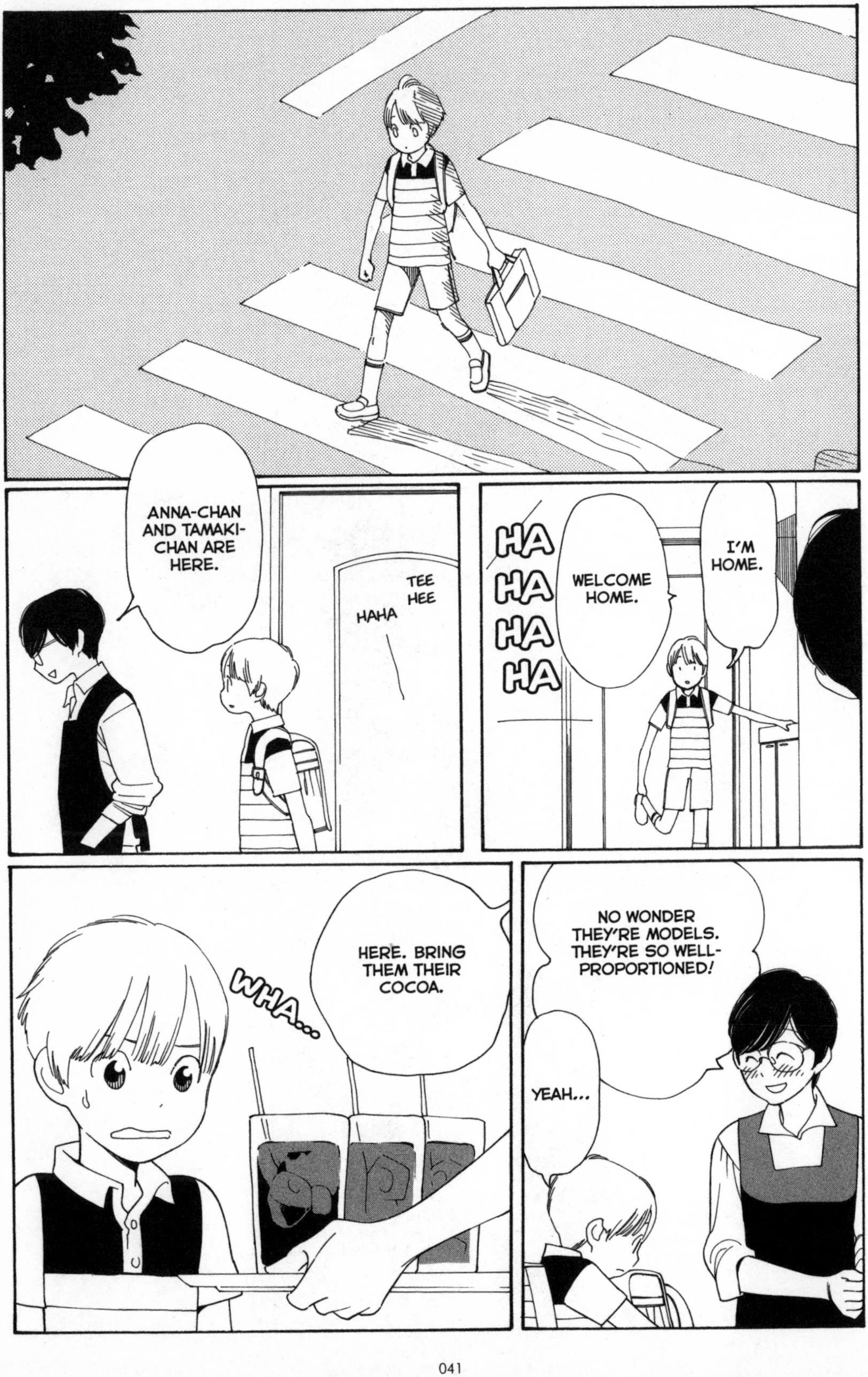
I'M HOME.
WELCOME HOME.
HA HA HA HA
TEE HEE
HAHA
ANNA-CHAN AND TAMAKI-CHAN ARE HERE.
NO WONDER THEY'RE MODELS. THEY'RE SO WELL-PROPORTIONED!
YEAH...
HERE. BRING THEM THEIR COCOA.
WHA...

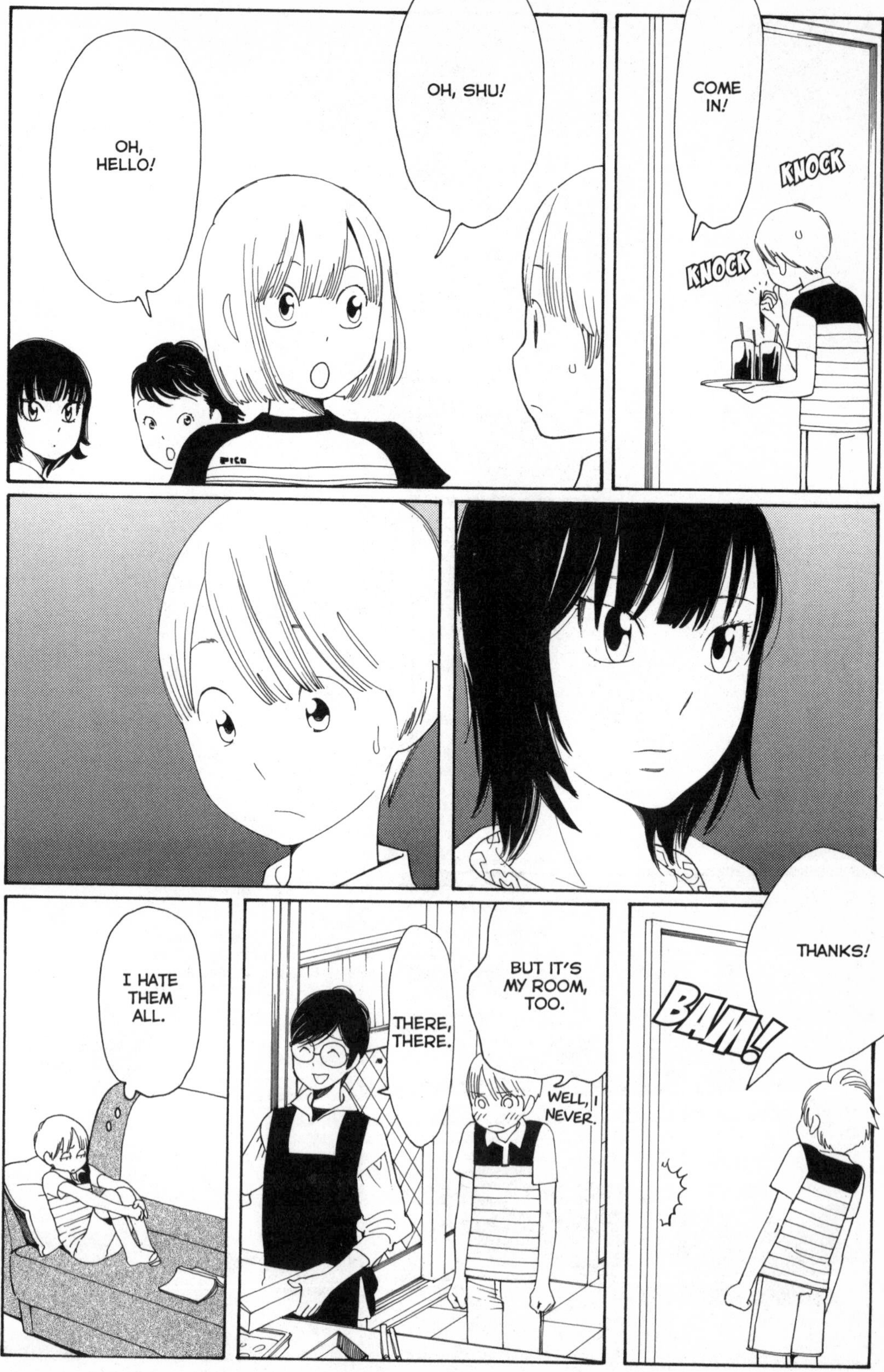
COME IN!
KNOCK
KNOCK
OH, SHU!
OH, HELLO!
THANKS!
BAM!
BUT IT'S MY ROOM, TOO.
THERE, THERE.
WELL, I NEVER.
I HATE THEM ALL.

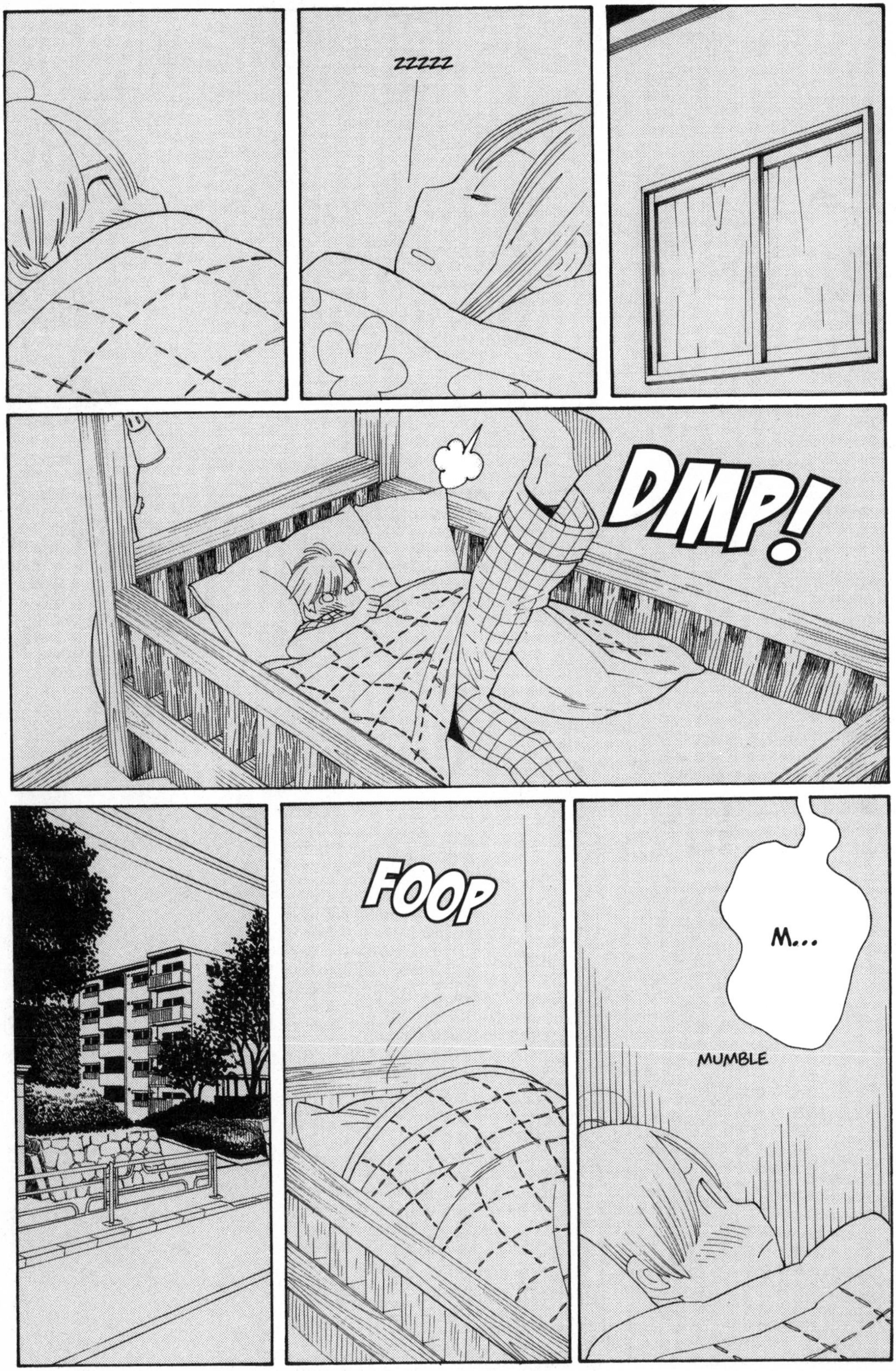
ZZZZZ
DMP!
M...
MUMBLE
FOOP

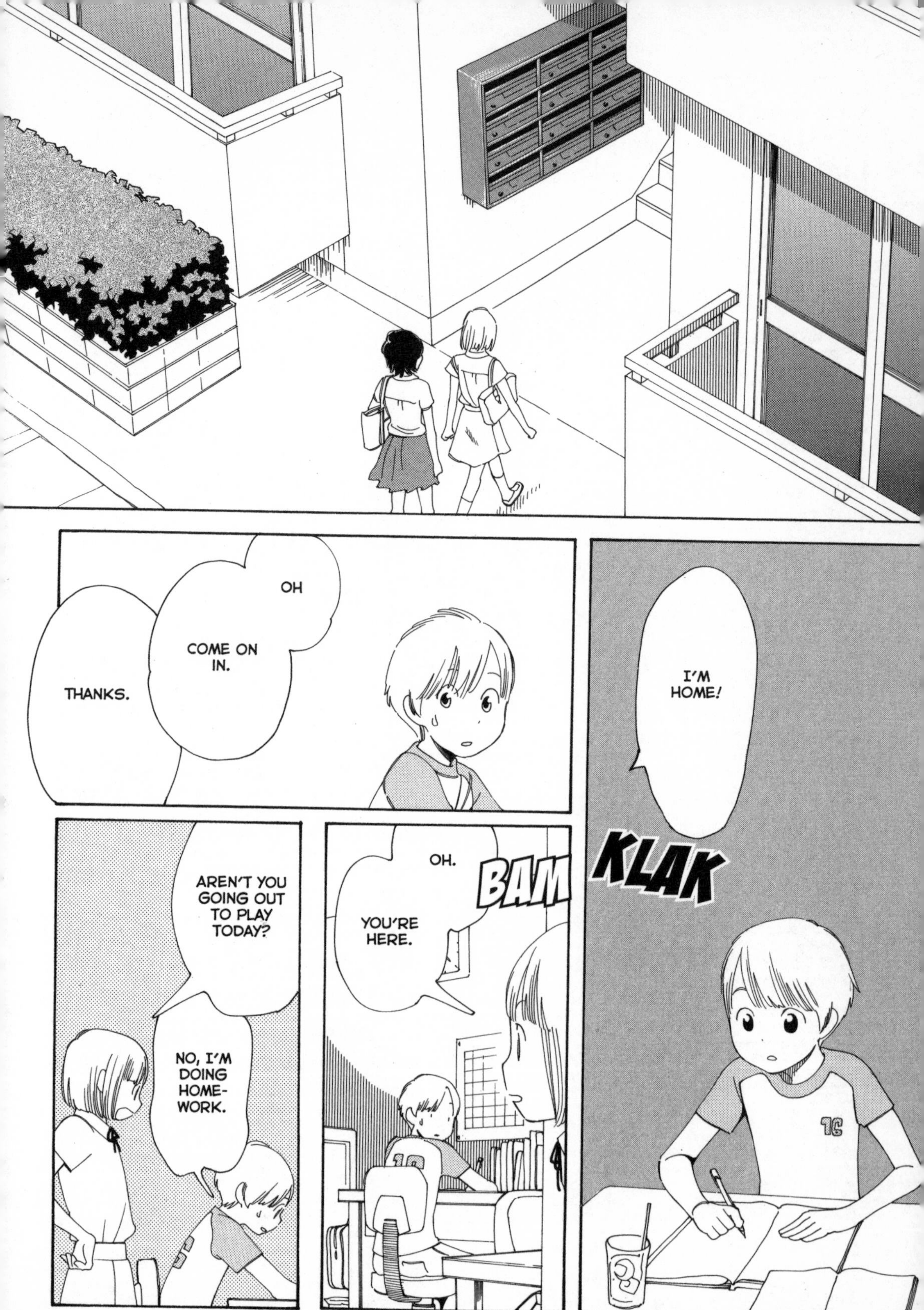

I'M HOME!
BAM
KLAK
OH
COME ON IN.
THANKS.
OH.
YOU'RE HERE.
AREN'T YOU GOING OUT TO PLAY TODAY?
NO, I'M DOING HOME-WORK.

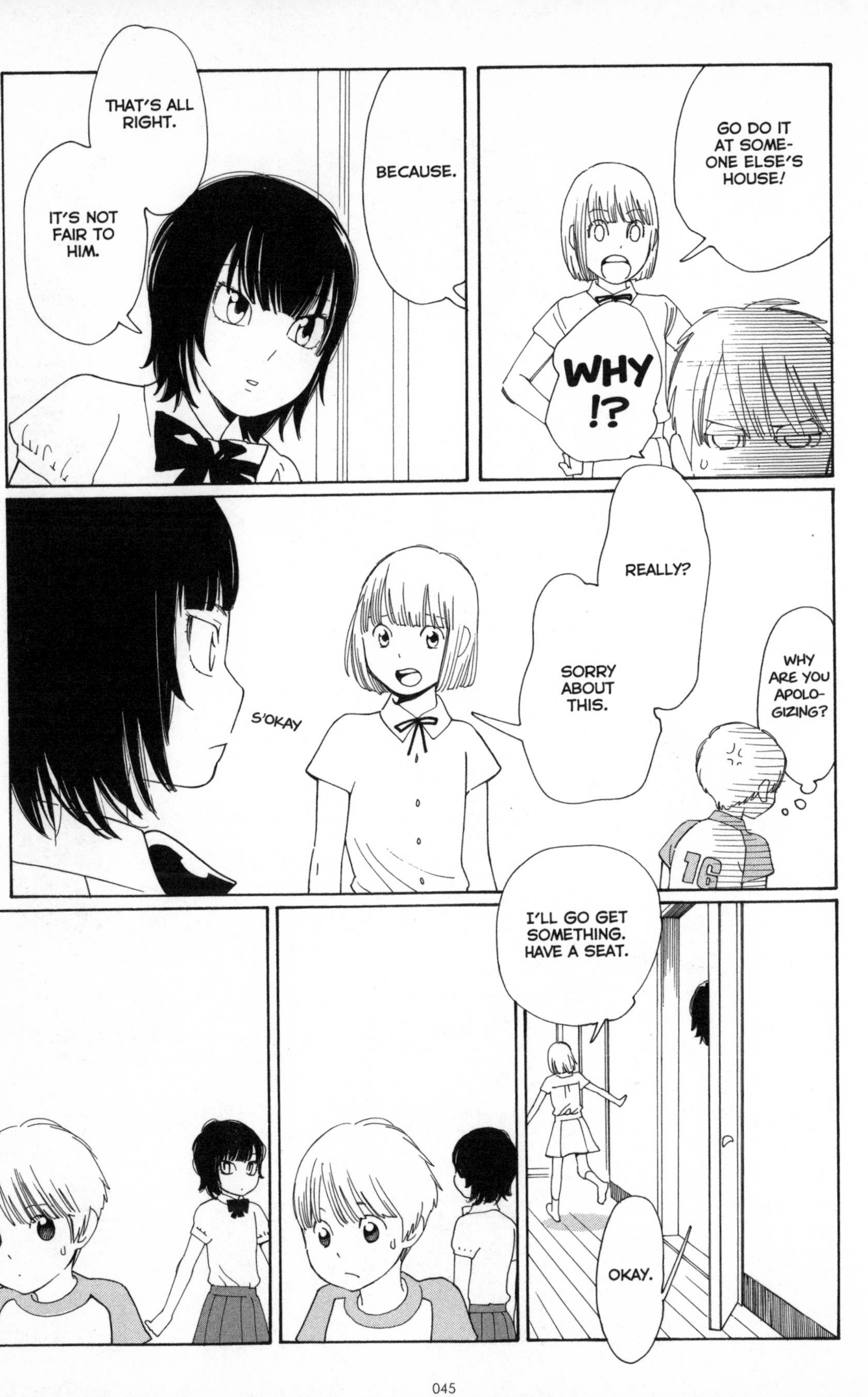
GO DO IT AT SOME-ONE ELSE'S HOUSE!
WHY !?
BECAUSE.
THAT'S ALL RIGHT.
IT'S NOT FAIR TO HIM.
REALLY?
WHY ARE YOU APOLO-GIZING?
SORRY ABOUT THIS.
S'OKAY
I'LL GO GET SOMETHING. HAVE A SEAT.
OKAY.

HI...

HI.

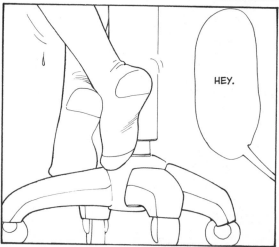

HEY.

HAVE YOU STOPPED DRESSING LIKE A GIRL?

AREN'T YOU THE GLOOMY ONE.

WAH!

HEY!

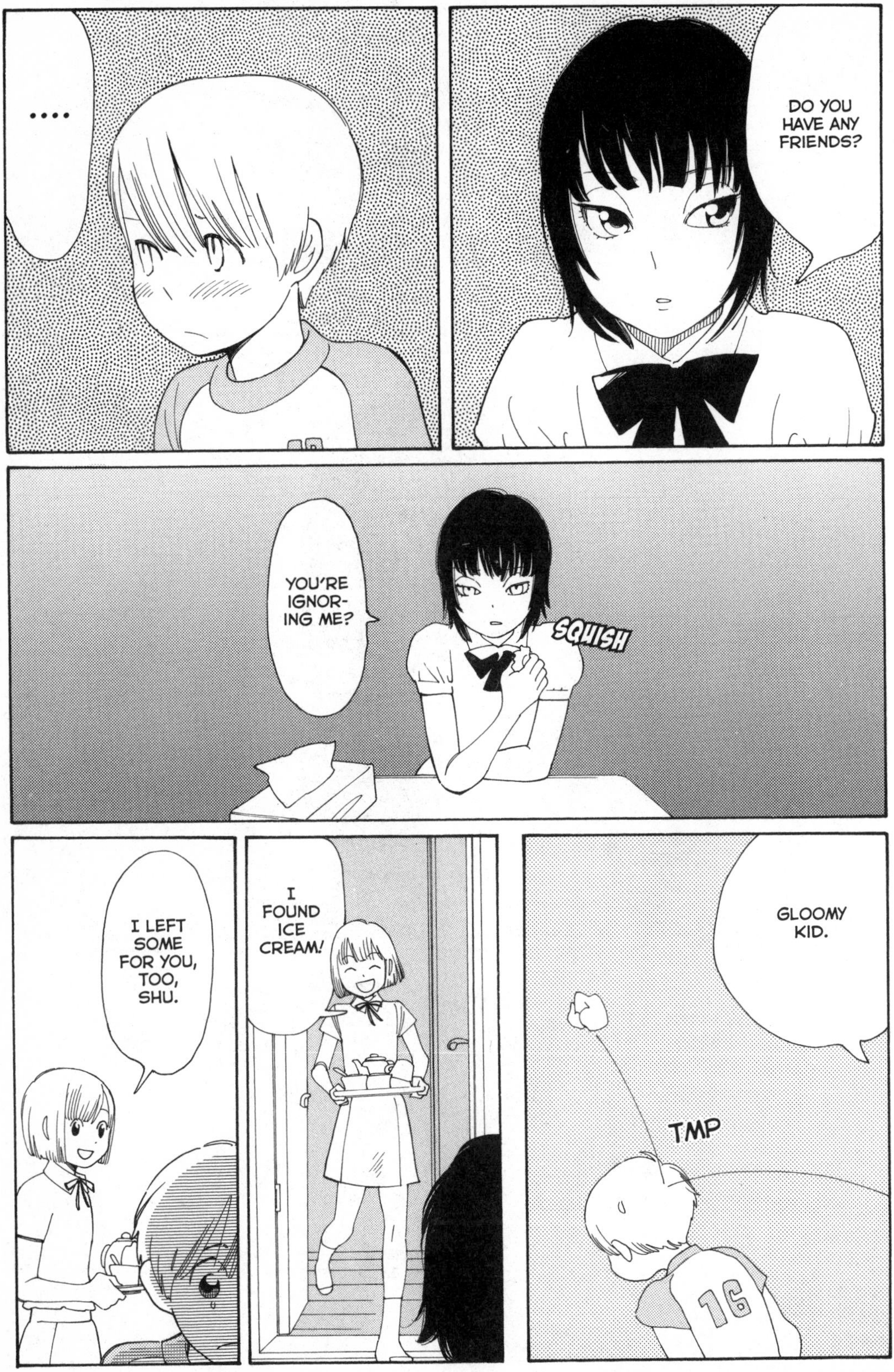
DO YOU HAVE ANY FRIENDS?
....
YOU'RE IGNORING ME?
SQUISH
GLOOMY KID.
TMP
I FOUND ICE CREAM!
I LEFT SOME FOR YOU, TOO, SHU.

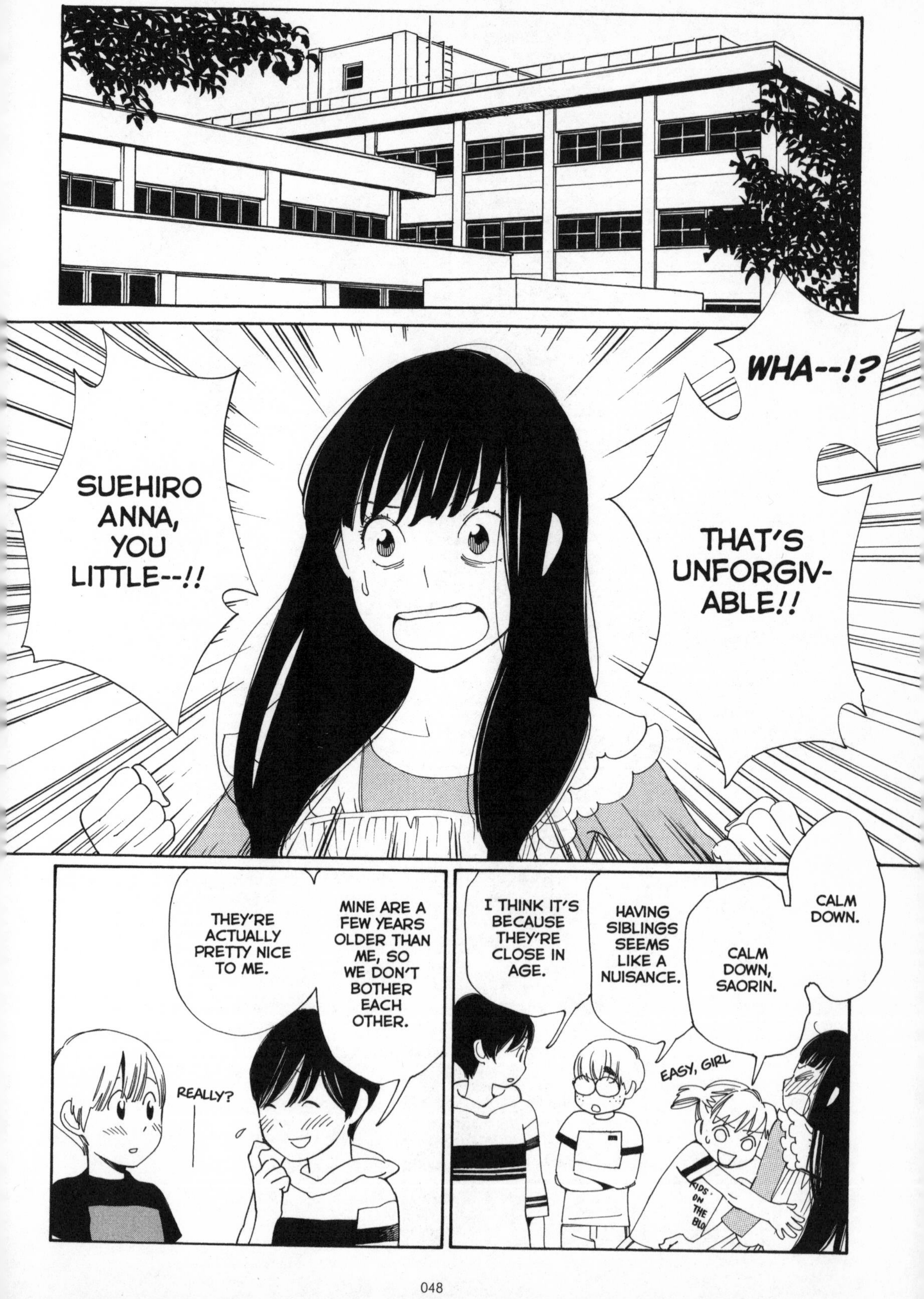
WHA--!?
THAT'S UNFORGIV-ABLE!!
SUEHIRO ANNA, YOU LITTLE--!!
CALM DOWN.
CALM DOWN, SAORIN.
EASY, GIRL
HAVING SIBLINGS SEEMS LIKE A NUISANCE.
I THINK IT'S BECAUSE THEY'RE CLOSE IN AGE.
MINE ARE A FEW YEARS OLDER THAN ME, SO WE DON'T BOTHER EACH OTHER.
THEY'RE ACTUALLY PRETTY NICE TO ME.
REALLY?

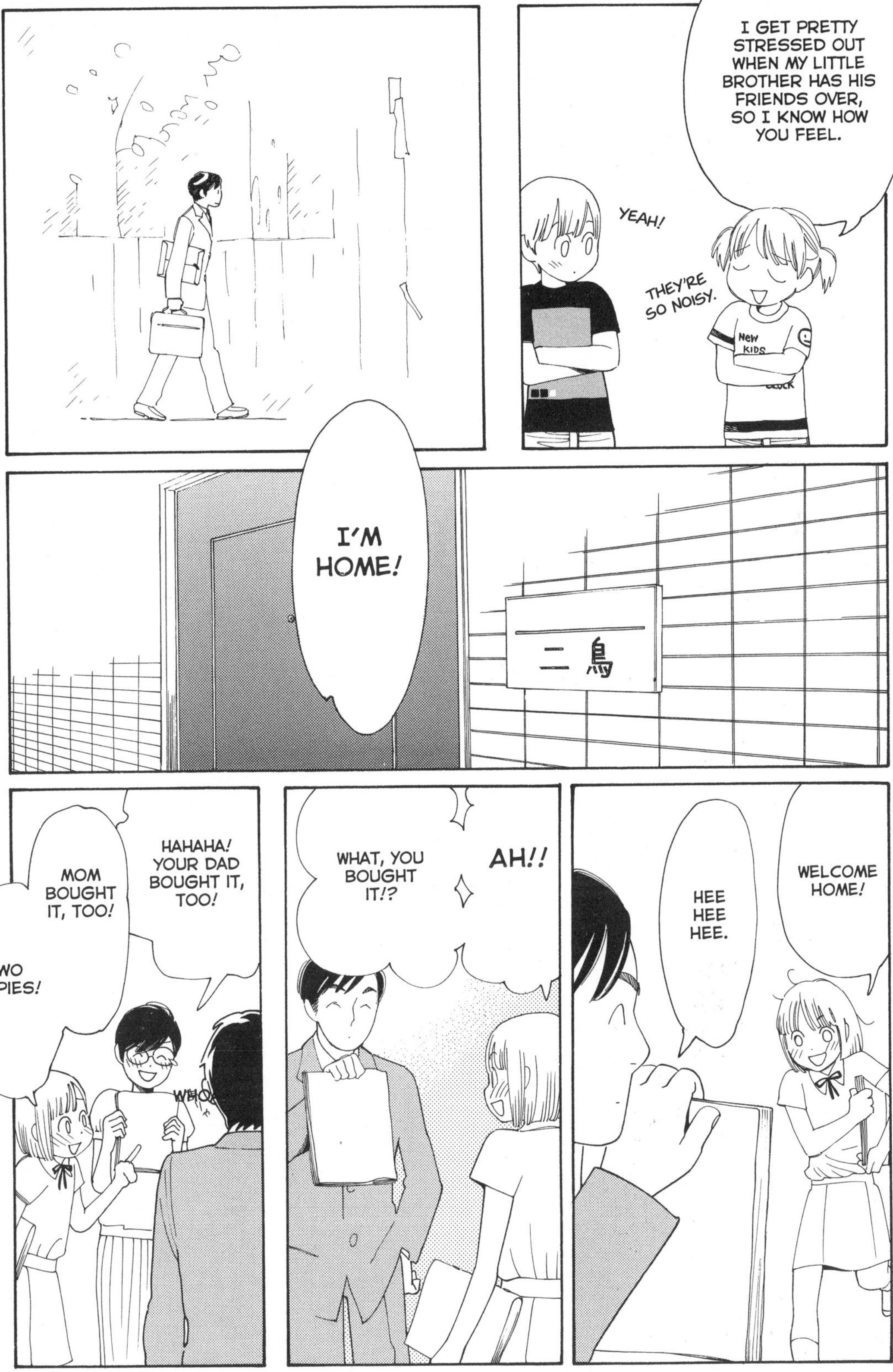
I GET PRETTY STRESSED OUT WHEN MY LITTLE BROTHER HAS HIS FRIENDS OVER, SO I KNOW HOW YOU FEEL.
YEAH!
THEY'RE SO NOISY.
New KIDS
I'M HOME!
二鳥
WELCOME HOME!
HEE HEE HEE.
AH!!
WHAT, YOU BOUGHT IT!?
HAHAHA! YOUR DAD BOUGHT IT, TOO!
MOM BOUGHT IT, TOO!
TWO COPIES!
WHOA

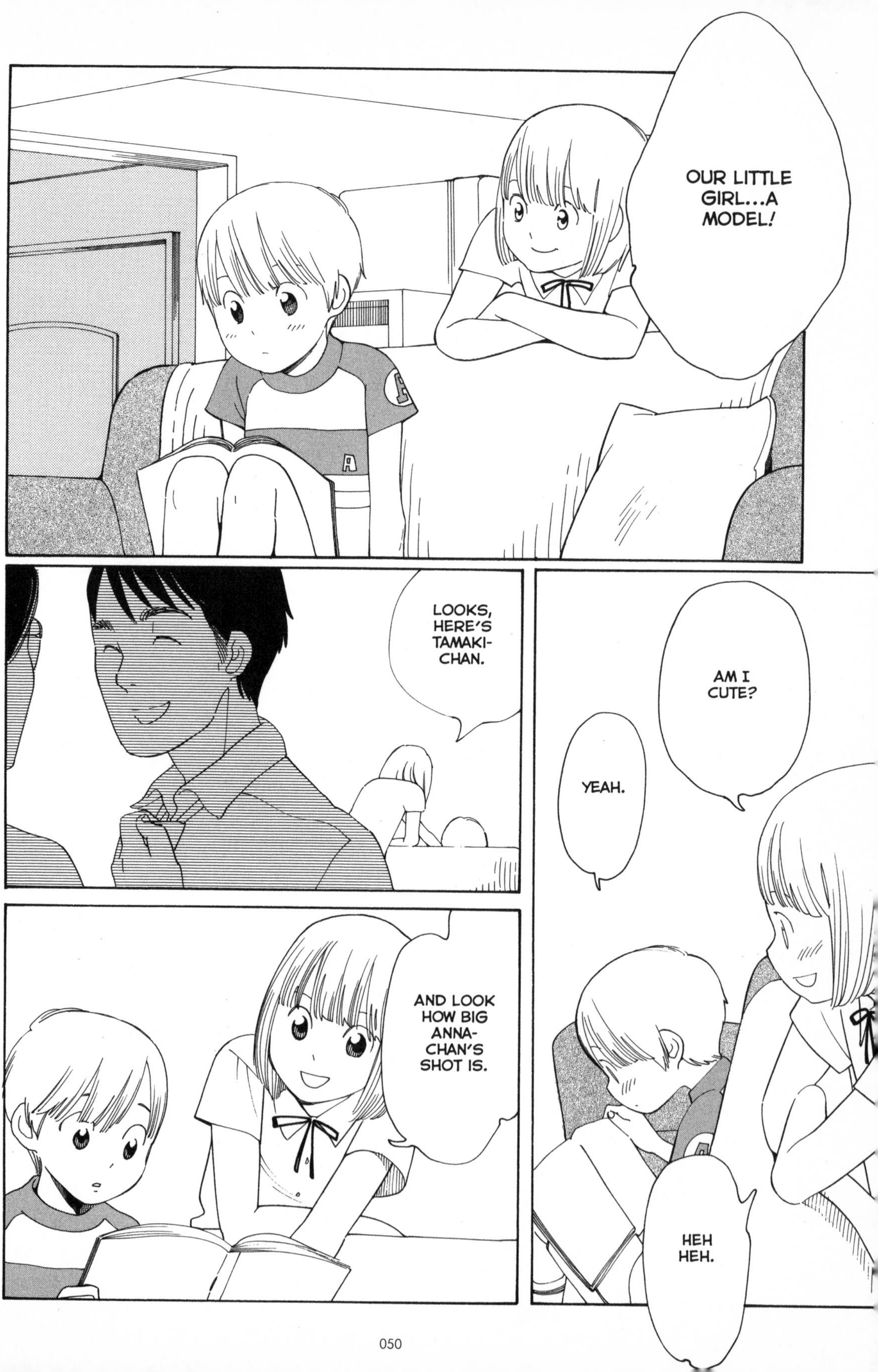
OUR LITTLE GIRL...A MODEL!
AM I CUTE?
YEAH.
HEH HEH.
LOOKS, HERE'S TAMAKI-CHAN.
AND LOOK HOW BIG ANNA-CHAN'S SHOT IS.

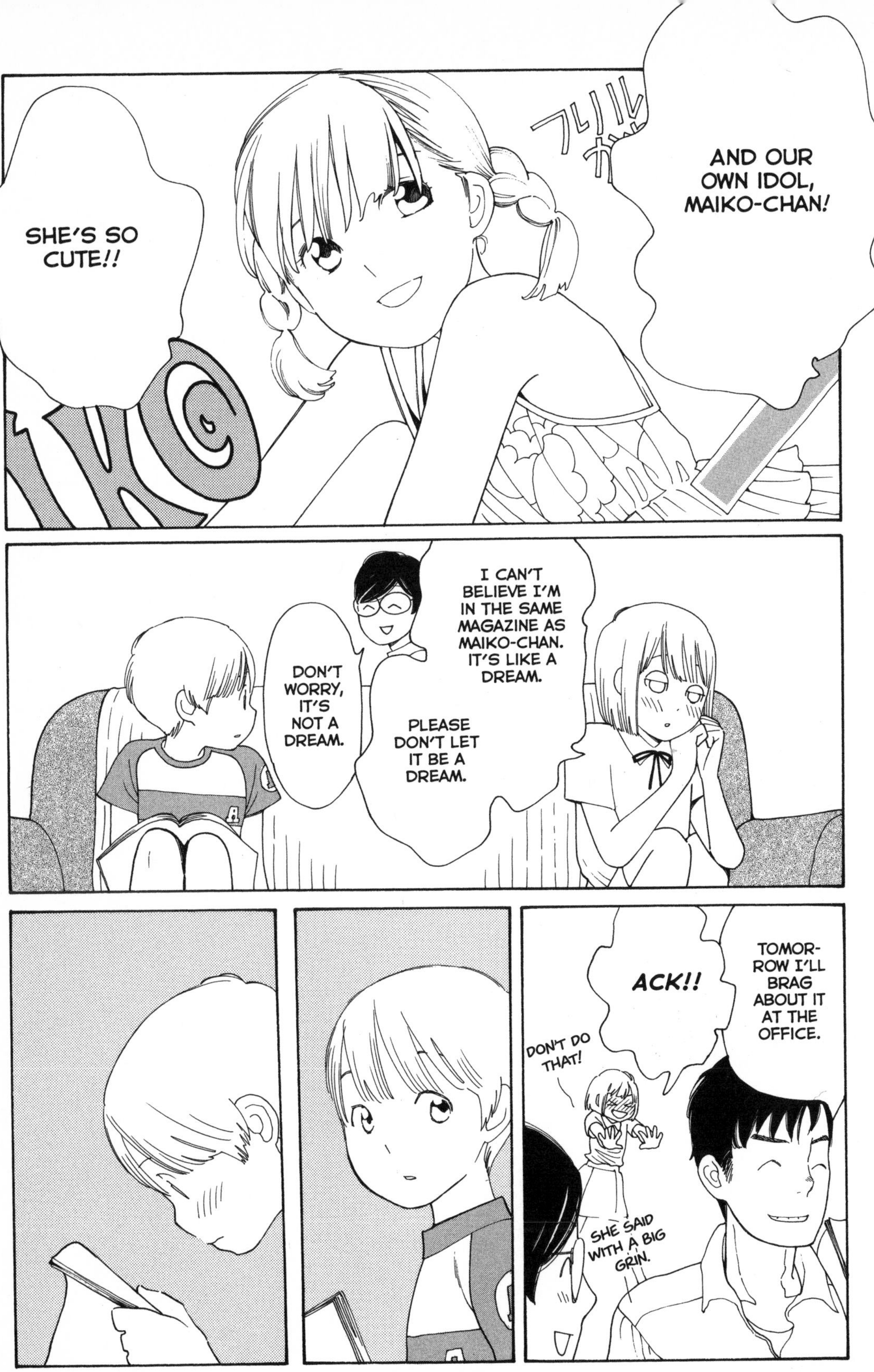
AND OUR OWN IDOL, MAIKO-CHAN!
SHE'S SO CUTE!!
I CAN'T BELIEVE I'M IN THE SAME MAGAZINE AS MAIKO-CHAN. IT'S LIKE A DREAM.
PLEASE DON'T LET IT BE A DREAM.
DON'T WORRY, IT'S NOT A DREAM.
TOMOR-ROW I'LL BRAG ABOUT IT AT THE OFFICE.
ACK!!
DON'T DO THAT!
SHE SAID WITH A BIG GRIN.

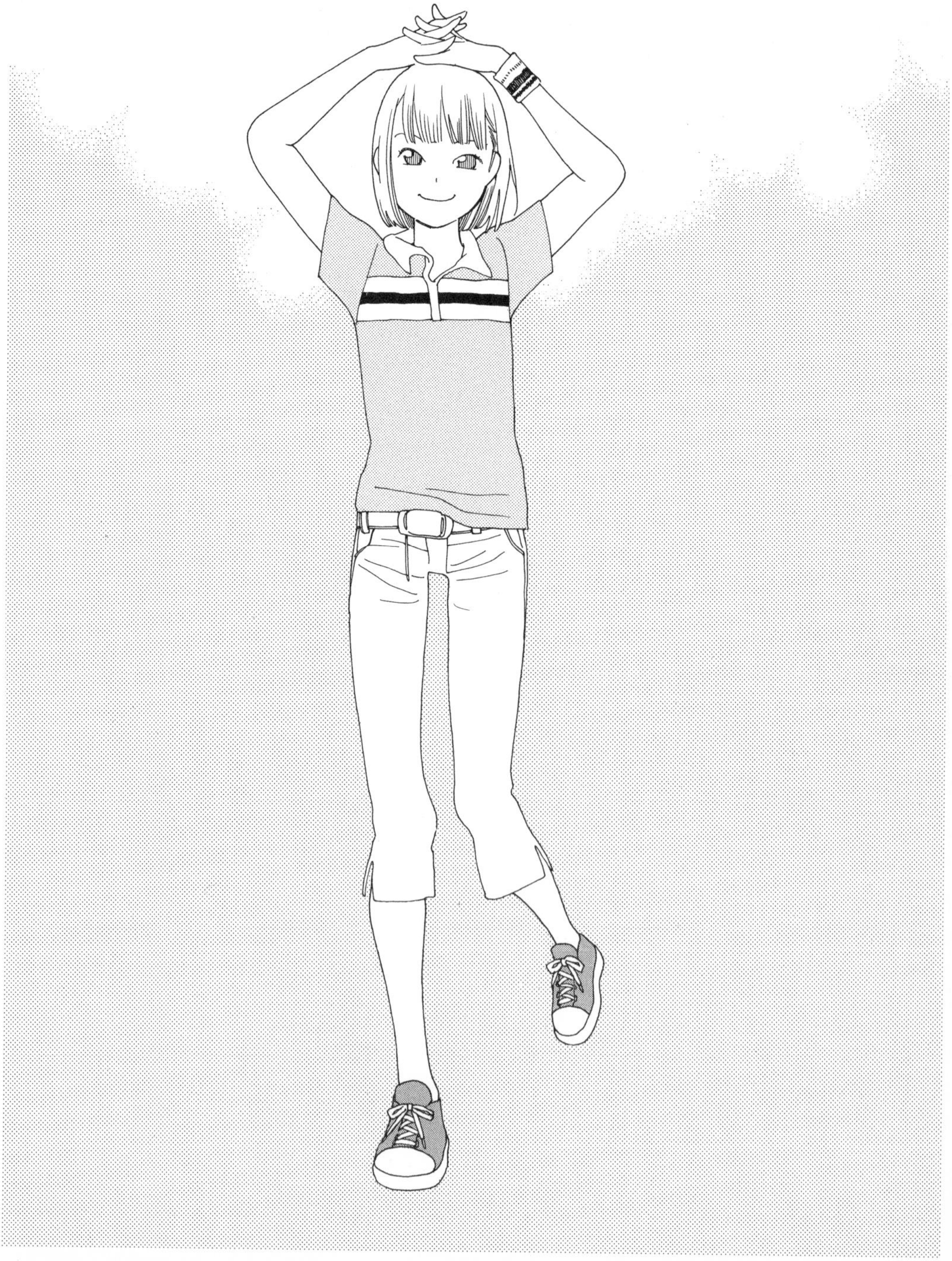

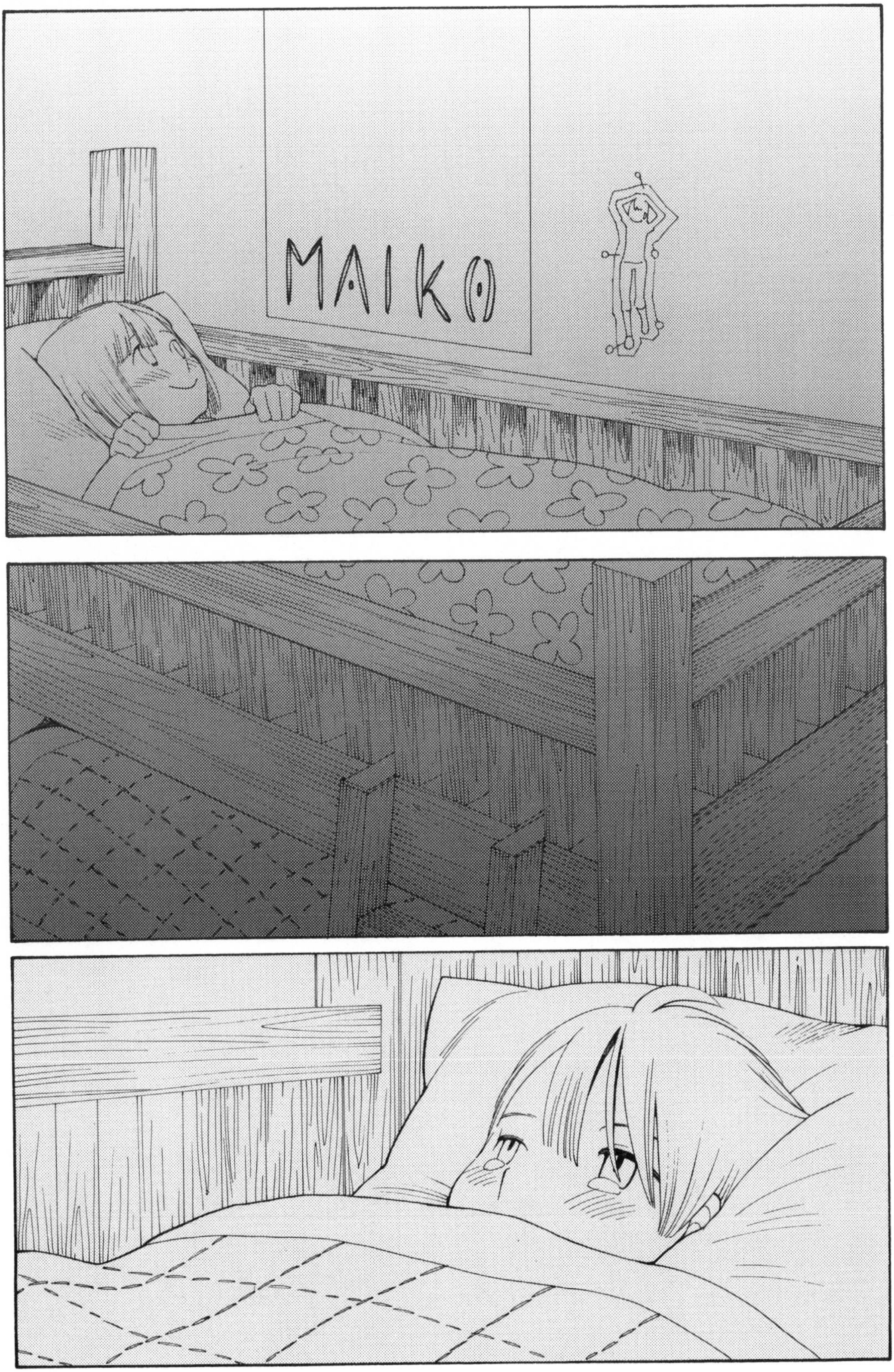
MAIKO

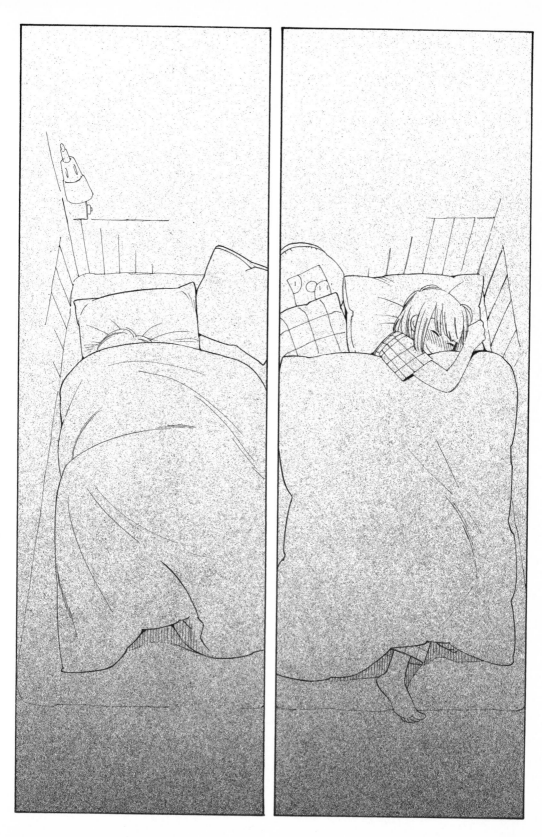

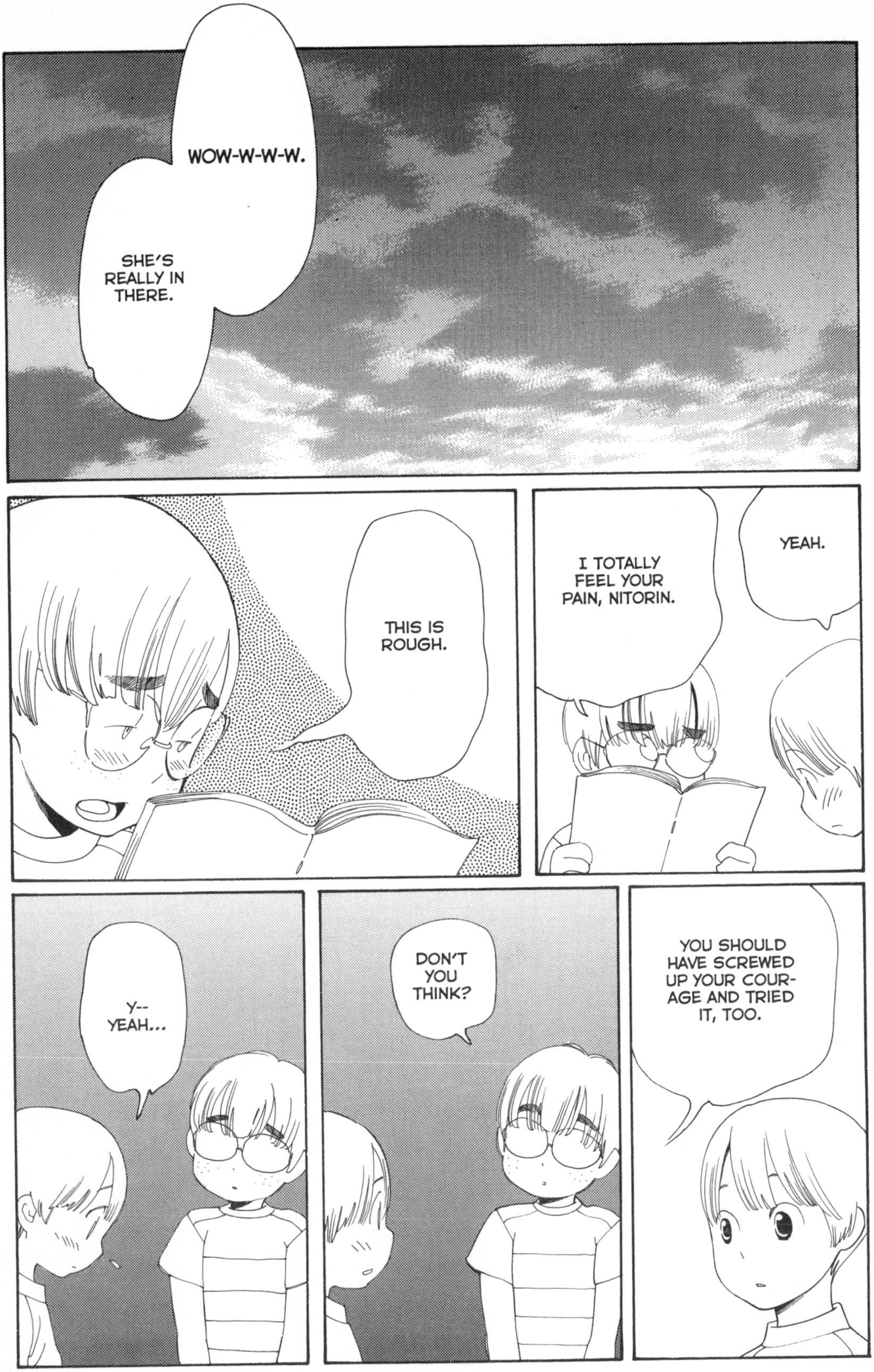
WOW-W-W-W.
SHE'S REALLY IN THERE.
YEAH.
I TOTALLY FEEL YOUR PAIN, NITORIN.
THIS IS ROUGH.
YOU SHOULD HAVE SCREWED UP YOUR COURAGE AND TRIED IT, TOO.
DON'T YOU THINK?
Y-- YEAH...

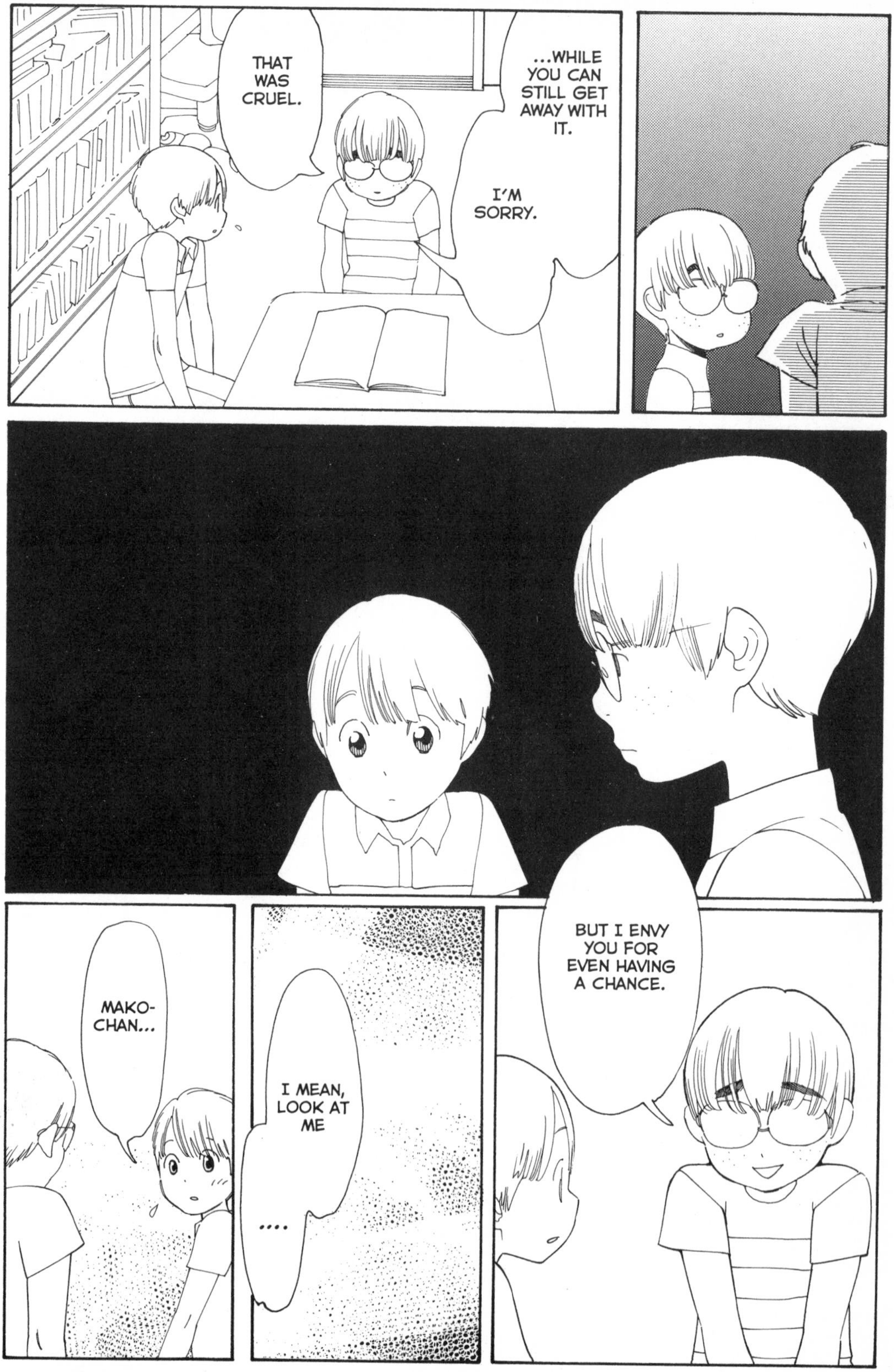
...WHILE YOU CAN STILL GET AWAY WITH IT.
I'M SORRY.
THAT WAS CRUEL.
BUT I ENVY YOU FOR EVEN HAVING A CHANCE.
I MEAN, LOOK AT ME
....
MAKO-CHAN...

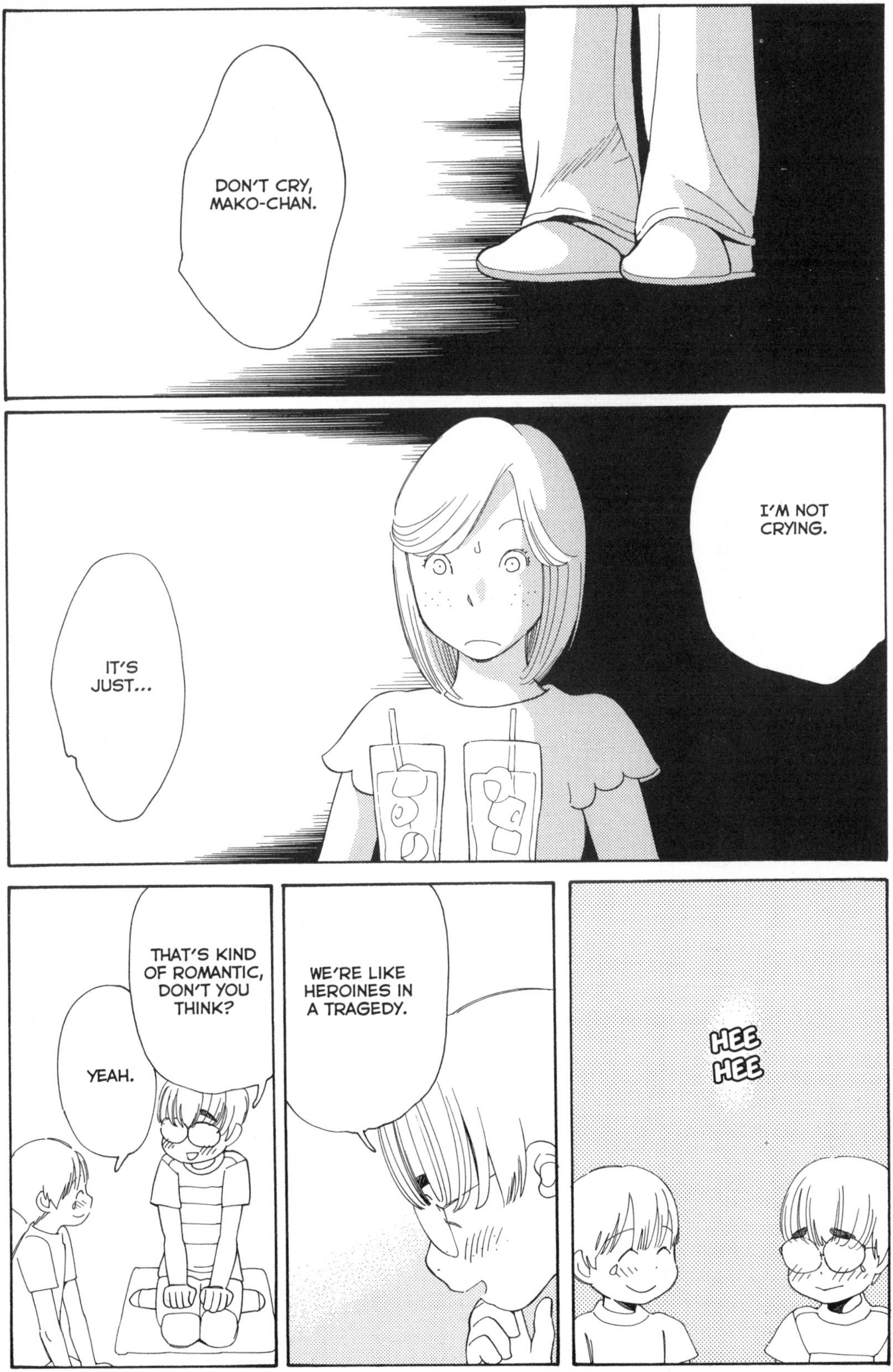
DON'T CRY, MAKO-CHAN.
I'M NOT CRYING.
IT'S JUST...
HEE HEE
WE'RE LIKE HEROINES IN A TRAGEDY.
THAT'S KIND OF ROMANTIC, DON'T YOU THINK?
YEAH.

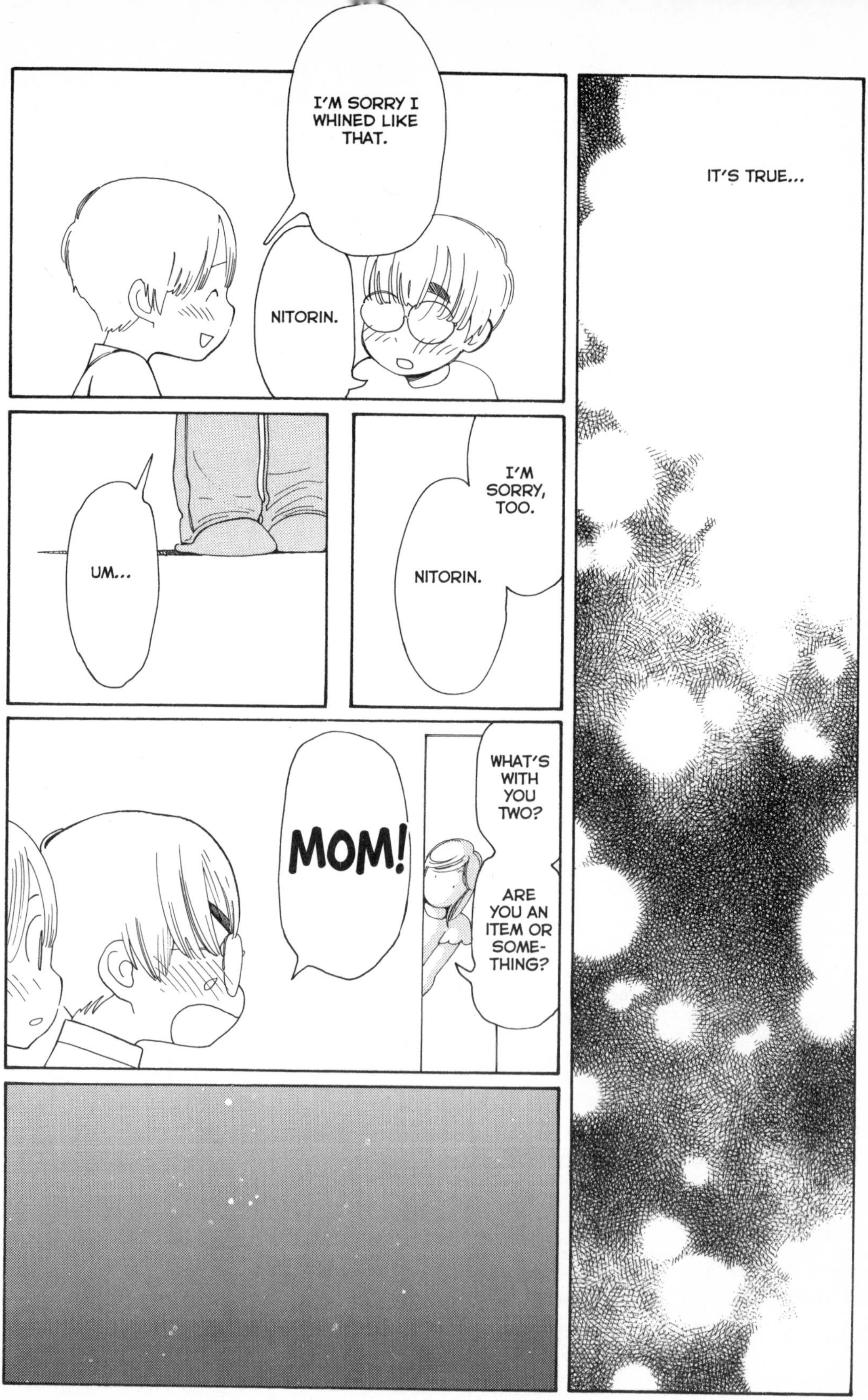
IT'S TRUE...
NITORIN.
I'M SORRY I WHINED LIKE THAT.
I'M SORRY, TOO.
NITORIN.
UM...
WHAT'S WITH YOU TWO?
ARE YOU AN ITEM OR SOME-THING?
MOM!

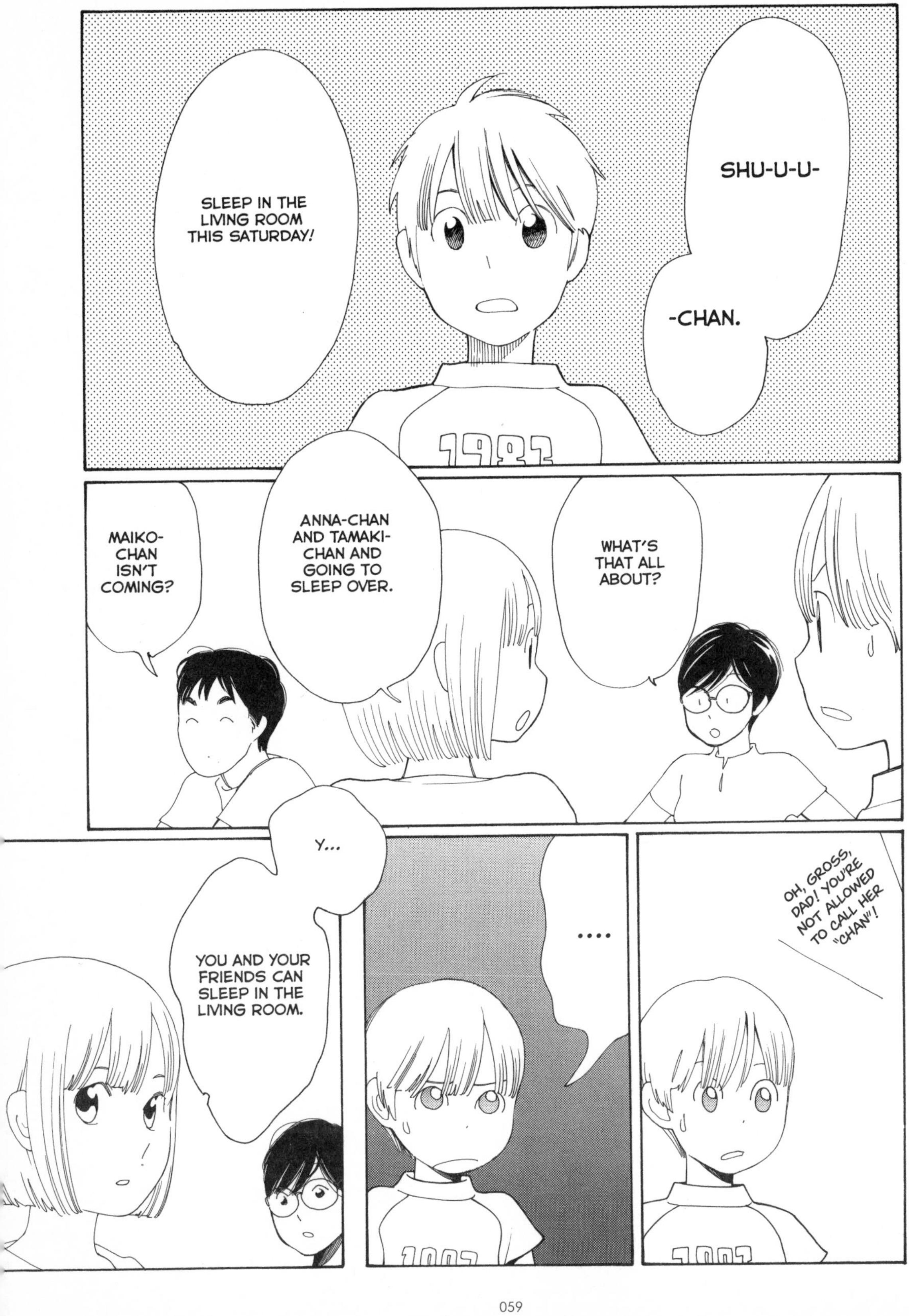
SHU-U-U-
-CHAN.
SLEEP IN THE LIVING ROOM THIS SATURDAY!
WHAT'S THAT ALL ABOUT?
ANNA-CHAN AND TAMAKI-CHAN AND GOING TO SLEEP OVER.
MAIKO-CHAN ISN'T COMING?
OH, GROSS, DAD! YOU'RE NOT ALLOWED TO CALL HER "CHAN"!
....
Y...
YOU AND YOUR FRIENDS CAN SLEEP IN THE LIVING ROOM.

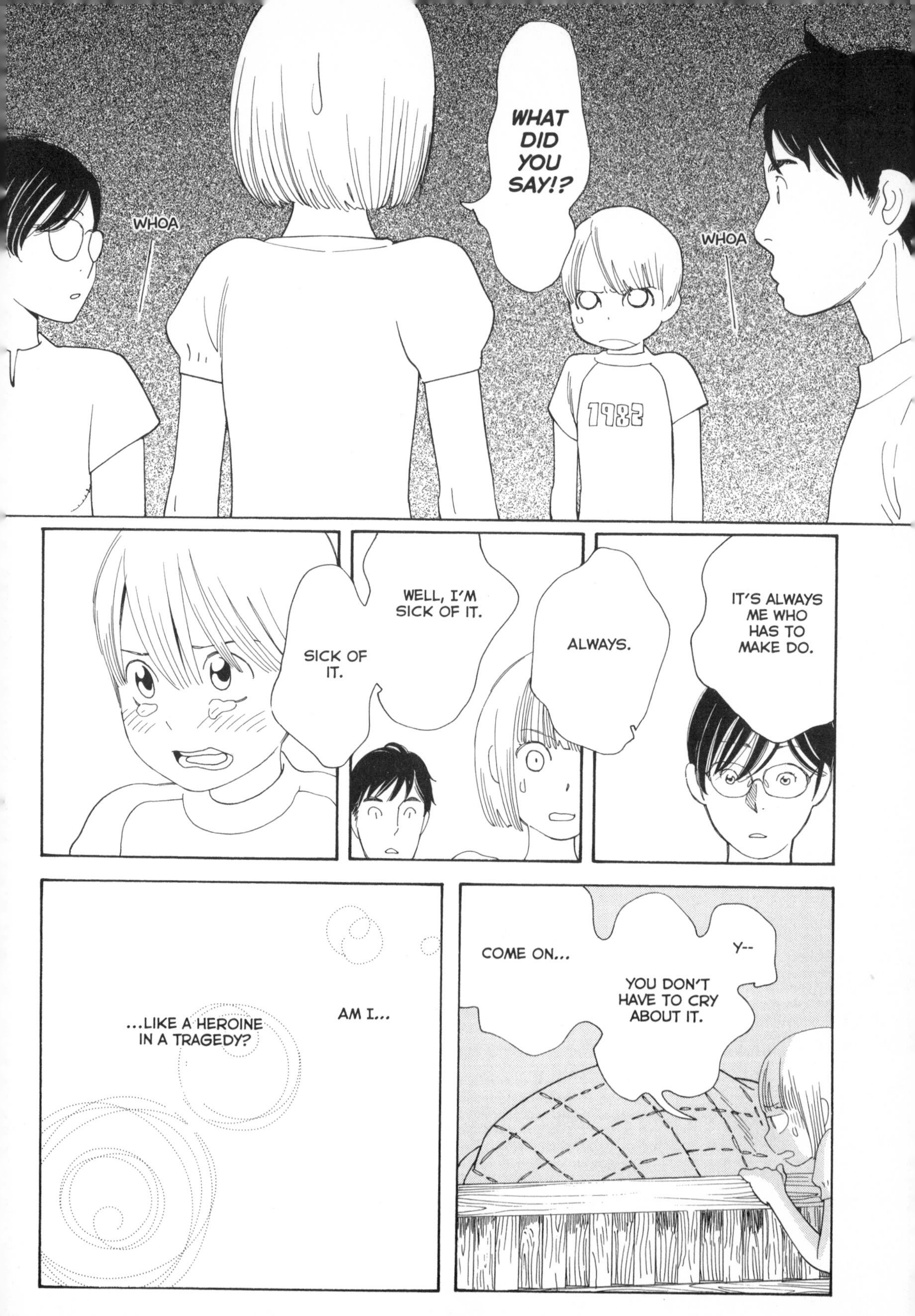
WHAT DID YOU SAY!?
WHOA
WHOA
IT'S ALWAYS ME WHO HAS TO MAKE DO.
ALWAYS.
WELL, I'M SICK OF IT.
SICK OF IT.
Y--
COME ON...
YOU DON'T HAVE TO CRY ABOUT IT.
AM I...
...LIKE A HEROINE IN A TRAGEDY?

28

A Romantic Escape

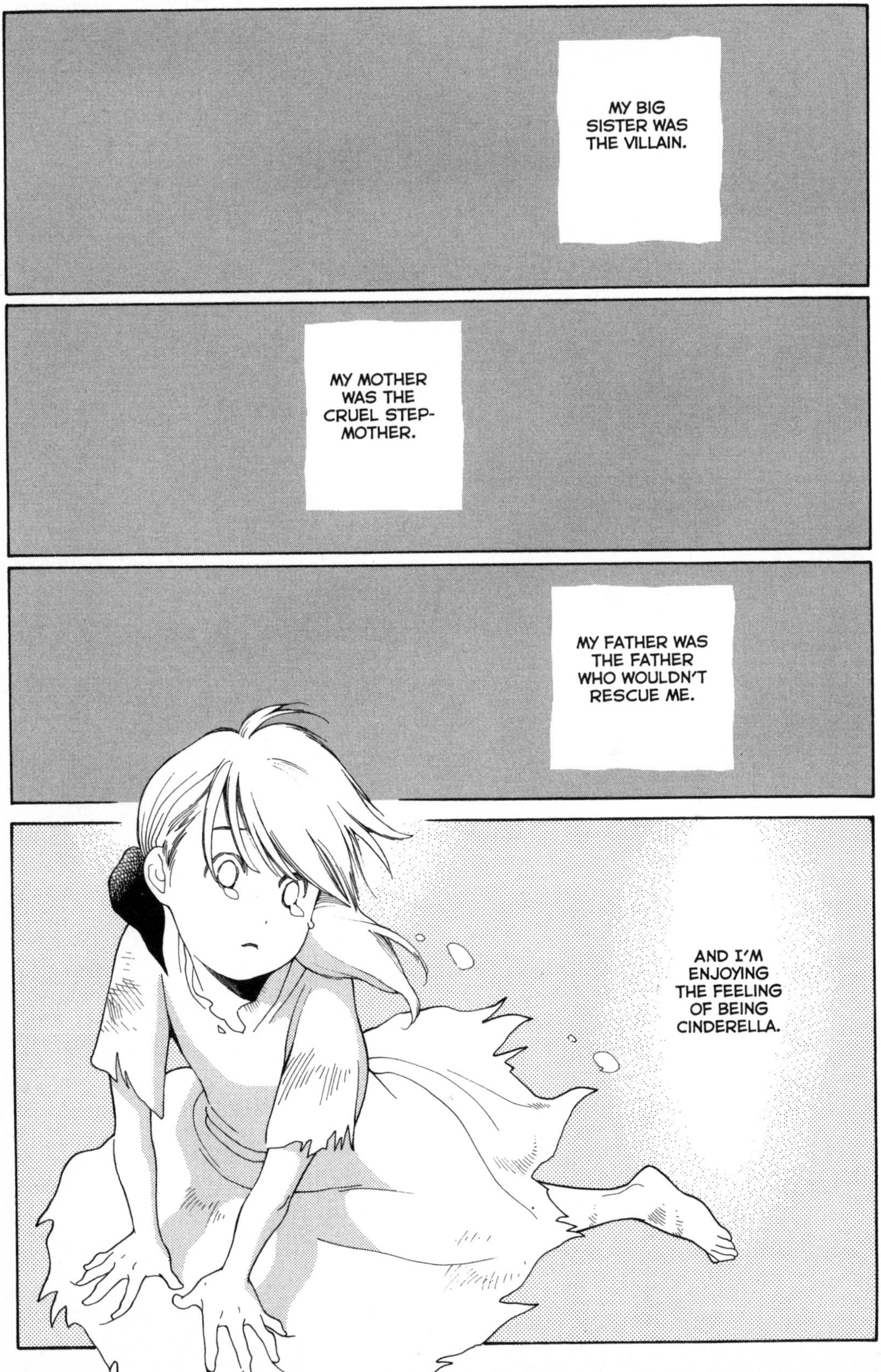
MY BIG SISTER WAS THE VILLAIN.
MY MOTHER WAS THE CRUEL STEP-MOTHER.
MY FATHER WAS THE FATHER WHO WOULDN'T RESCUE ME.
AND I'M ENJOYING THE FEELING OF BEING CINDERELLA.

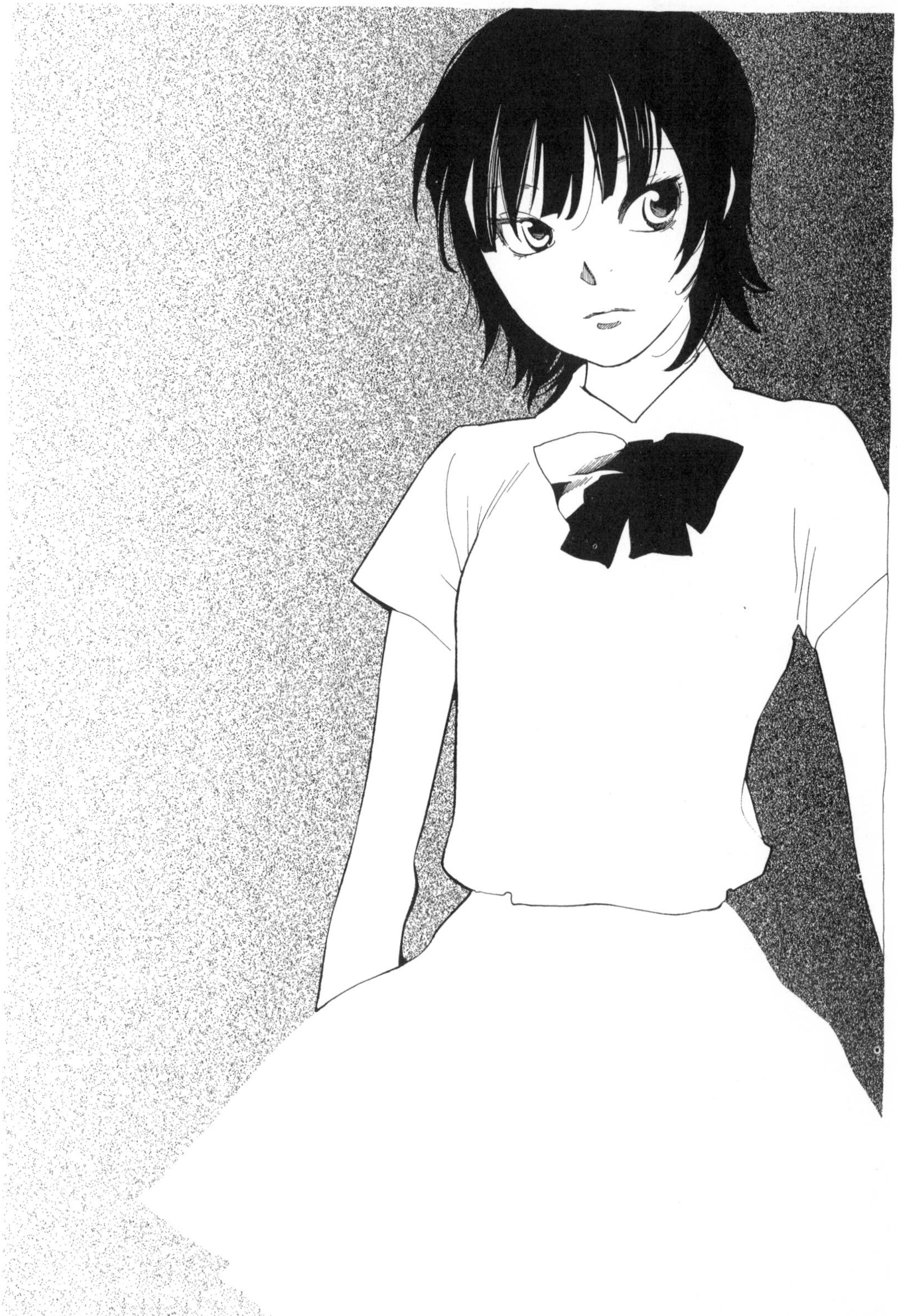

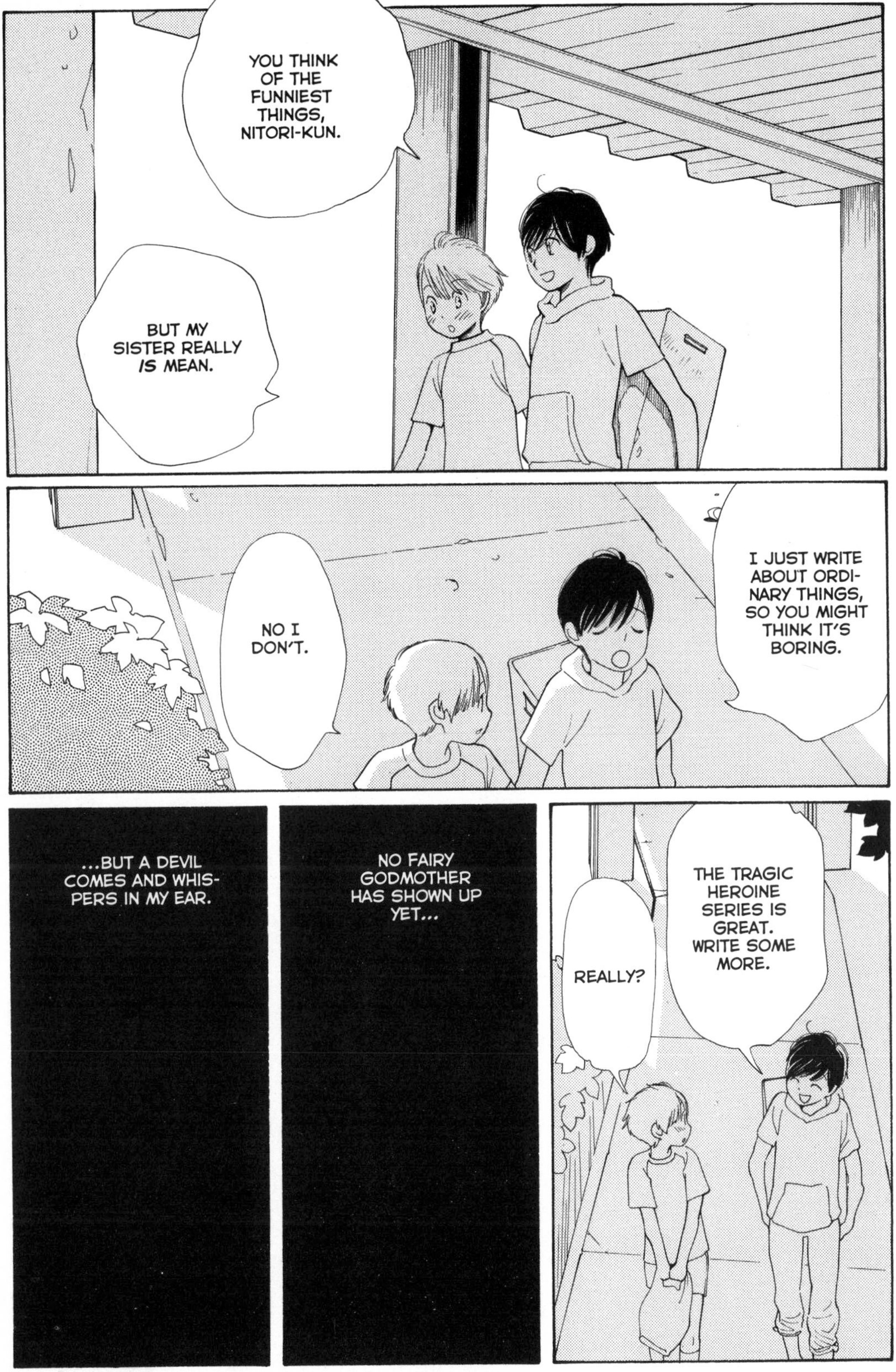
YOU THINK OF THE FUNNIEST THINGS, NITORI-KUN.
BUT MY SISTER REALLY *IS* MEAN.
I JUST WRITE ABOUT ORDINARY THINGS, SO YOU MIGHT THINK IT'S BORING.
NO I DON'T.
THE TRAGIC HEROINE SERIES IS GREAT. WRITE SOME MORE.
REALLY?
NO FAIRY GODMOTHER HAS SHOWN UP YET...
...BUT A DEVIL COMES AND WHISPERS IN MY EAR.

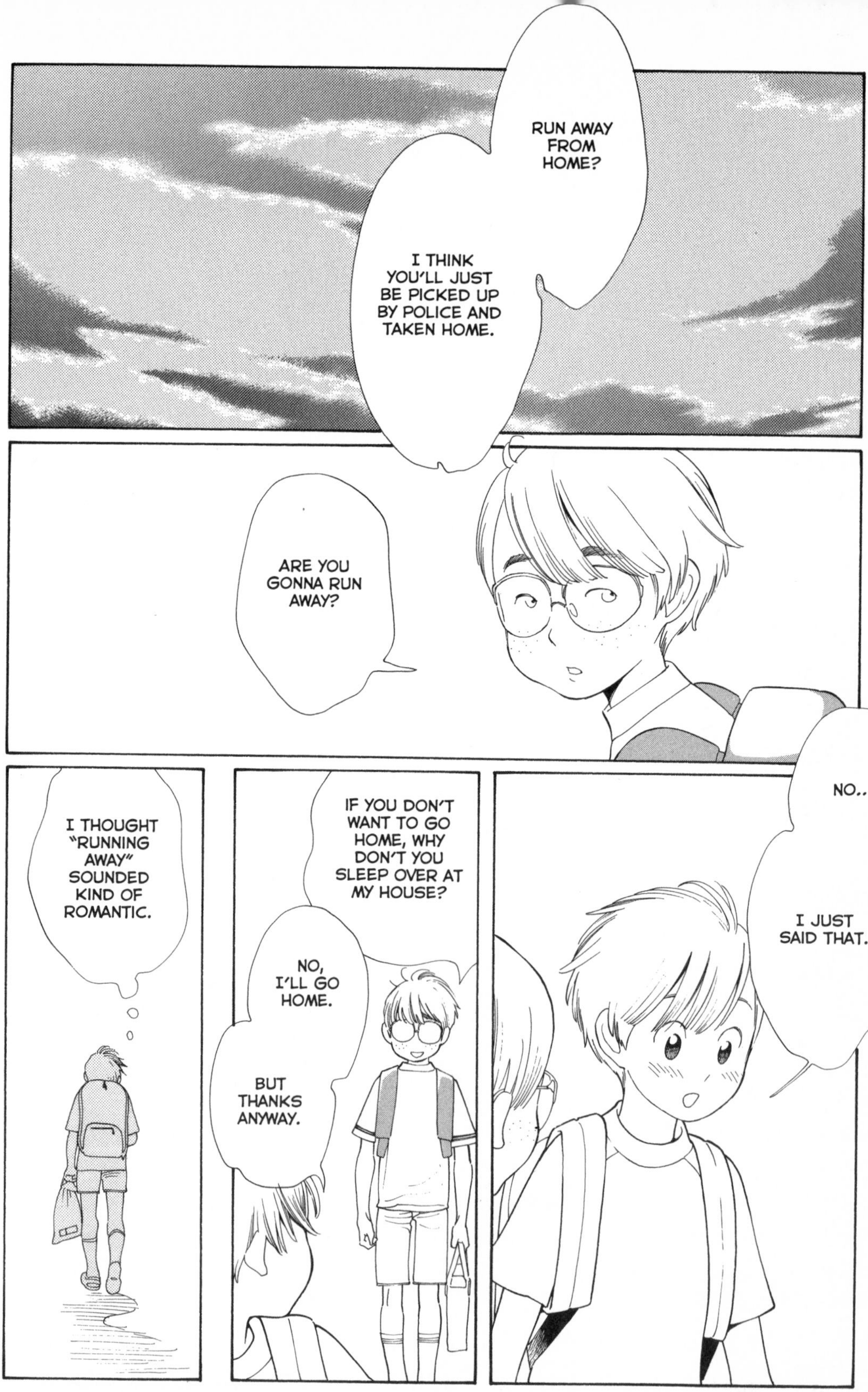
RUN AWAY FROM HOME?
I THINK YOU'LL JUST BE PICKED UP BY POLICE AND TAKEN HOME.
ARE YOU GONNA RUN AWAY?
NO...
I JUST SAID THAT.
IF YOU DON'T WANT TO GO HOME, WHY DON'T YOU SLEEP OVER AT MY HOUSE?
NO, I'LL GO HOME.
BUT THANKS ANYWAY.
I THOUGHT "RUNNING AWAY" SOUNDED KIND OF ROMANTIC.

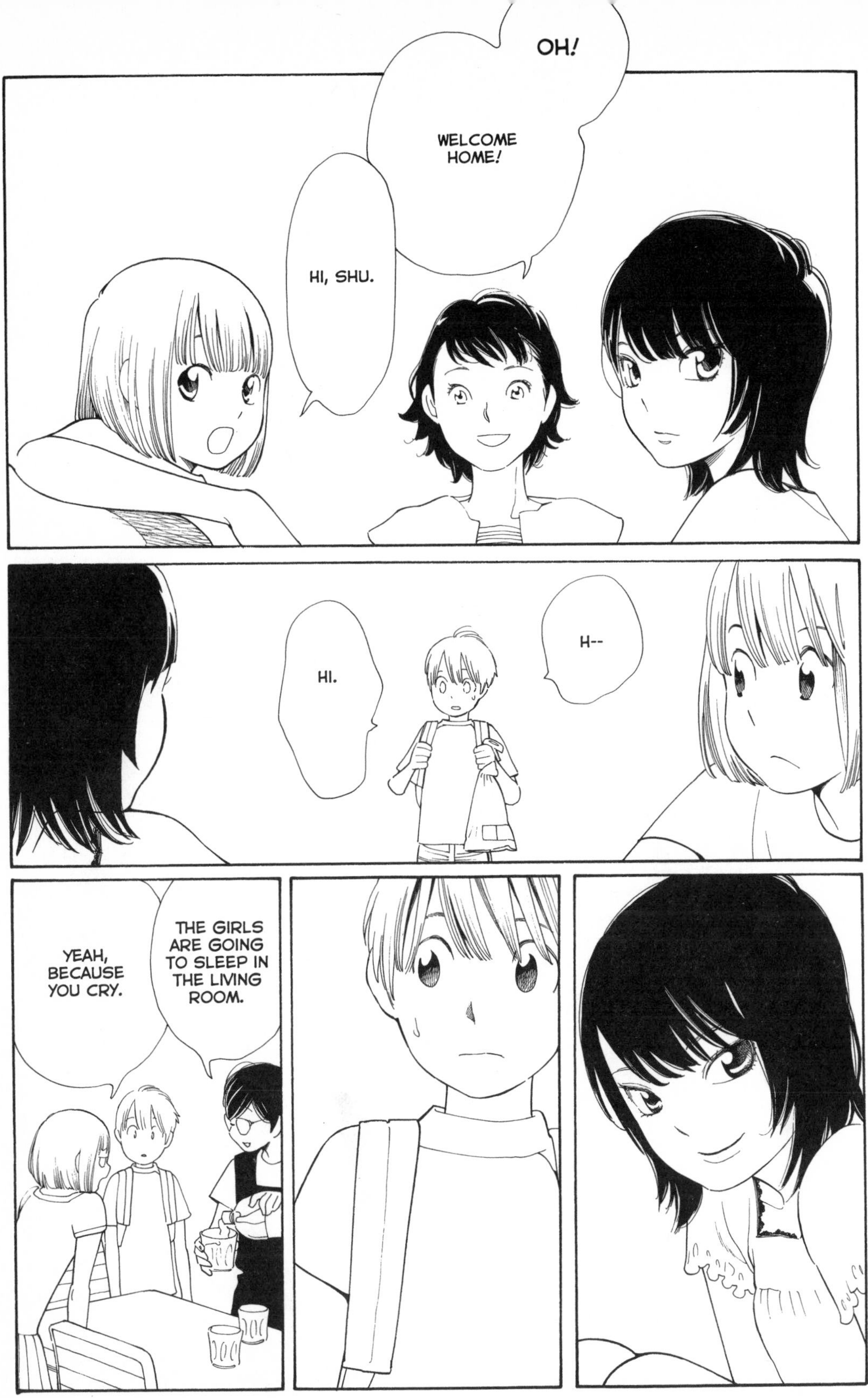
OH!
WELCOME HOME!
HI, SHU.
H--
HI.
THE GIRLS ARE GOING TO SLEEP IN THE LIVING ROOM.
YEAH, BECAUSE YOU CRY.

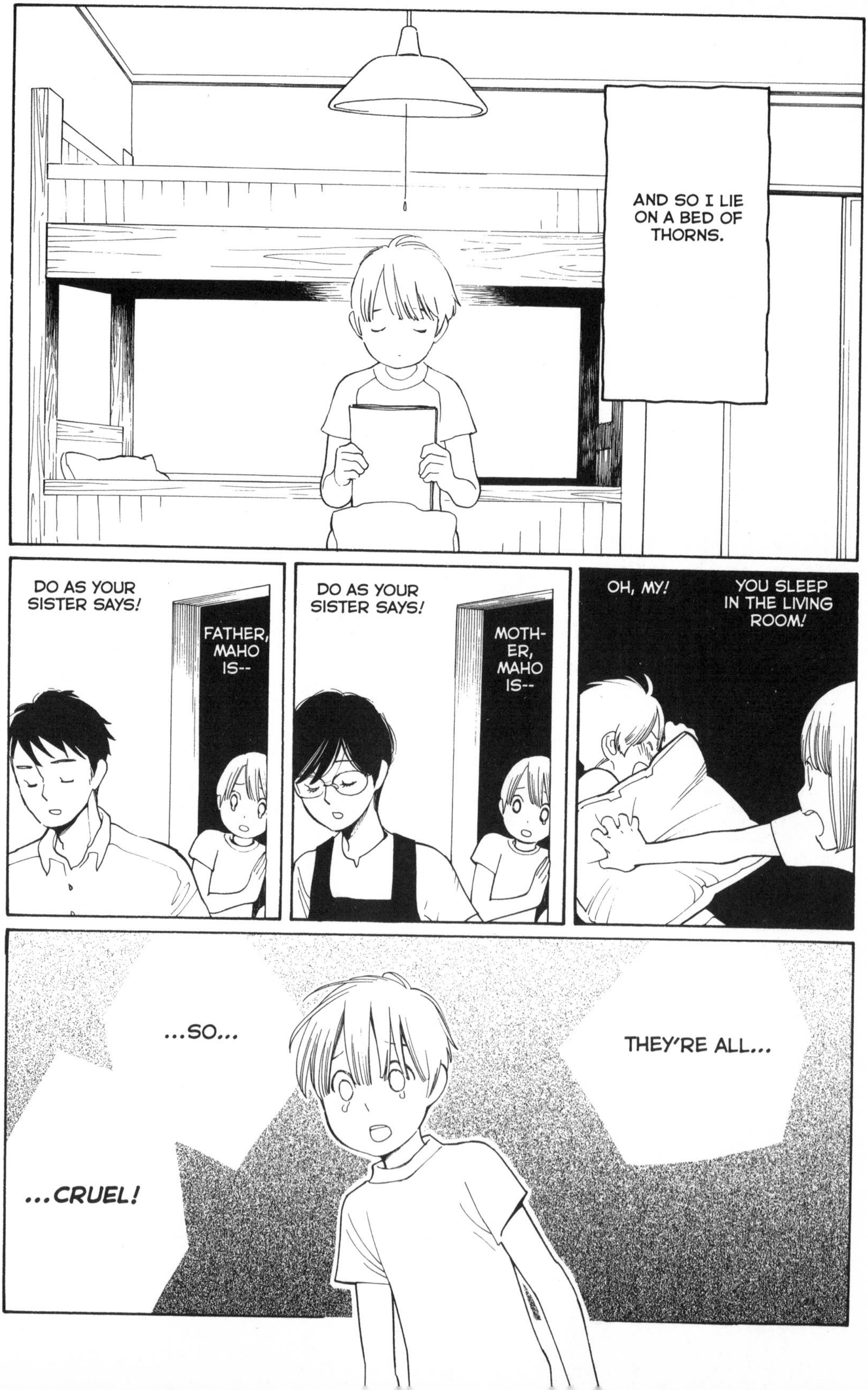
AND SO I LIE ON A BED OF THORNS.
YOU SLEEP IN THE LIVING ROOM!
OH, MY!
MOTH-ER, MAHO IS--
DO AS YOUR SISTER SAYS!
FATHER, MAHO IS--
DO AS YOUR SISTER SAYS!
THEY'RE ALL...
...SO...
...CRUEL!

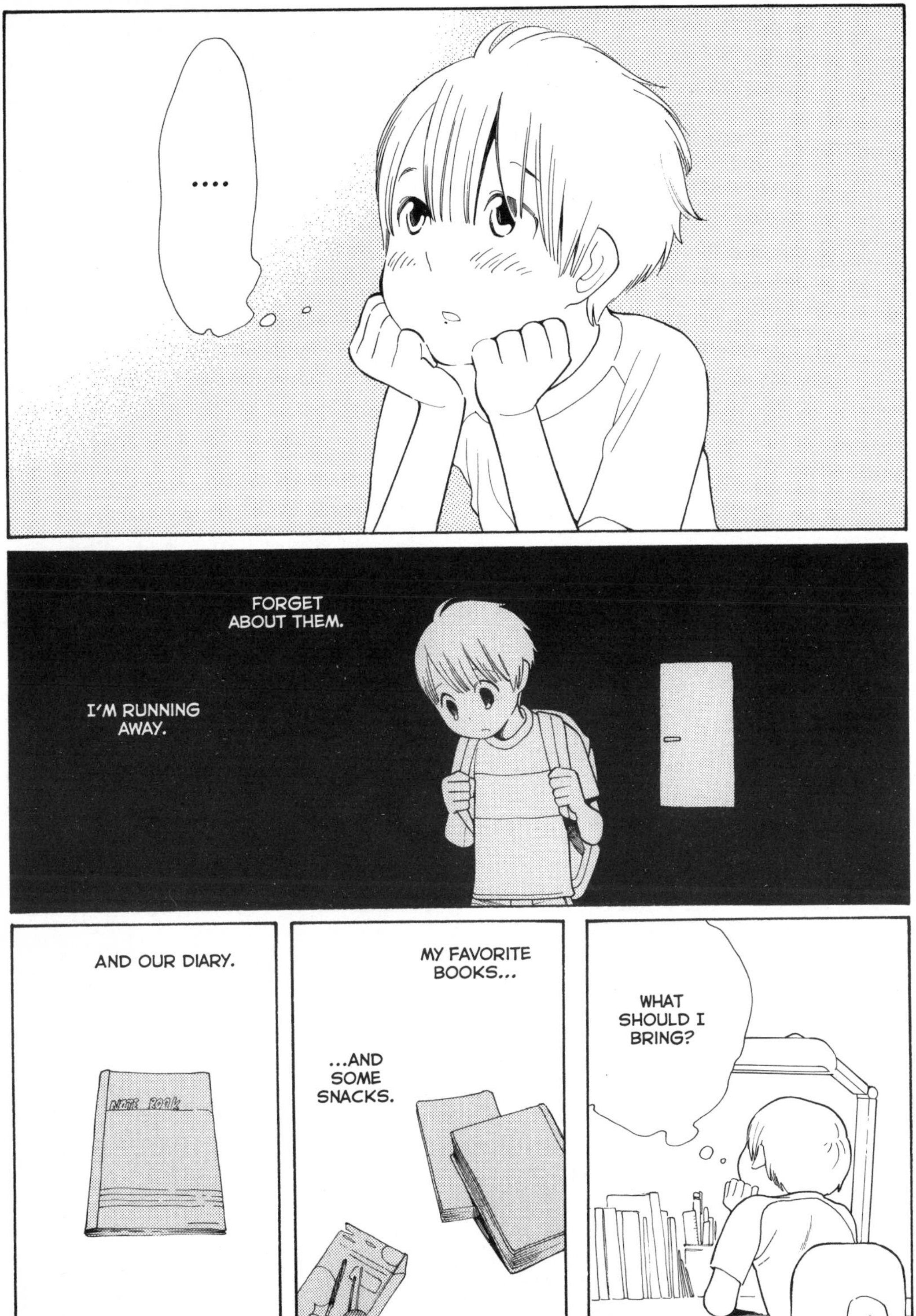
....
FORGET ABOUT THEM.
I'M RUNNING AWAY.
WHAT SHOULD I BRING?
MY FAVORITE BOOKS...
...AND SOME SNACKS.
AND OUR DIARY.

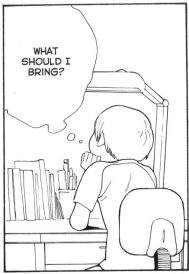

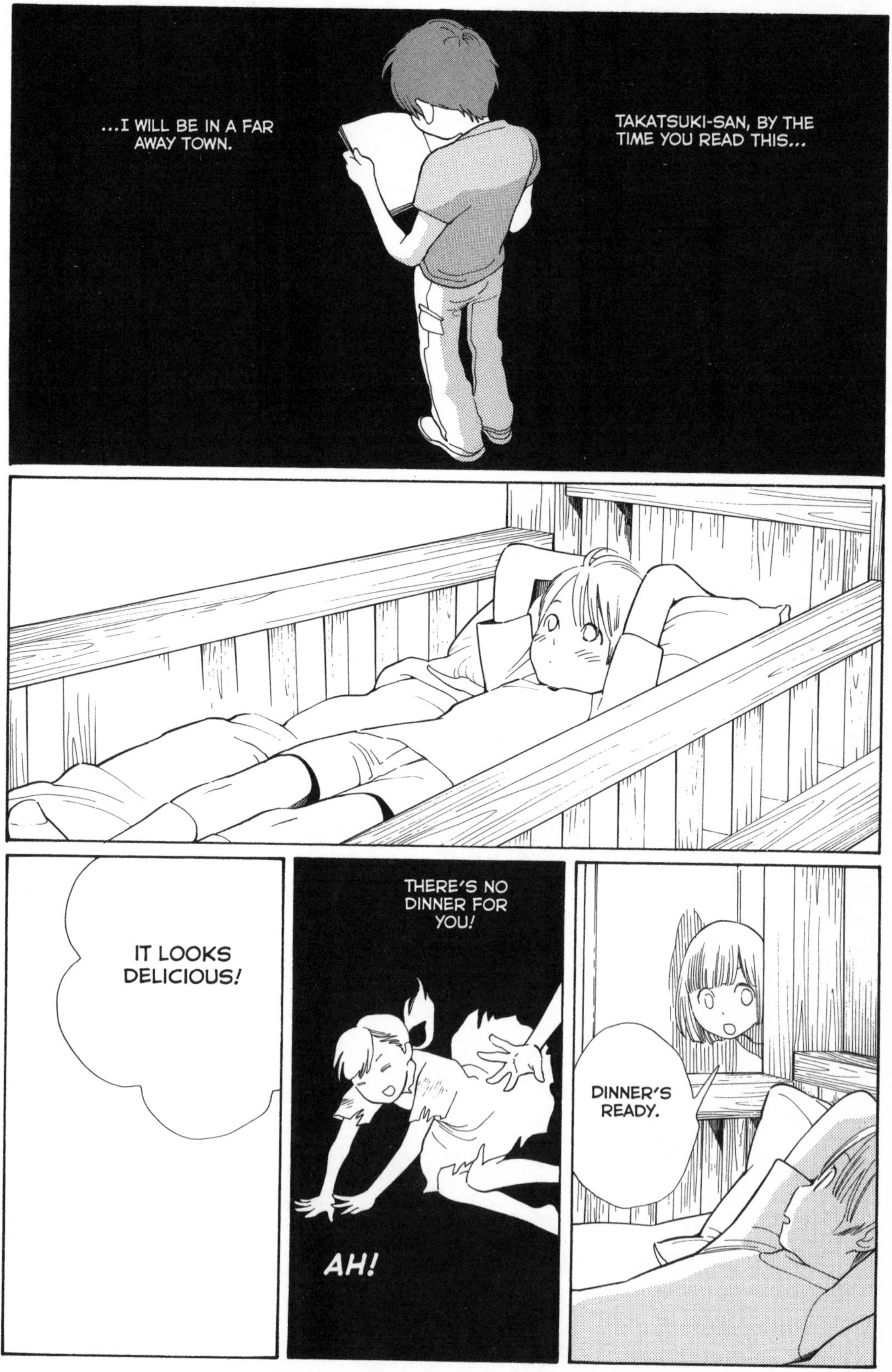
TAKATSUKI-SAN, BY THE TIME YOU READ THIS...
...I WILL BE IN A FAR AWAY TOWN.
DINNER'S READY.
THERE'S NO DINNER FOR YOU!
AH!
IT LOOKS DELICIOUS!

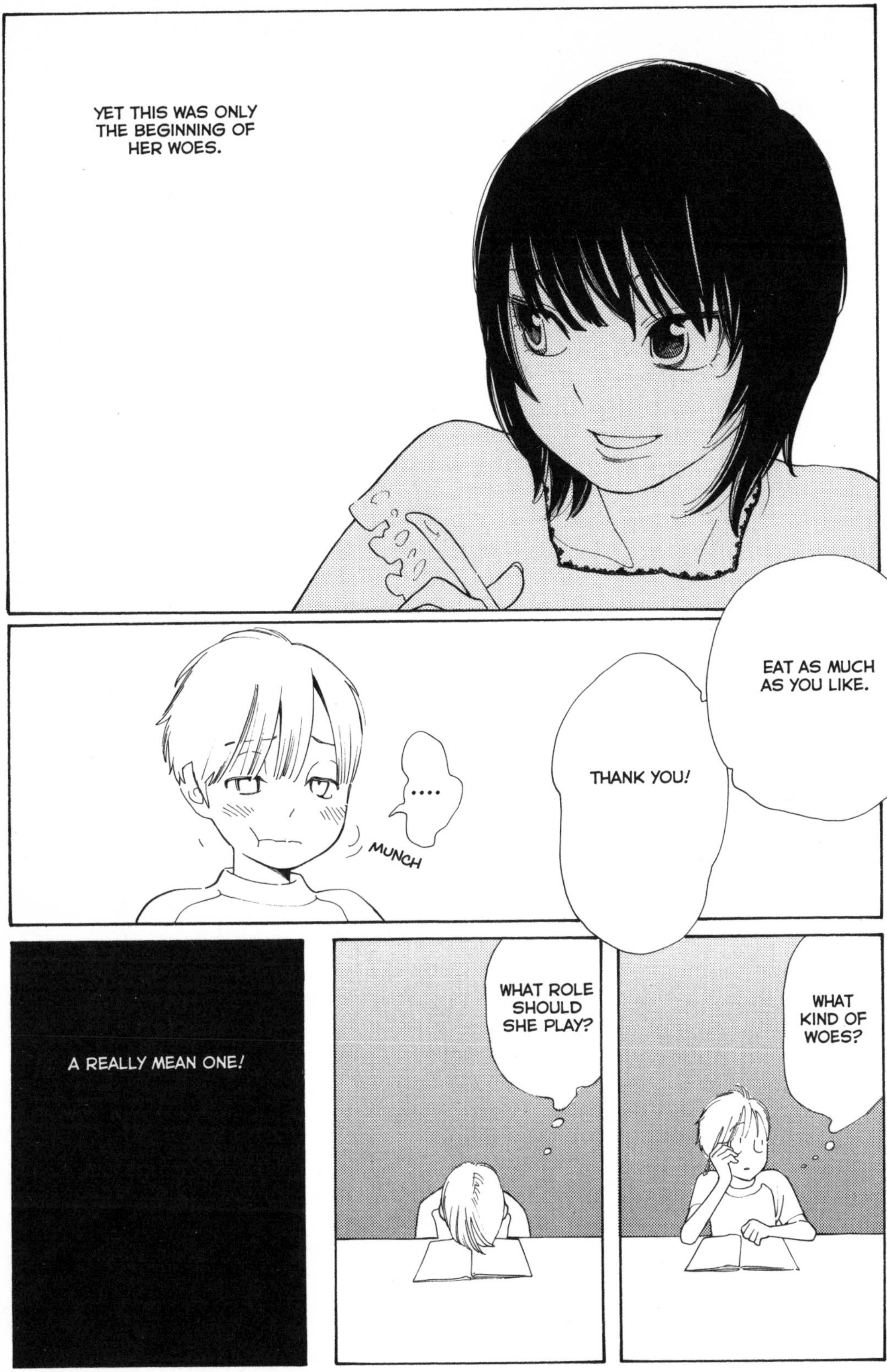
YET THIS WAS ONLY THE BEGINNING OF HER WOES.
EAT AS MUCH AS YOU LIKE.
THANK YOU!
....
MUNCH
WHAT KIND OF WOES?
WHAT ROLE SHOULD SHE PLAY?
A REALLY MEAN ONE!

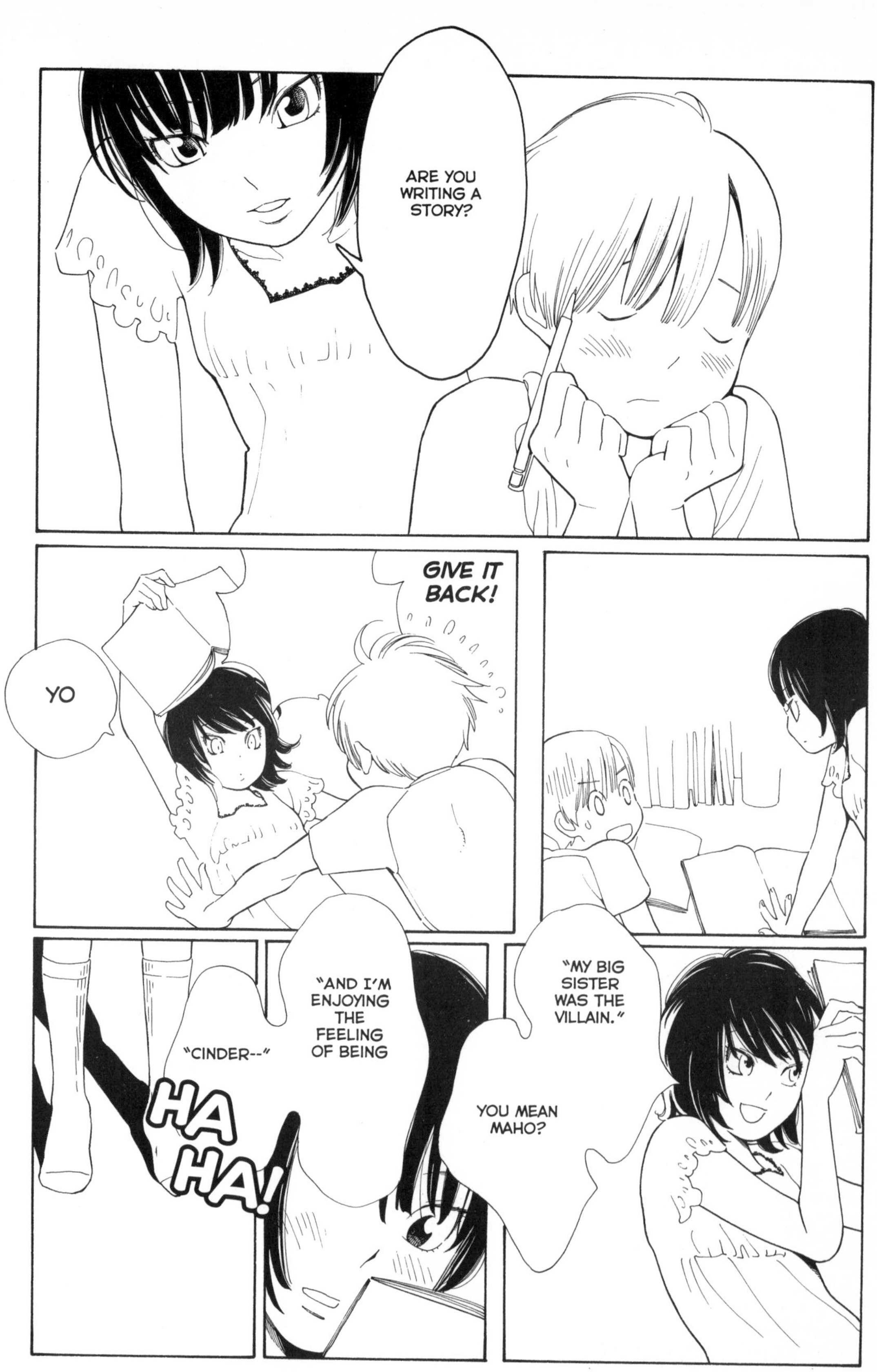
ARE YOU WRITING A STORY?
GIVE IT BACK!
YO
"MY BIG SISTER WAS THE VILLAIN."
YOU MEAN MAHO?
"AND I'M ENJOYING THE FEELING OF BEING
"CINDER--"
HA HA!

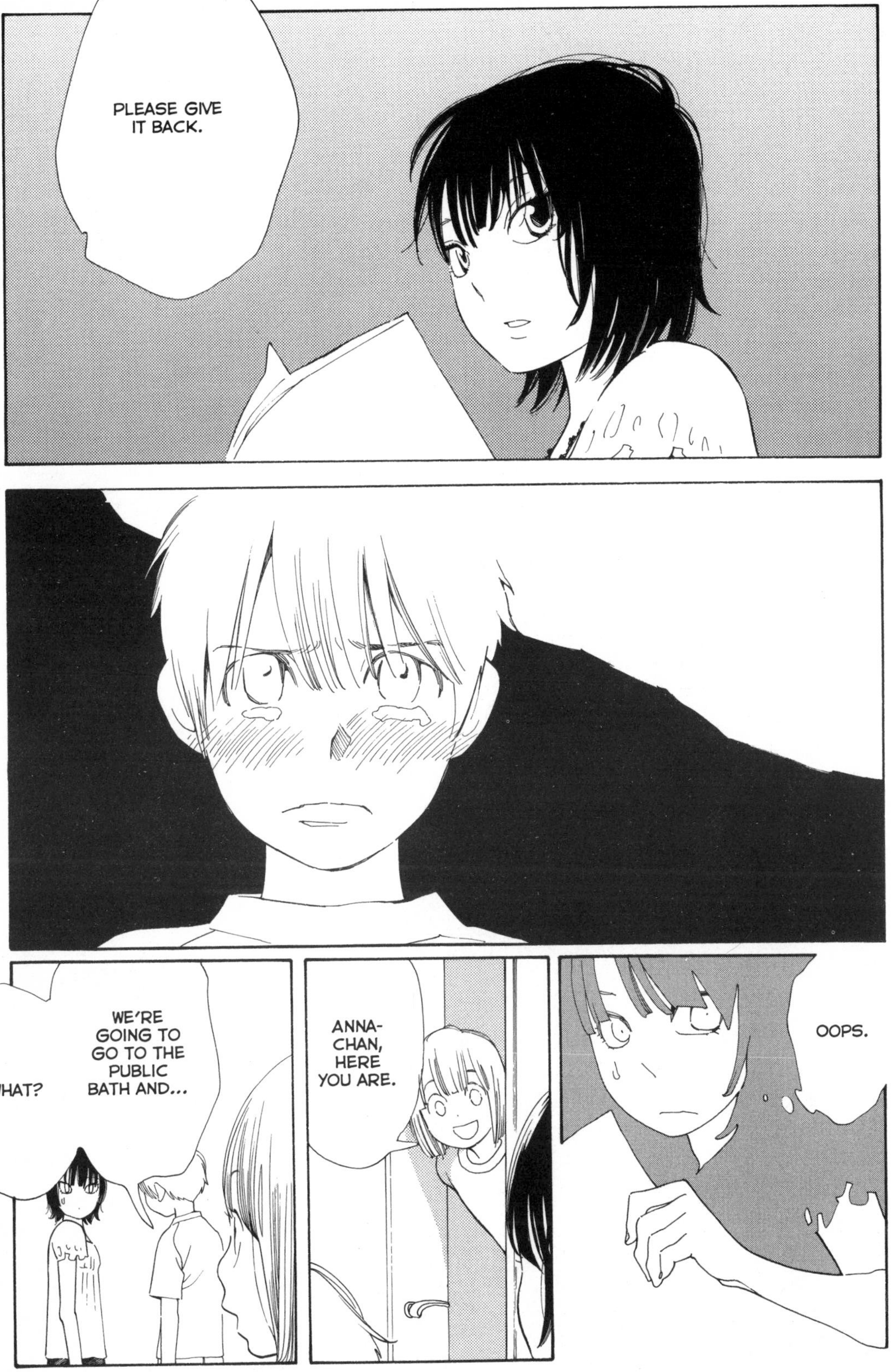
PLEASE GIVE IT BACK.
OOPS.
ANNA-CHAN, HERE YOU ARE.
WE'RE GOING TO GO TO THE PUBLIC BATH AND...
WHAT?

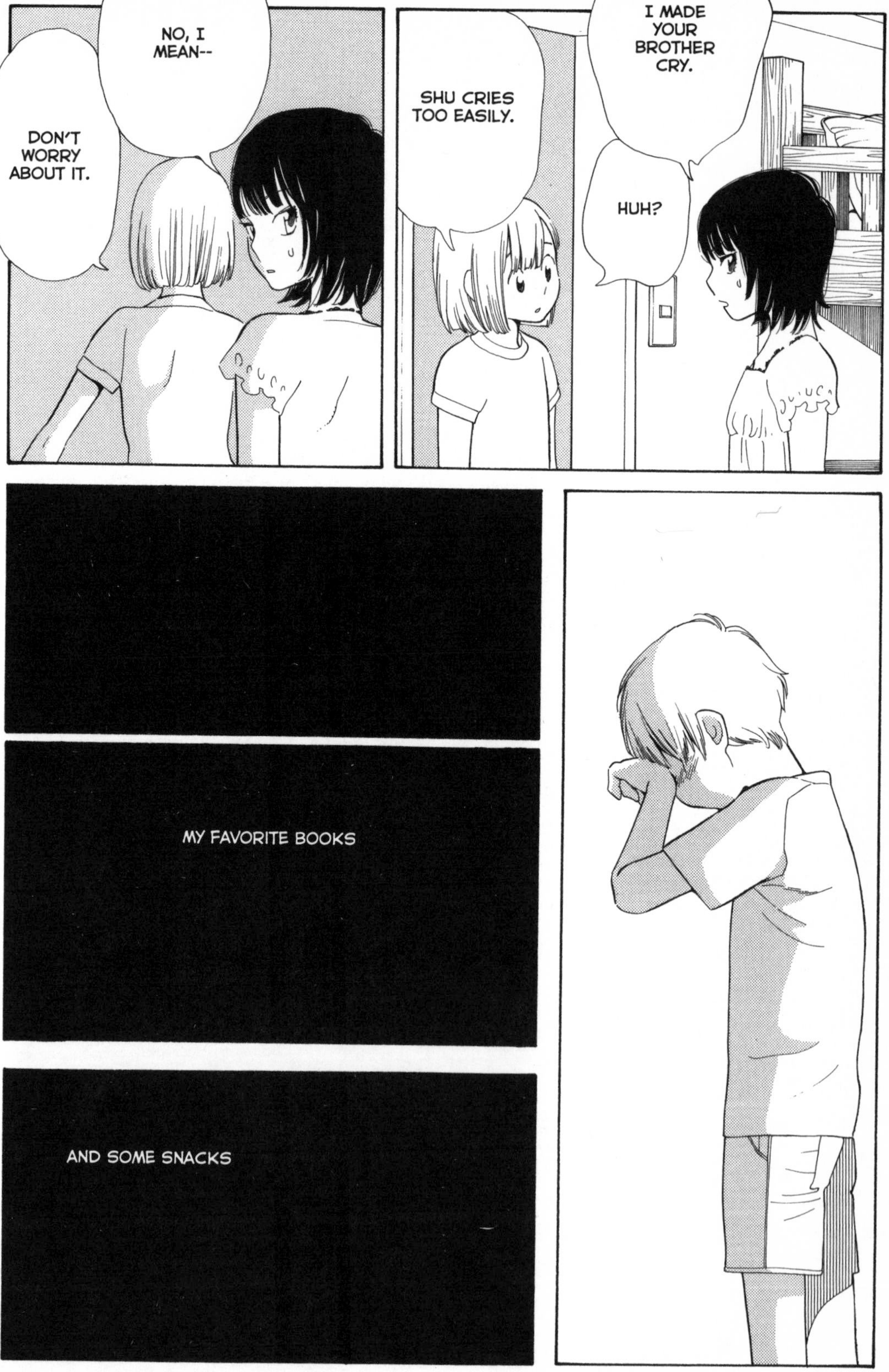
I MADE YOUR BROTHER CRY.
HUH?
SHU CRIES TOO EASILY.
NO, I MEAN--
DON'T WORRY ABOUT IT.
MY FAVORITE BOOKS
AND SOME SNACKS

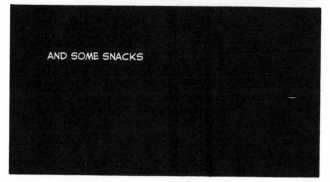

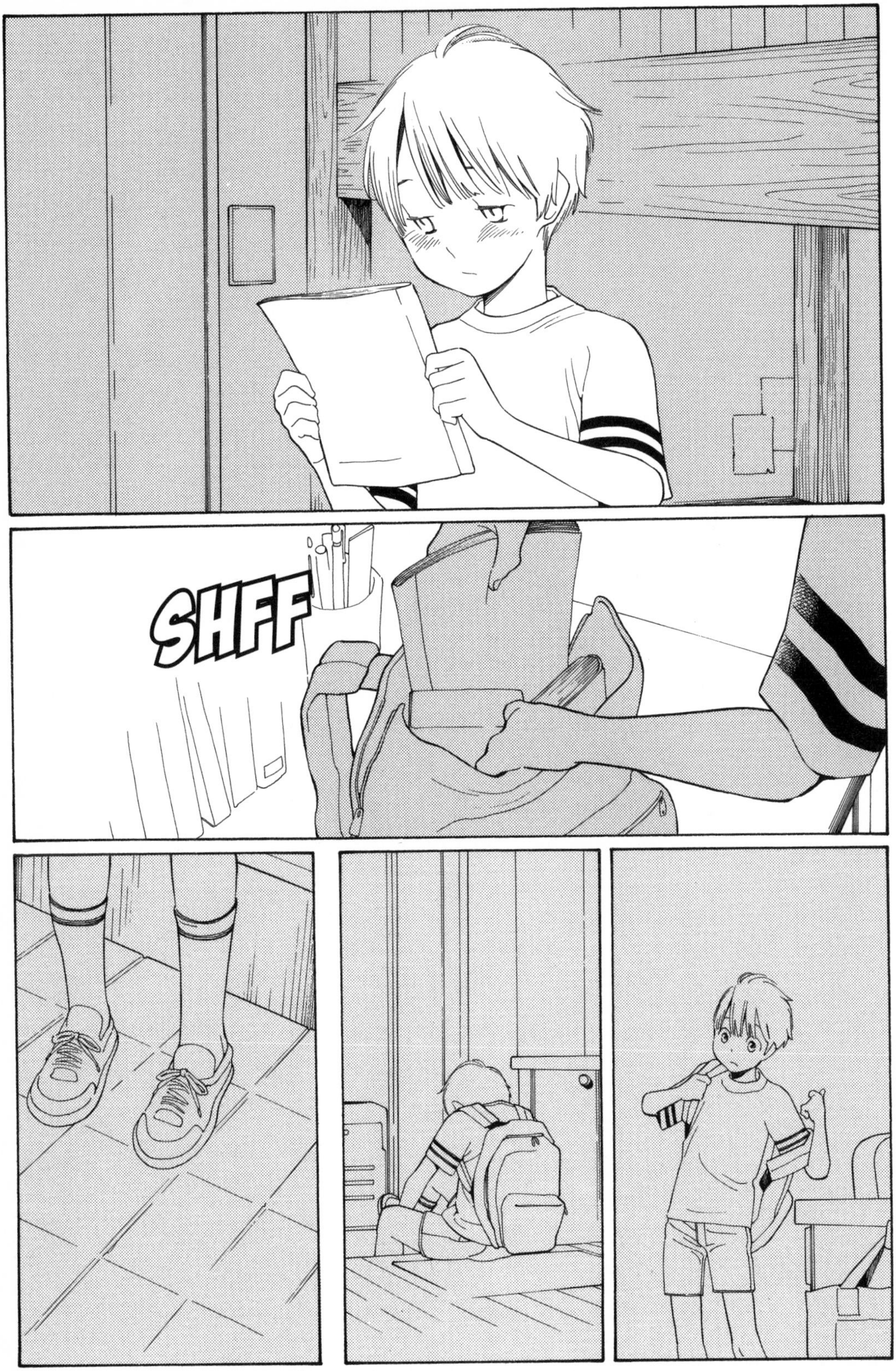
SHFF

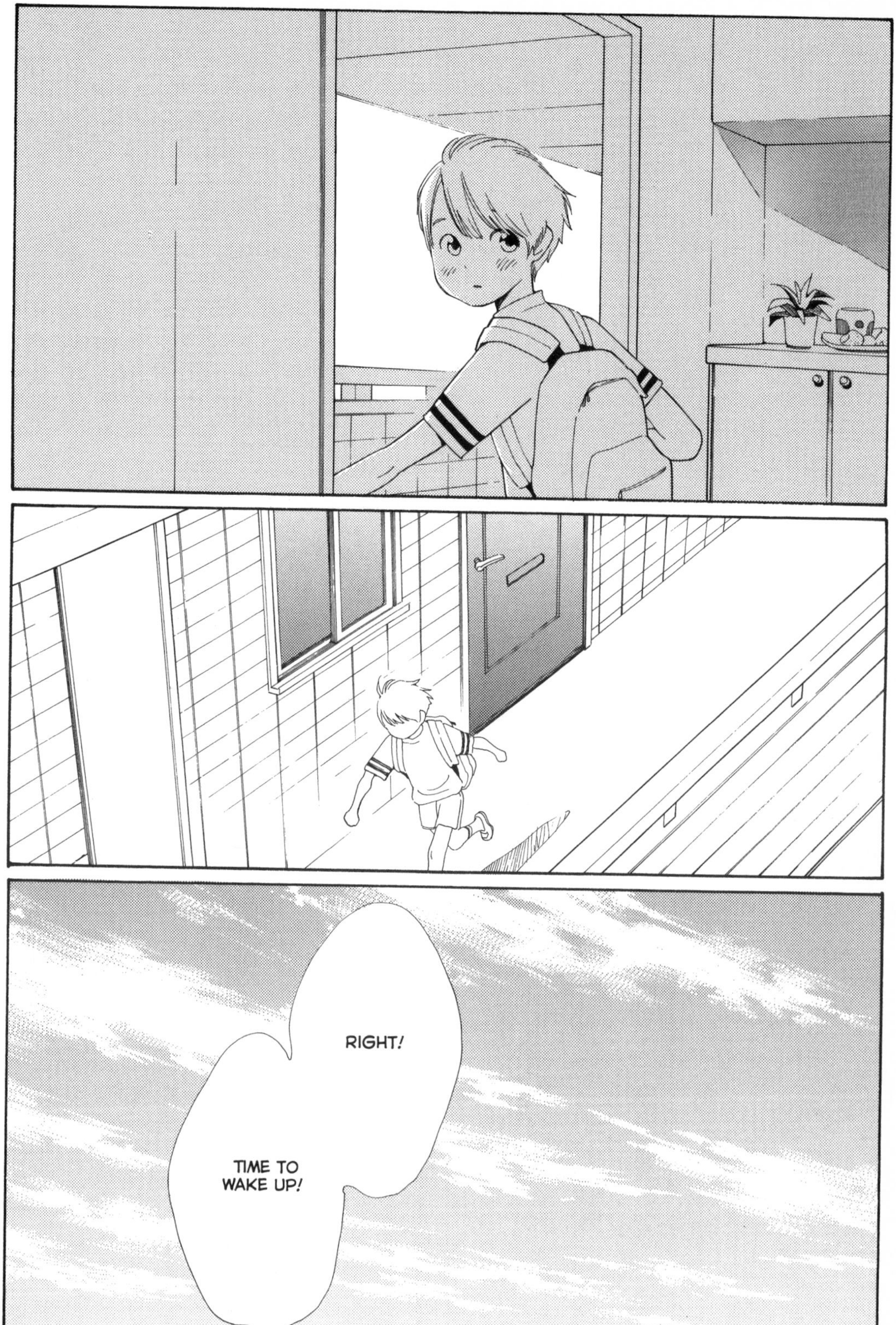
RIGHT!
TIME TO WAKE UP!

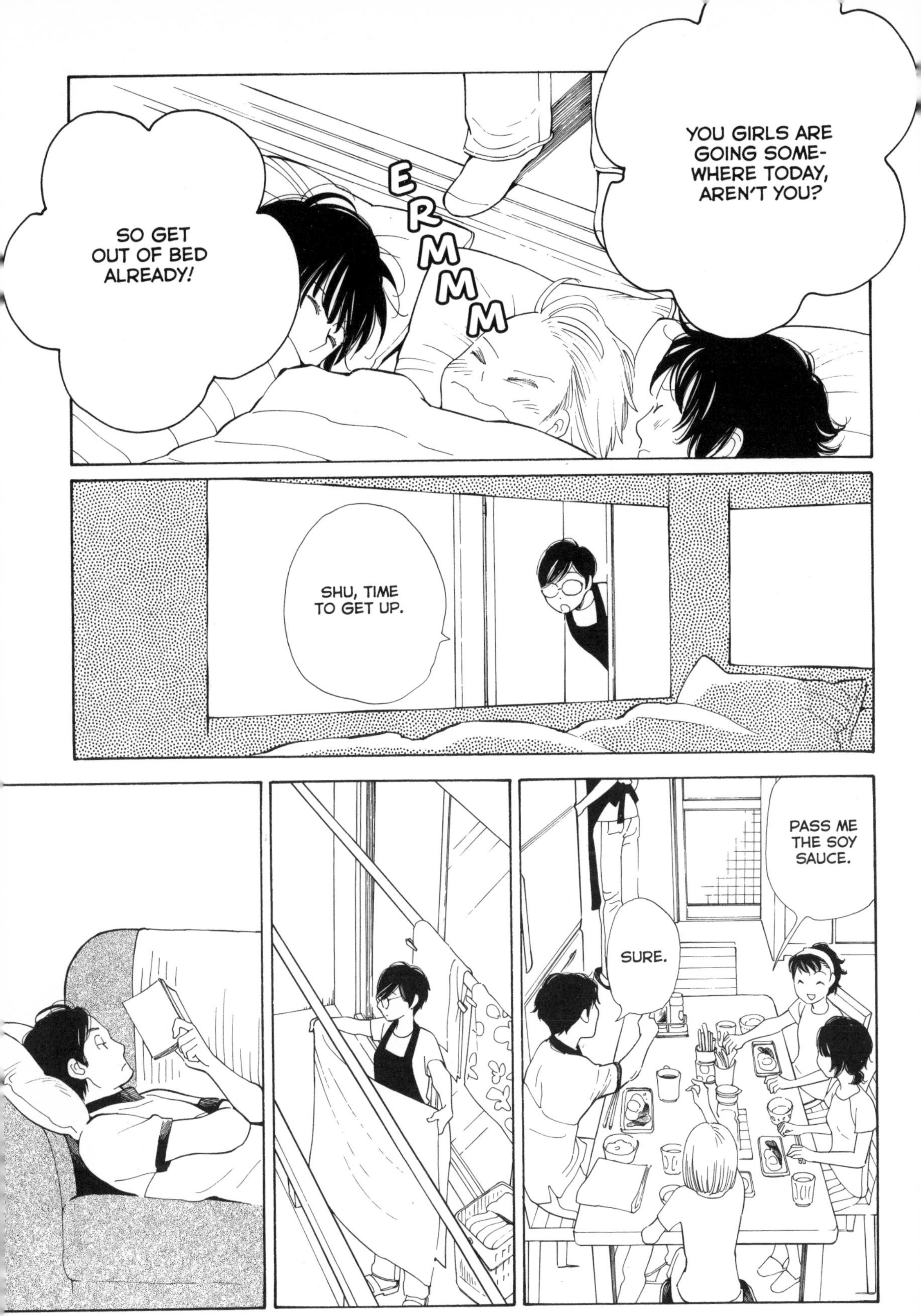
YOU GIRLS ARE GOING SOME-WHERE TODAY, AREN'T YOU?
ERMMM
SO GET OUT OF BED ALREADY!
SHU, TIME TO GET UP.
PASS ME THE SOY SAUCE.
SURE.

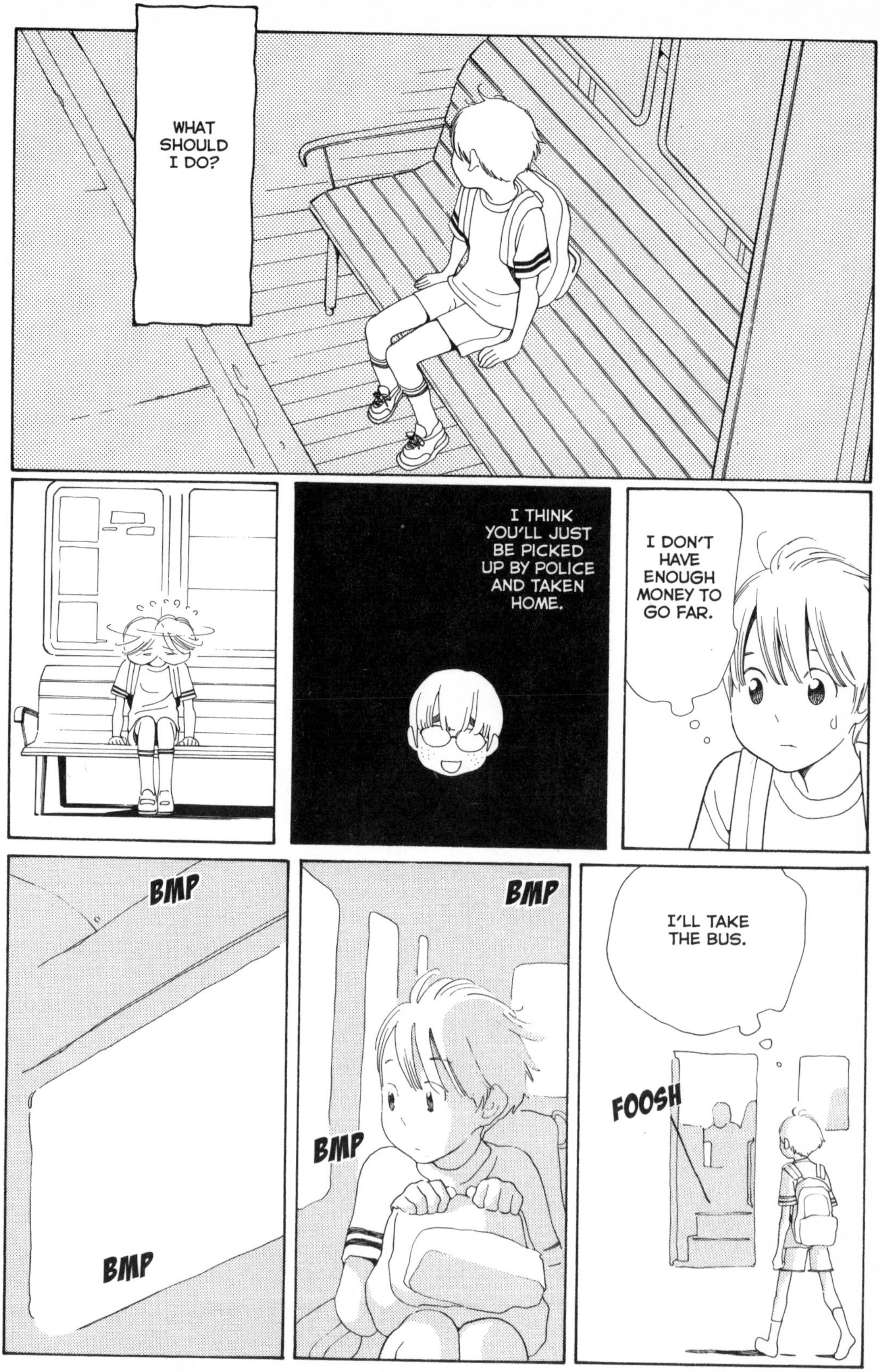
WHAT SHOULD I DO?
I DON'T HAVE ENOUGH MONEY TO GO FAR.
I THINK YOU'LL JUST BE PICKED UP BY POLICE AND TAKEN HOME.
I'LL TAKE THE BUS.
FOOSH
BMP
BMP
BMP
BMP

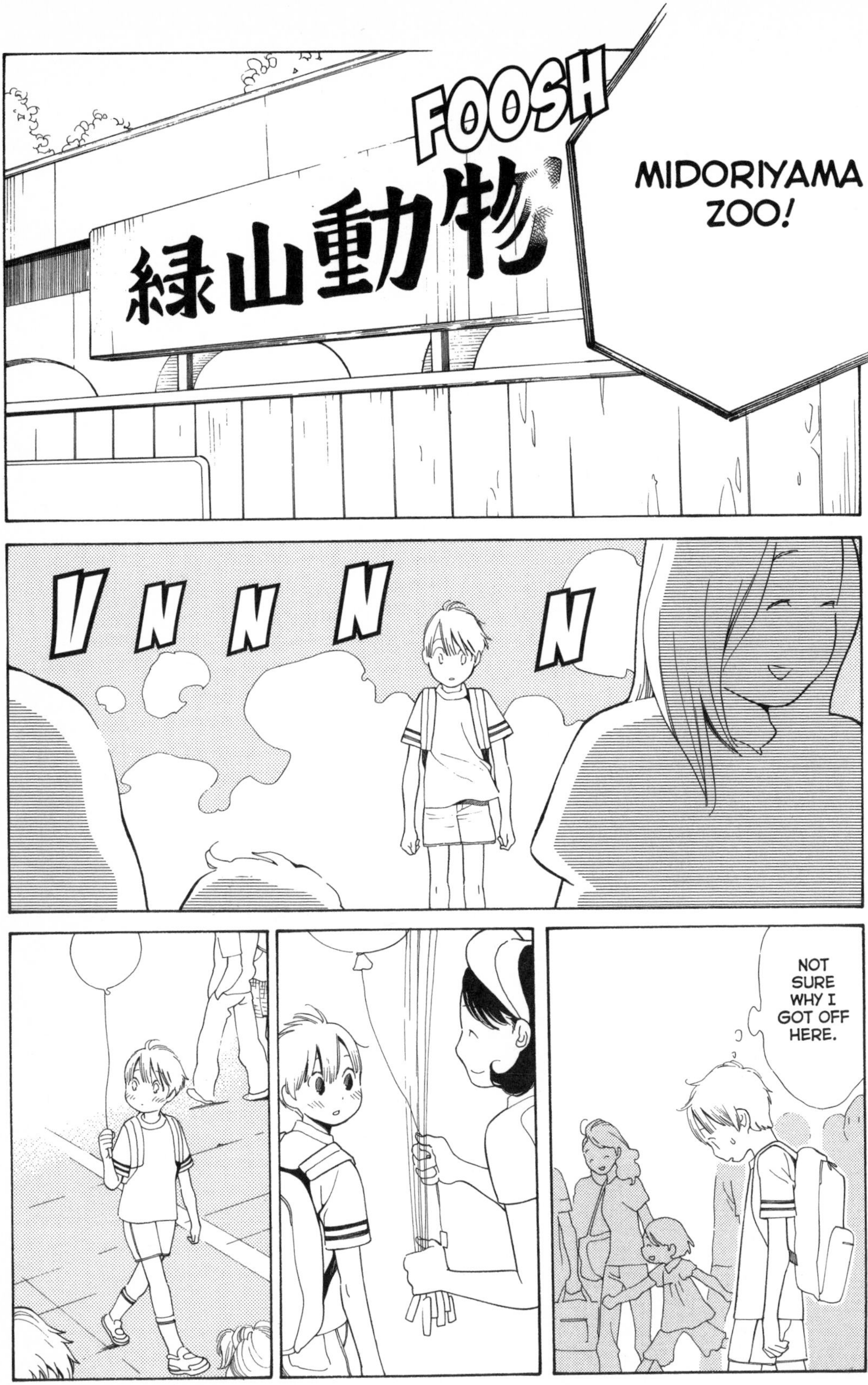
FOOSH
MIDORIYAMA ZOO!
緑山動物
VNNNN
NOT SURE WHY I GOT OFF HERE.

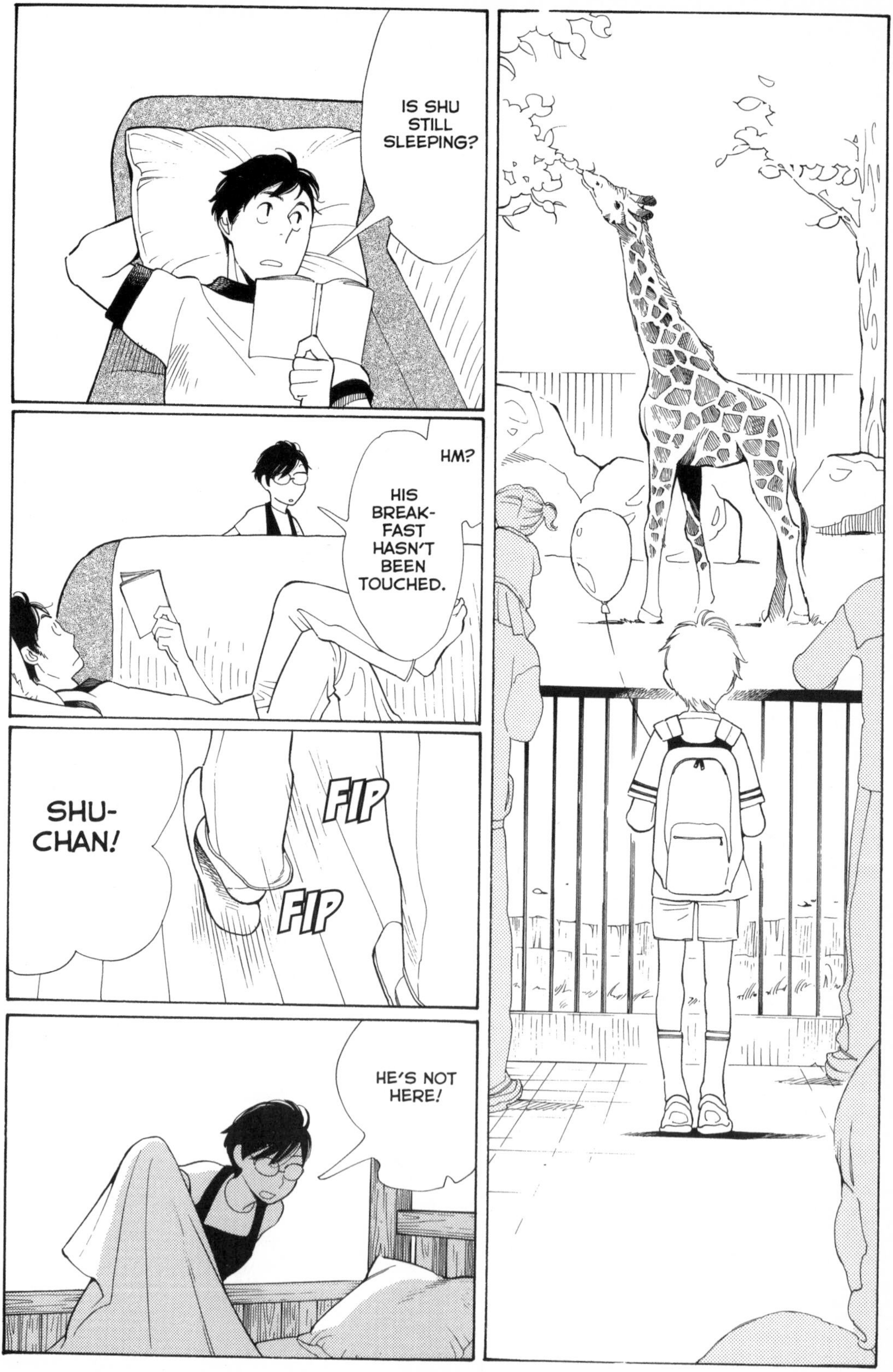
IS SHU STILL SLEEPING?
HM?
HIS BREAK-FAST HASN'T BEEN TOUCHED.
SHU-CHAN!
FIP
FIP
HE'S NOT HERE!

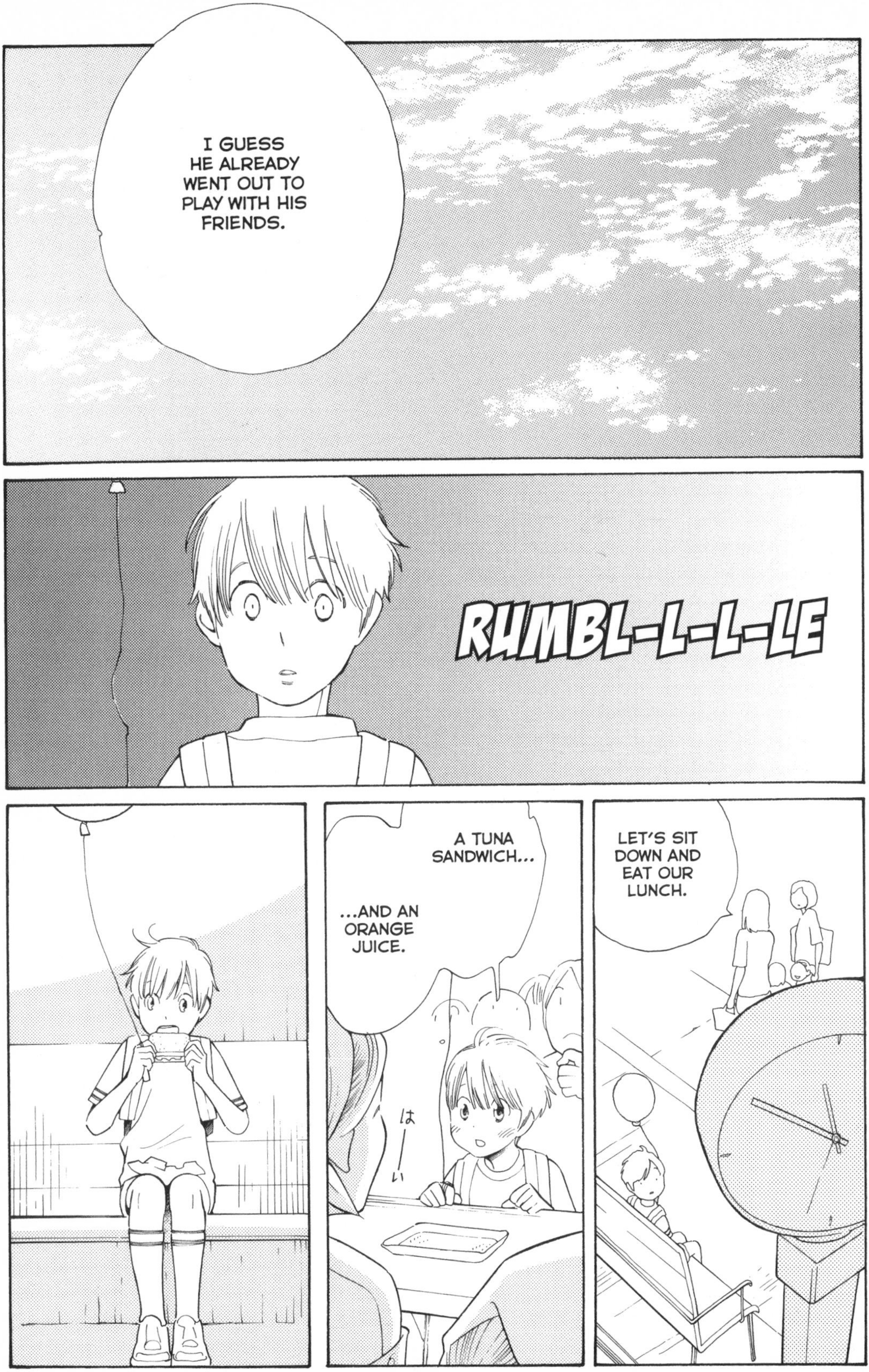
I GUESS HE ALREADY WENT OUT TO PLAY WITH HIS FRIENDS.
RUMBL-L-L-LE
LET'S SIT DOWN AND EAT OUR LUNCH.
A TUNA SANDWICH...
...AND AN ORANGE JUICE.
はーい

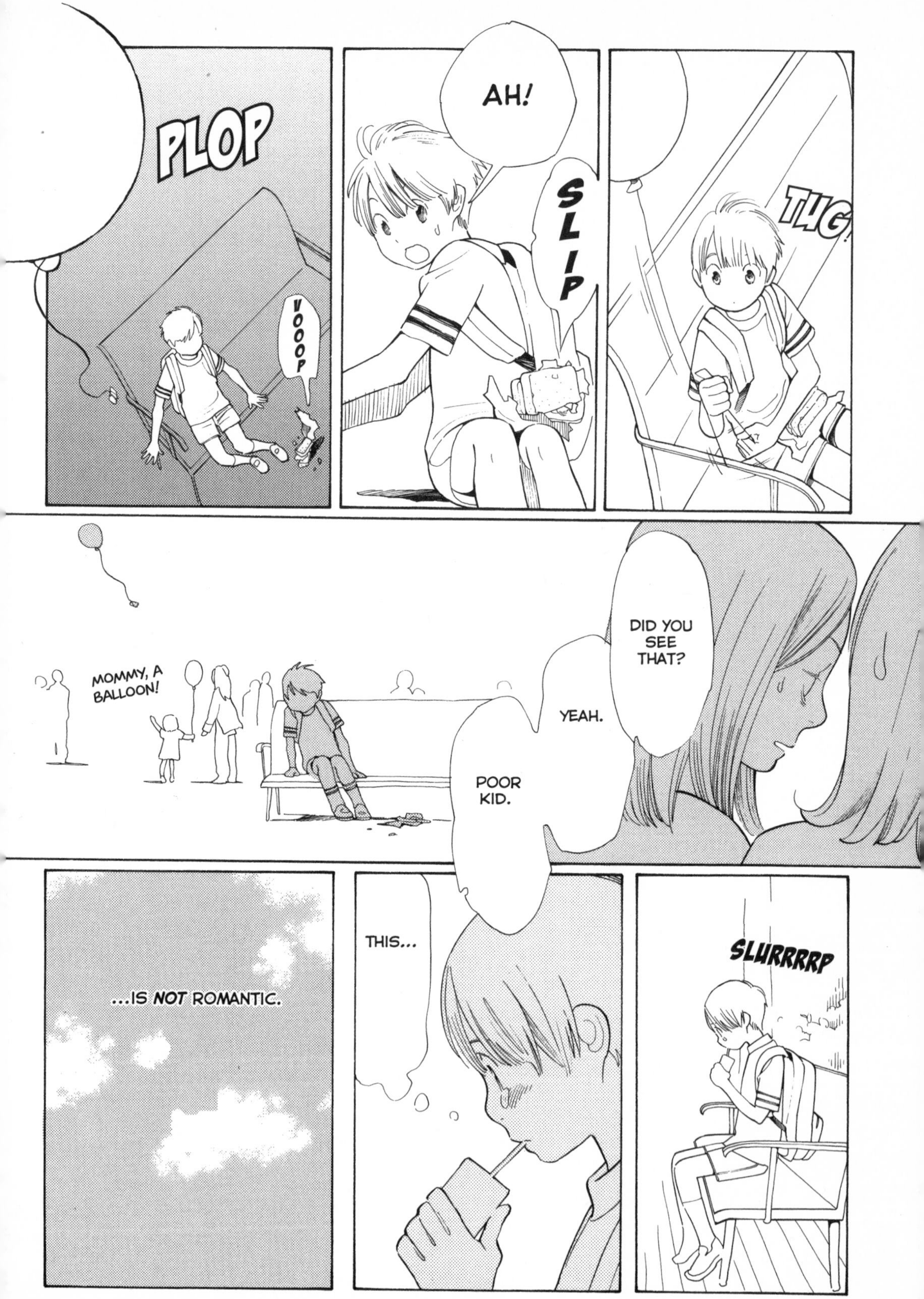
TUG!
AH!
SLIP
PLOP
VOOOP
DID YOU SEE THAT?
YEAH.
POOR KID.
MOMMY, A BALLOON!
SLURRRRP
THIS...
...IS NOT ROMANTIC.

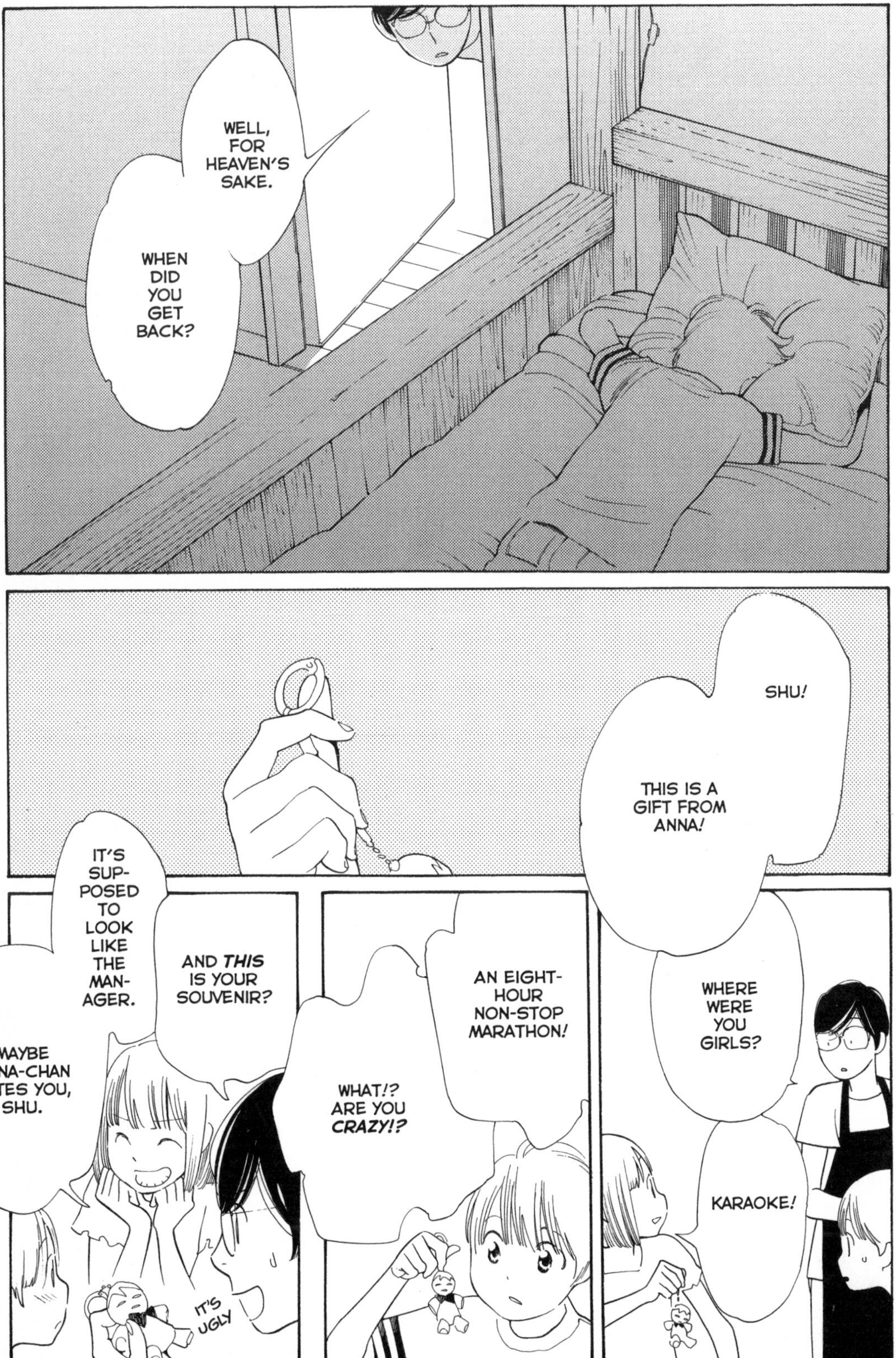
WELL, FOR HEAVEN'S SAKE.
WHEN DID YOU GET BACK?
SHU!
THIS IS A GIFT FROM ANNA!
WHERE WERE YOU GIRLS?
KARAOKE!
AN EIGHT-HOUR NON-STOP MARATHON!
WHAT!? ARE YOU *CRAZY!?*
AND *THIS* IS YOUR SOUVENIR?
IT'S SUP-POSED TO LOOK LIKE THE MAN-AGER.
MAYBE ANNA-CHAN HATES YOU, SHU.
IT'S UGLY

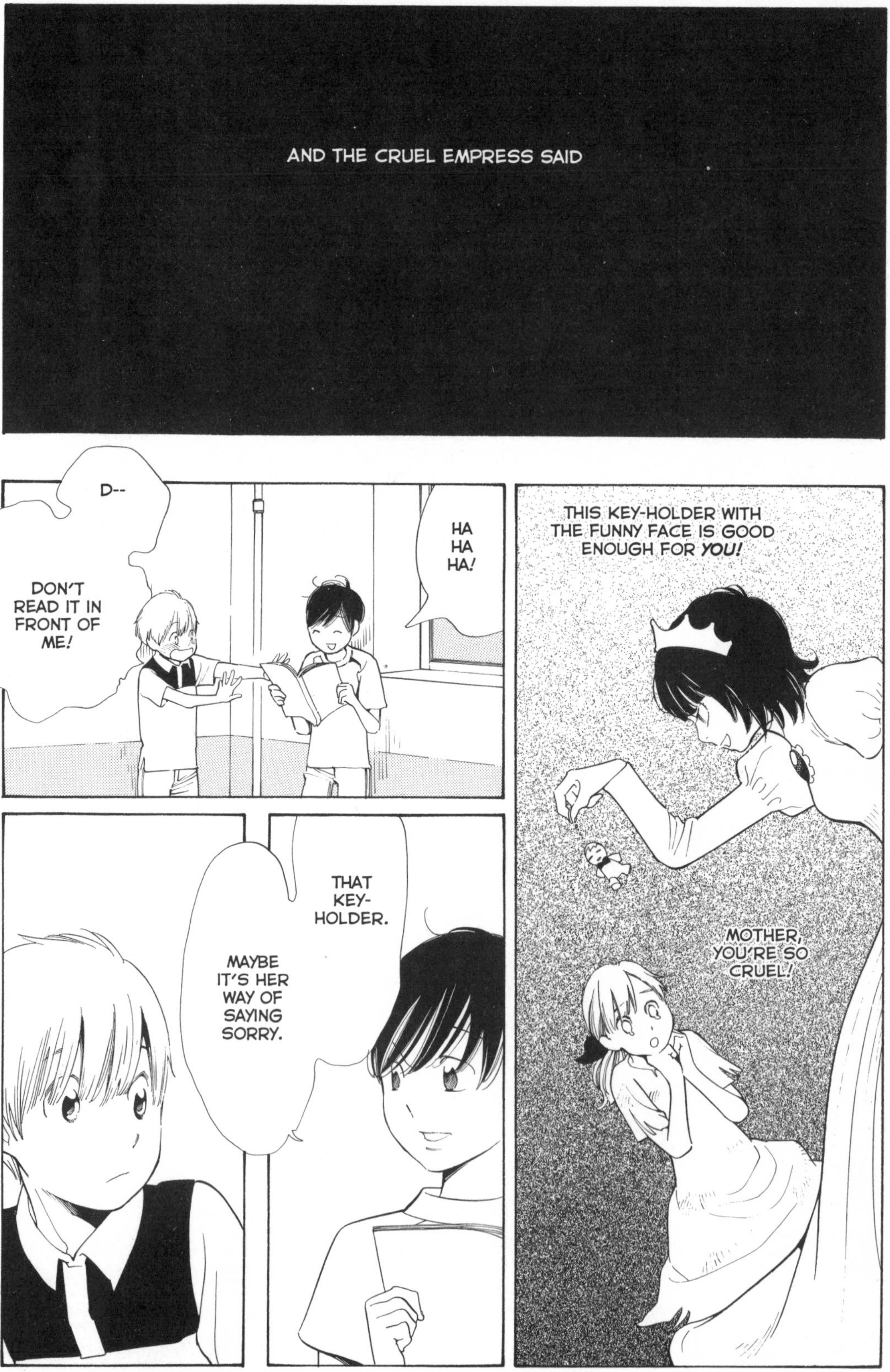
AND THE CRUEL EMPRESS SAID
THIS KEY-HOLDER WITH THE FUNNY FACE IS GOOD ENOUGH FOR ***YOU!***
MOTHER, YOU'RE SO CRUEL!
HA HA HA!
D--
DON'T READ IT IN FRONT OF ME!
THAT KEY-HOLDER.
MAYBE IT'S HER WAY OF SAYING SORRY.

I'M HOME!

MOM, JUICE!

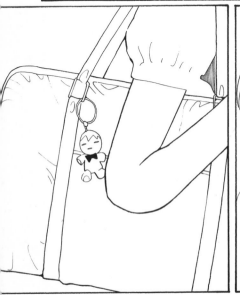

HEL-LO...

HELLO.

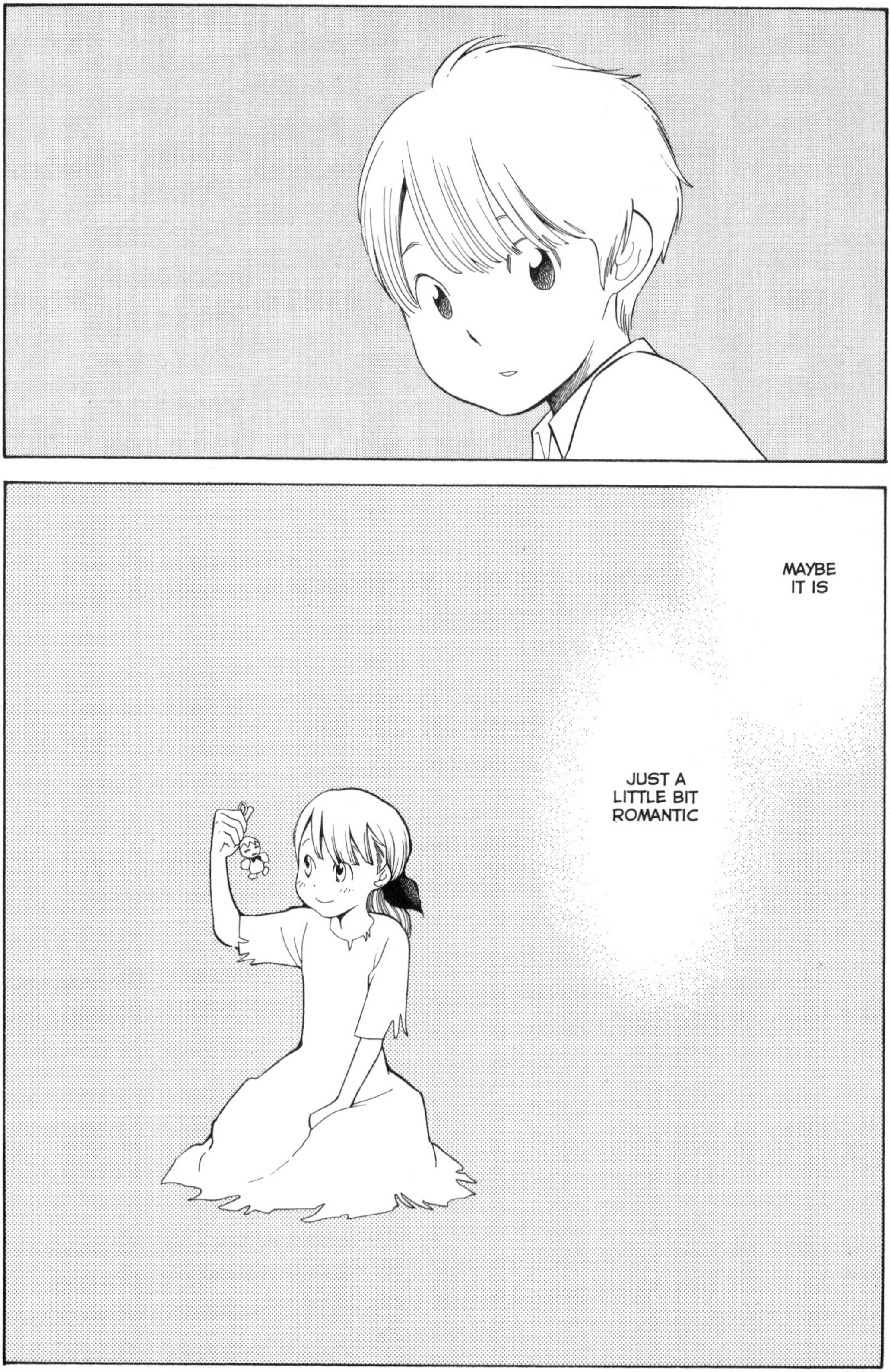
MAYBE IT IS
JUST A LITTLE BIT ROMANTIC

29

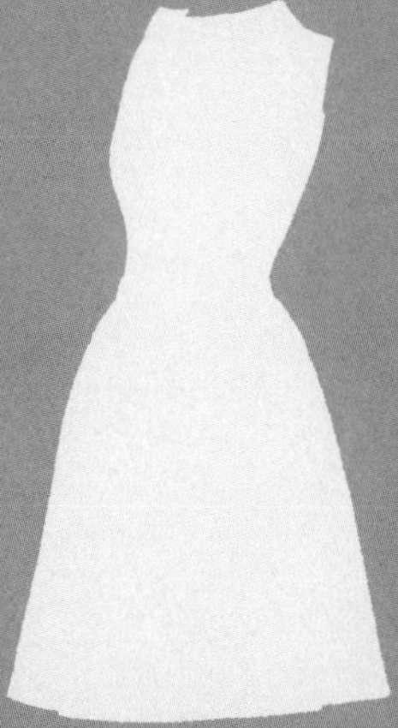

The Kissing Incident

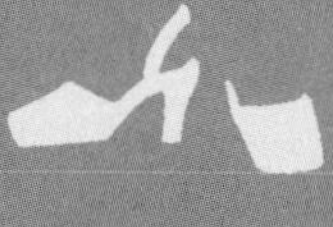

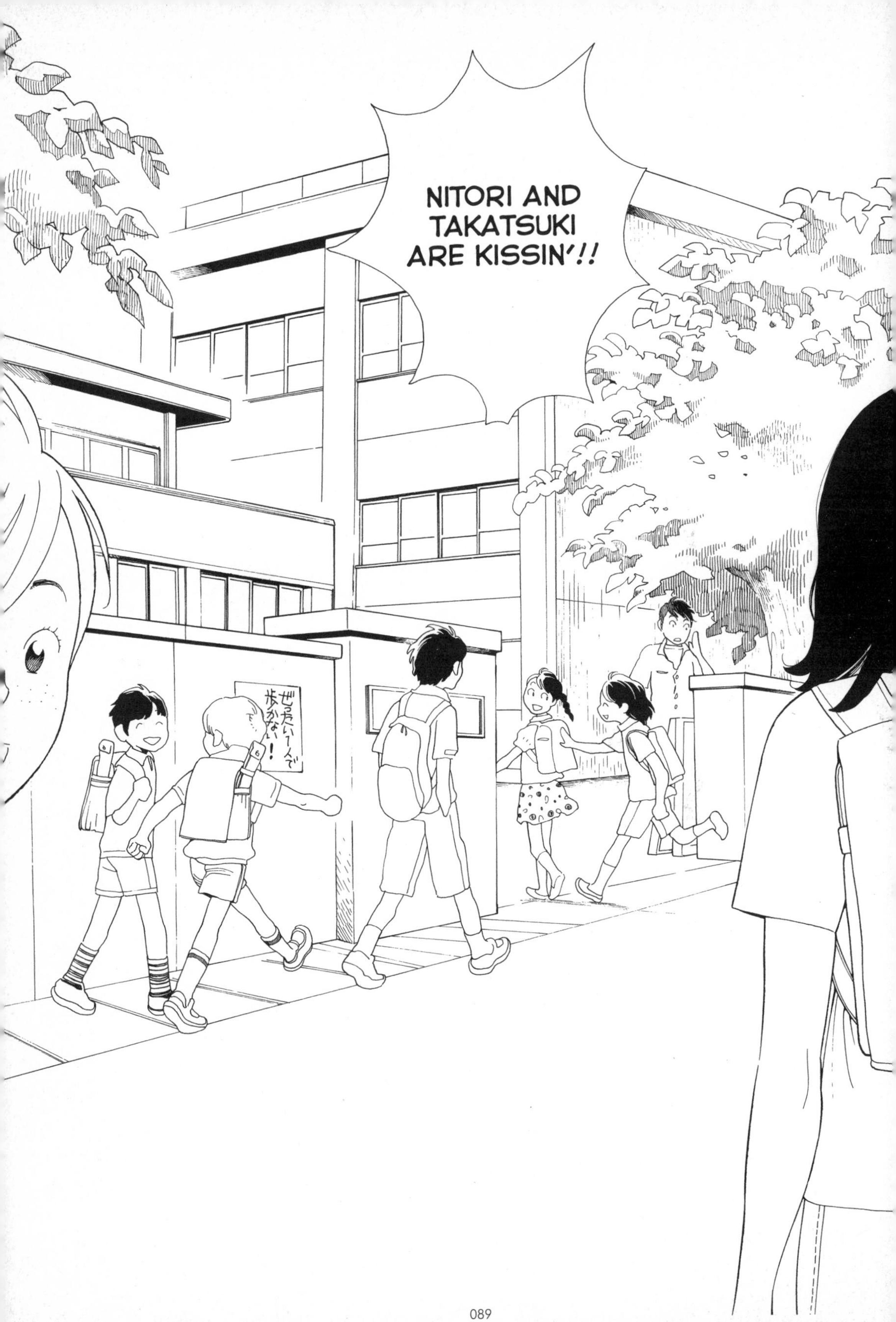
NITORI AND TAKATSUKI ARE KISSIN'!!
ぜったい1人で歩かない!

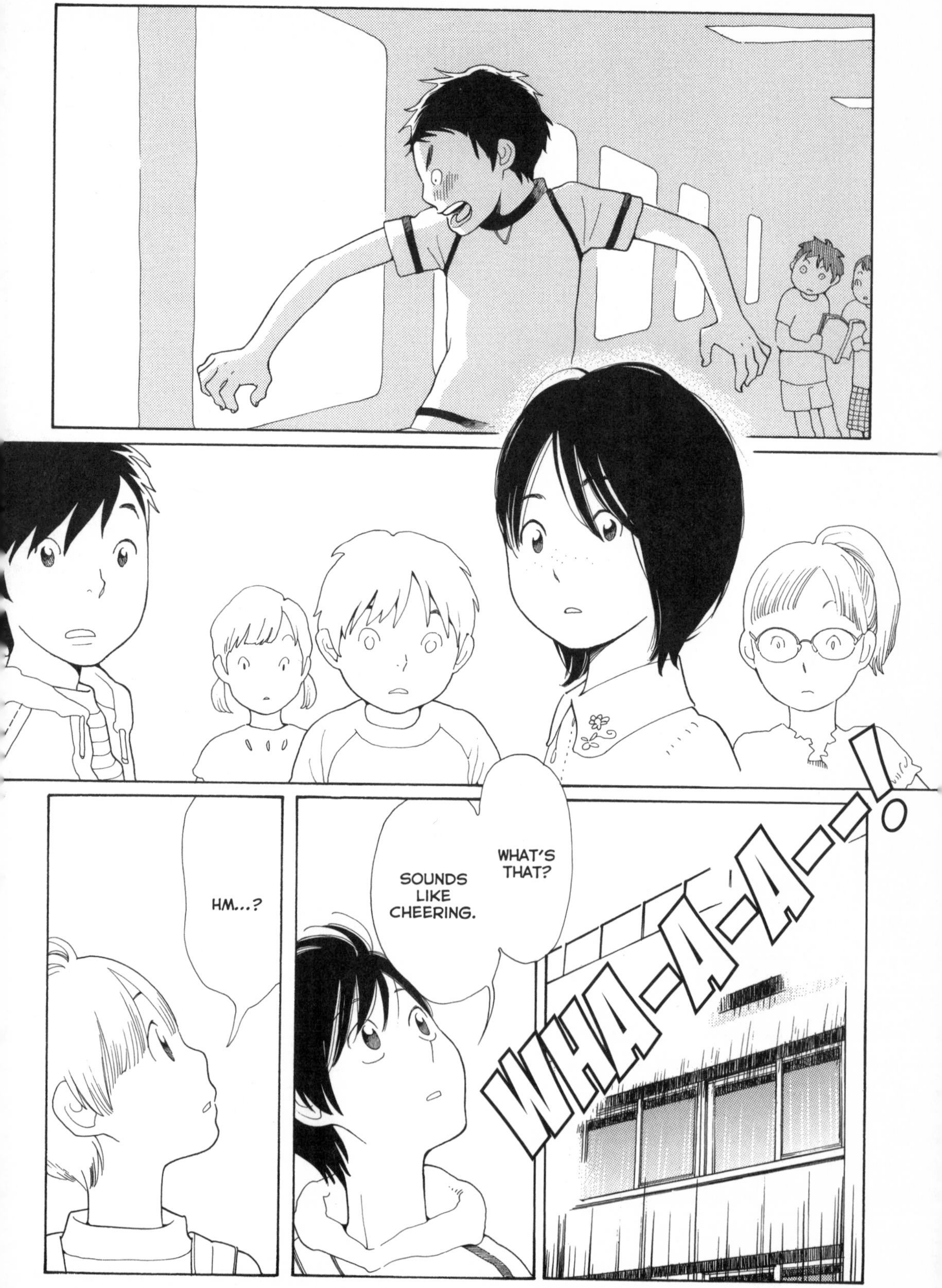
WHA-A-A--!
WHAT'S THAT?
SOUNDS LIKE CHEERING.
HM...?

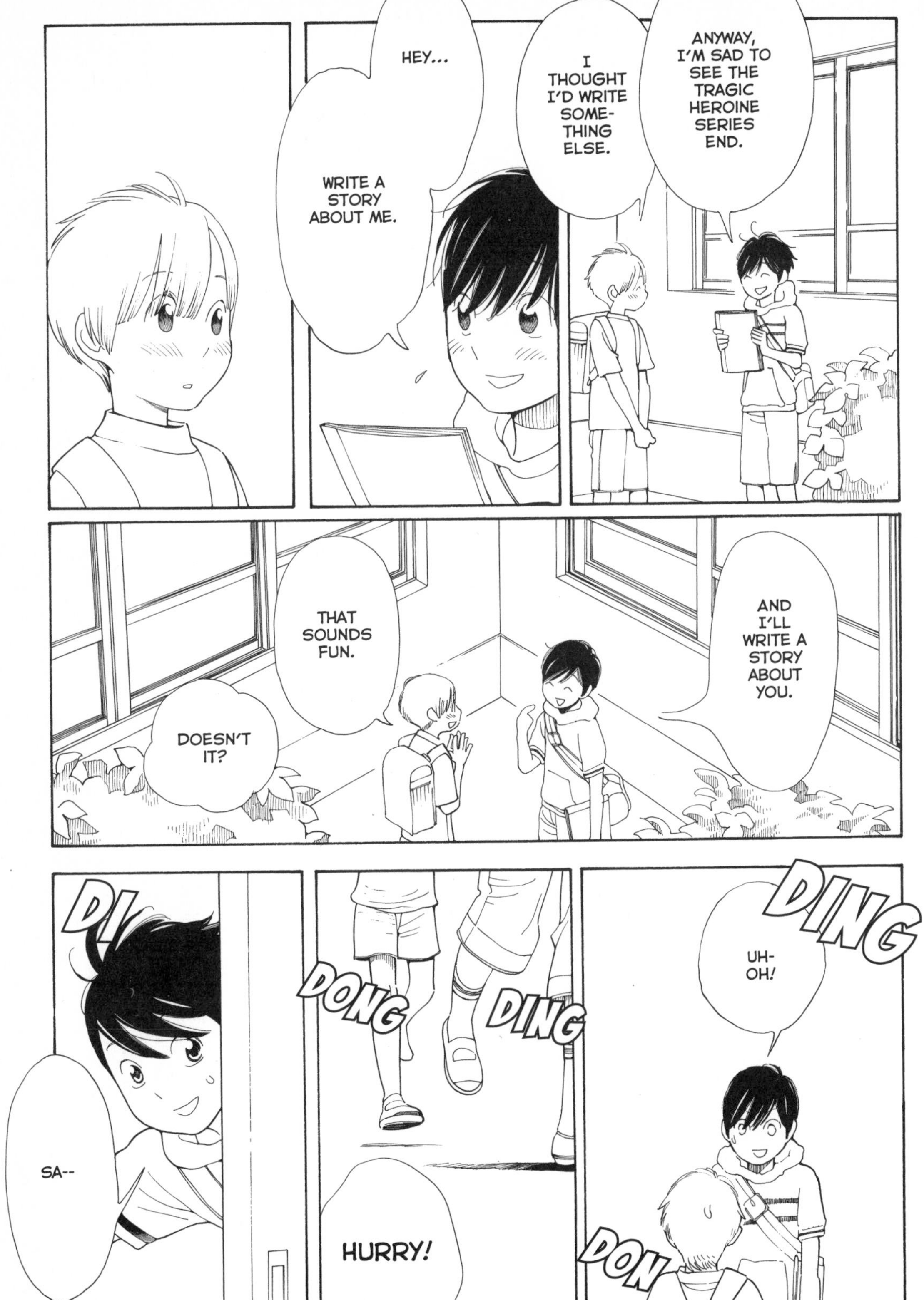
ANYWAY, I'M SAD TO SEE THE TRAGIC HEROINE SERIES END.
I THOUGHT I'D WRITE SOME-THING ELSE.
HEY...
WRITE A STORY ABOUT ME.
AND I'LL WRITE A STORY ABOUT YOU.
THAT SOUNDS FUN.
DOESN'T IT?
DING
UH-OH!
DON
DONG
DING
HURRY!
DI
SA--

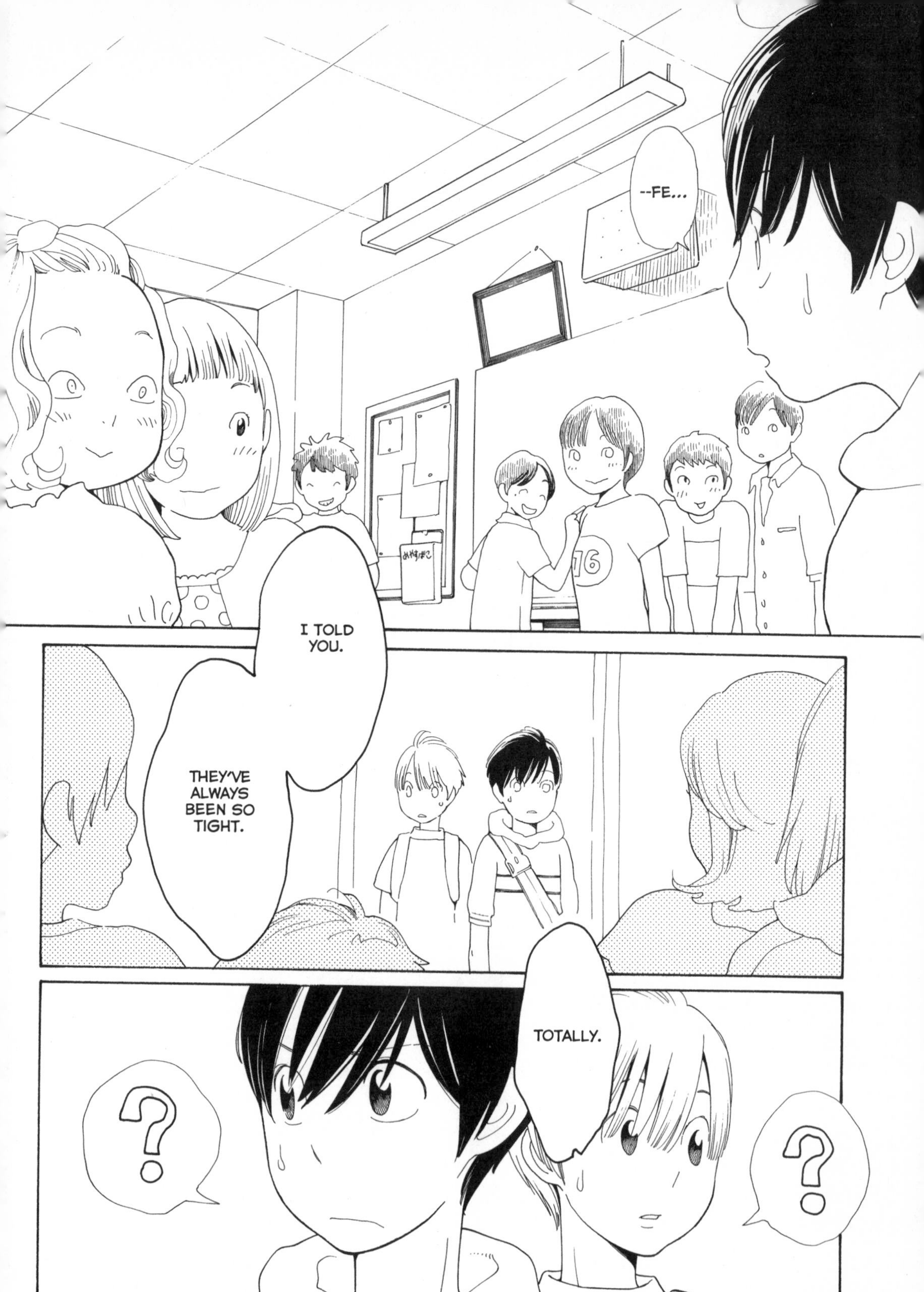
--FE...
I TOLD YOU.
THEY'VE ALWAYS BEEN SO TIGHT.
TOTALLY.
?
?

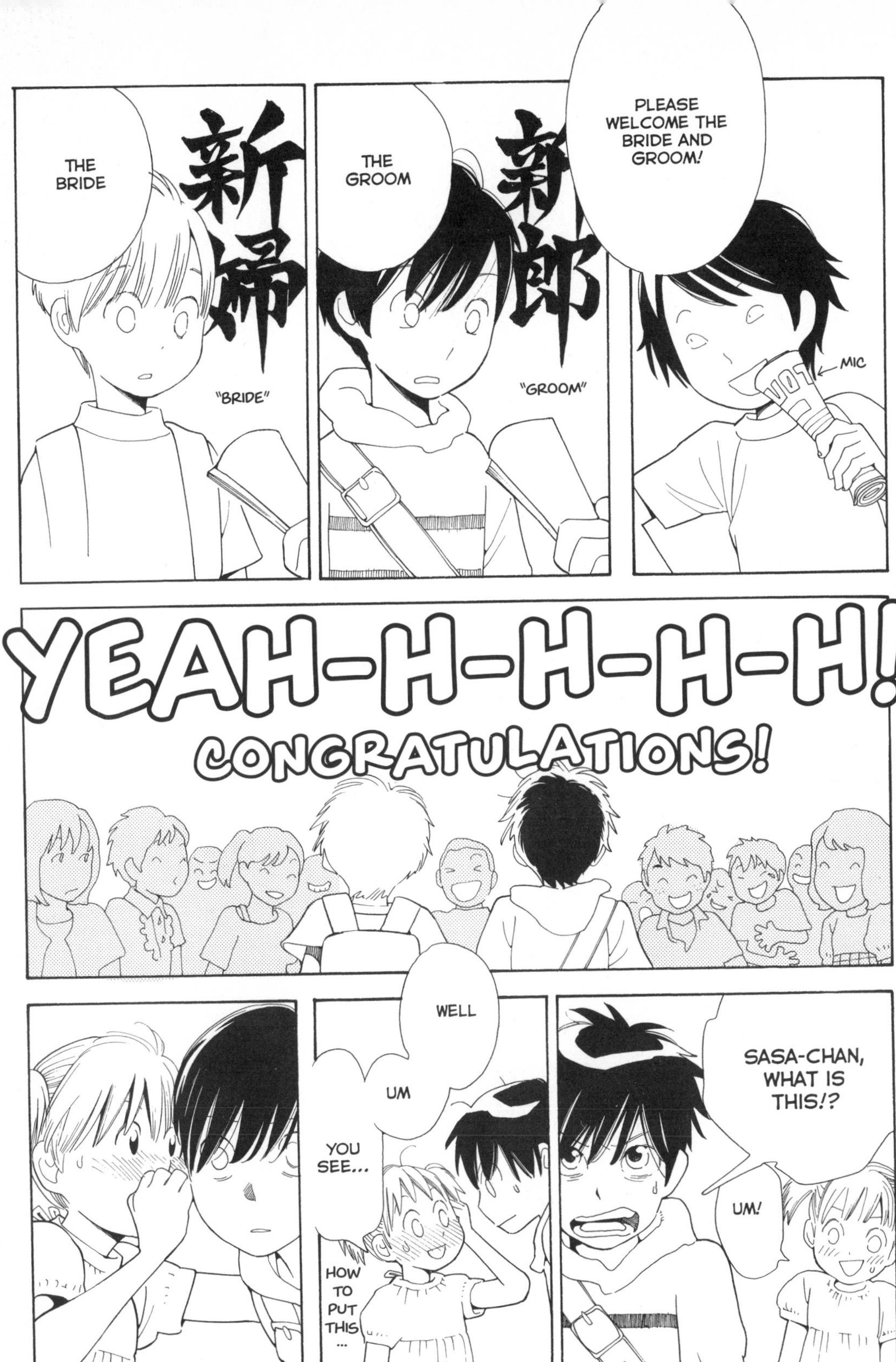
PLEASE WELCOME THE BRIDE AND GROOM!
MIC
THE GROOM
新郎
"GROOM"
THE BRIDE
新婦
"BRIDE"
YEAH-H-H-H-H!
CONGRATULATIONS!
SASA-CHAN, WHAT IS THIS!?
UM!
WELL
UM
YOU SEE...
HOW TO PUT THIS ...

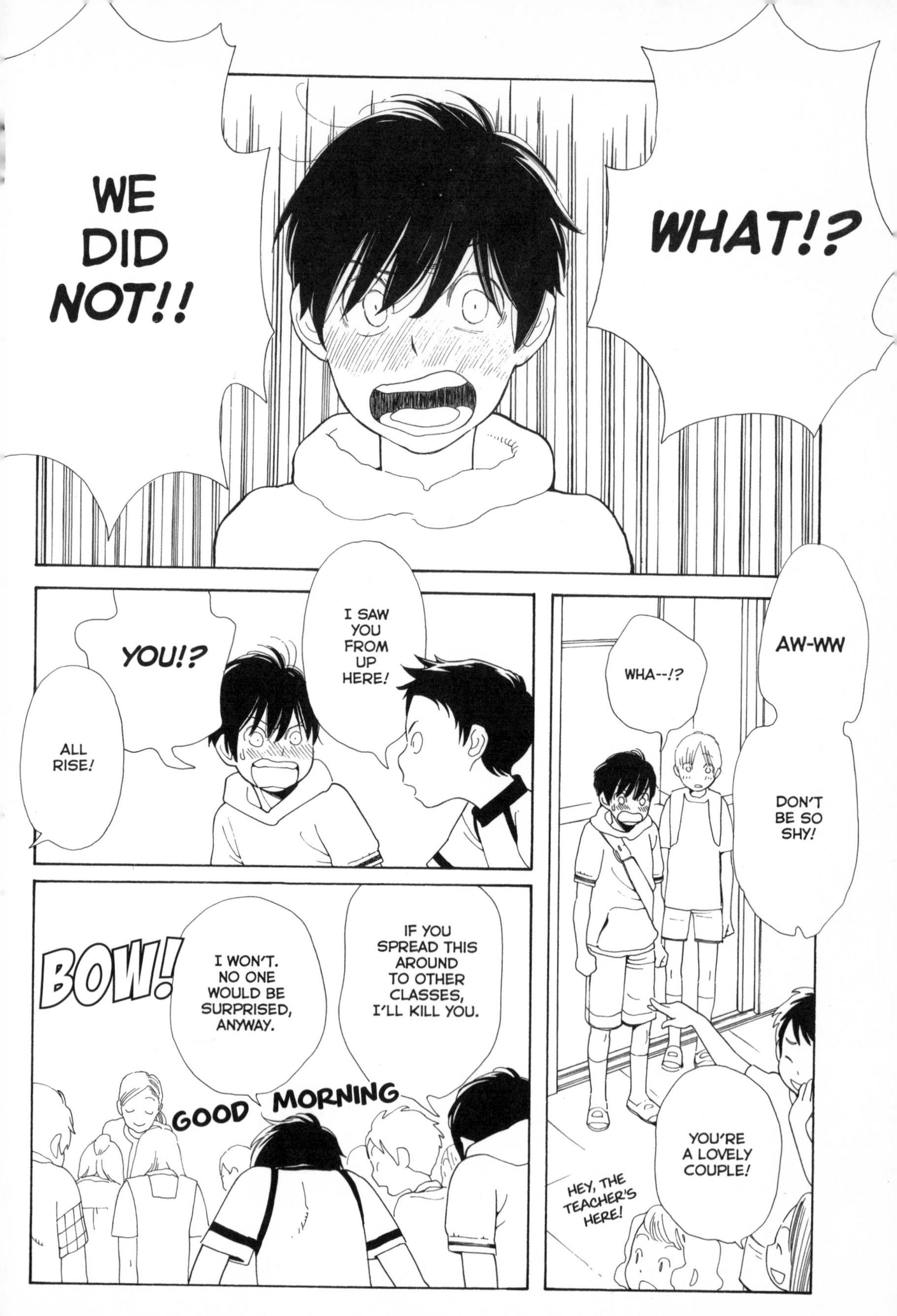
WHAT!?
WE DID NOT!!
AW-WW
WHA--!?
DON'T BE SO SHY!
YOU'RE A LOVELY COUPLE!
HEY, THE TEACHER'S HERE!
I SAW YOU FROM UP HERE!
YOU!?
ALL RISE!
IF YOU SPREAD THIS AROUND TO OTHER CLASSES, I'LL KILL YOU.
I WON'T. NO ONE WOULD BE SURPRISED, ANYWAY.
BOW!
GOOD MORNING

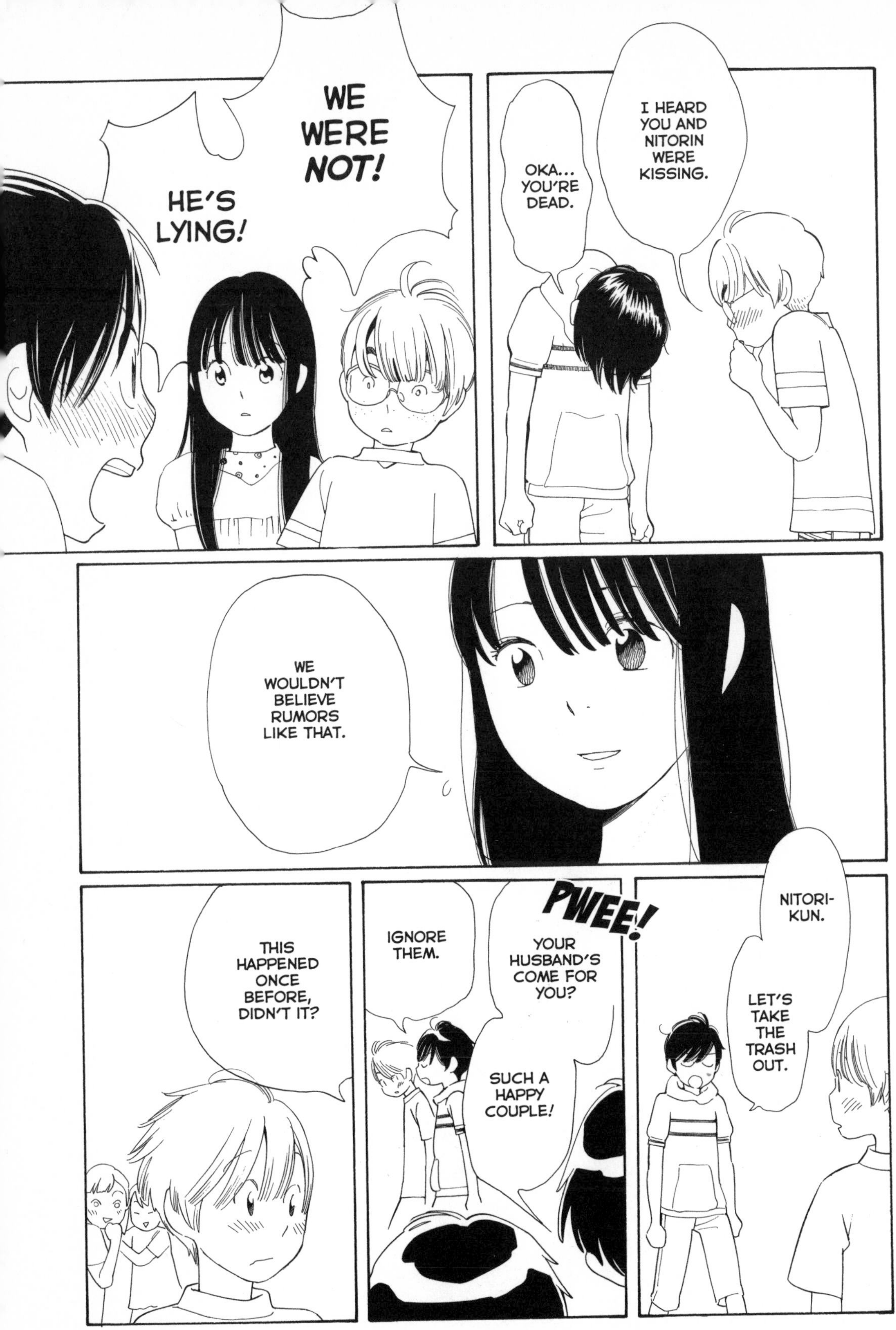
I HEARD YOU AND NITORIN WERE KISSING.
OKA... YOU'RE DEAD.
WE WERE NOT!
HE'S LYING!
WE WOULDN'T BELIEVE RUMORS LIKE THAT.
NITORI-KUN.
LET'S TAKE THE TRASH OUT.
PWEE!
YOUR HUSBAND'S COME FOR YOU?
IGNORE THEM.
SUCH A HAPPY COUPLE!
THIS HAPPENED ONCE BEFORE, DIDN'T IT?

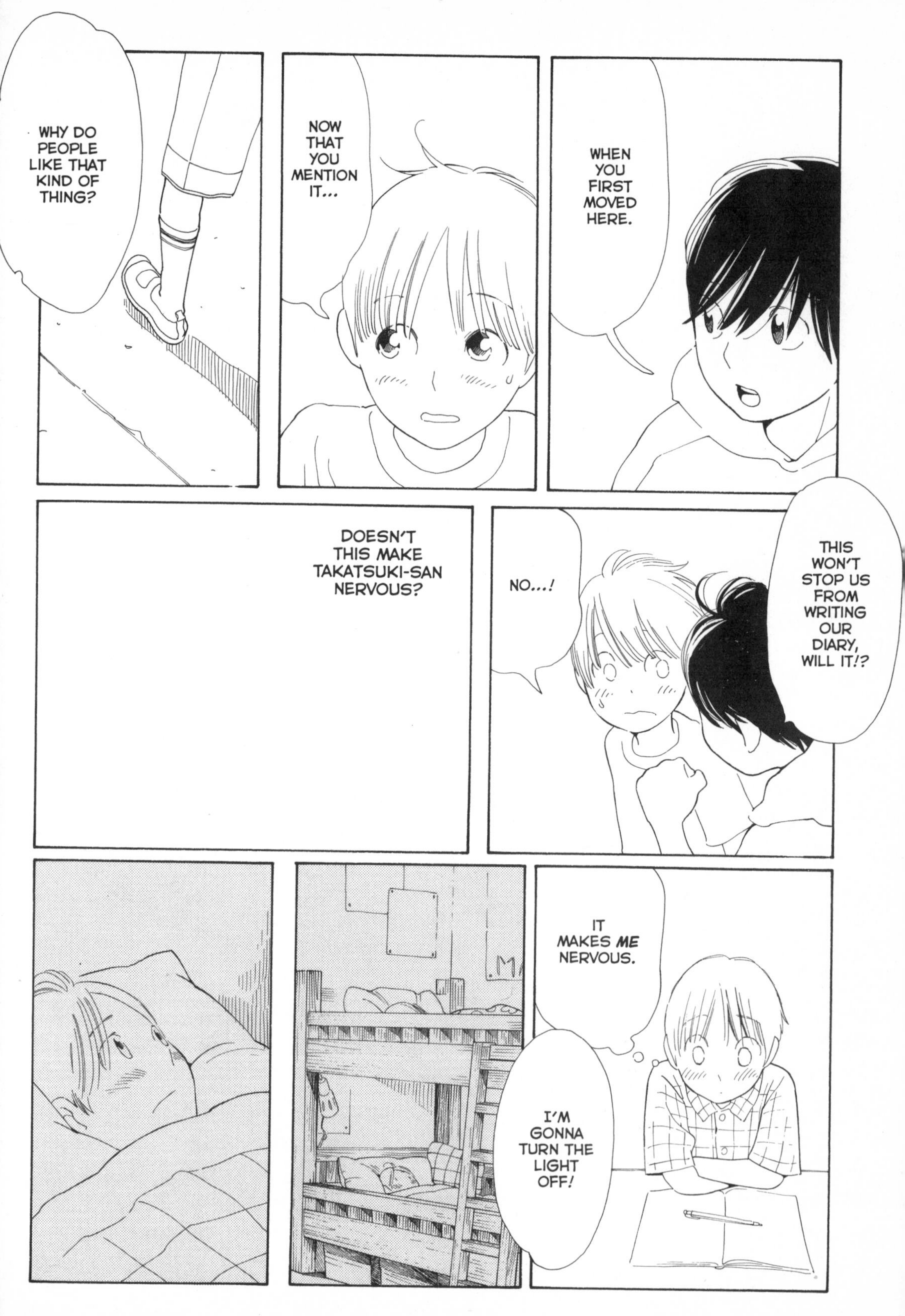
WHEN YOU FIRST MOVED HERE.
NOW THAT YOU MENTION IT...
WHY DO PEOPLE LIKE THAT KIND OF THING?
THIS WON'T STOP US FROM WRITING OUR DIARY, WILL IT!?
NO...!
DOESN'T THIS MAKE TAKATSUKI-SAN NERVOUS?
IT MAKES *ME* NERVOUS.
I'M GONNA TURN THE LIGHT OFF!

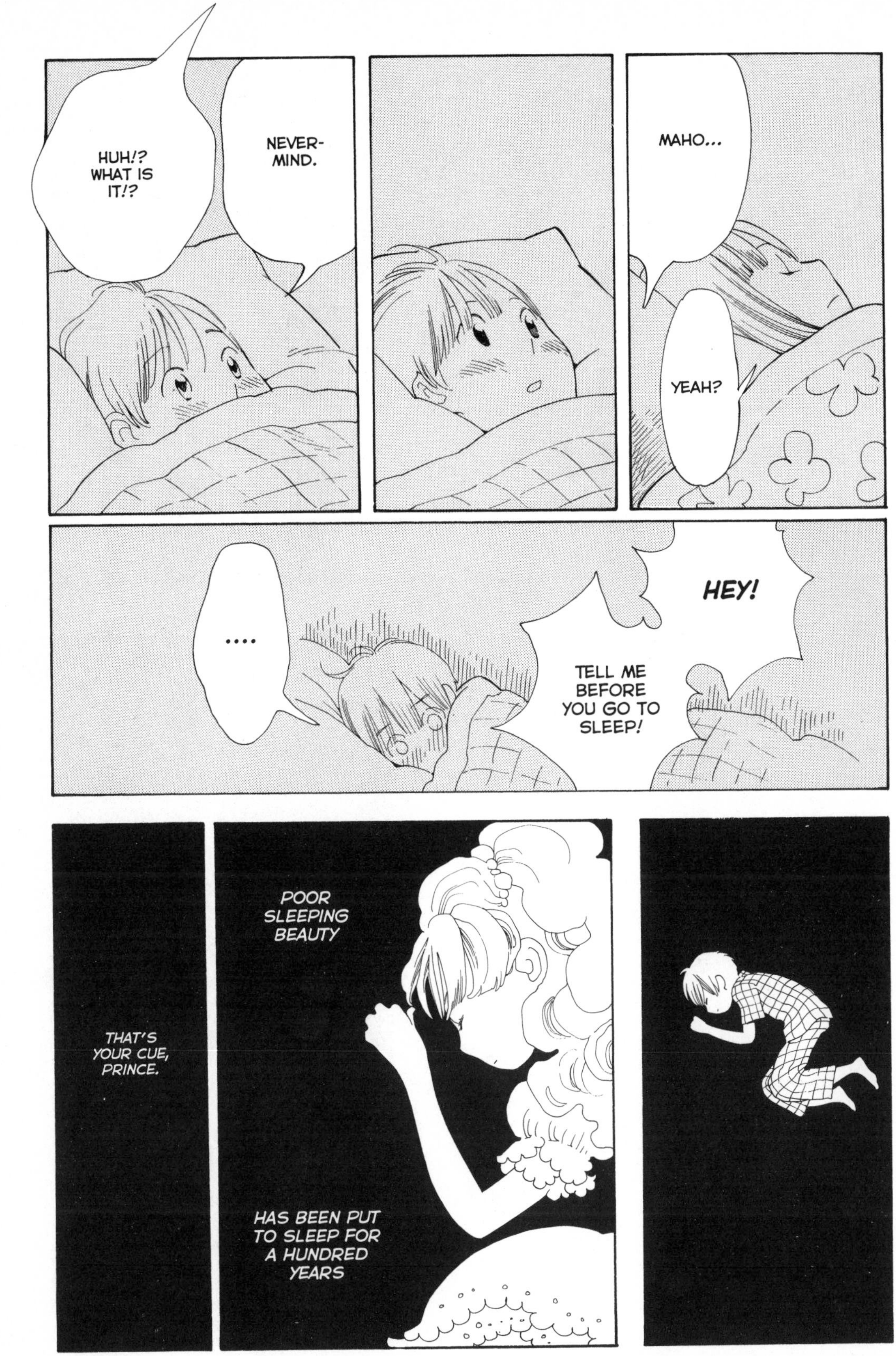
MAHO...
YEAH?
NEVER-MIND.
HUH!? WHAT IS IT!?
HEY!
TELL ME BEFORE YOU GO TO SLEEP!
....
POOR SLEEPING BEAUTY
HAS BEEN PUT TO SLEEP FOR A HUNDRED YEARS
THAT'S YOUR CUE, PRINCE.

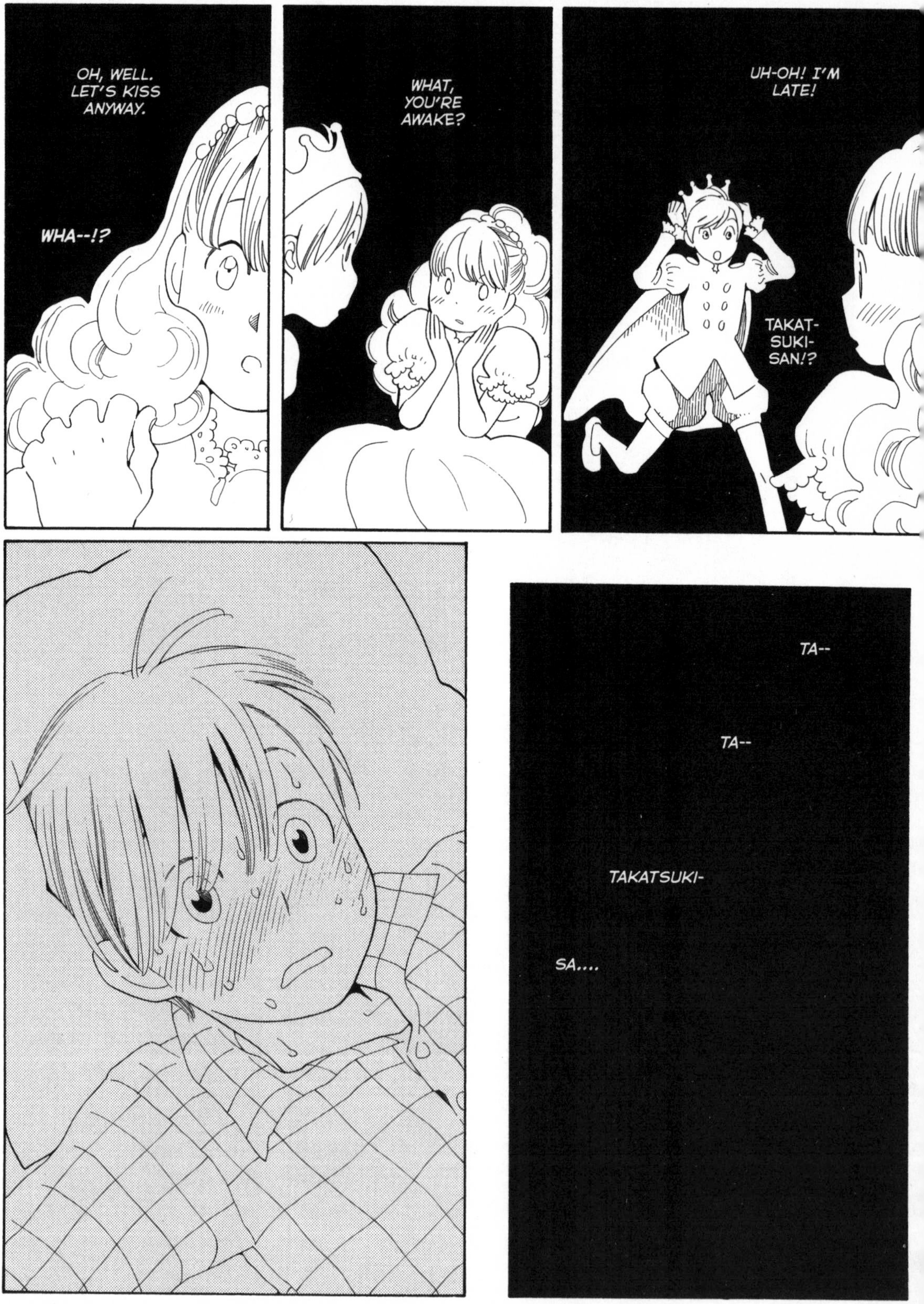
UH-OH! I'M LATE!
TAKAT-SUKI-SAN!?
WHAT, YOU'RE AWAKE?
OH, WELL. LET'S KISS ANYWAY.
WHA--!?
TA--
TA--
TAKATSUKI-
SA....

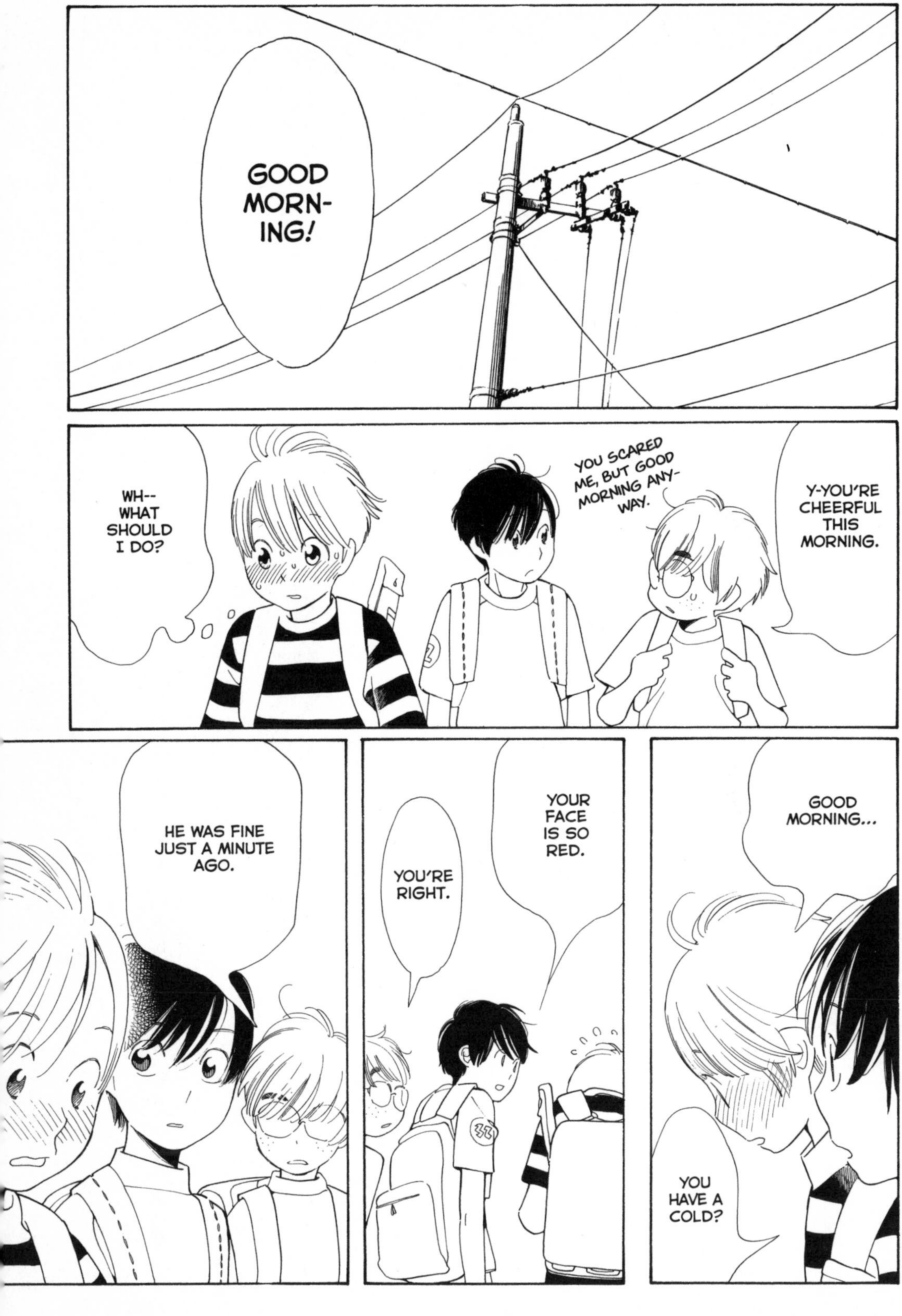
GOOD MORN-ING!
Y-YOU'RE CHEERFUL THIS MORNING.
YOU SCARED ME, BUT GOOD MORNING ANY-WAY.
WH-- WHAT SHOULD I DO?
GOOD MORNING...
YOU HAVE A COLD?
YOUR FACE IS SO RED.
YOU'RE RIGHT.
HE WAS FINE JUST A MINUTE AGO.

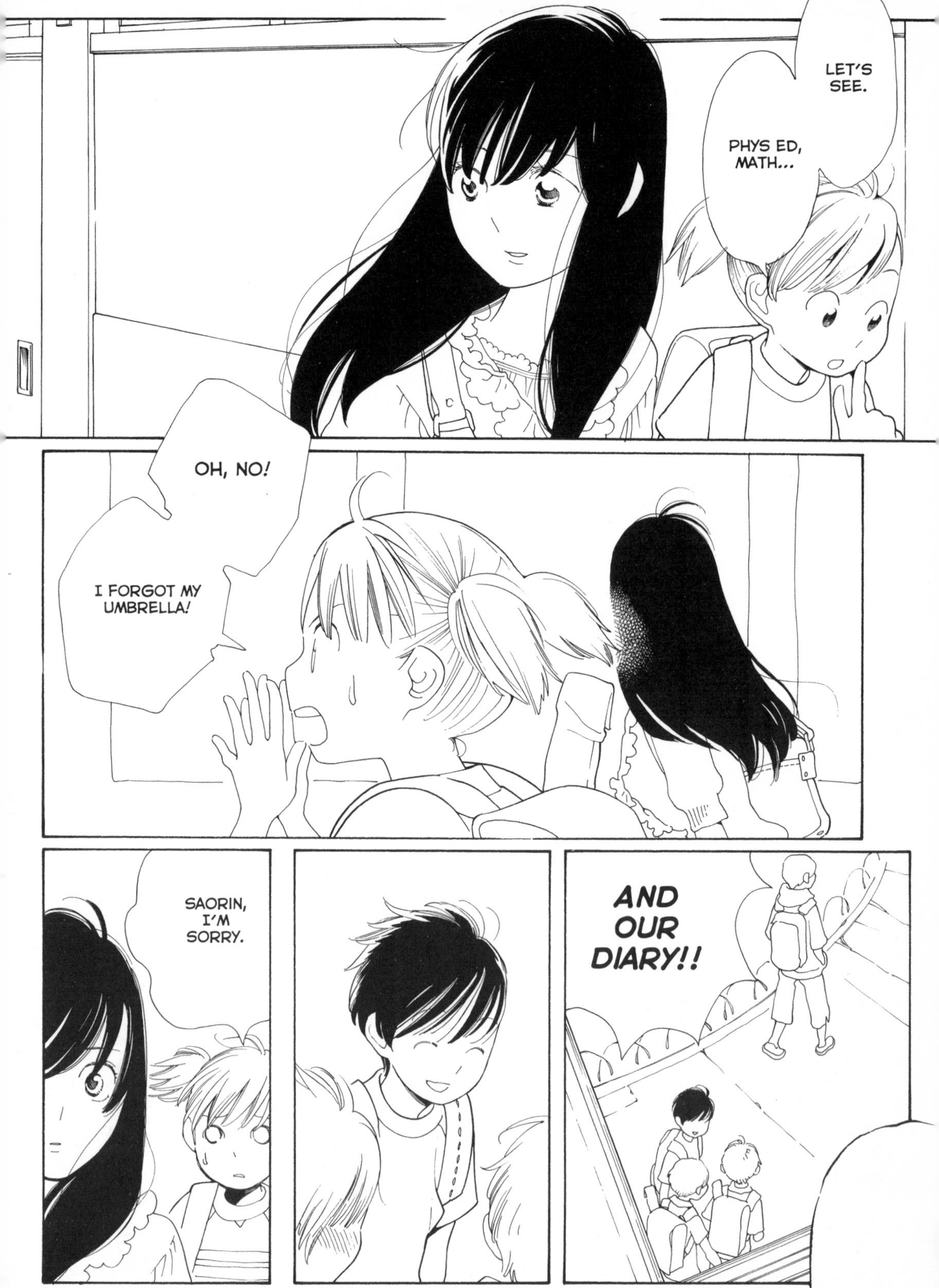
LET'S SEE.
PHYS ED, MATH...
OH, NO!
I FORGOT MY UMBRELLA!
AND OUR DIARY!!
SAORIN, I'M SORRY.

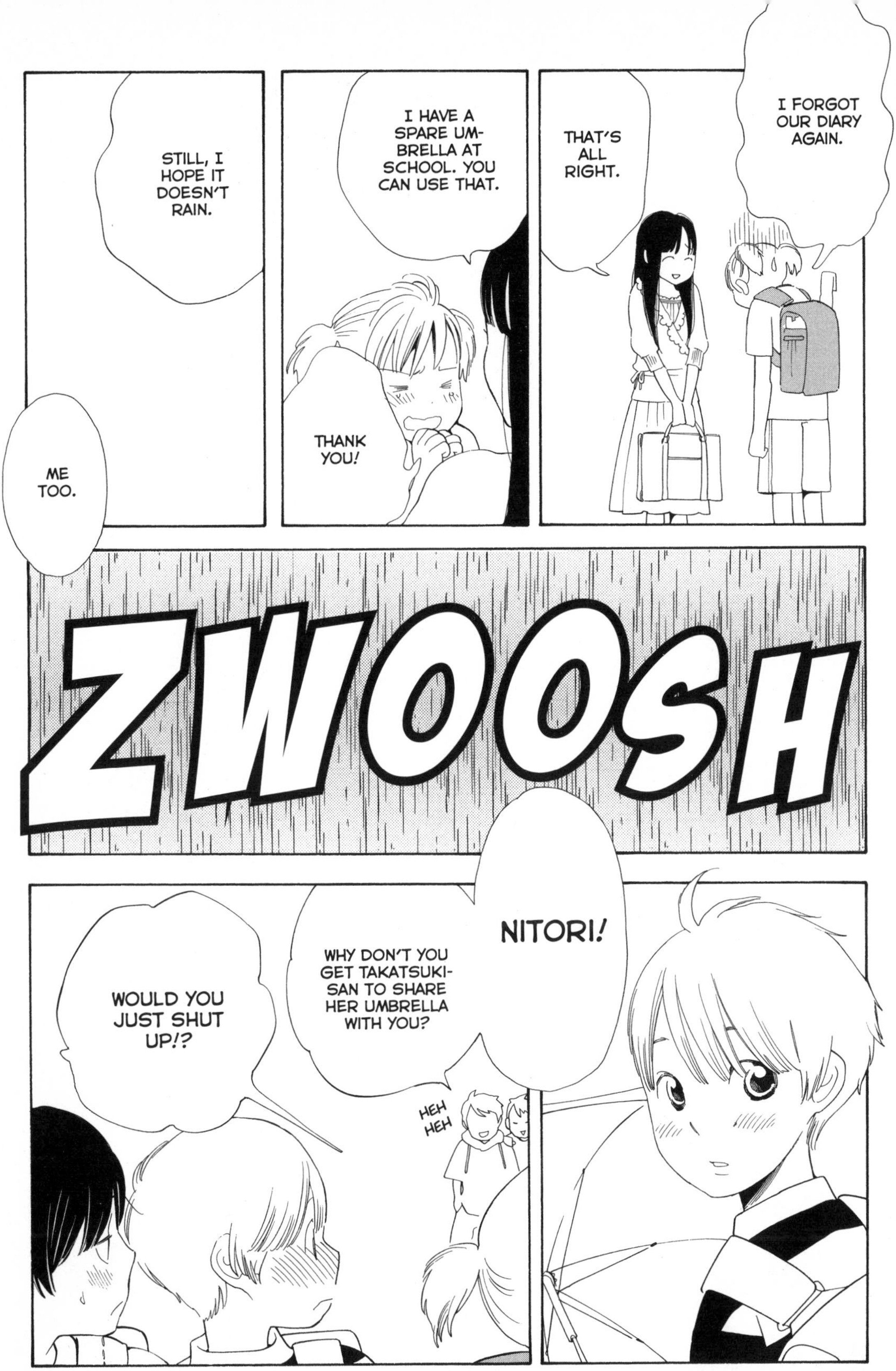
I FORGOT OUR DIARY AGAIN.
THAT'S ALL RIGHT.
I HAVE A SPARE UMBRELLA AT SCHOOL. YOU CAN USE THAT.
THANK YOU!
STILL, I HOPE IT DOESN'T RAIN.
ME TOO.
ZWOOSH
NITORI!
WHY DON'T YOU GET TAKATSUKI-SAN TO SHARE HER UMBRELLA WITH YOU?
HEH HEH
WOULD YOU JUST SHUT UP!?

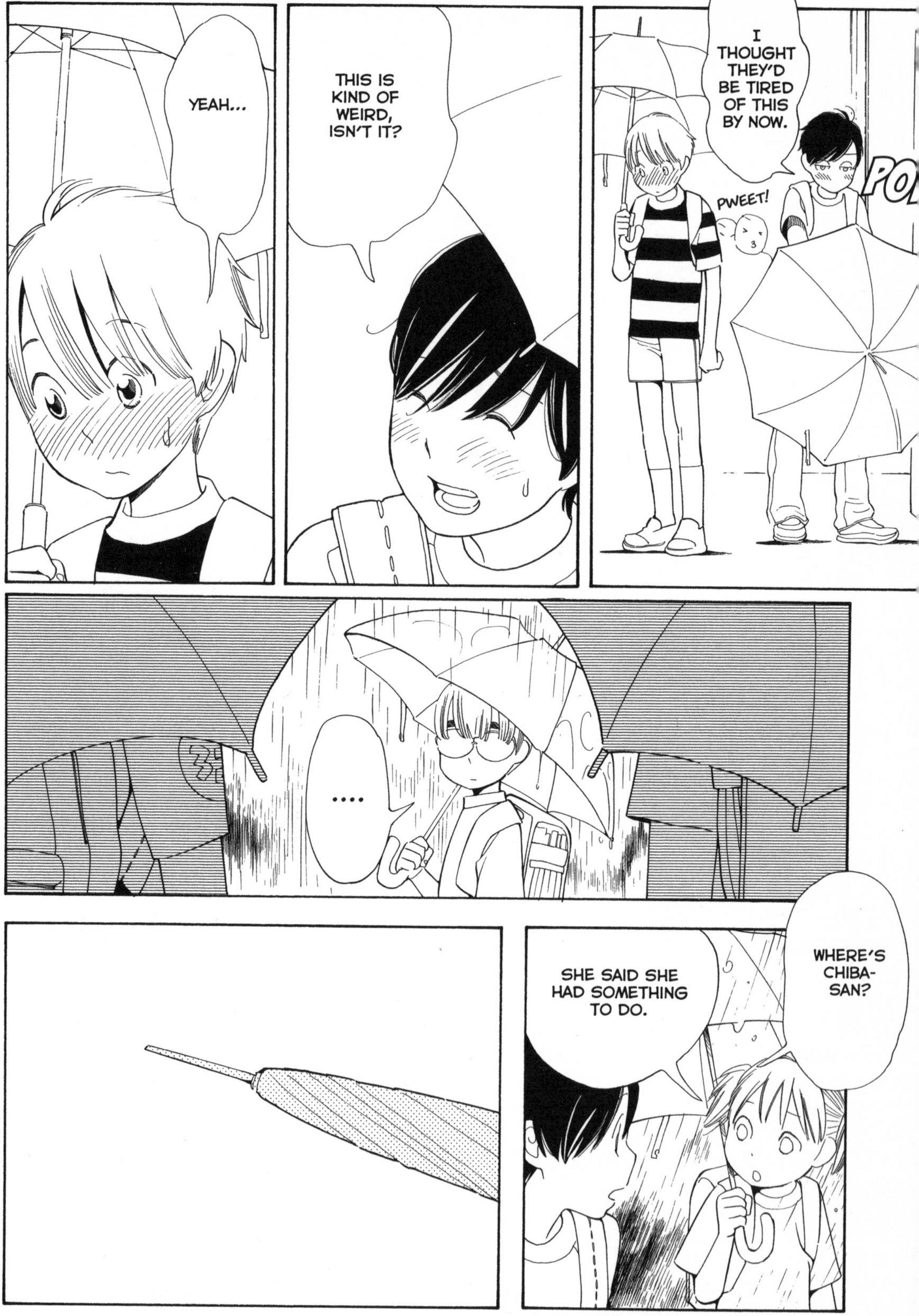
I THOUGHT THEY'D BE TIRED OF THIS BY NOW.
PWEET!
THIS IS KIND OF WEIRD, ISN'T IT?
YEAH...
....
WHERE'S CHIBA-SAN?
SHE SAID SHE HAD SOMETHING TO DO.

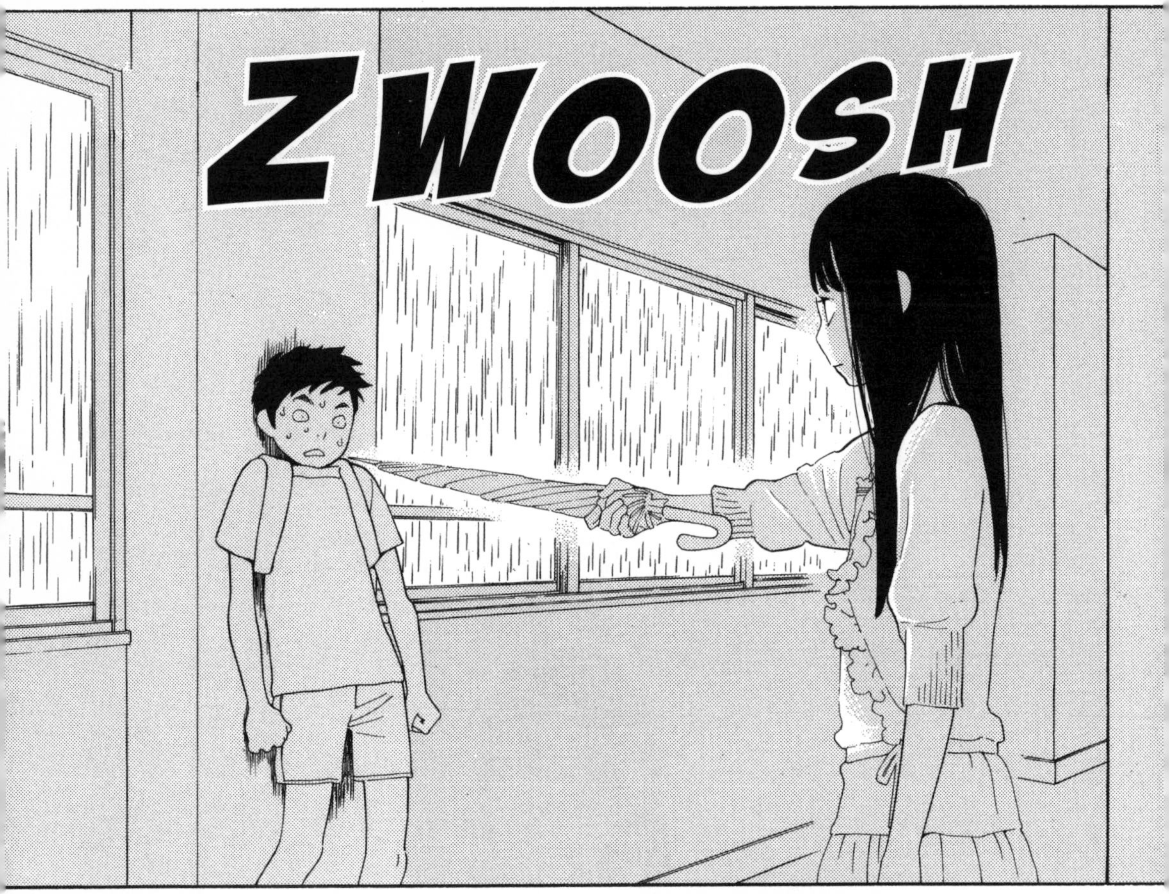
ZWOOSH

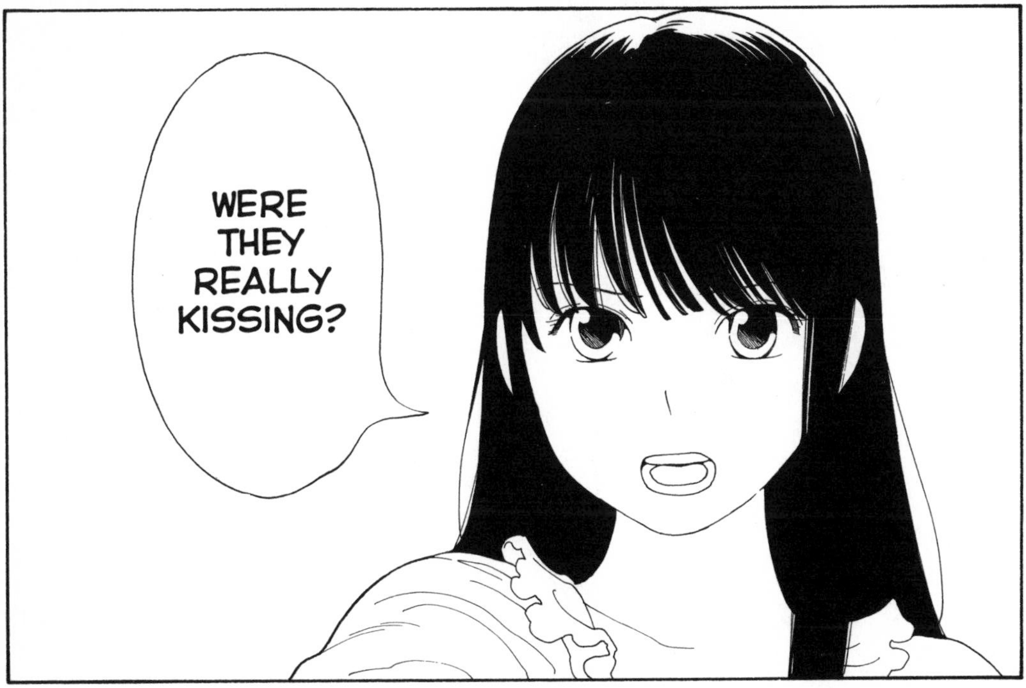
WERE THEY REALLY KISSING?

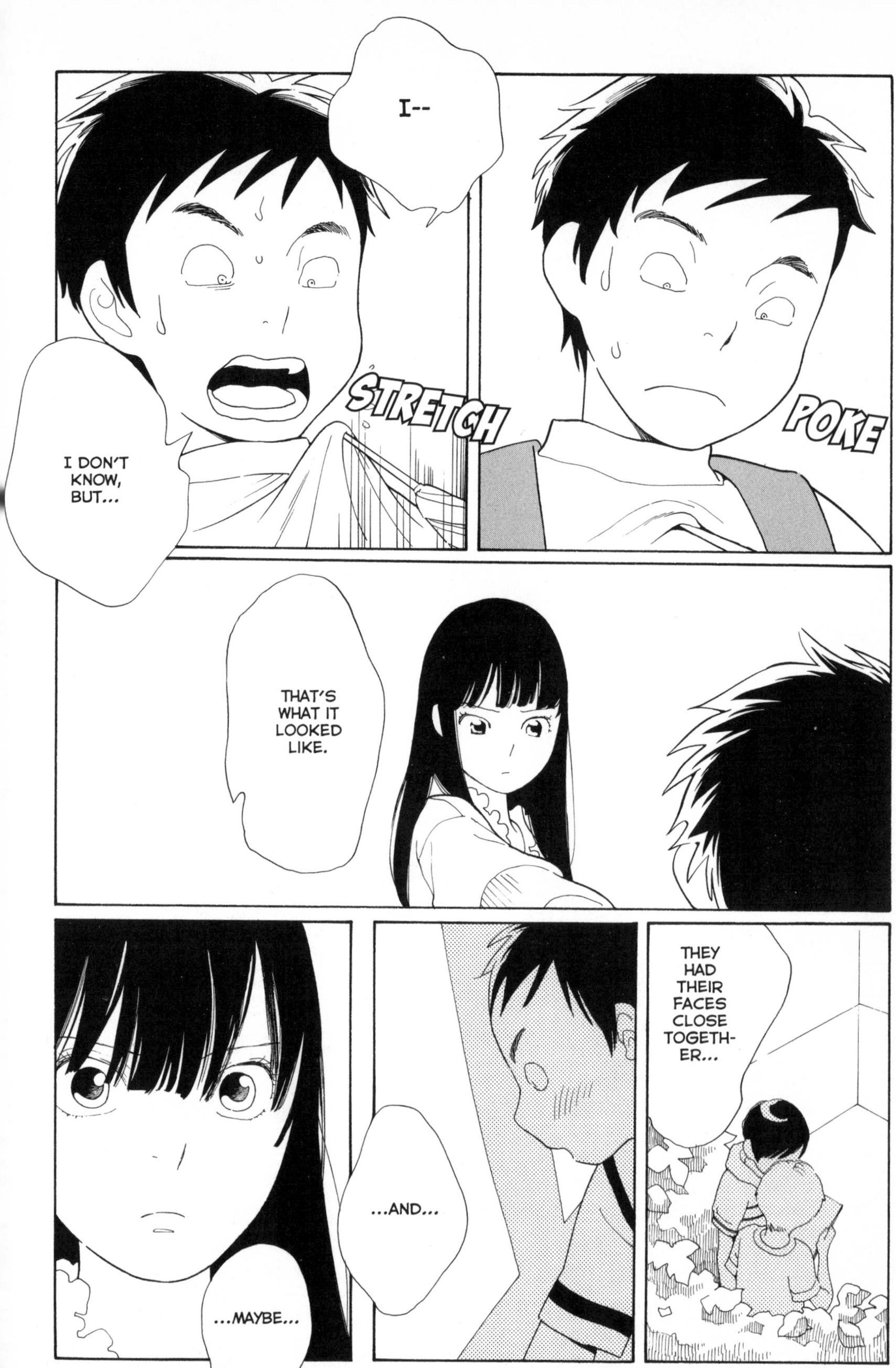
POKE
I--
STRETCH
I DON'T KNOW, BUT...
THAT'S WHAT IT LOOKED LIKE.
THEY HAD THEIR FACES CLOSE TOGETH-ER...
...AND...
...MAYBE...

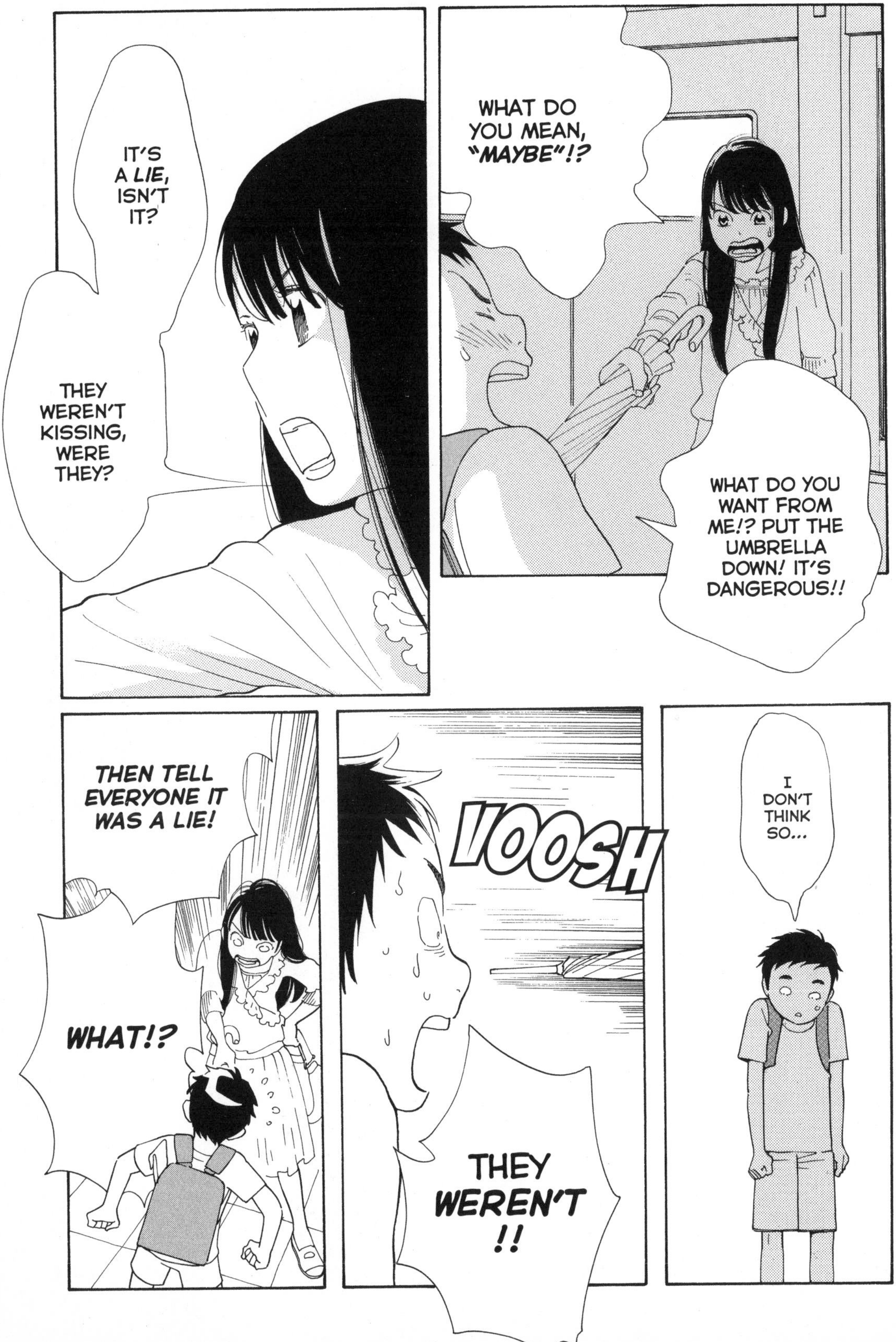
WHAT DO YOU MEAN, "MAYBE"!?
WHAT DO YOU WANT FROM ME!? PUT THE UMBRELLA DOWN! IT'S DANGEROUS!!
IT'S A LIE, ISN'T IT?
THEY WEREN'T KISSING, WERE THEY?
I DON'T THINK SO...
VOOSH
THEY WEREN'T !!
THEN TELL EVERYONE IT WAS A LIE!
WHAT!?

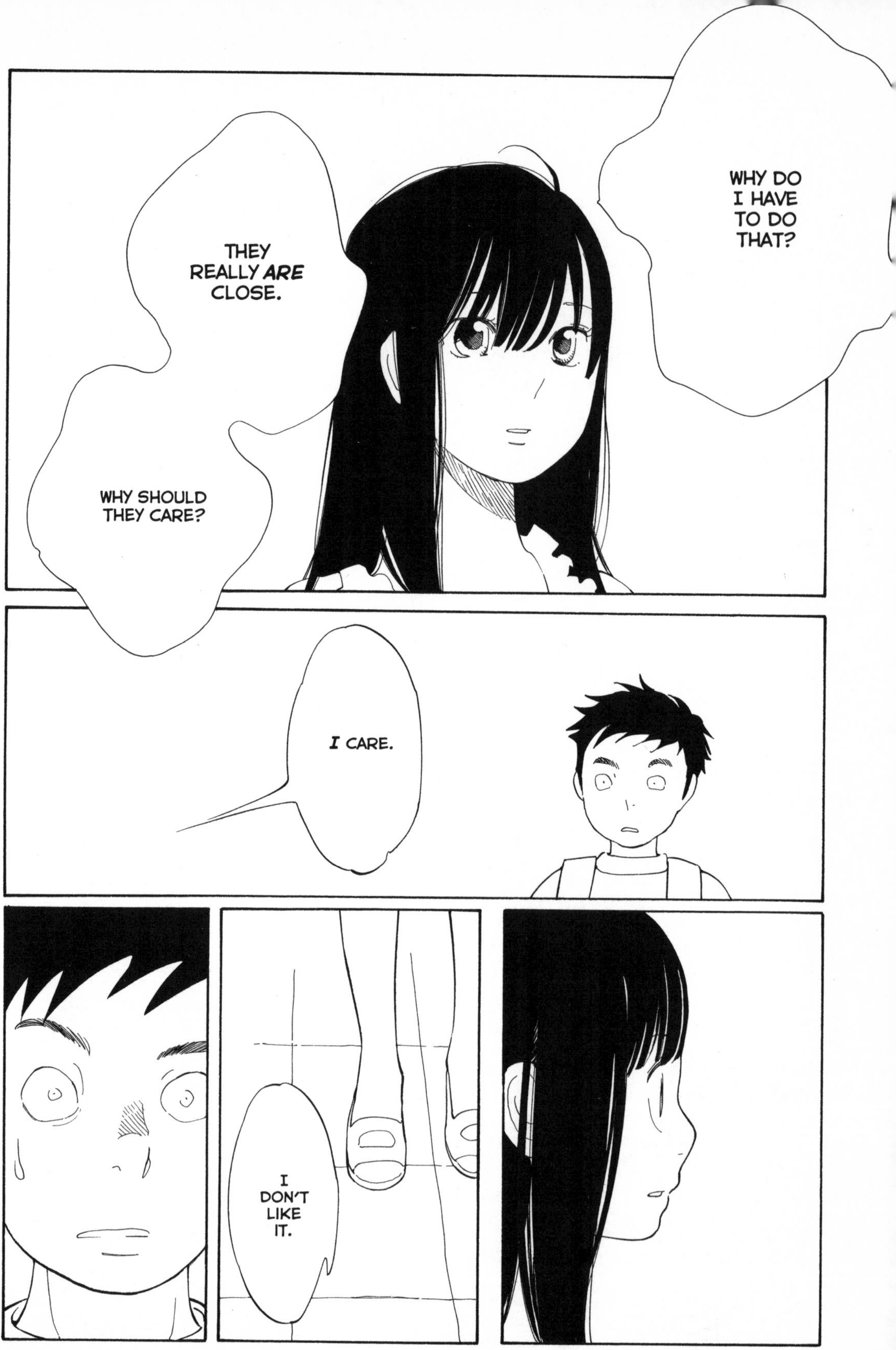
WHY DO I HAVE TO DO THAT?
THEY REALLY ***ARE*** CLOSE.
WHY SHOULD THEY CARE?
I CARE.
I DON'T LIKE IT.

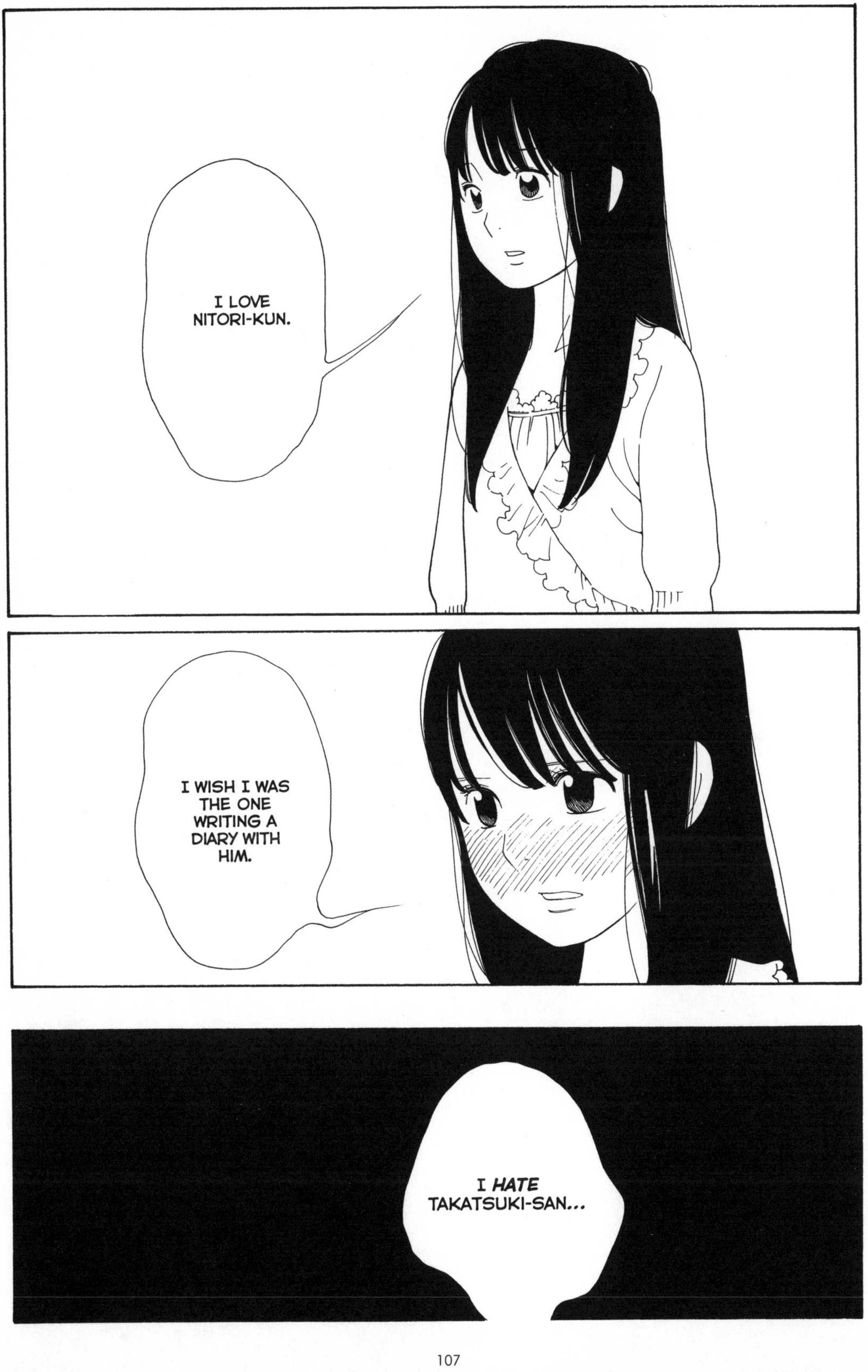
I LOVE NITORI-KUN.
I WISH I WAS THE ONE WRITING A DIARY WITH HIM.
I *HATE* TAKATSUKI-SAN...

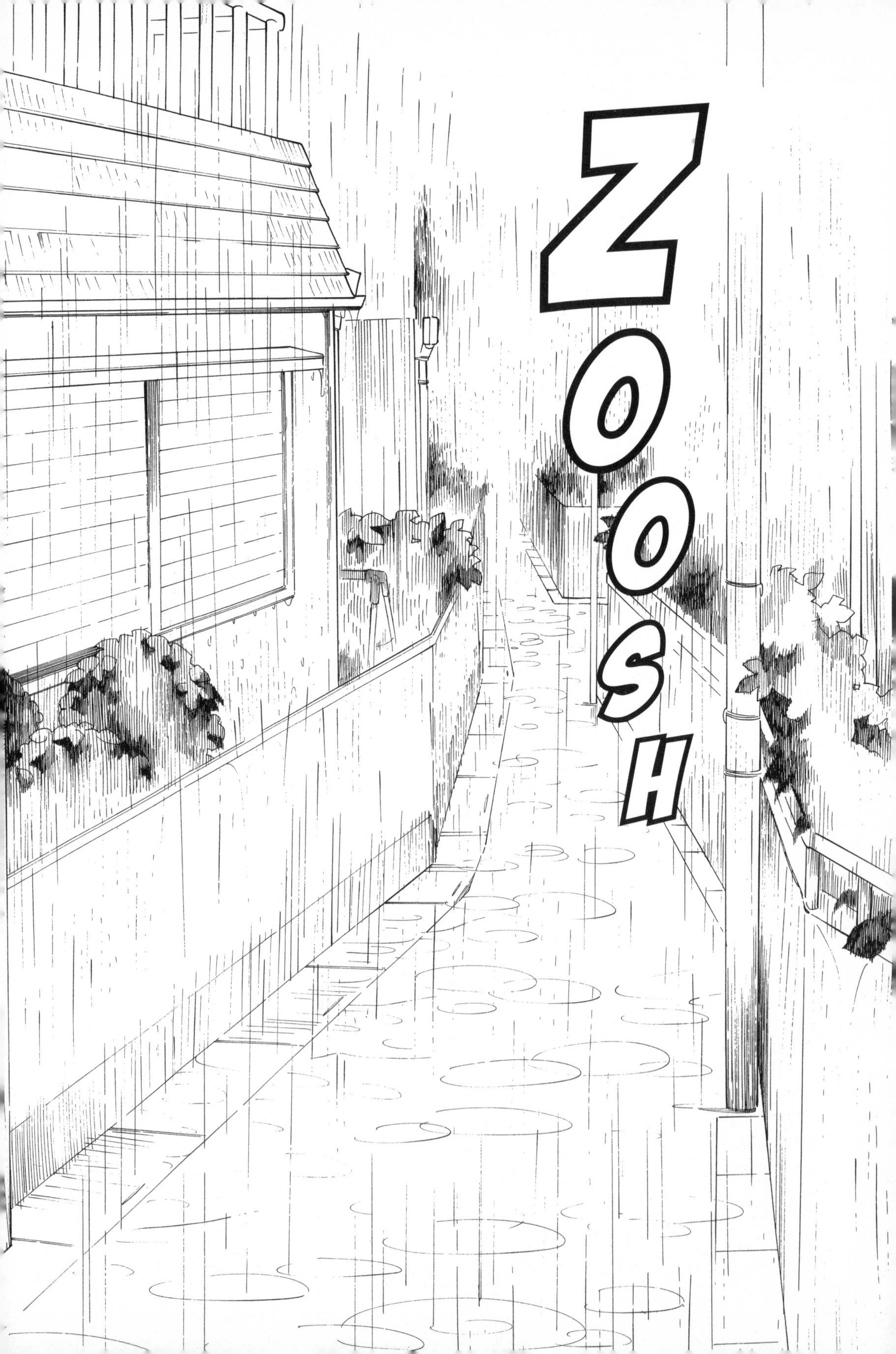
ZOOSH

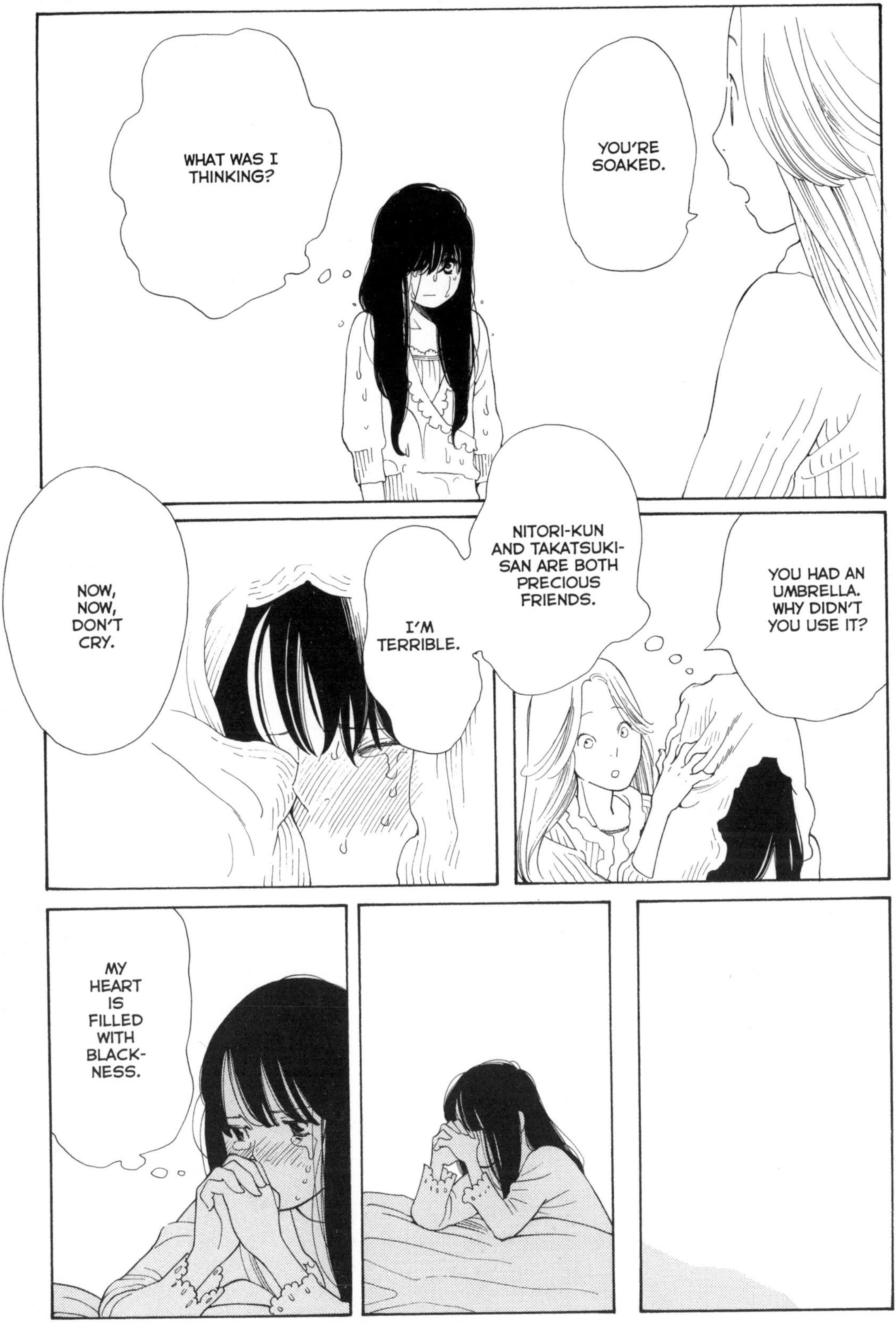
YOU'RE SOAKED.
WHAT WAS I THINKING?
YOU HAD AN UMBRELLA. WHY DIDN'T YOU USE IT?
NITORI-KUN AND TAKATSUKI-SAN ARE BOTH PRECIOUS FRIENDS.
I'M TERRIBLE.
NOW, NOW, DON'T CRY.
MY HEART IS FILLED WITH BLACKNESS.

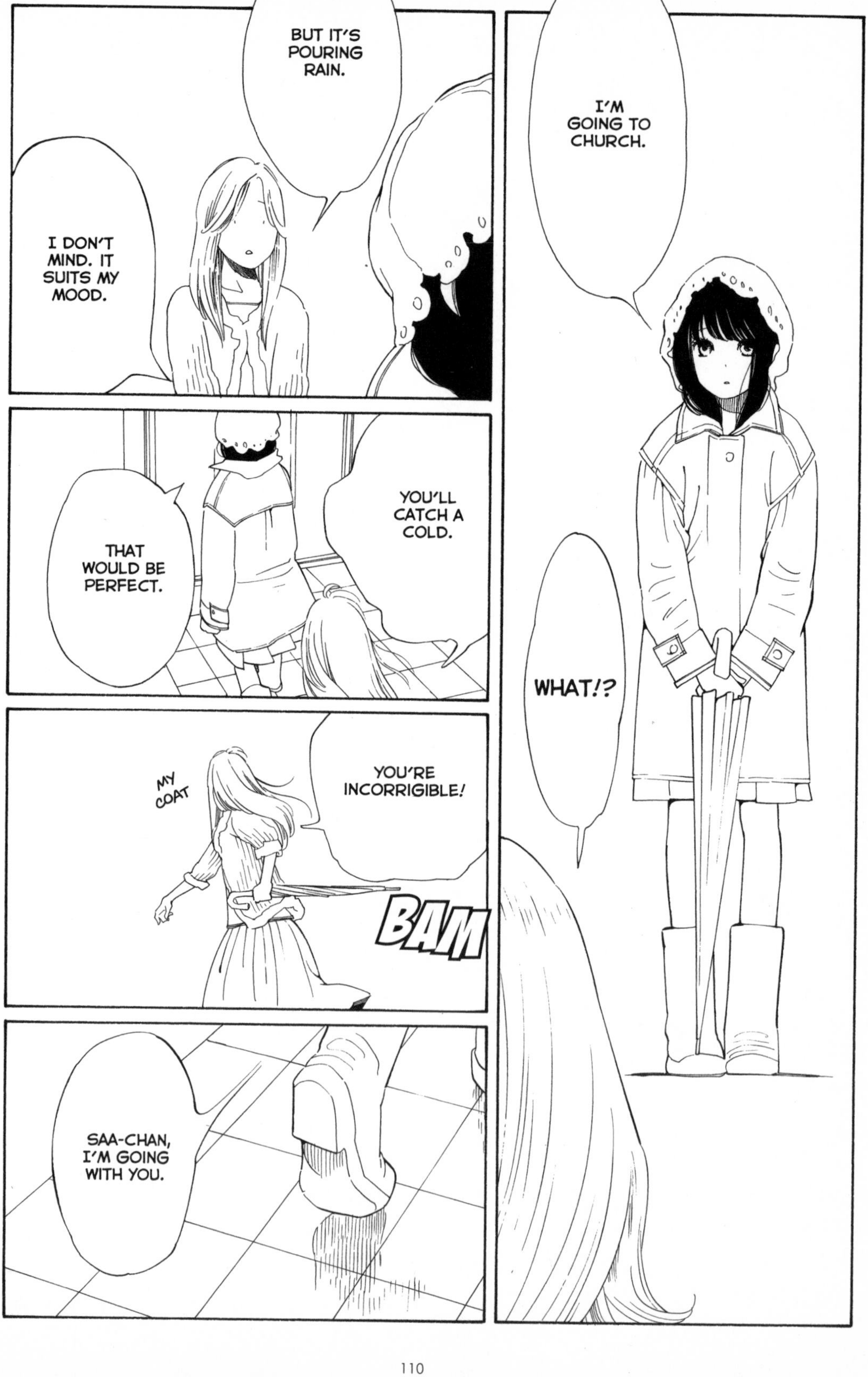
I'M GOING TO CHURCH.
WHAT!?
BUT IT'S POURING RAIN.
I DON'T MIND. IT SUITS MY MOOD.
YOU'LL CATCH A COLD.
THAT WOULD BE PERFECT.
YOU'RE INCORRIGIBLE!
MY COAT
BAM
SAA-CHAN, I'M GOING WITH YOU.

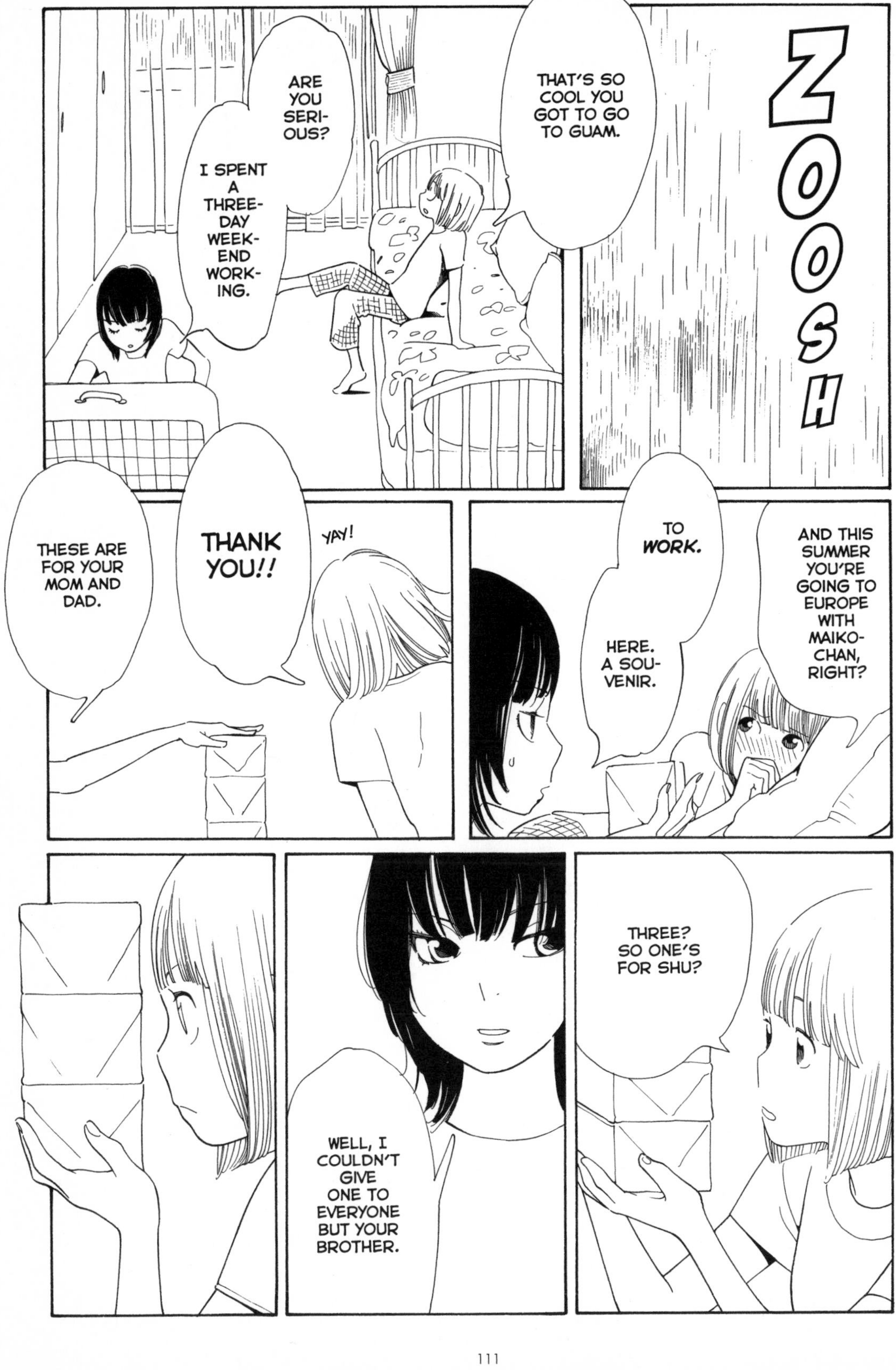
ZOOSH
THAT'S SO COOL YOU GOT TO GO TO GUAM.
ARE YOU SERI-OUS?
I SPENT A THREE-DAY WEEK-END WORKING.
AND THIS SUMMER YOU'RE GOING TO EUROPE WITH MAIKO-CHAN, RIGHT?
TO *WORK.*
HERE. A SOU-VENIR.
YAY!
THANK YOU!!
THESE ARE FOR YOUR MOM AND DAD.
THREE? SO ONE'S FOR SHU?
WELL, I COULDN'T GIVE ONE TO EVERYONE BUT YOUR BROTHER.

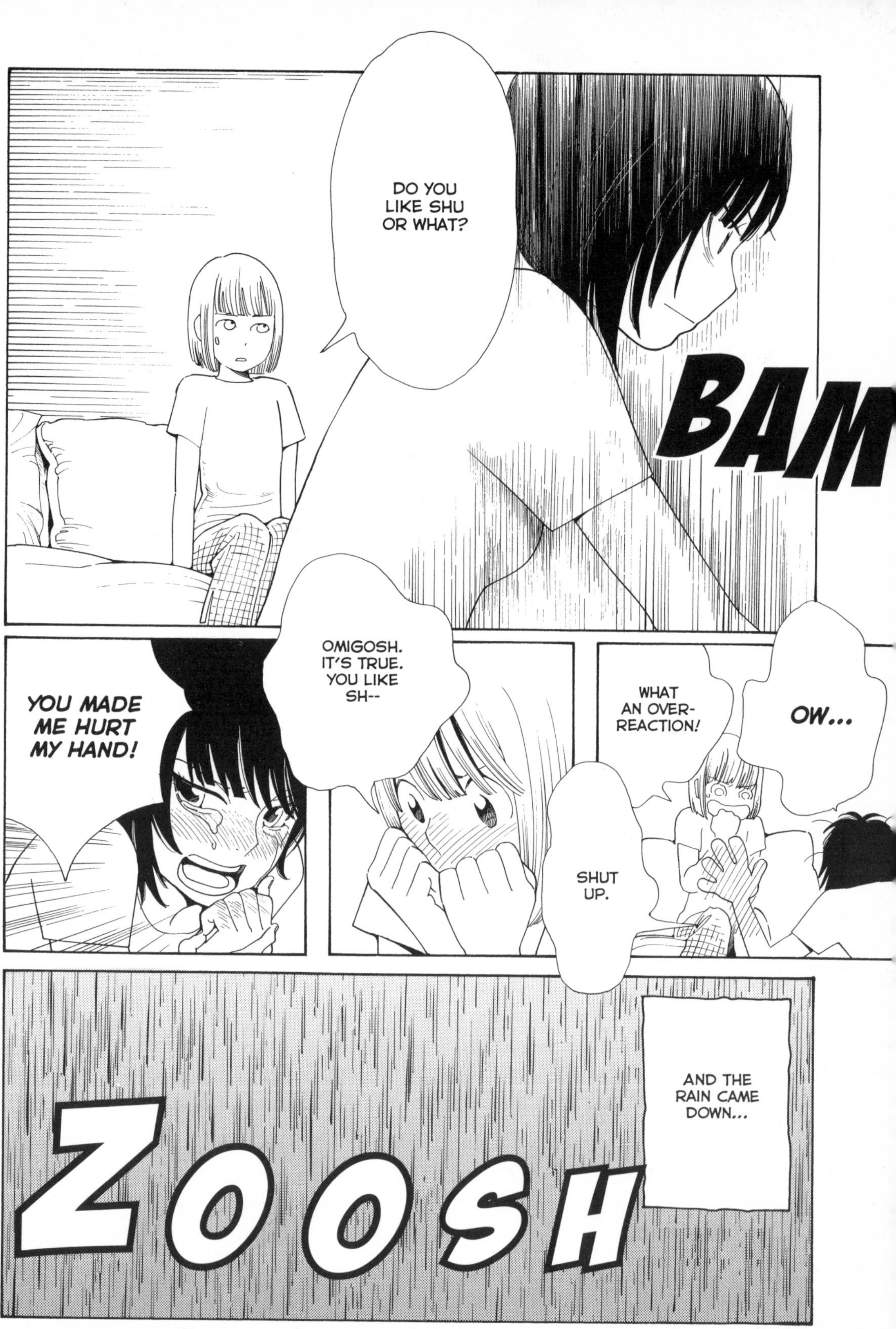
DO YOU LIKE SHU OR WHAT?
BAM
OW...
WHAT AN OVER-REACTION!
SHUT UP.
OMIGOSH. IT'S TRUE. YOU LIKE SH--
YOU MADE ME HURT MY HAND!
AND THE RAIN CAME DOWN...
ZOOSH

30

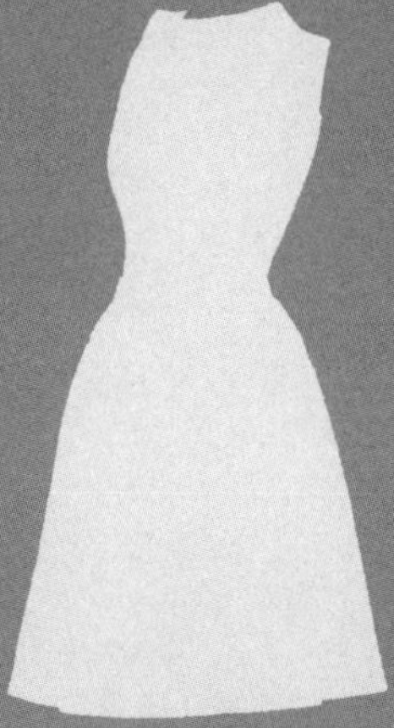

And It's Not Even Spring

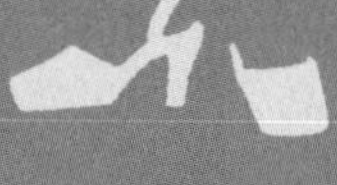

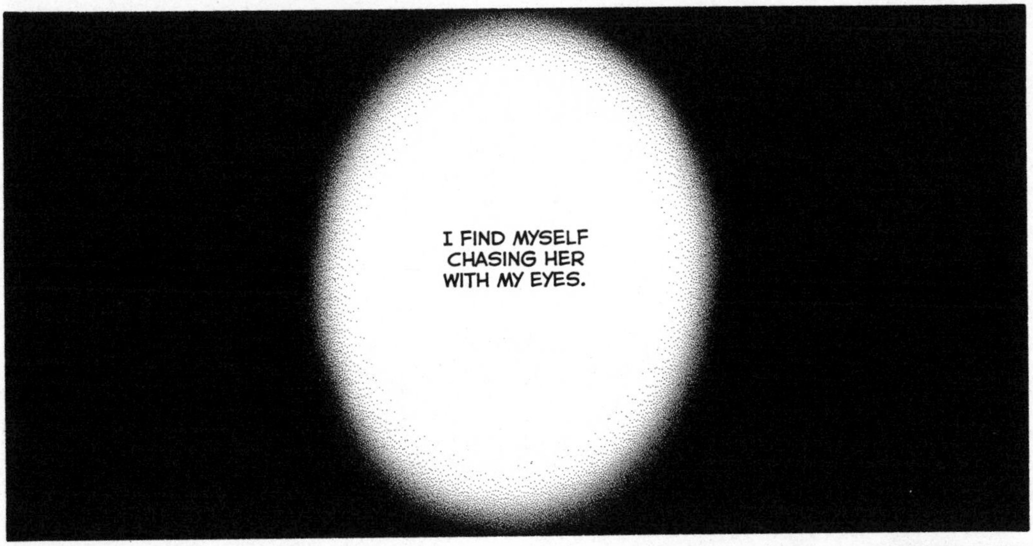
I FIND MYSELF
CHASING HER
WITH MY EYES.

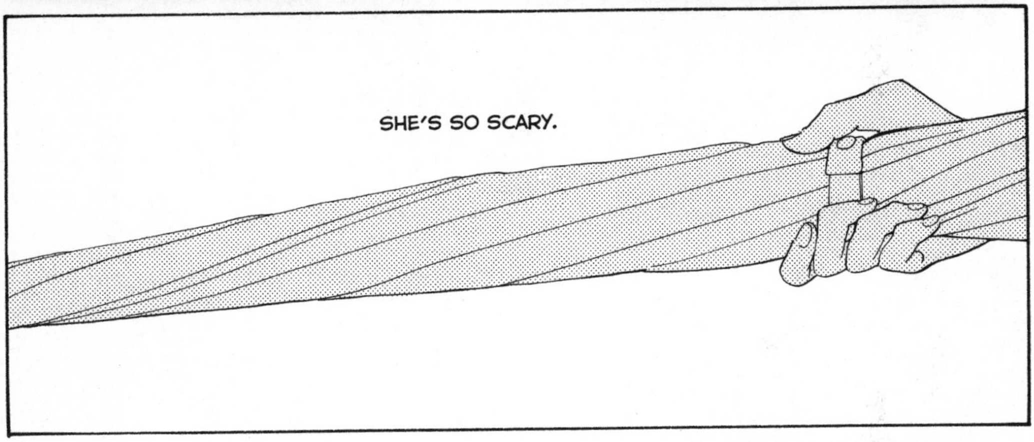
SHE'S SO SCARY.

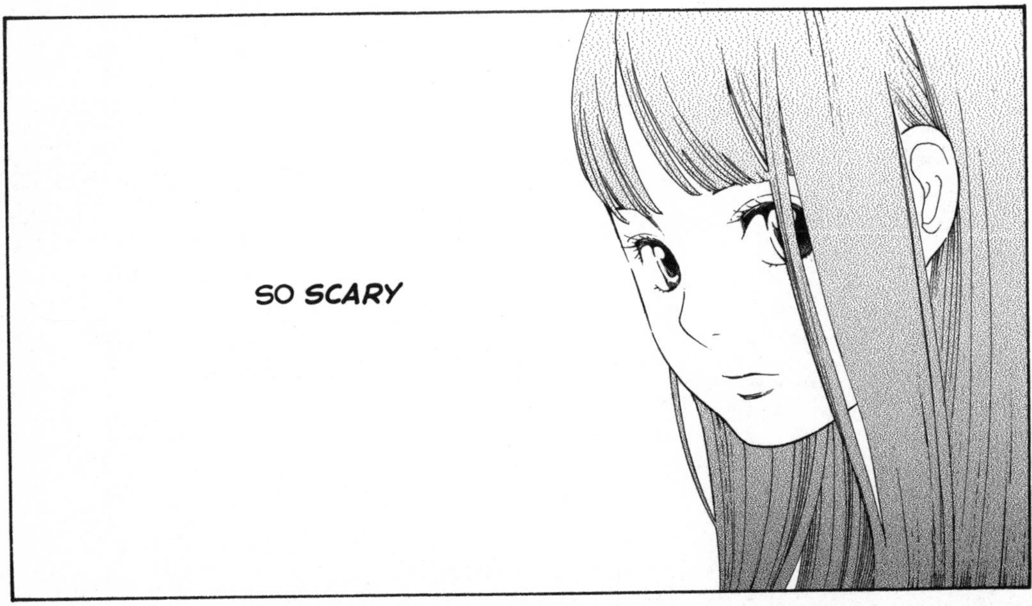
SO SCARY

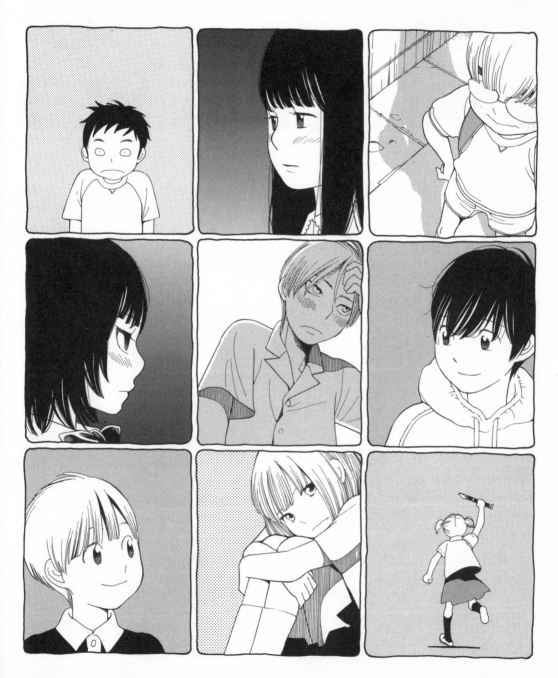

116

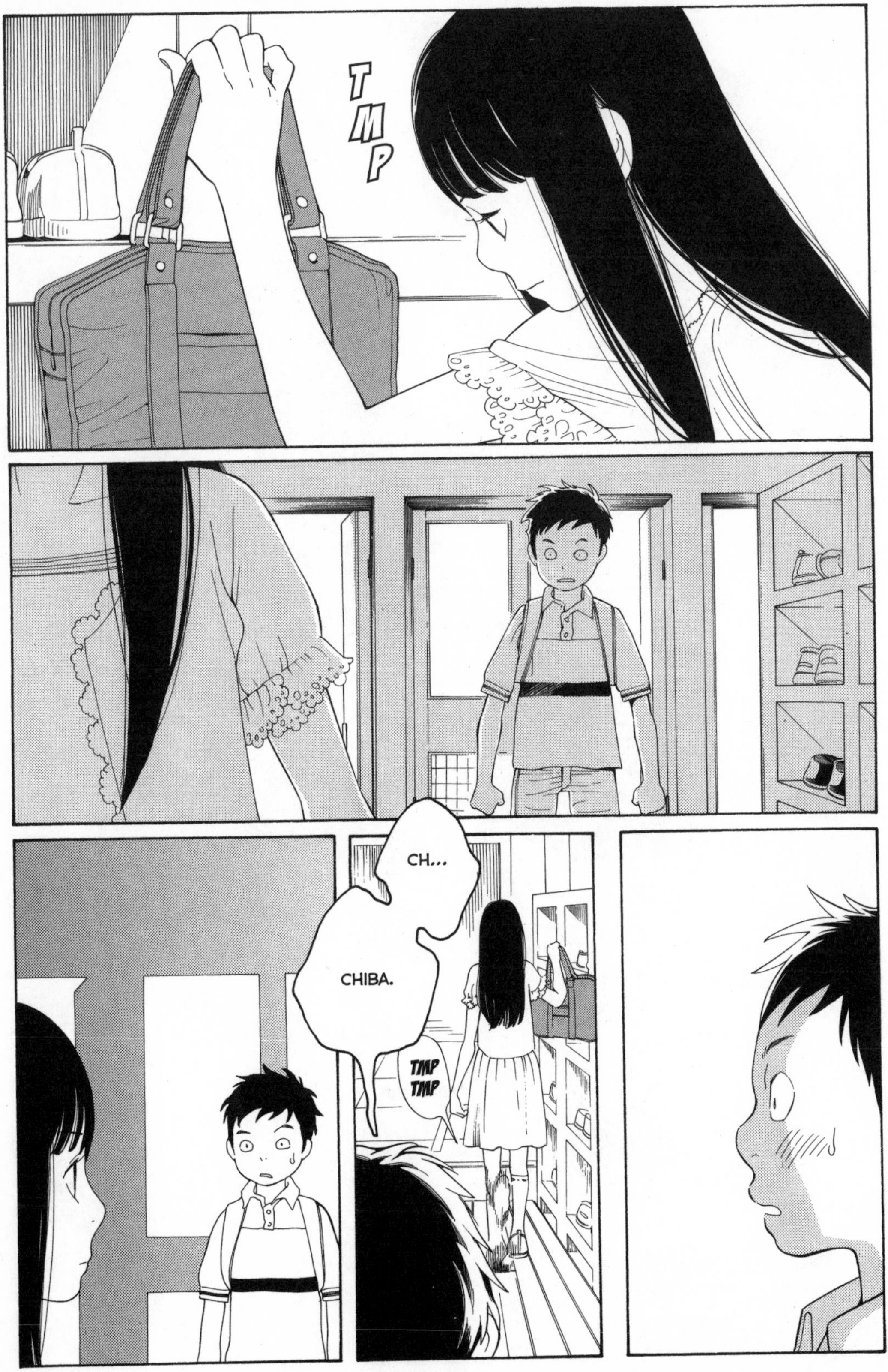
TMP
CH...
CHIBA.
TMP TMP

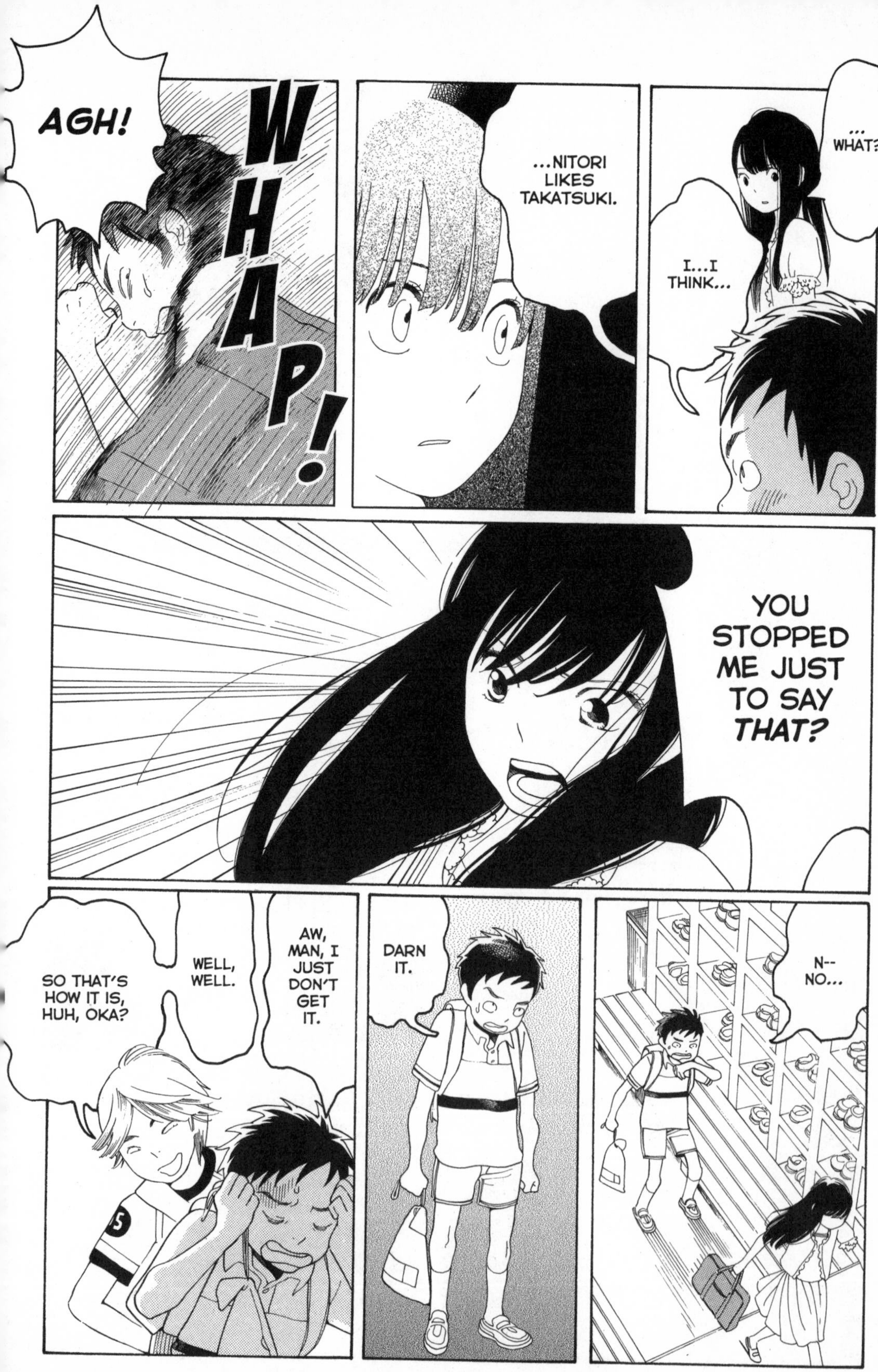
...WHAT?
I...I THINK...
...NITORI LIKES TAKATSUKI.
WHAP!
AGH!
YOU STOPPED ME JUST TO SAY *THAT?*
N-- NO...
DARN IT.
AW, MAN, I JUST DON'T GET IT.
WELL, WELL.
SO THAT'S HOW IT IS, HUH, OKA?

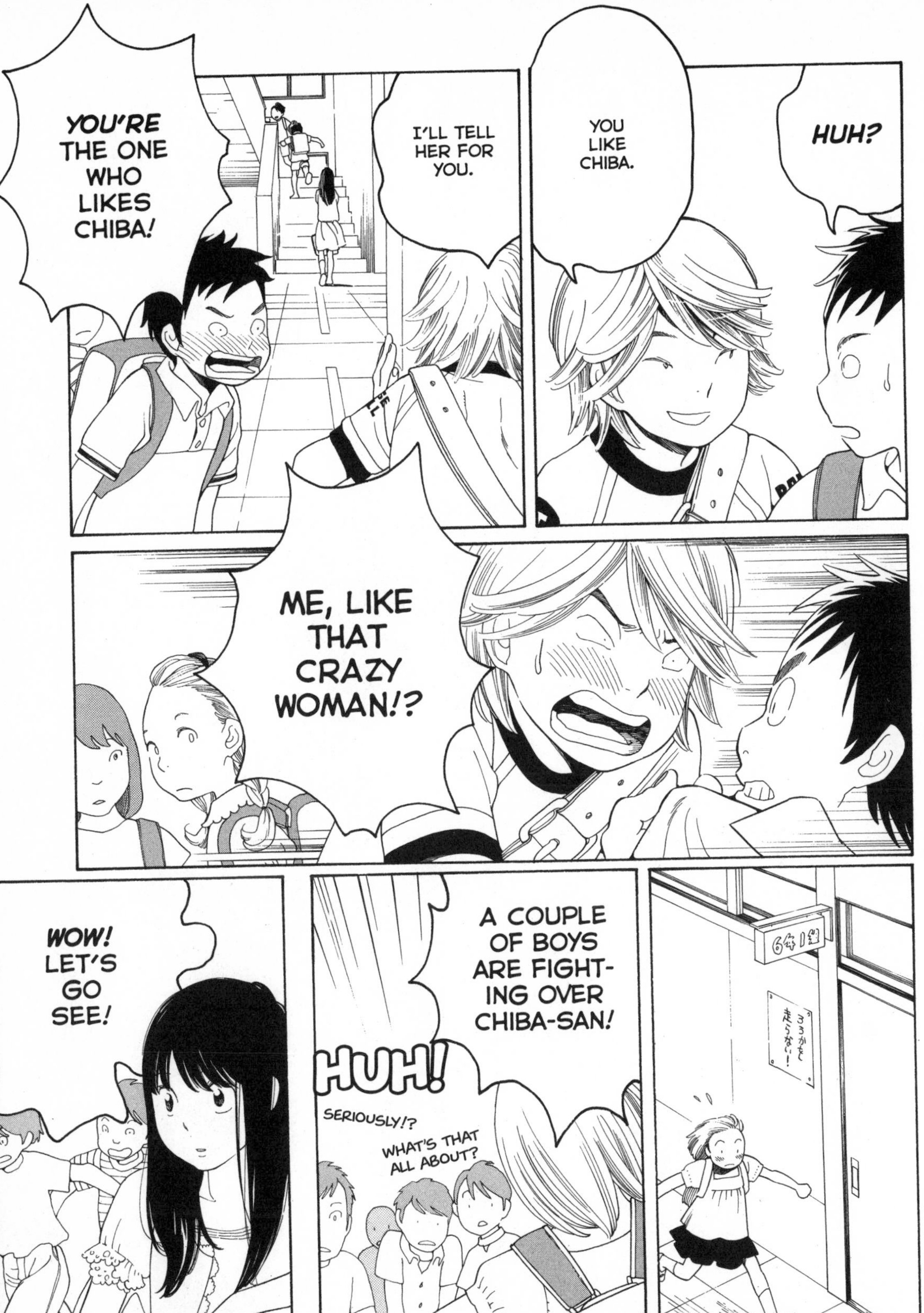
HUH?
YOU LIKE CHIBA.
I'LL TELL HER FOR YOU.
YOU'RE THE ONE WHO LIKES CHIBA!
ME, LIKE THAT CRAZY WOMAN!?
6年1組
ろうかを走らない!
A COUPLE OF BOYS ARE FIGHTING OVER CHIBA-SAN!
HUH!
SERIOUSLY!?
WHAT'S THAT ALL ABOUT?
WOW! LET'S GO SEE!

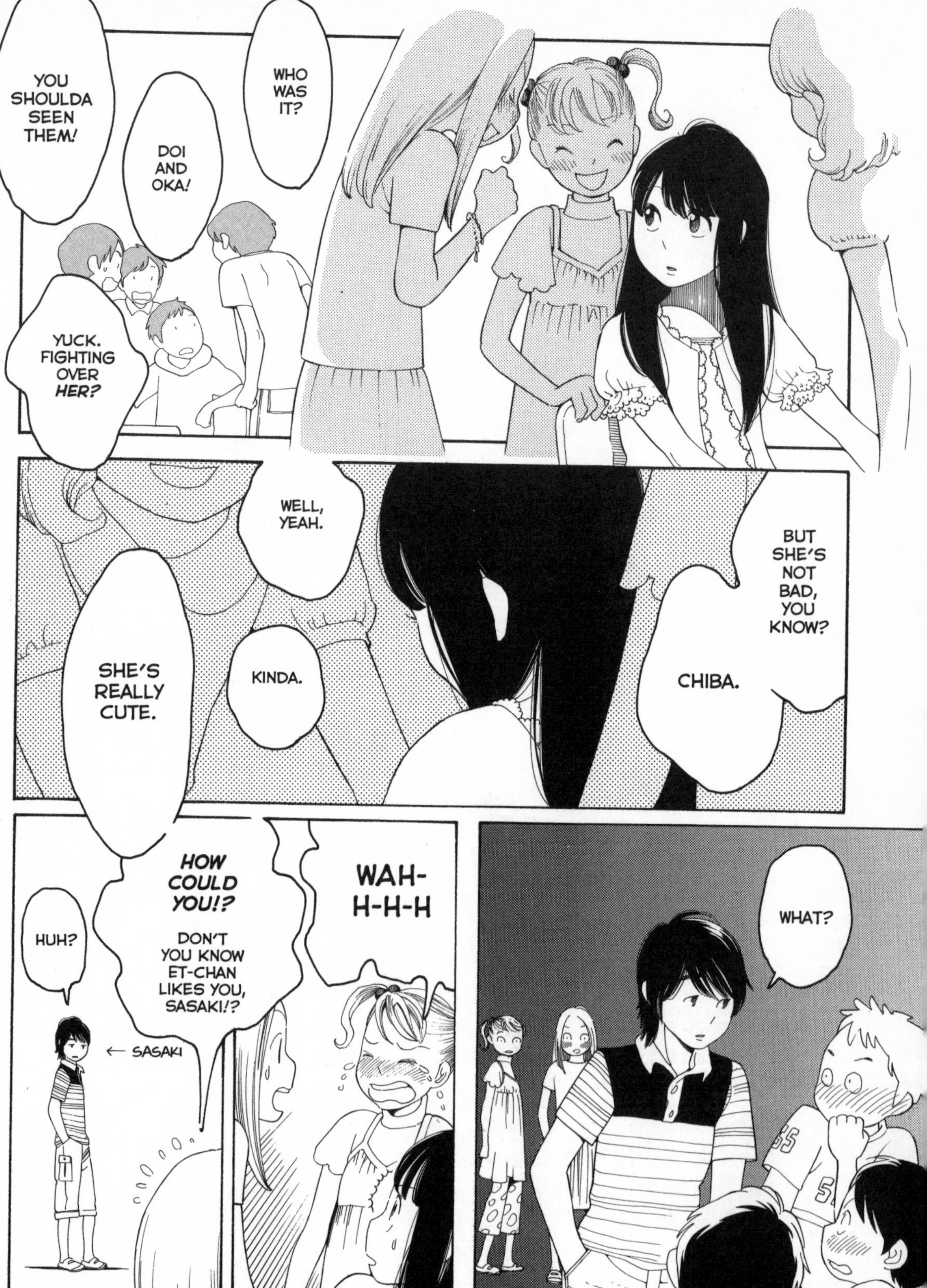

WHO WAS IT?
DOI AND OKA!
YOU SHOULDA SEEN THEM!
YUCK. FIGHTING OVER *HER?*
BUT SHE'S NOT BAD, YOU KNOW?
CHIBA.
WELL, YEAH.
KINDA.
SHE'S REALLY CUTE.
WHAT?
WAH-H-H-H
HOW COULD YOU!?
DON'T YOU KNOW ET-CHAN LIKES YOU, SASAKI!?
HUH?
← SASAKI

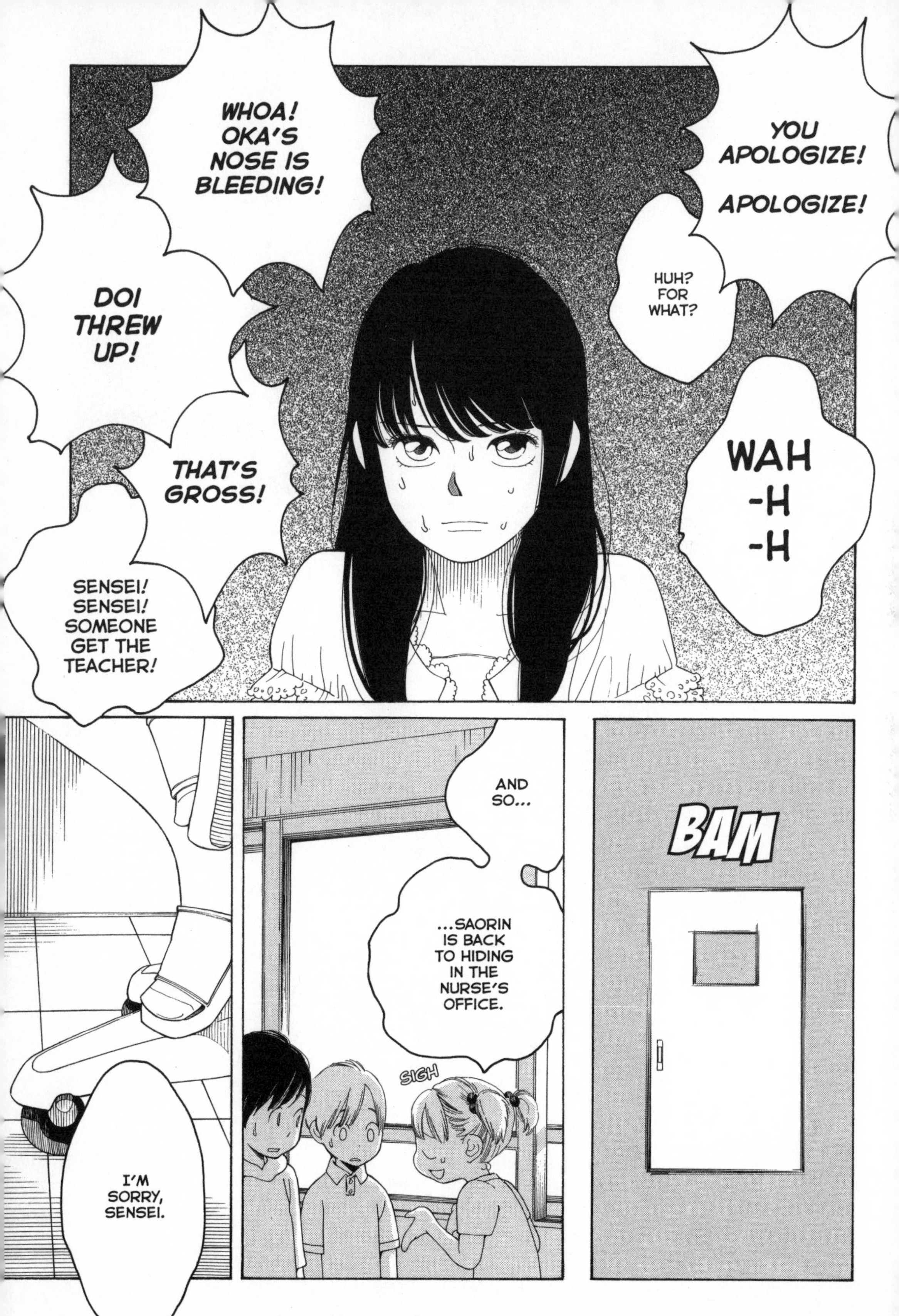
YOU APOLOGIZE!
APOLOGIZE!
WHOA! OKA'S NOSE IS BLEEDING!
HUH? FOR WHAT?
DOI THREW UP!
WAH -H -H
THAT'S GROSS!
SENSEI! SENSEI! SOMEONE GET THE TEACHER!
BAM
AND SO...
...SAORIN IS BACK TO HIDING IN THE NURSE'S OFFICE.
SIGH
I'M SORRY, SENSEI.

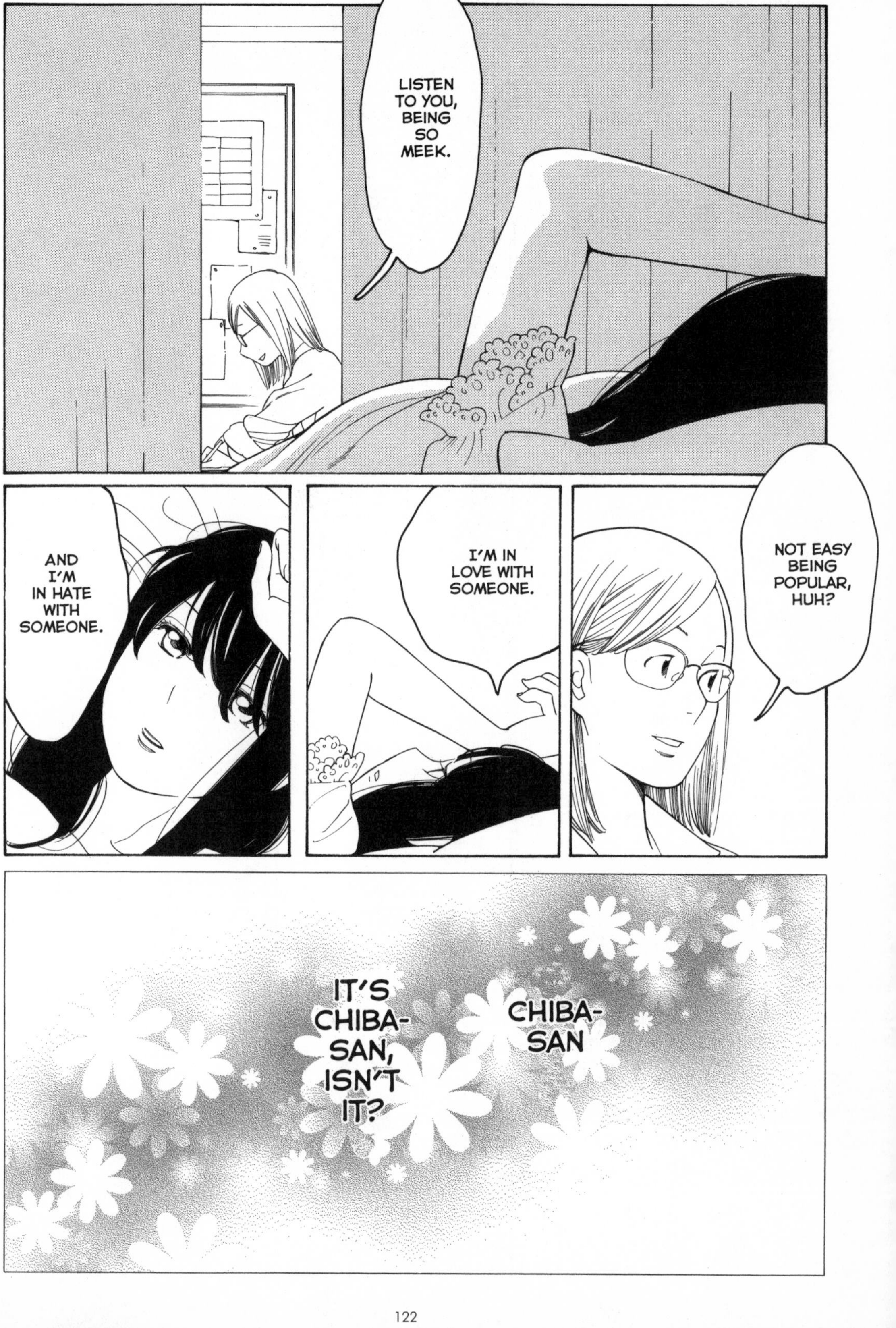
LISTEN TO YOU, BEING SO MEEK.
NOT EASY BEING POPULAR, HUH?
I'M IN LOVE WITH SOMEONE.
AND I'M IN HATE WITH SOMEONE.
CHIBA-SAN
IT'S CHIBA-SAN, ISN'T IT?

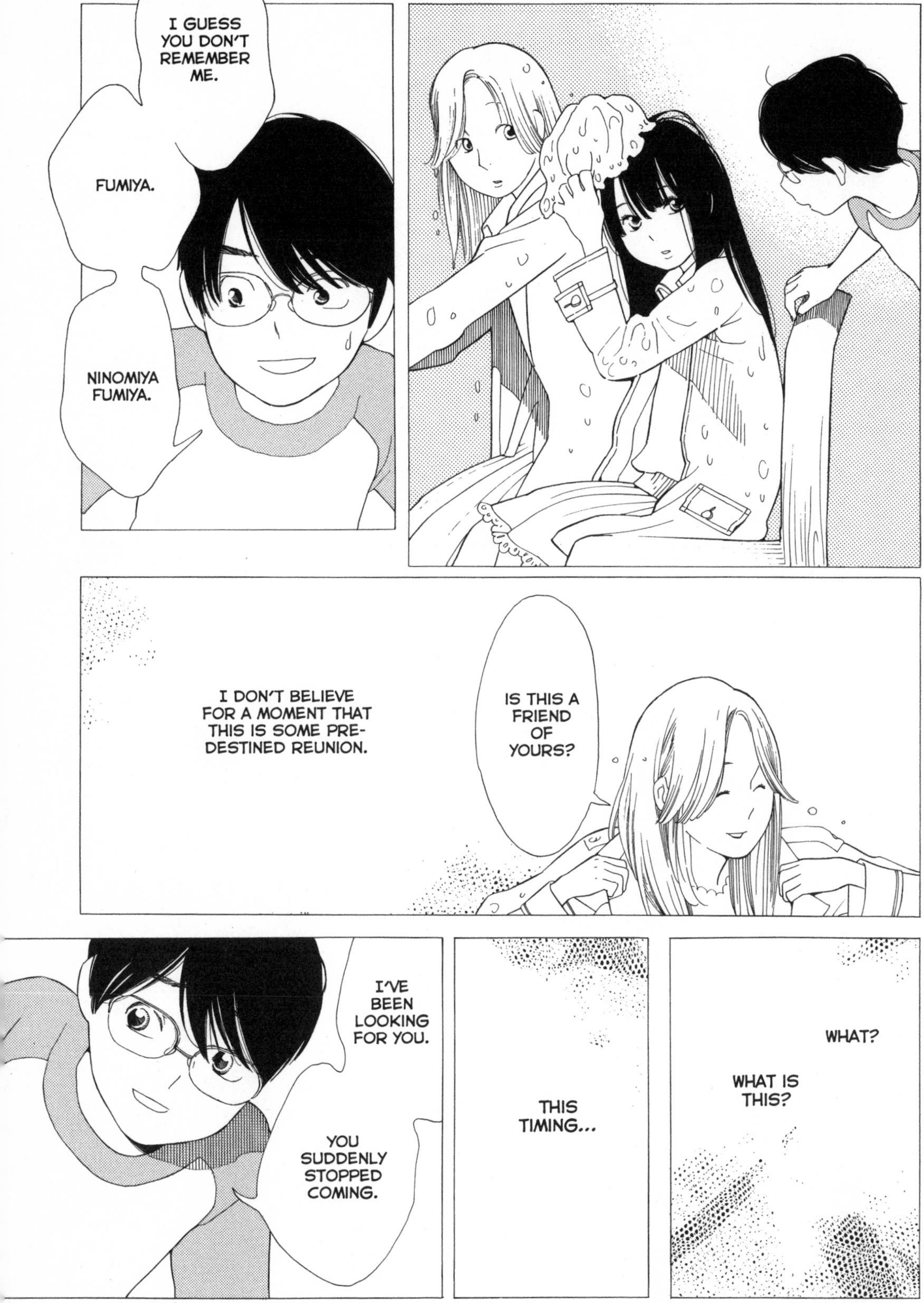
I GUESS YOU DON'T REMEMBER ME.
FUMIYA.
NINOMIYA FUMIYA.
IS THIS A FRIEND OF YOURS?
I DON'T BELIEVE FOR A MOMENT THAT THIS IS SOME PRE-DESTINED REUNION.
WHAT?
WHAT IS THIS?
THIS TIMING...
I'VE BEEN LOOKING FOR YOU.
YOU SUDDENLY STOPPED COMING.

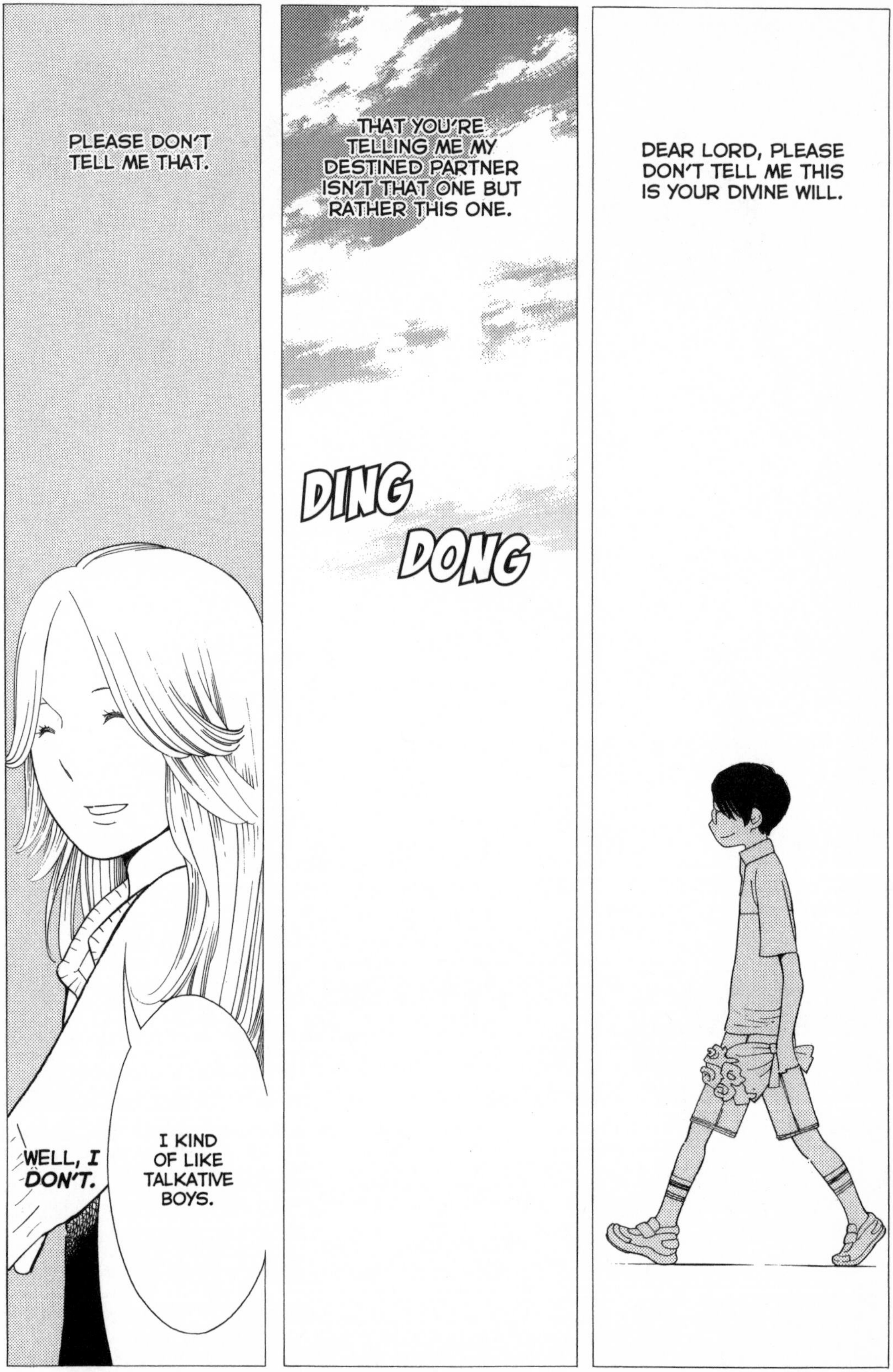
DEAR LORD, PLEASE DON'T TELL ME THIS IS YOUR DIVINE WILL.
THAT YOU'RE TELLING ME MY DESTINED PARTNER ISN'T THAT ONE BUT RATHER THIS ONE.
DING
DONG
PLEASE DON'T TELL ME THAT.
I KIND OF LIKE TALKATIVE BOYS.
WELL, I DON'T.

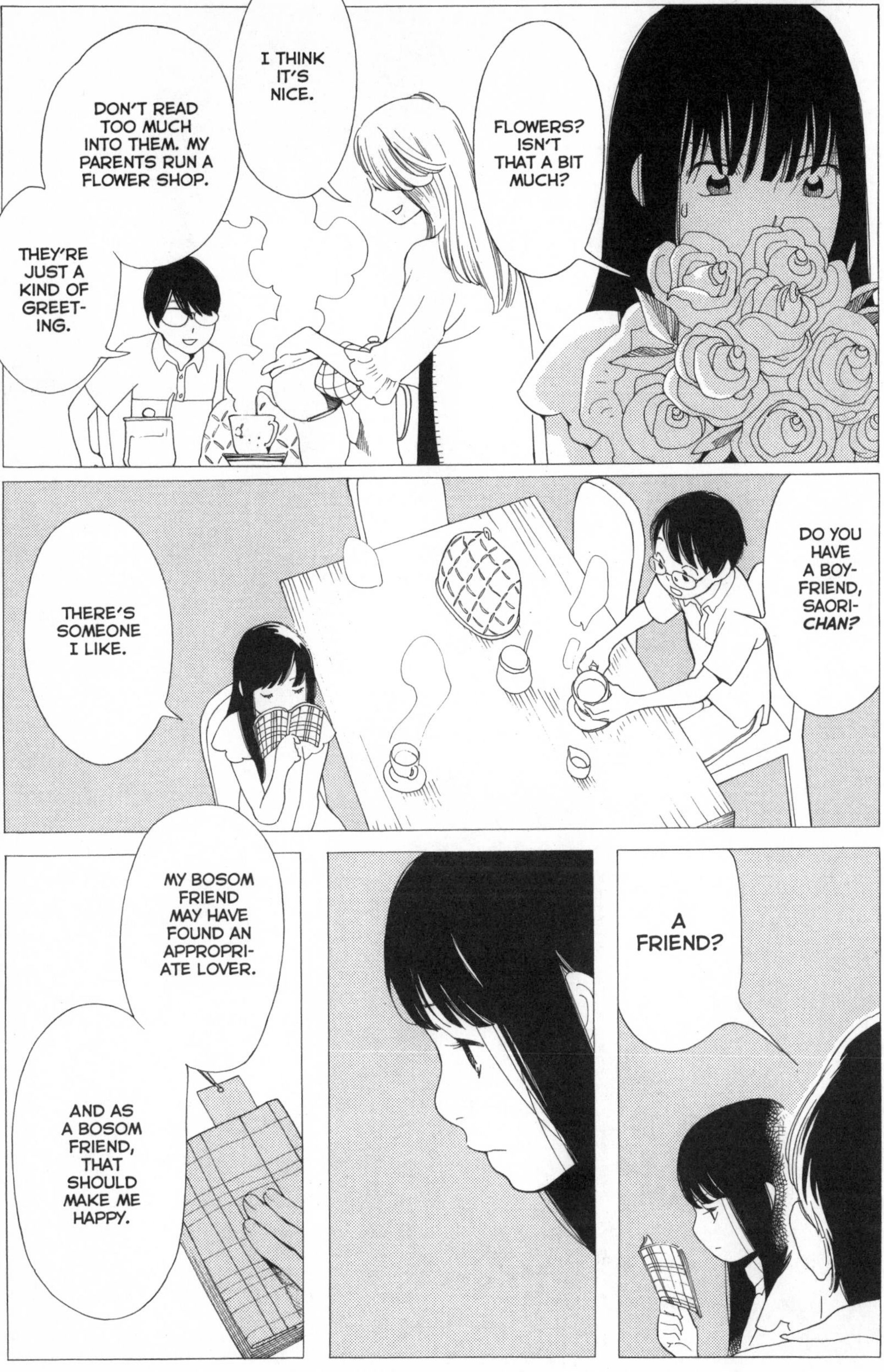
FLOWERS? ISN'T THAT A BIT MUCH?
I THINK IT'S NICE.
DON'T READ TOO MUCH INTO THEM. MY PARENTS RUN A FLOWER SHOP.
THEY'RE JUST A KIND OF GREETING.
DO YOU HAVE A BOYFRIEND, SAORI-*CHAN?*
THERE'S SOMEONE I LIKE.
A FRIEND?
MY BOSOM FRIEND MAY HAVE FOUND AN APPROPRIATE LOVER.
AND AS A BOSOM FRIEND, THAT SHOULD MAKE ME HAPPY.

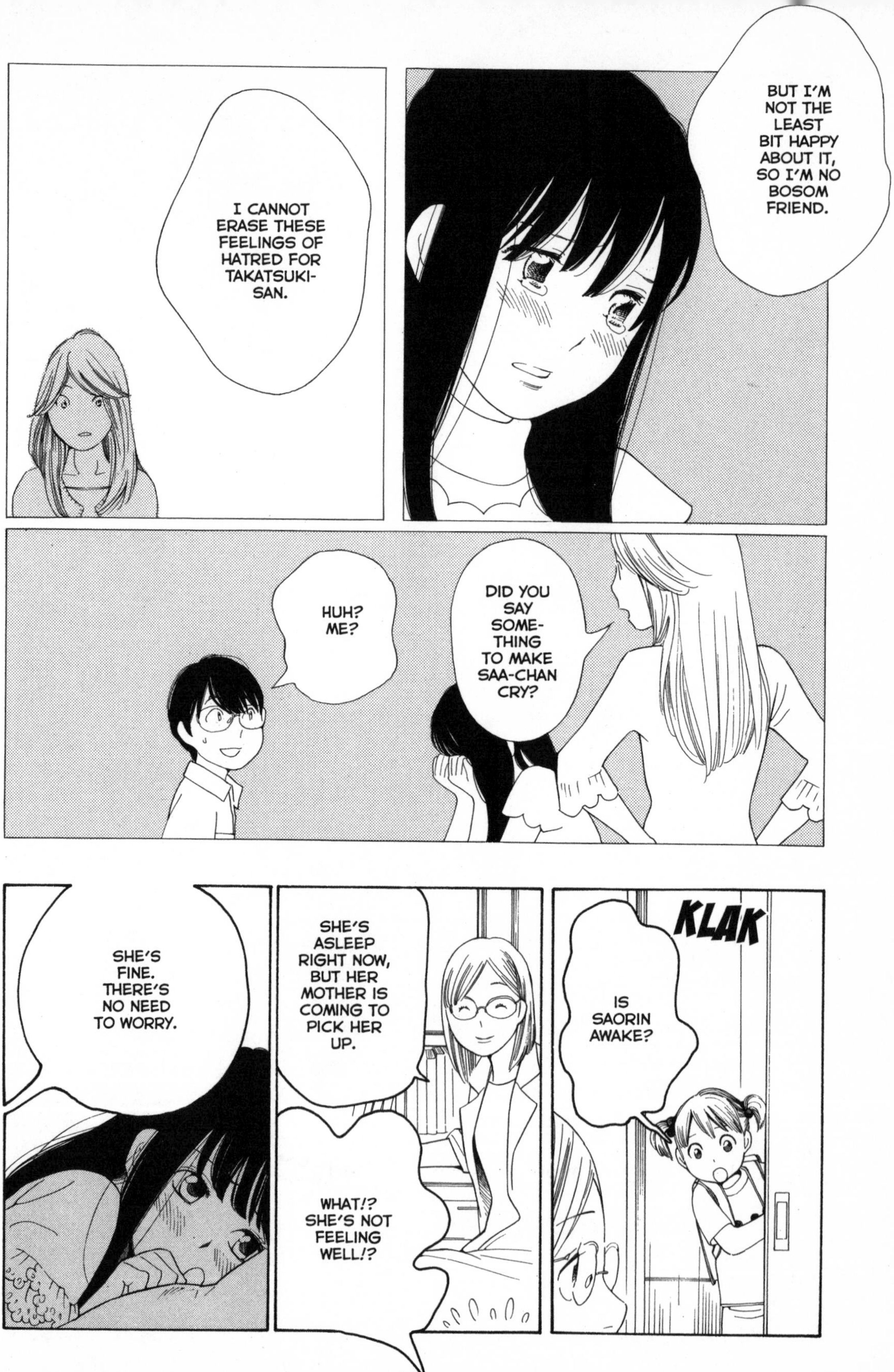
BUT I'M NOT THE LEAST BIT HAPPY ABOUT IT, SO I'M NO BOSOM FRIEND.
I CANNOT ERASE THESE FEELINGS OF HATRED FOR TAKATSUKI-SAN.
DID YOU SAY SOME-THING TO MAKE SAA-CHAN CRY?
HUH? ME?
KLAK
IS SAORIN AWAKE?
SHE'S ASLEEP RIGHT NOW, BUT HER MOTHER IS COMING TO PICK HER UP.
WHAT!? SHE'S NOT FEELING WELL!?
SHE'S FINE. THERE'S NO NEED TO WORRY.

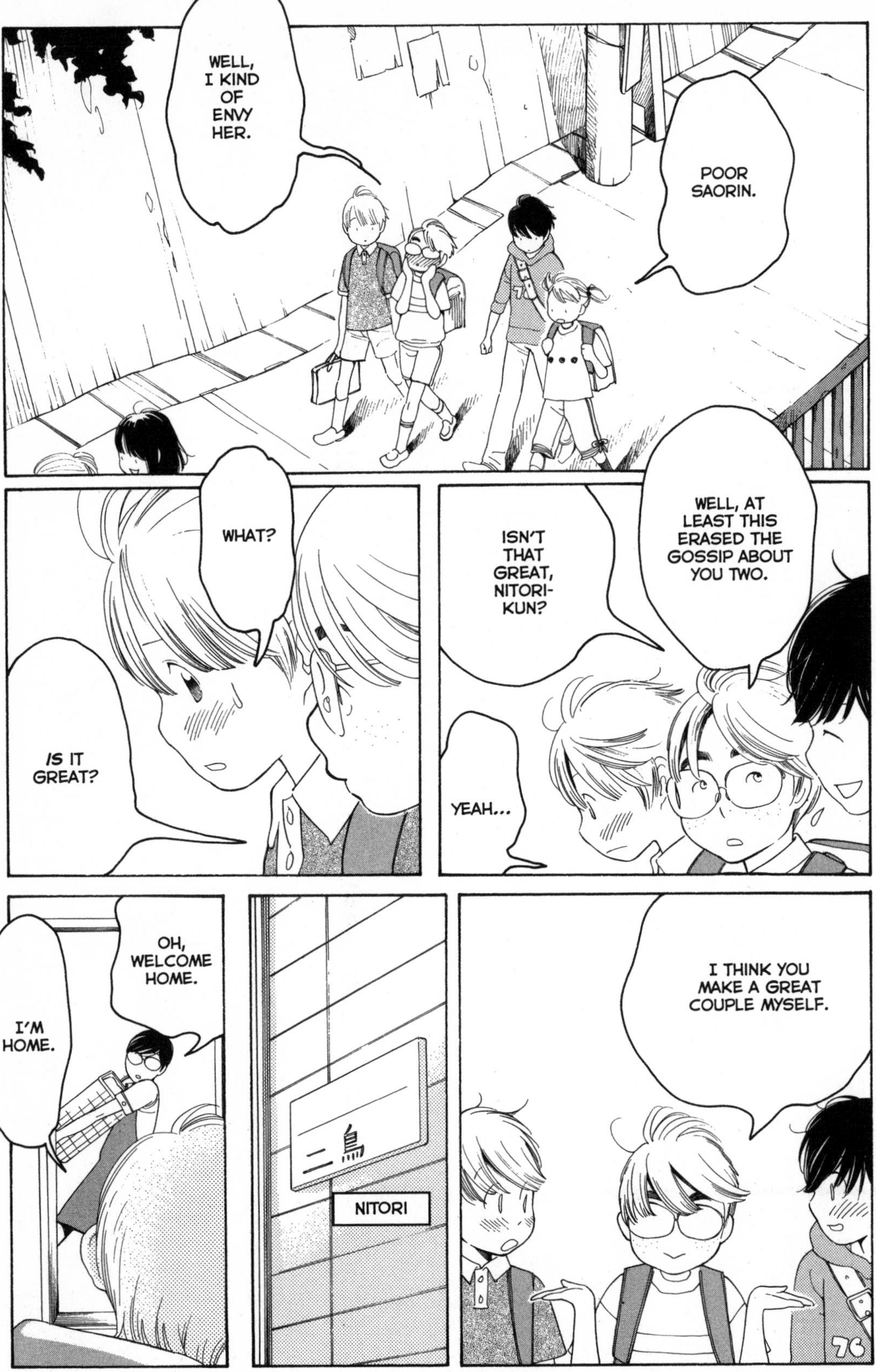
POOR SAORIN.
WELL, I KIND OF ENVY HER.
WELL, AT LEAST THIS ERASED THE GOSSIP ABOUT YOU TWO.
ISN'T THAT GREAT, NITORI-KUN?
YEAH...
WHAT?
IS IT GREAT?
I THINK YOU MAKE A GREAT COUPLE MYSELF.
二鳥
NITORI
OH, WELCOME HOME.
I'M HOME.

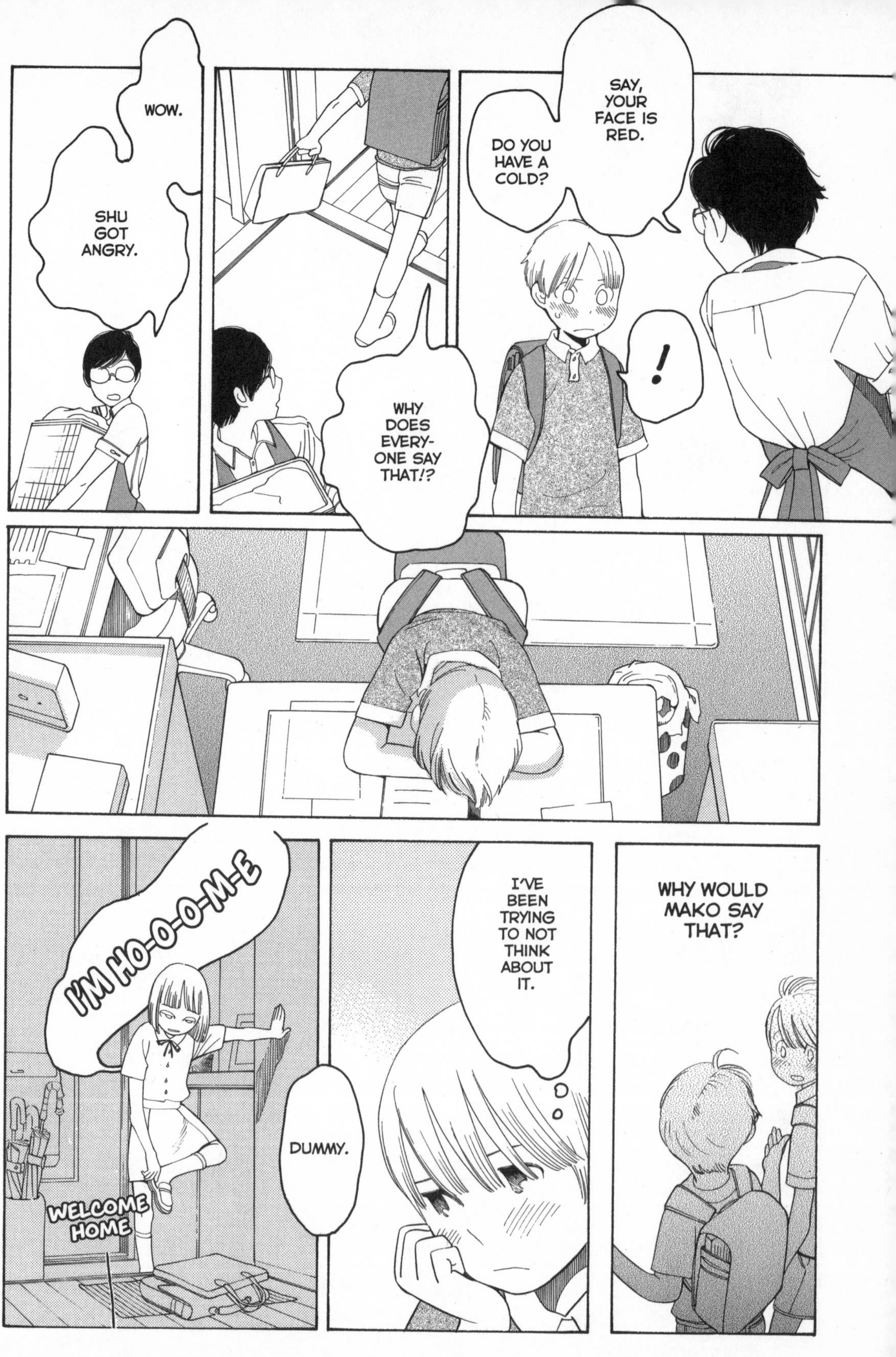
SAY, YOUR FACE IS RED.
DO YOU HAVE A COLD?
!
WHY DOES EVERY-ONE SAY THAT!?
WOW.
SHU GOT ANGRY.
WHY WOULD MAKO SAY THAT?
I'VE BEEN TRYING TO NOT THINK ABOUT IT.
DUMMY.
I'M HO-O-O-M-E
WELCOME HOME

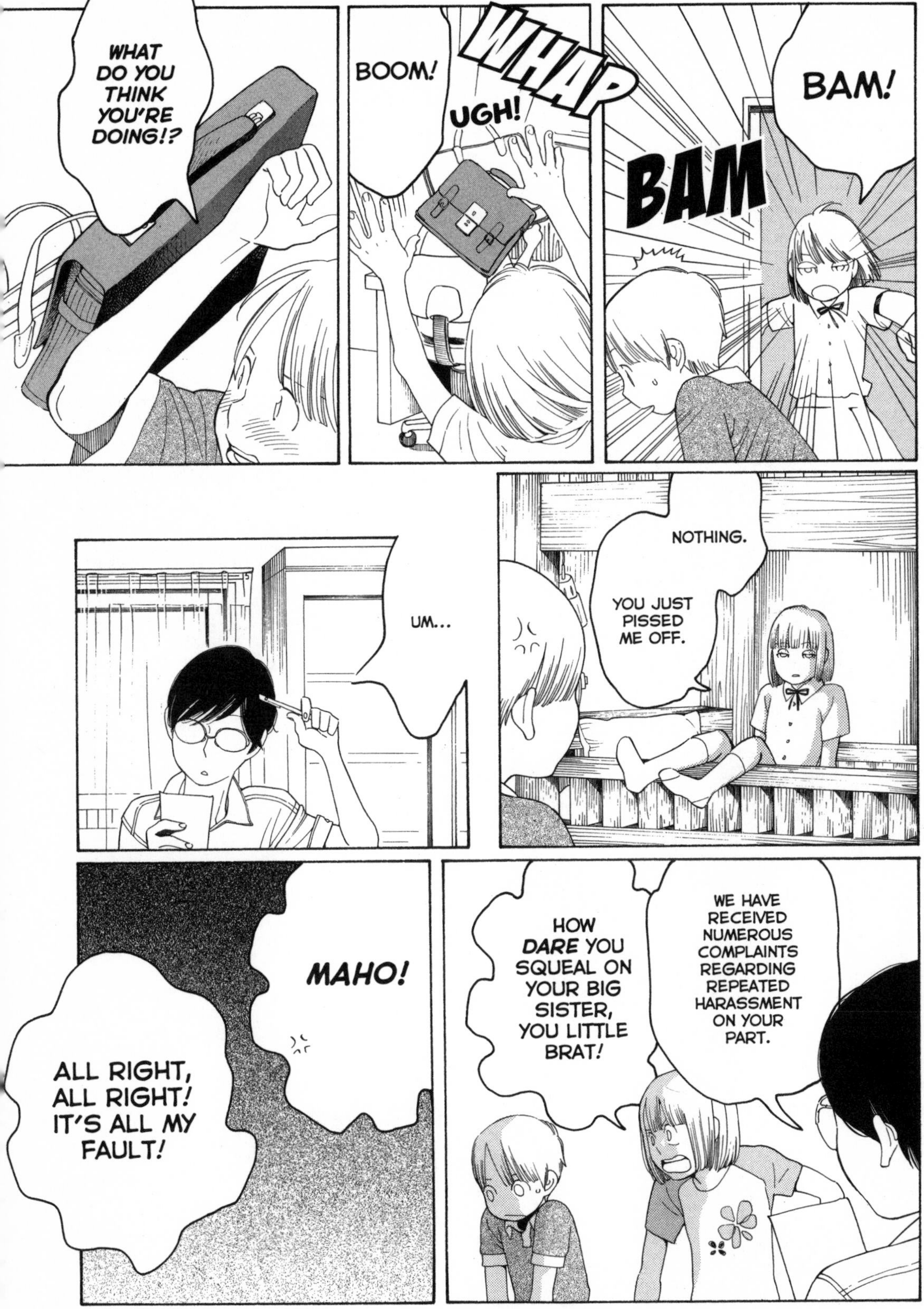
BAM!
BAM
WHAP
BOOM!
UGH!
WHAT DO YOU THINK YOU'RE DOING!?
NOTHING.
YOU JUST PISSED ME OFF.
UM...
WE HAVE RECEIVED NUMEROUS COMPLAINTS REGARDING REPEATED HARASSMENT ON YOUR PART.
HOW *DARE* YOU SQUEAL ON YOUR BIG SISTER, YOU LITTLE BRAT!
MAHO!
ALL RIGHT, ALL RIGHT! IT'S ALL MY FAULT!

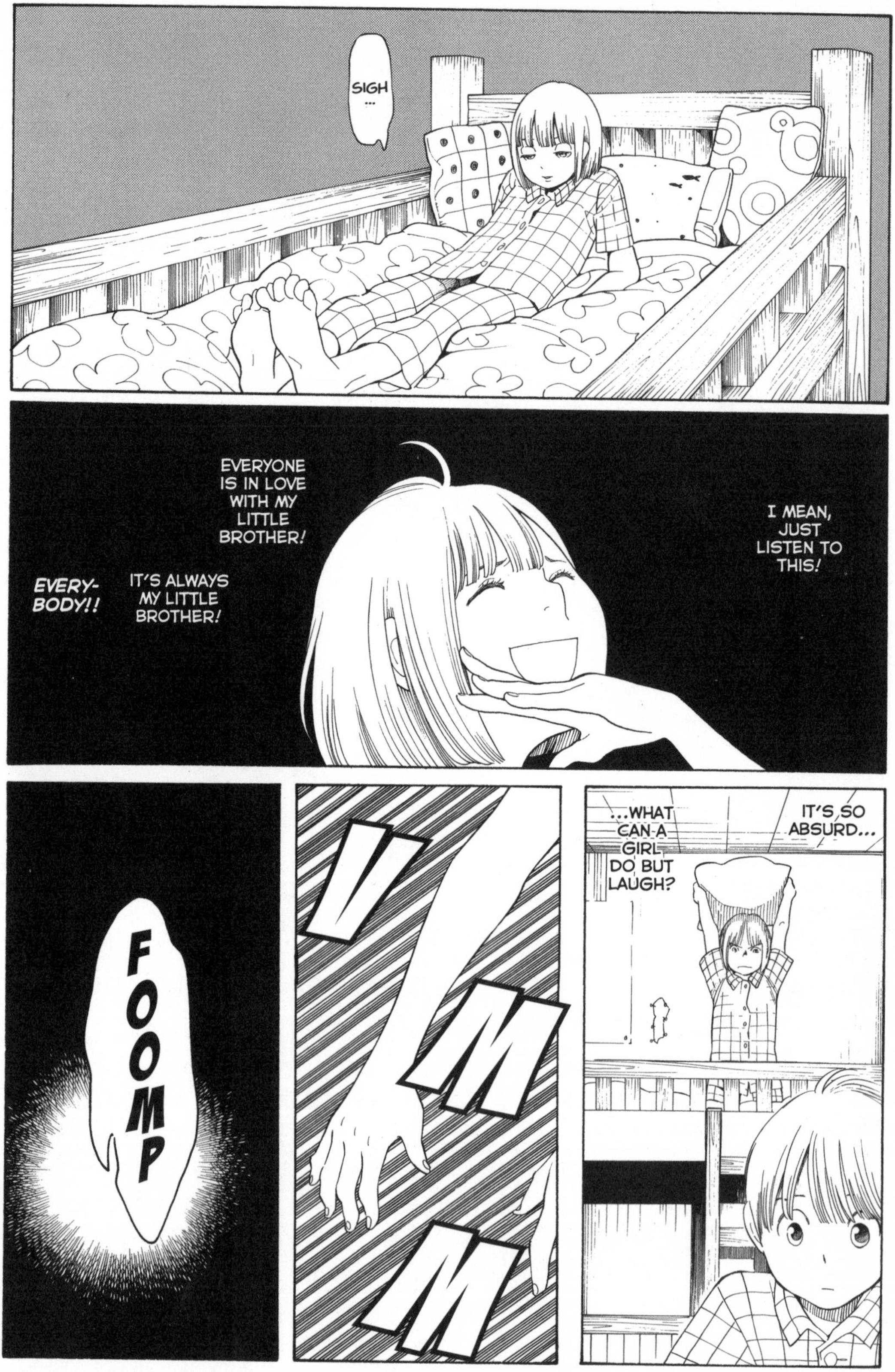
SIGH ...
I MEAN, JUST LISTEN TO THIS!
EVERYONE IS IN LOVE WITH MY LITTLE BROTHER!
IT'S ALWAYS MY LITTLE BROTHER!
EVERY-BODY!!
IT'S SO ABSURD...
...WHAT CAN A GIRL DO BUT LAUGH?
VMM
FOOMP

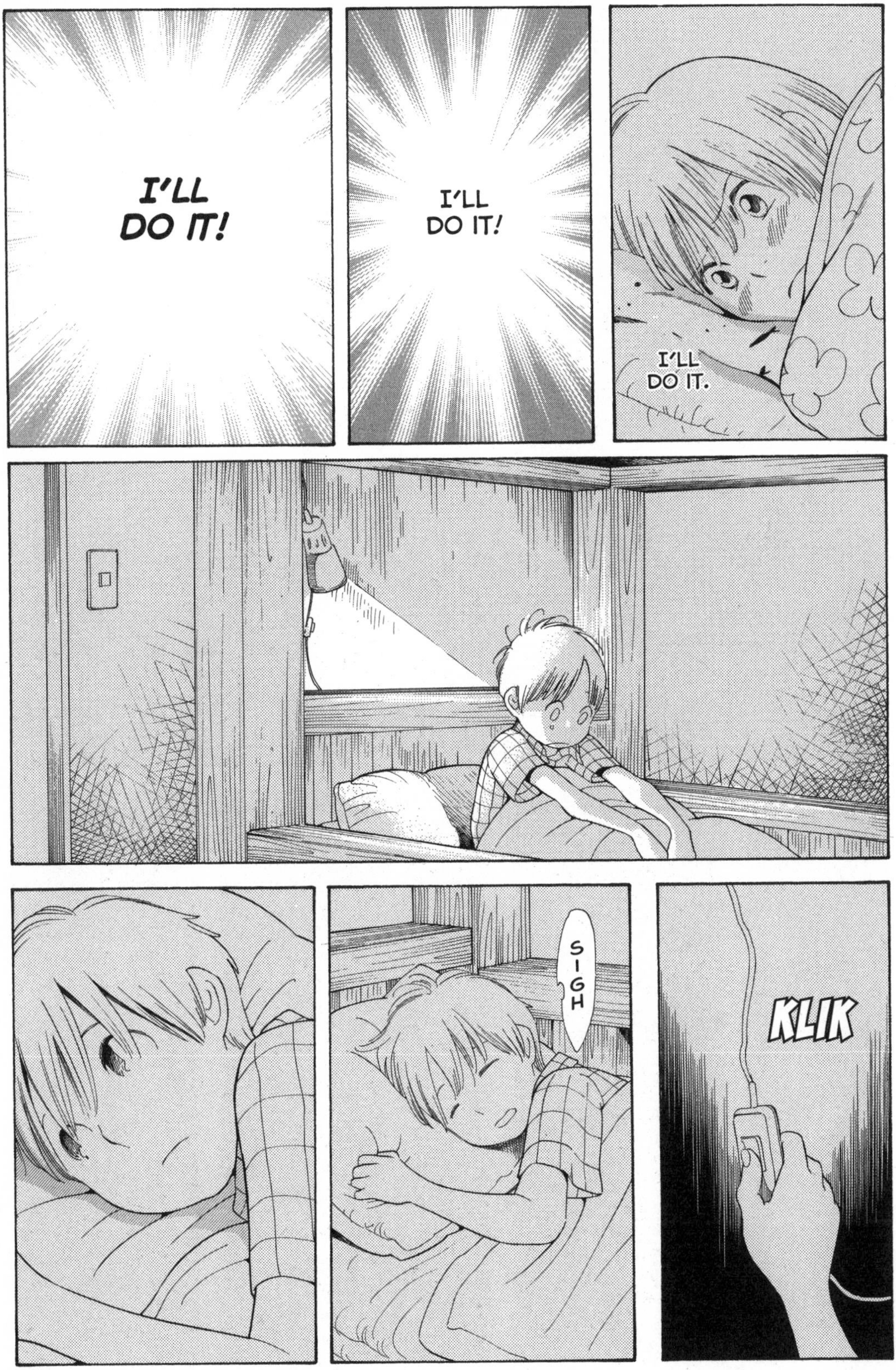
I'LL DO IT.
I'LL DO IT!
I'LL DO IT!
KLIK
SIGH

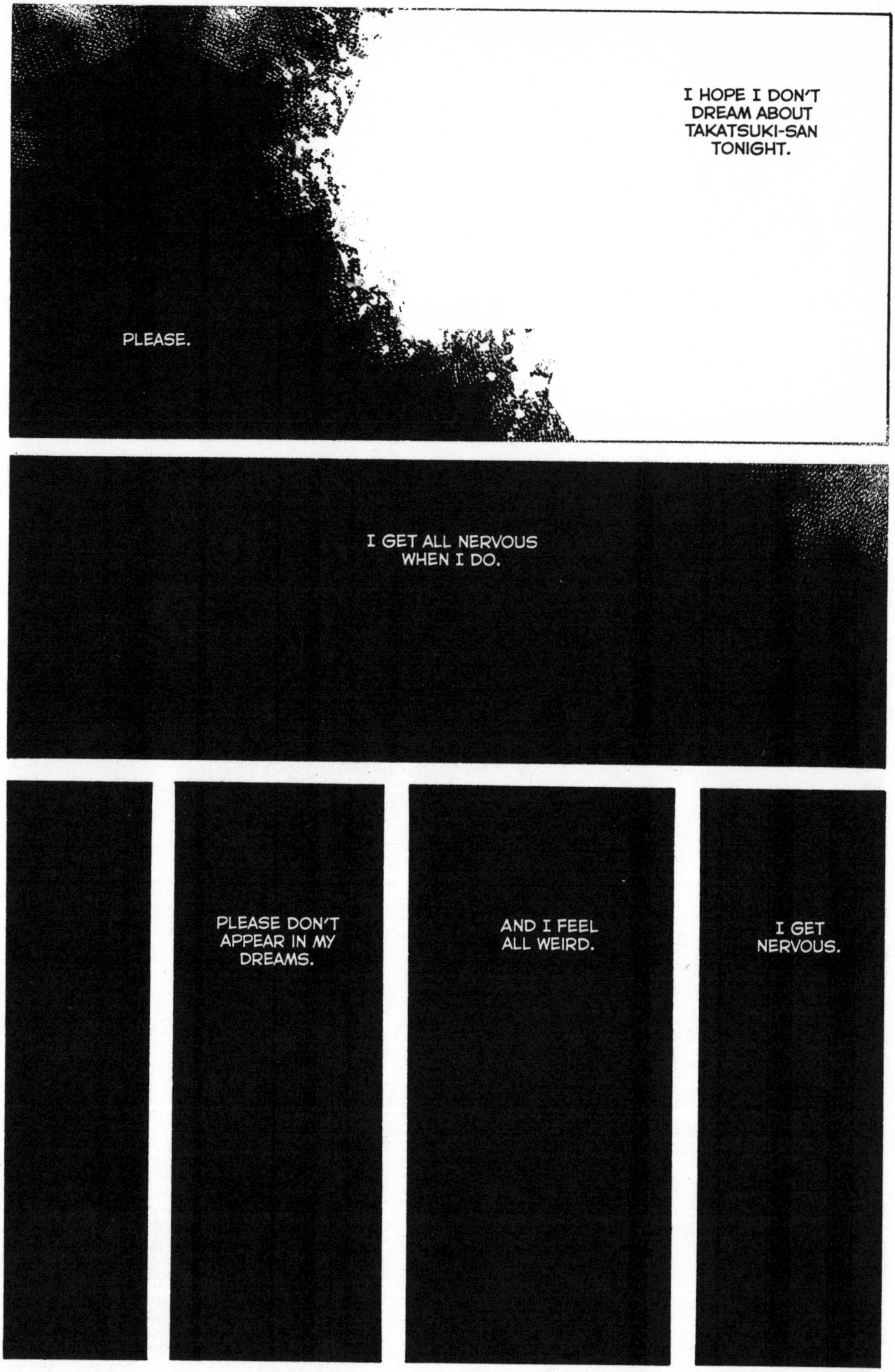
I HOPE I DON'T DREAM ABOUT TAKATSUKI-SAN TONIGHT.
PLEASE.
I GET ALL NERVOUS WHEN I DO.
I GET NERVOUS.
AND I FEEL ALL WEIRD.
PLEASE DON'T APPEAR IN MY DREAMS.

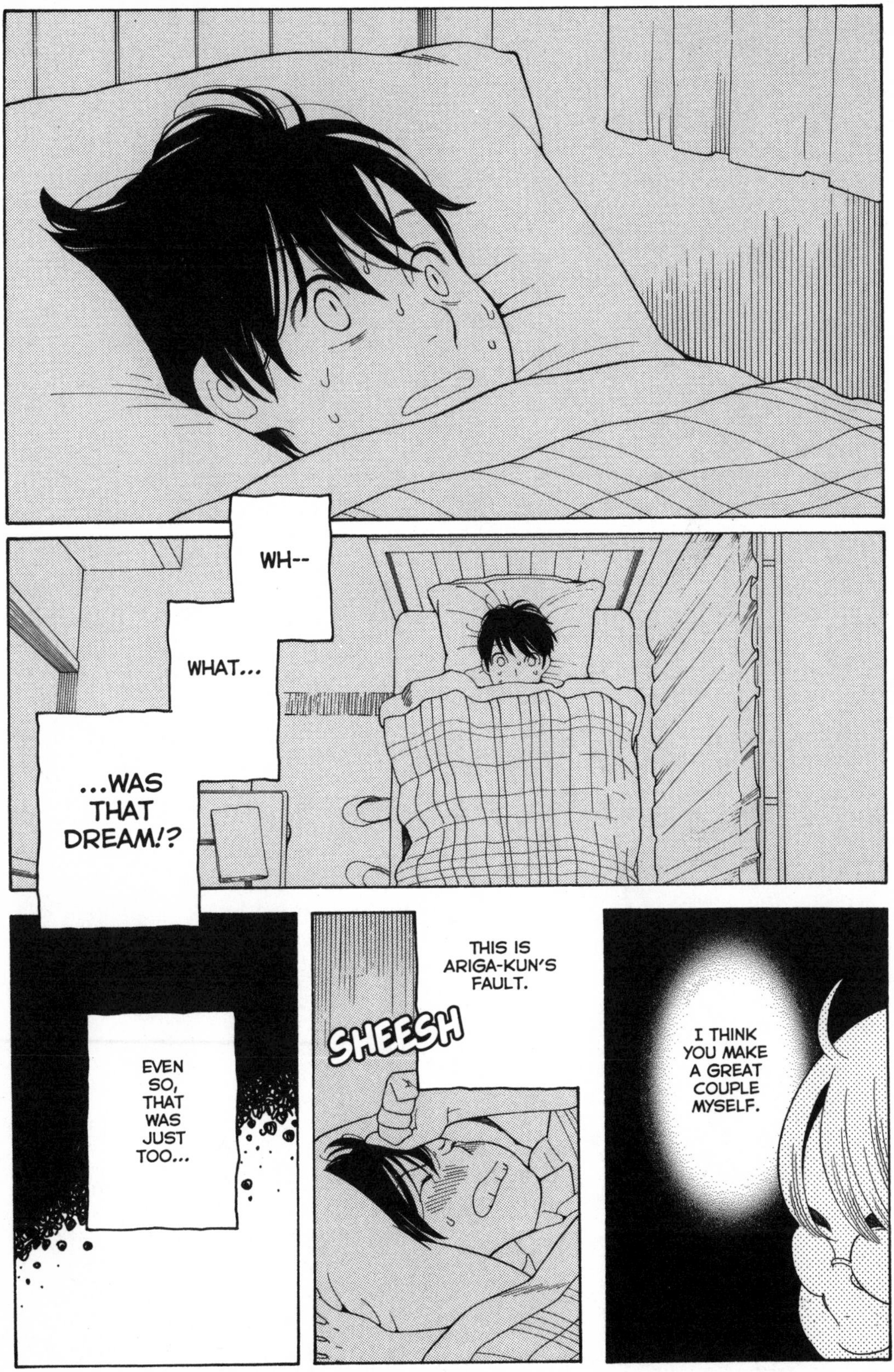
WH--
WHAT...
...WAS THAT DREAM!?
I THINK YOU MAKE A GREAT COUPLE MYSELF.
THIS IS ARIGA-KUN'S FAULT.
SHEESH
EVEN SO, THAT WAS JUST TOO...

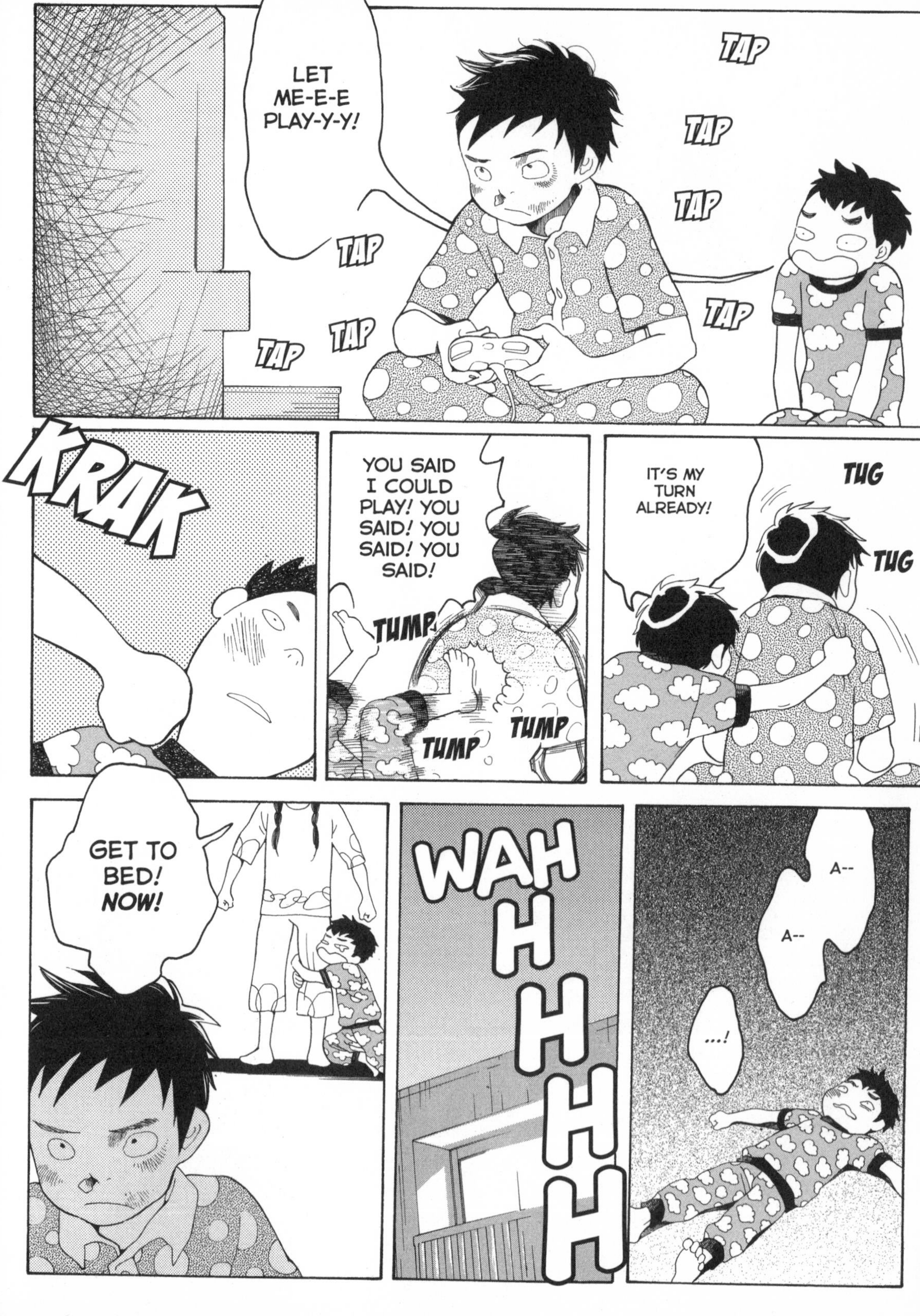
TAP
TAP
TAP
TAP
LET ME-E-E PLAY-Y-Y!
TAP
TAP
TAP
IT'S MY TURN ALREADY!
TUG
TUG
YOU SAID I COULD PLAY! YOU SAID! YOU SAID! YOU SAID!
TUMP
TUMP
TUMP
KRAK
A--
A--
...!
WAHHHHHH
GET TO BED! NOW!

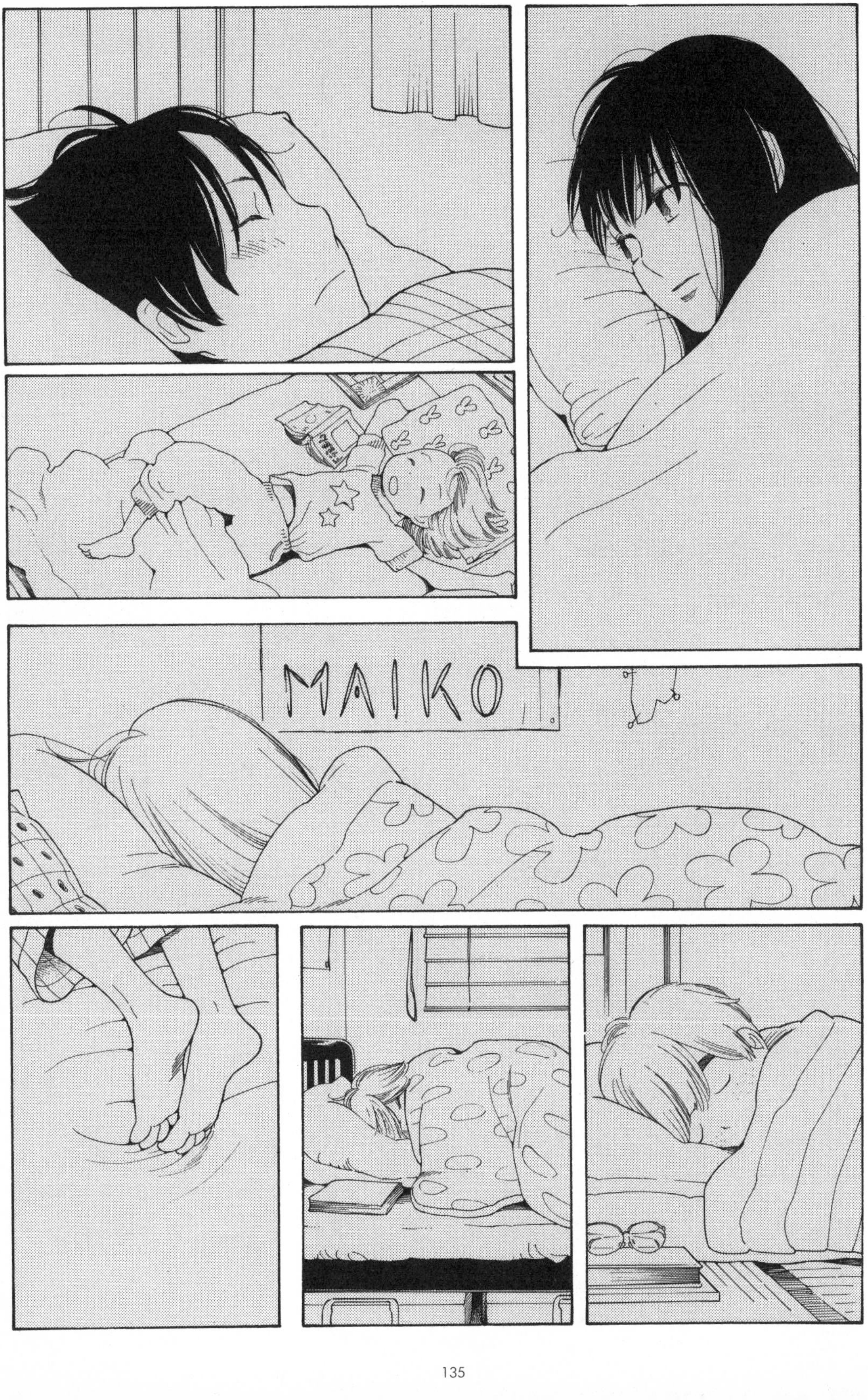
MAIKO

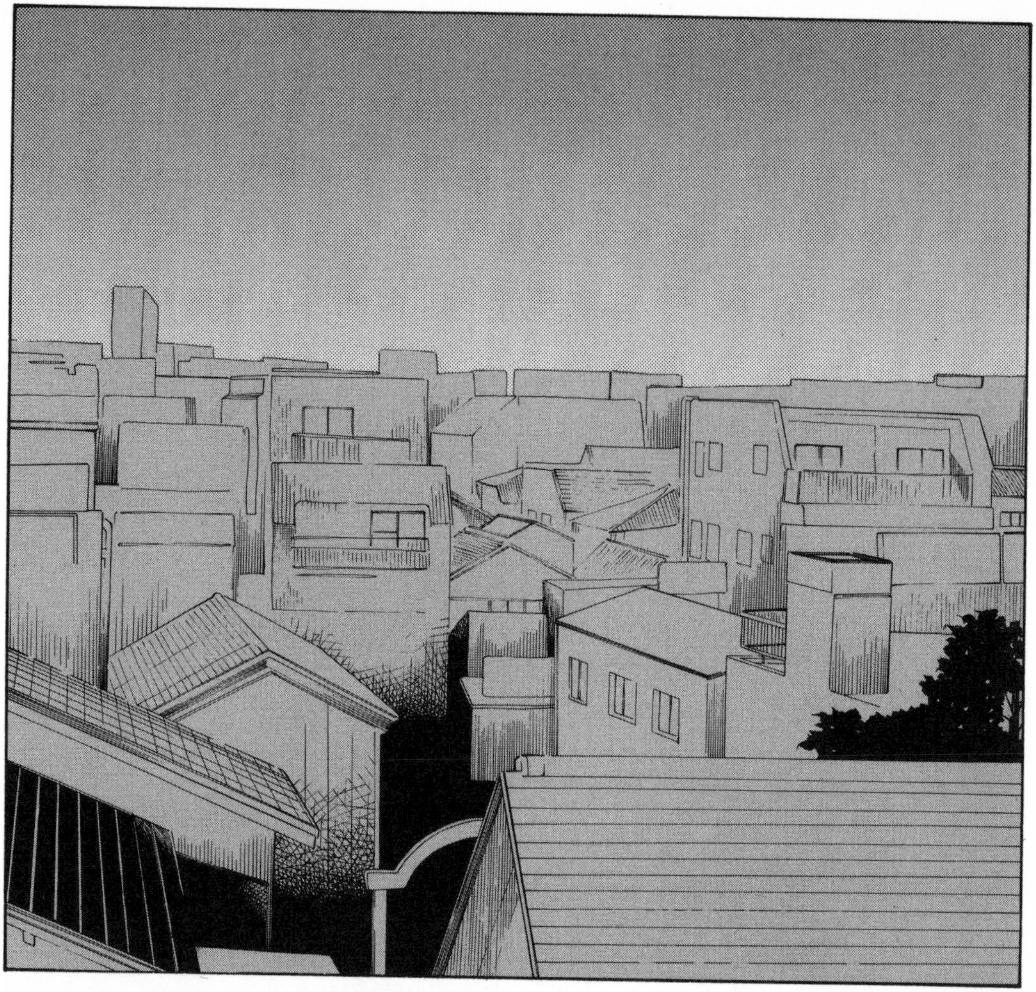

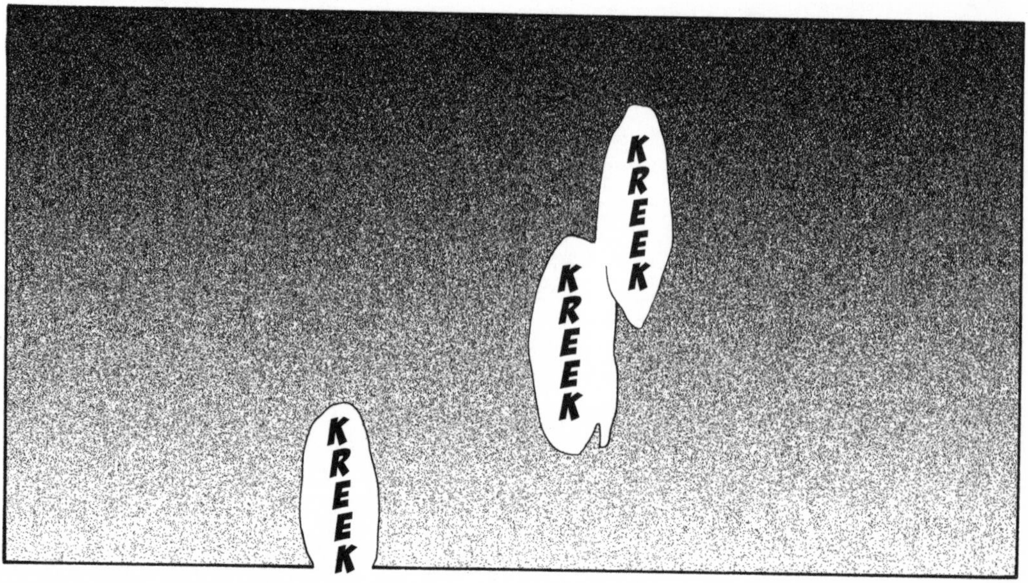
KREEK
KREEK
KREEK

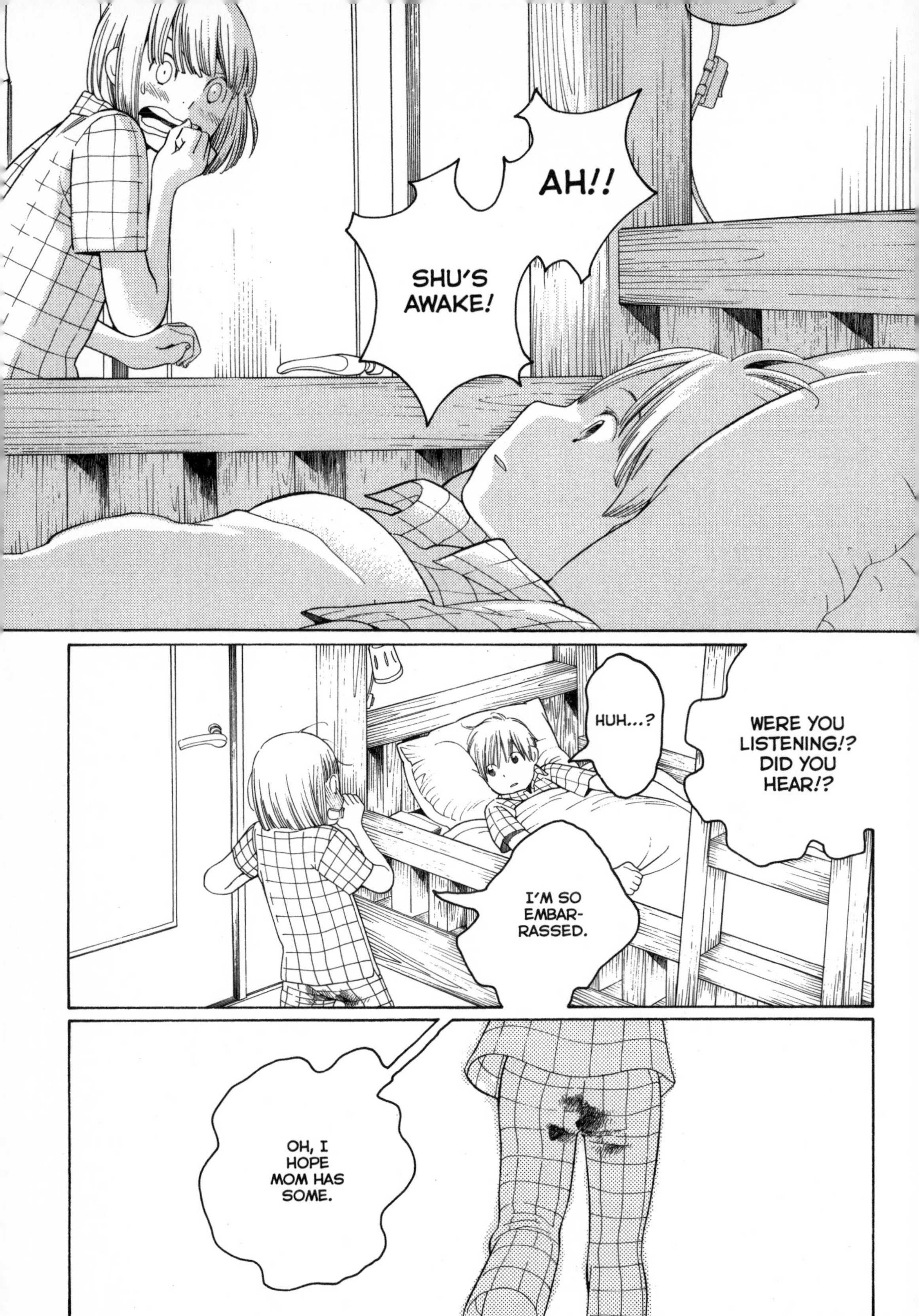
AH!!
SHU'S AWAKE!
WERE YOU LISTENING!? DID YOU HEAR!?
HUH...?
I'M SO EMBAR-RASSED.
OH, I HOPE MOM HAS SOME.

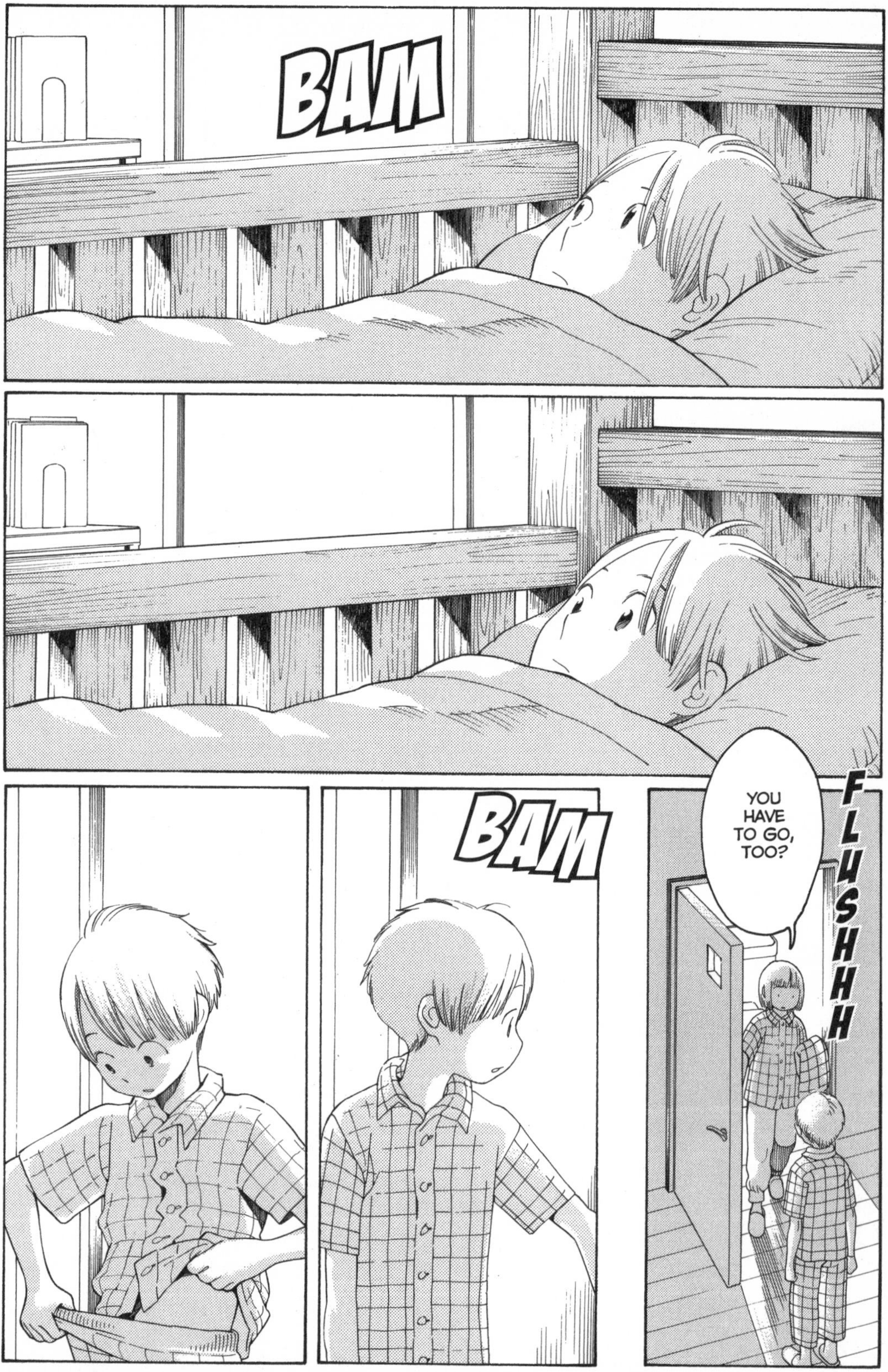
BAM
FLUSHHH
YOU HAVE TO GO, TOO?
BAM

31

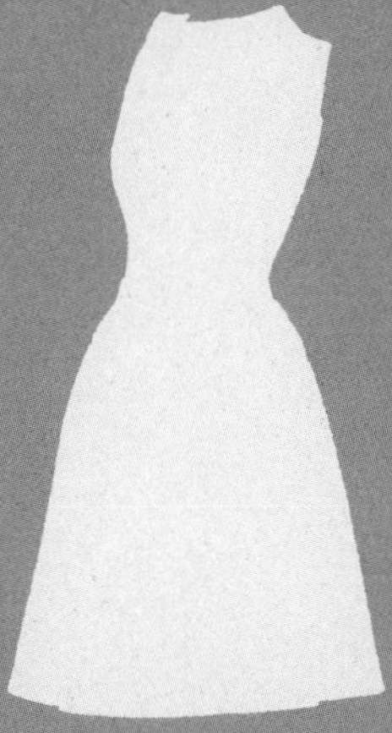

Confessions of Love

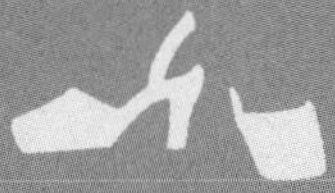

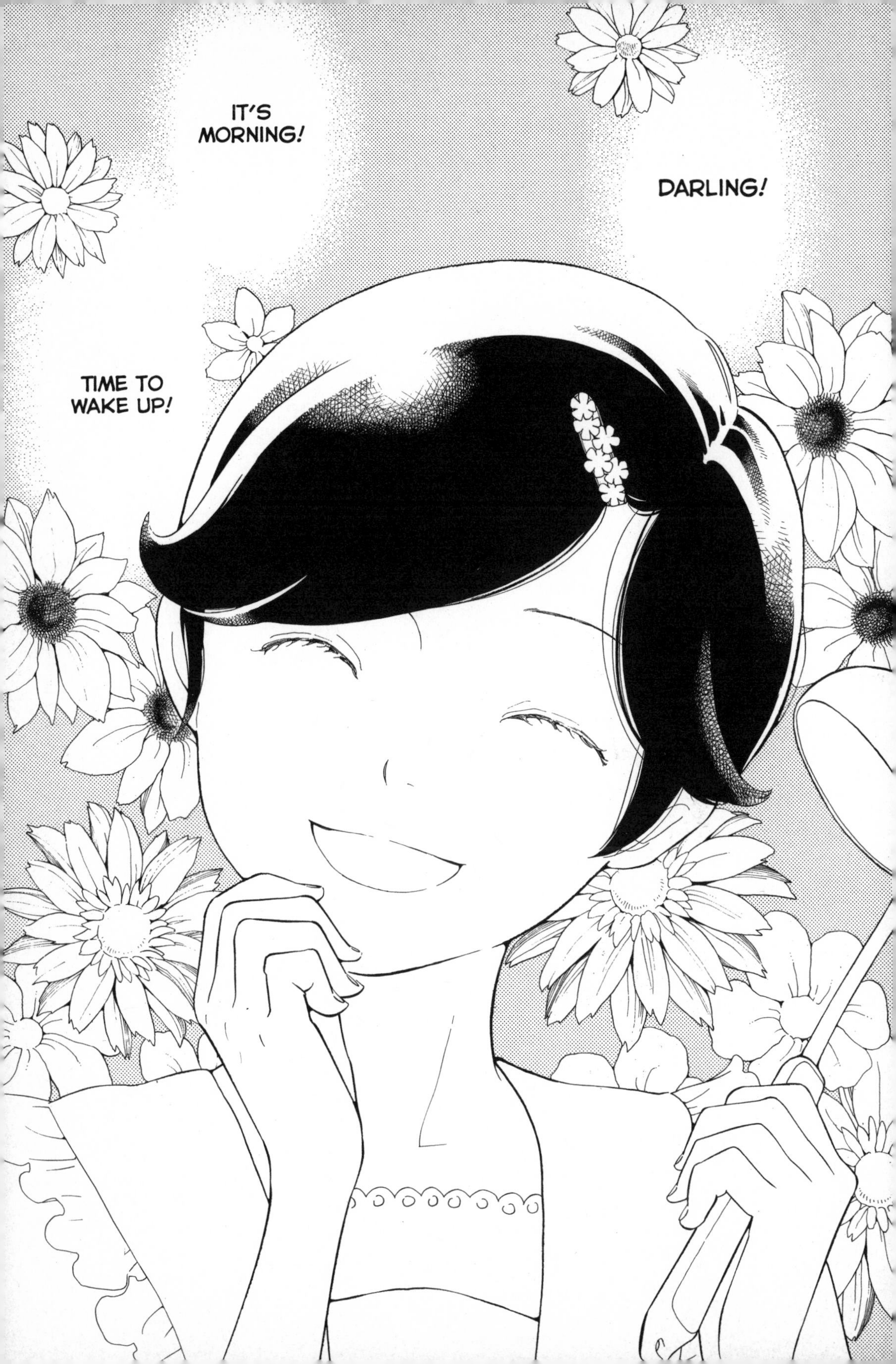
IT'S MORNING!
DARLING!
TIME TO WAKE UP!

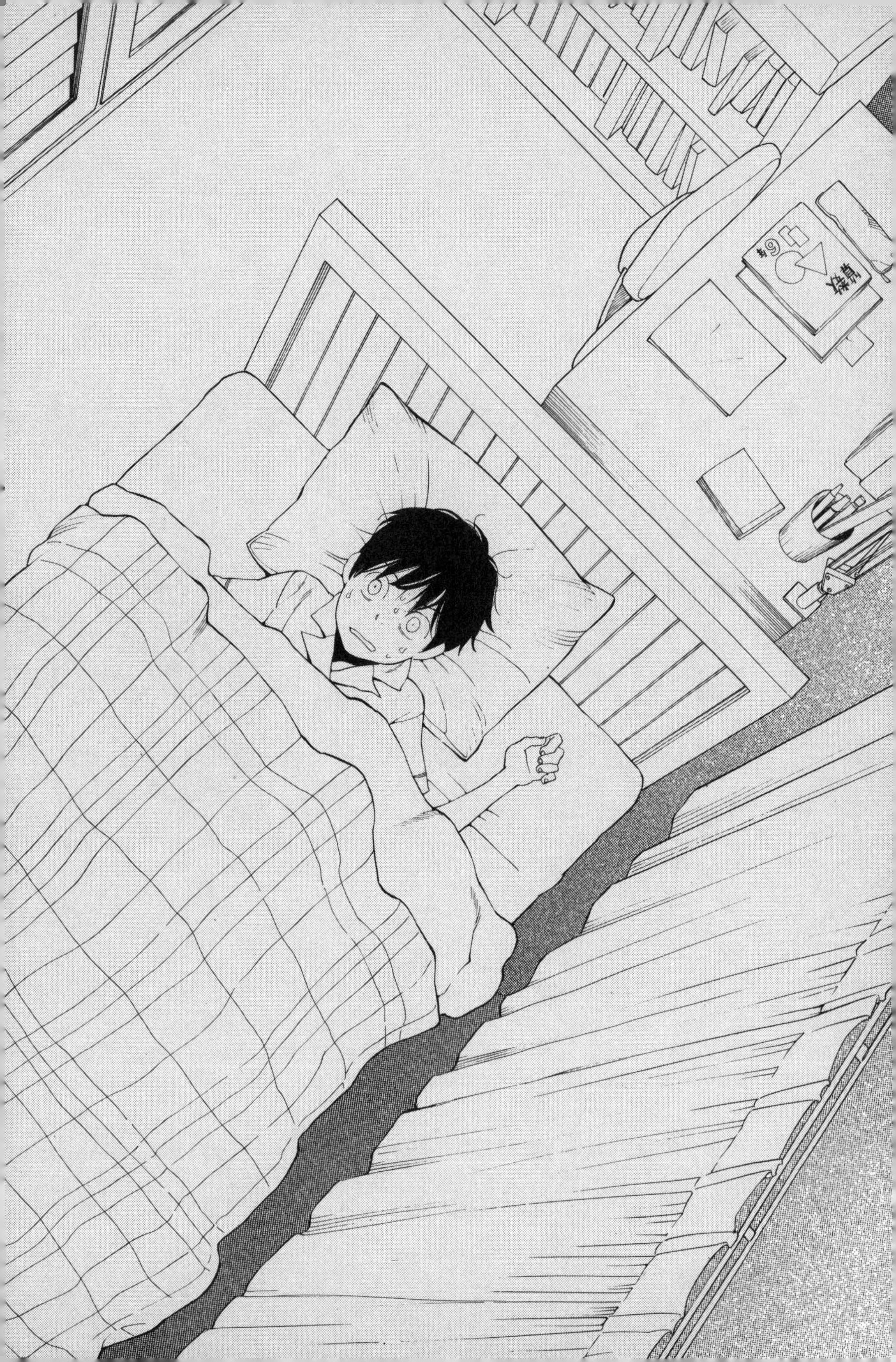
算数
6年

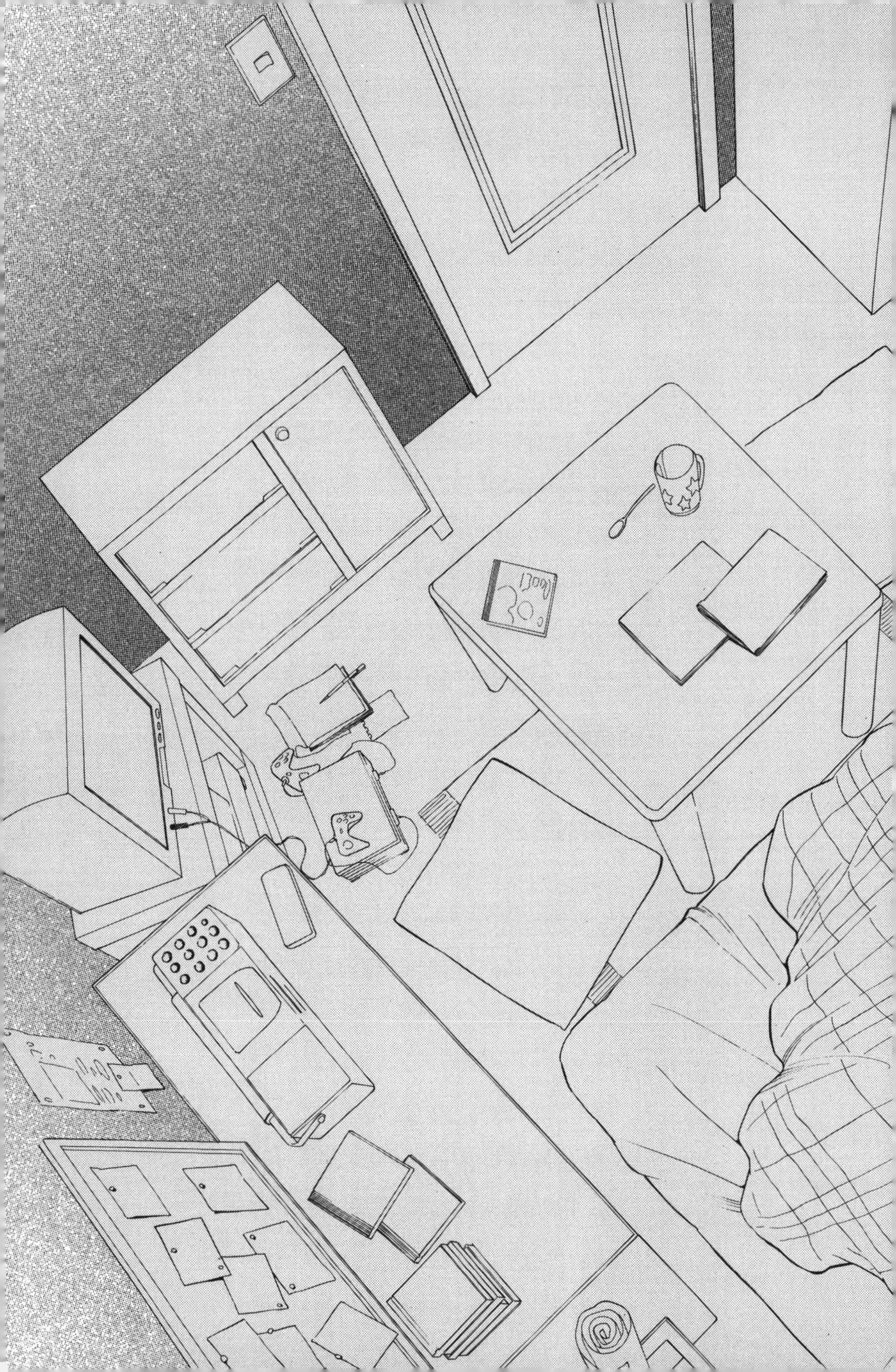

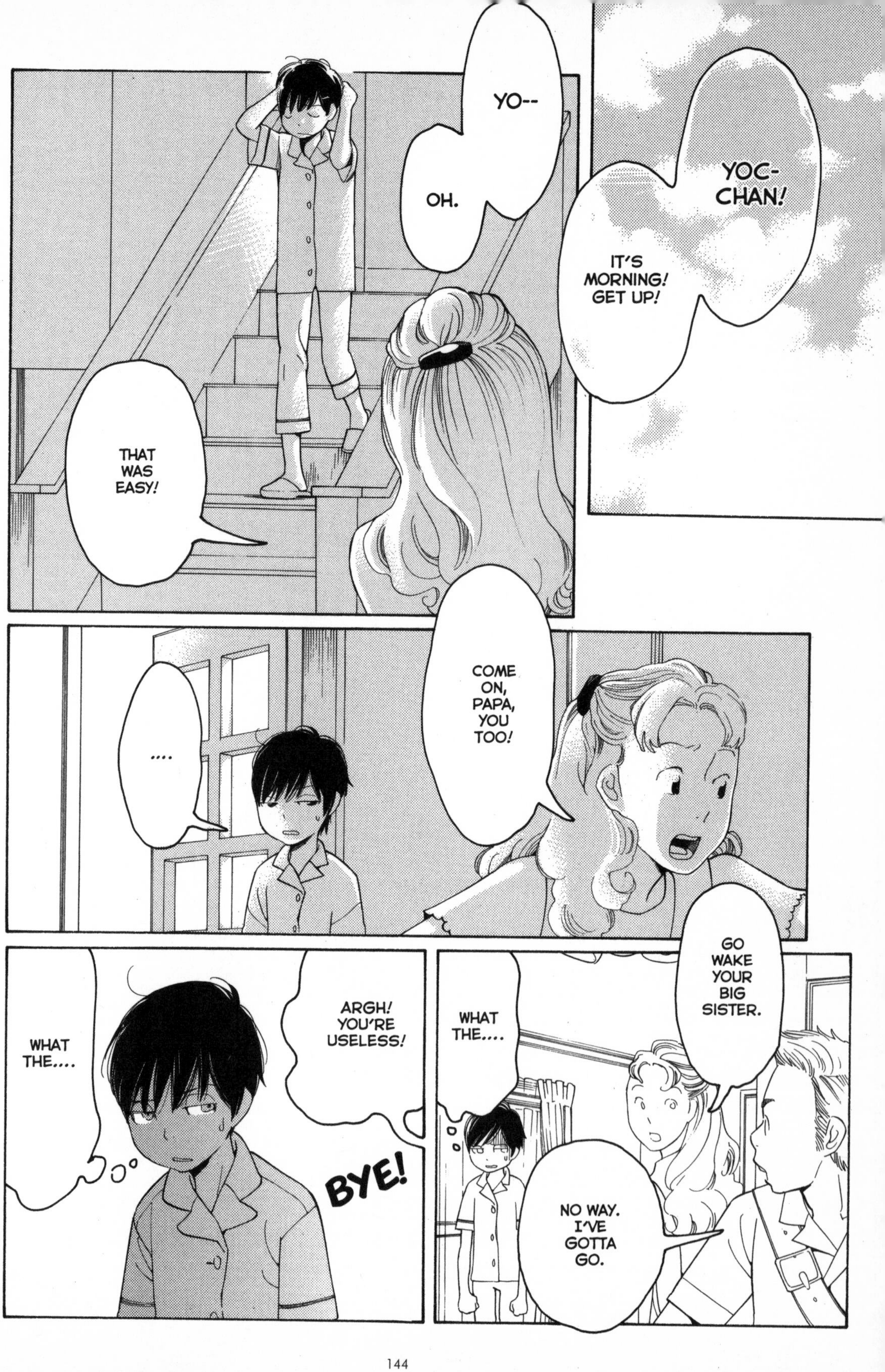
YOC-CHAN!
IT'S MORNING! GET UP!
YO--
OH.
THAT WAS EASY!
COME ON, PAPA, YOU TOO!
....
GO WAKE YOUR BIG SISTER.
NO WAY. I'VE GOTTA GO.
WHAT THE....
ARGH! YOU'RE USELESS!
BYE!
WHAT THE....

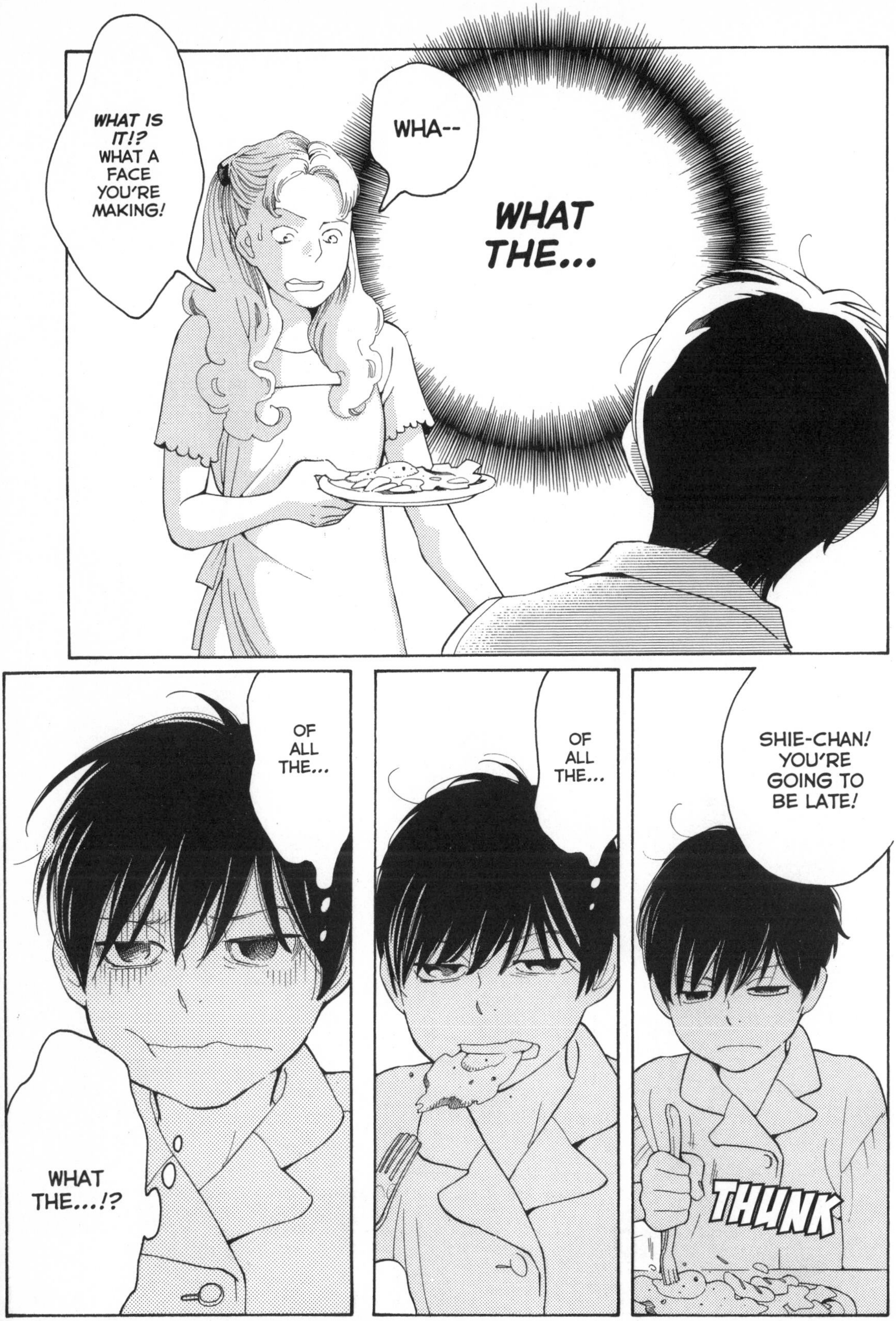

WHAT THE...
WHA--
WHAT IS IT!? WHAT A FACE YOU'RE MAKING!
SHIE-CHAN! YOU'RE GOING TO BE LATE!
THUNK
OF ALL THE...
OF ALL THE...
WHAT THE...!?

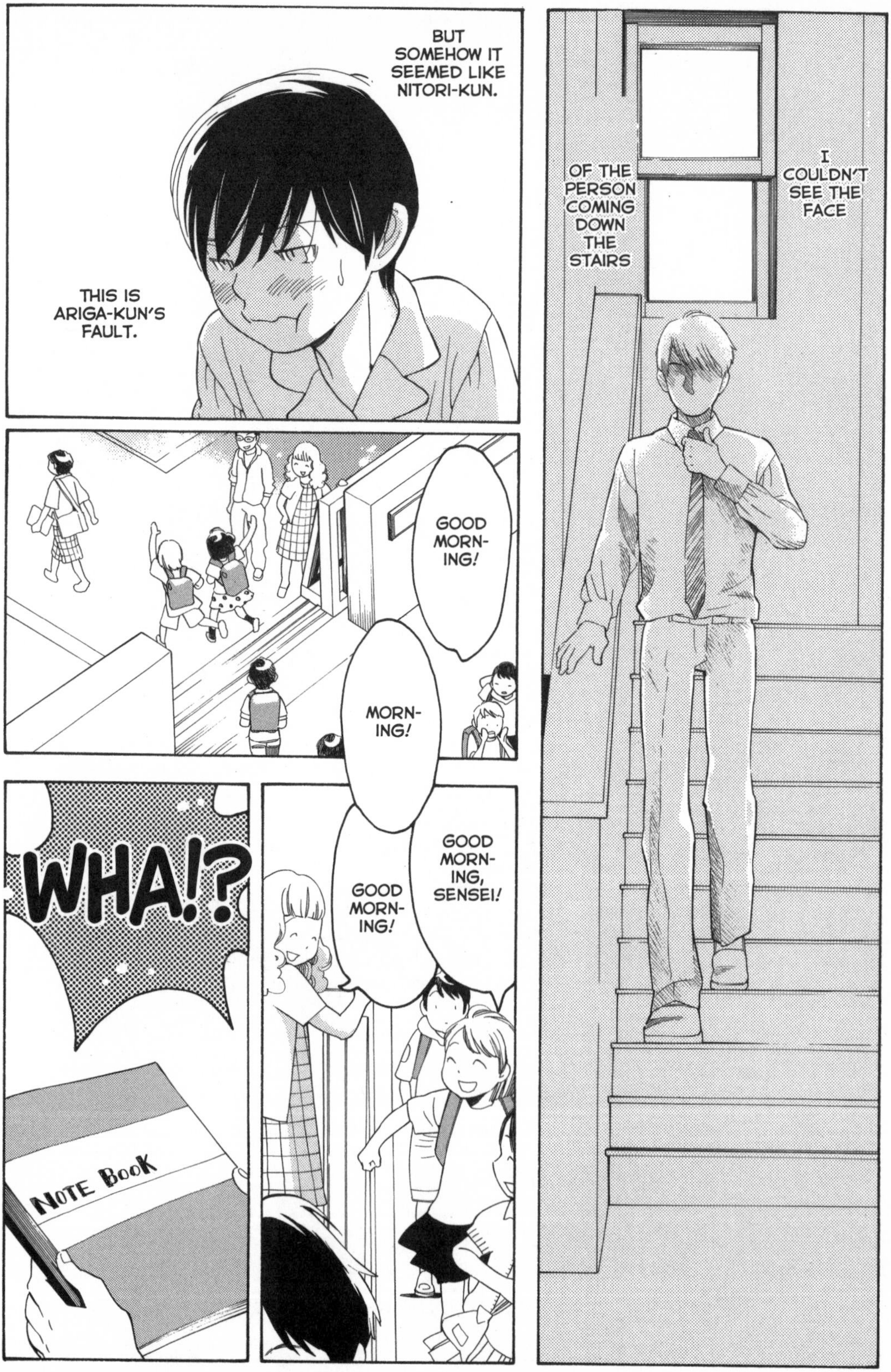
I COULDN'T SEE THE FACE
OF THE PERSON COMING DOWN THE STAIRS
BUT SOMEHOW IT SEEMED LIKE NITORI-KUN.
THIS IS ARIGA-KUN'S FAULT.
GOOD MORNING!
MORNING!
GOOD MORNING, SENSEI!
GOOD MORNING!
WHA!?
NOTE BOOK

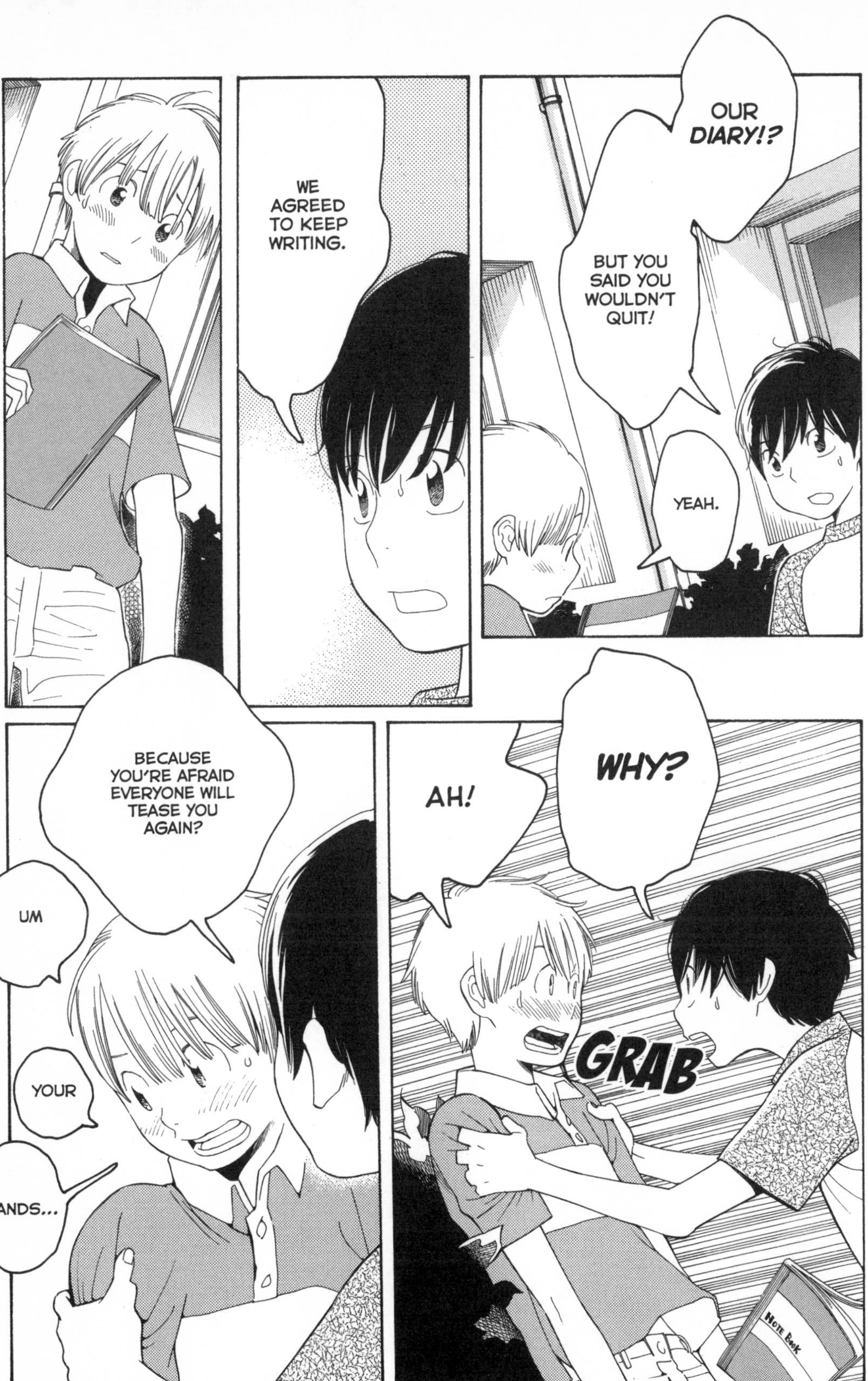
OUR DIARY!?
BUT YOU SAID YOU WOULDN'T QUIT!
YEAH.
WE AGREED TO KEEP WRITING.
WHY?
AH!
GRAB
NOTE Book
BECAUSE YOU'RE AFRAID EVERYONE WILL TEASE YOU AGAIN?
UM
YOUR
HANDS...

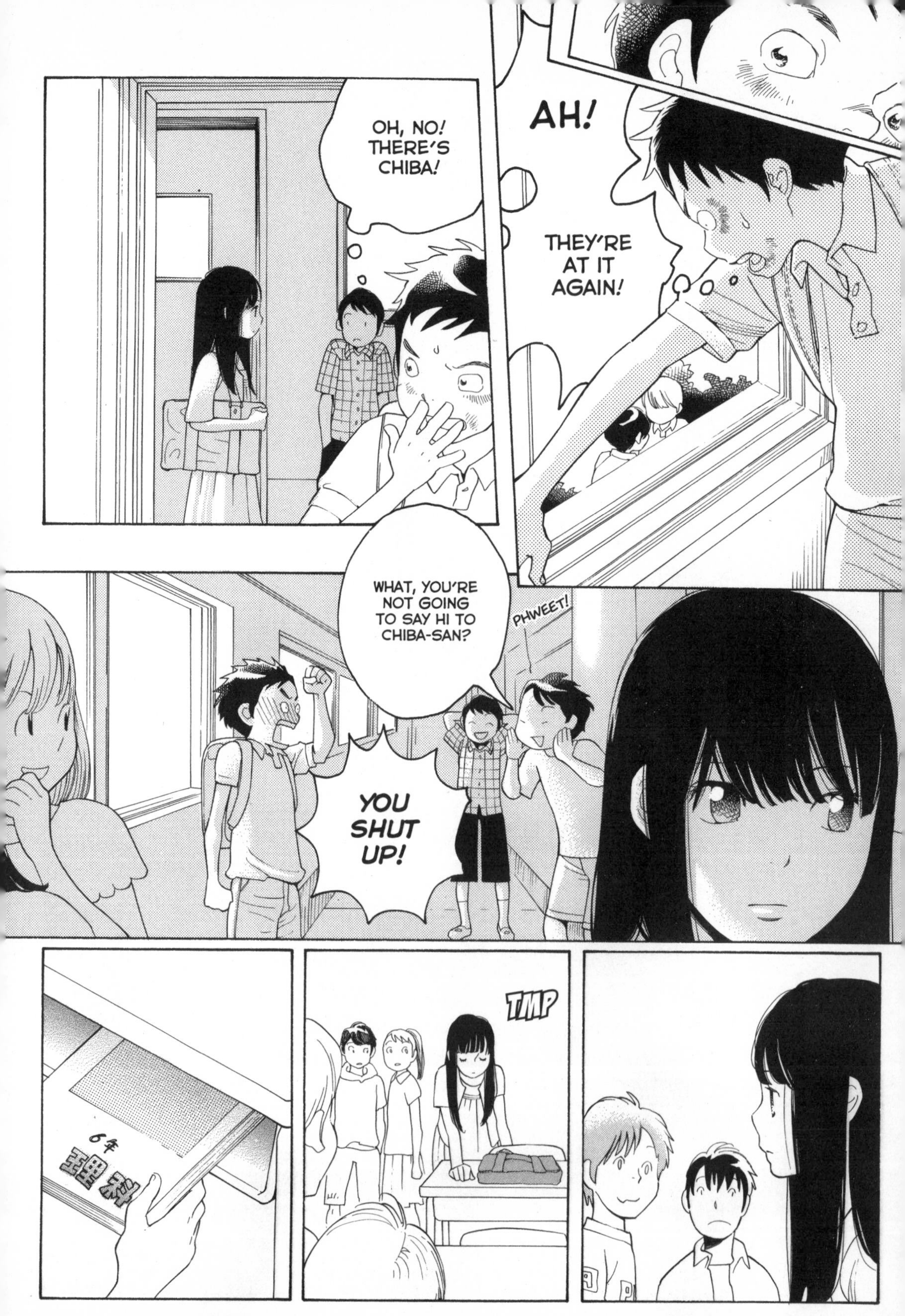
AH!
THEY'RE AT IT AGAIN!
OH, NO! THERE'S CHIBA!
WHAT, YOU'RE NOT GOING TO SAY HI TO CHIBA-SAN?
PHWEET!
YOU SHUT UP!
TMP
6年
理科

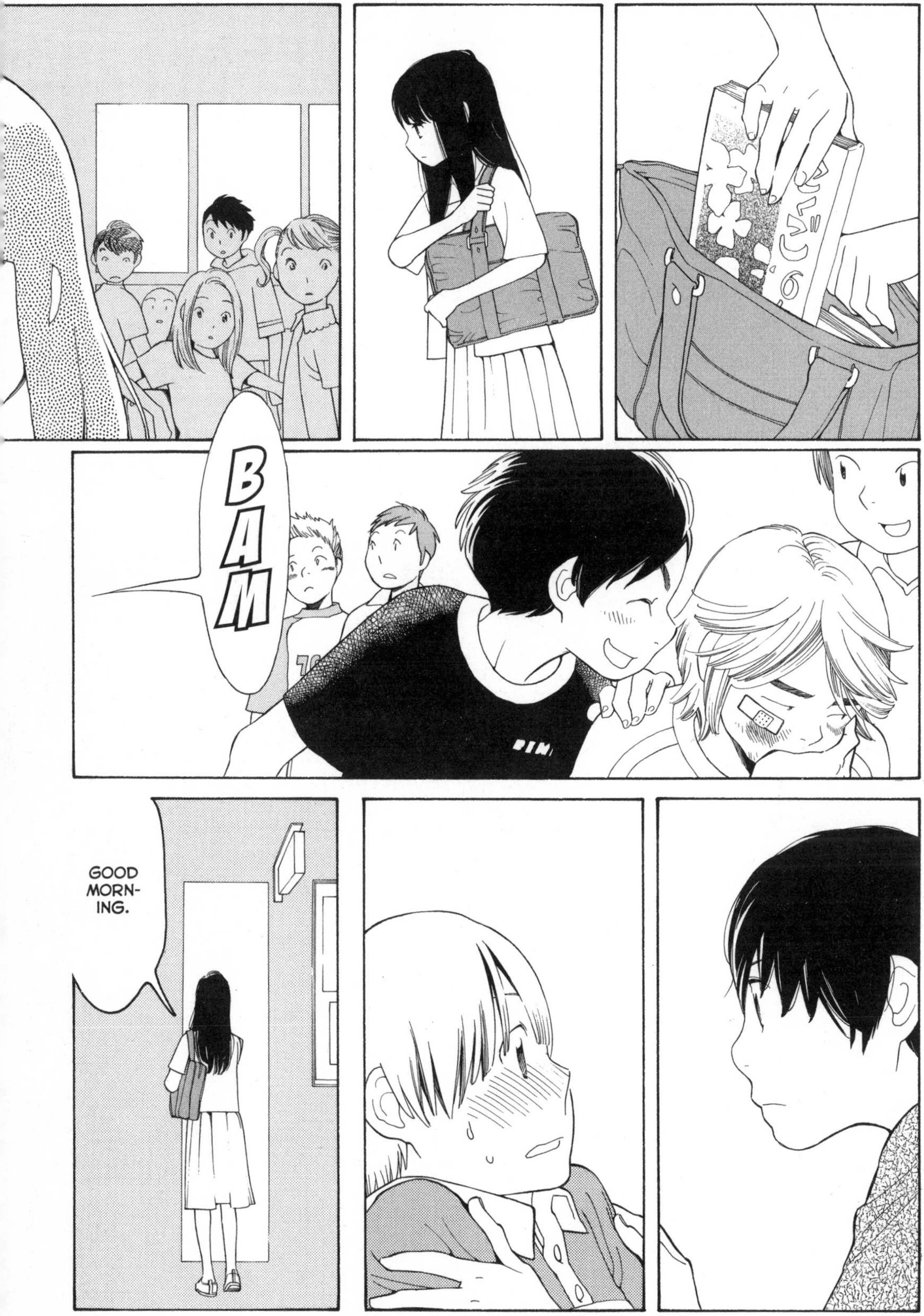
BAM
GOOD MORN-ING.

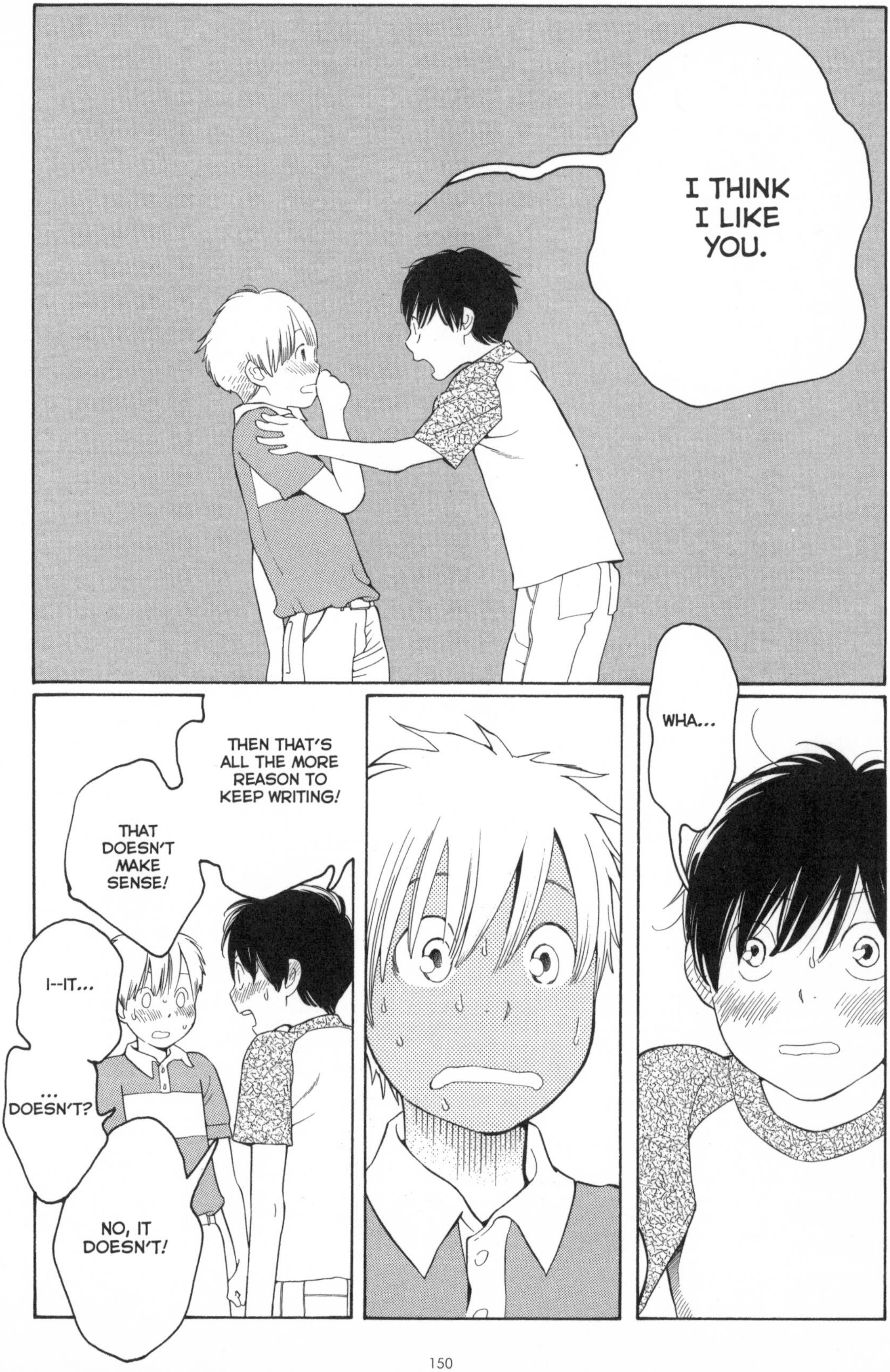
I THINK I LIKE YOU.
WHA...
THEN THAT'S ALL THE MORE REASON TO KEEP WRITING!
THAT DOESN'T MAKE SENSE!
I--IT...
... DOESN'T?
NO, IT DOESN'T!

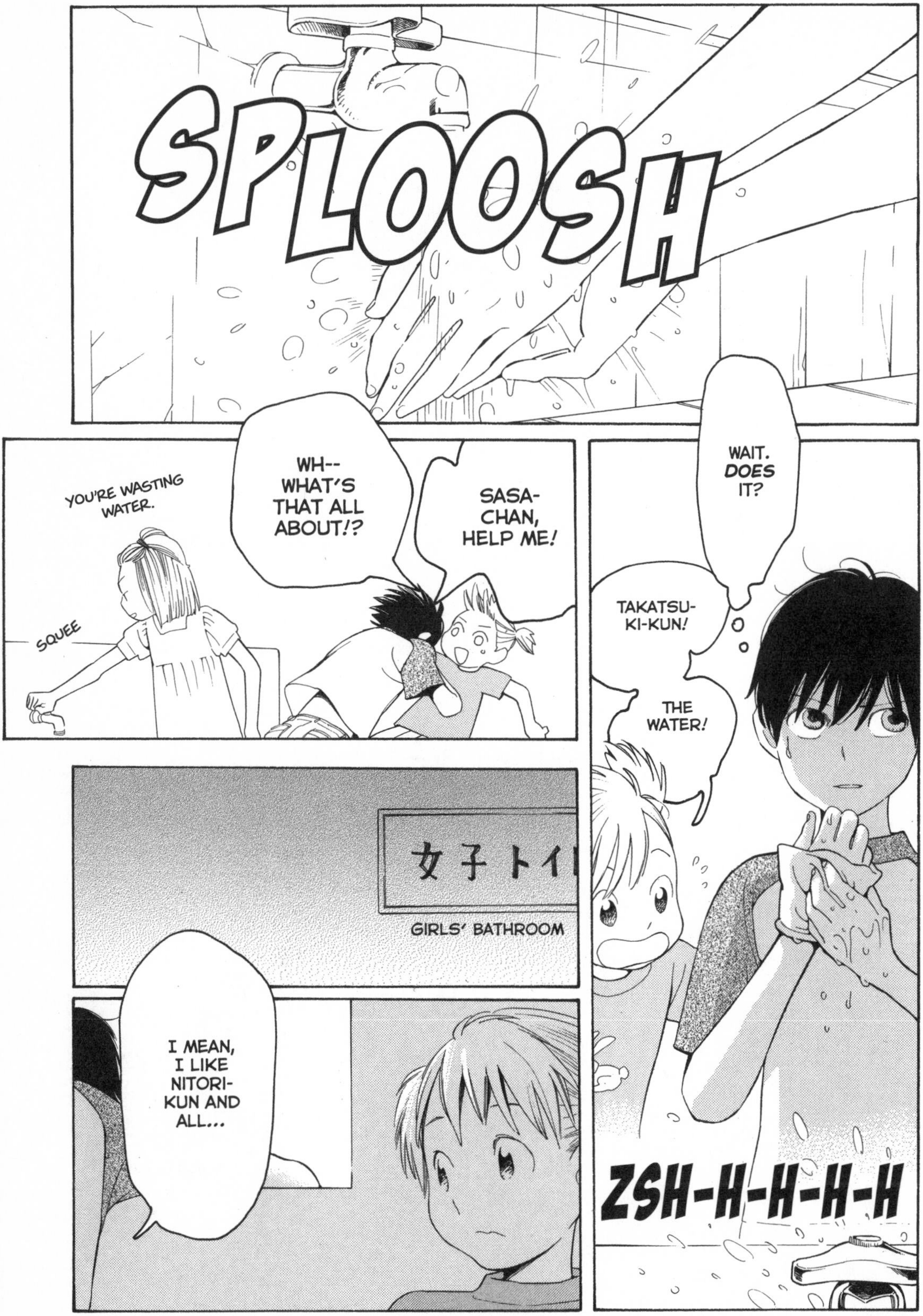
SPLOOSH
WAIT. DOES IT?
TAKATSU-KI-KUN!
THE WATER!
ZSH-H-H-H-H
SASA-CHAN, HELP ME!
WH-- WHAT'S THAT ALL ABOUT!?
YOU'RE WASTING WATER.
SQUEE
女子トイ
GIRLS' BATHROOM
I MEAN, I LIKE NITORI-KUN AND ALL...

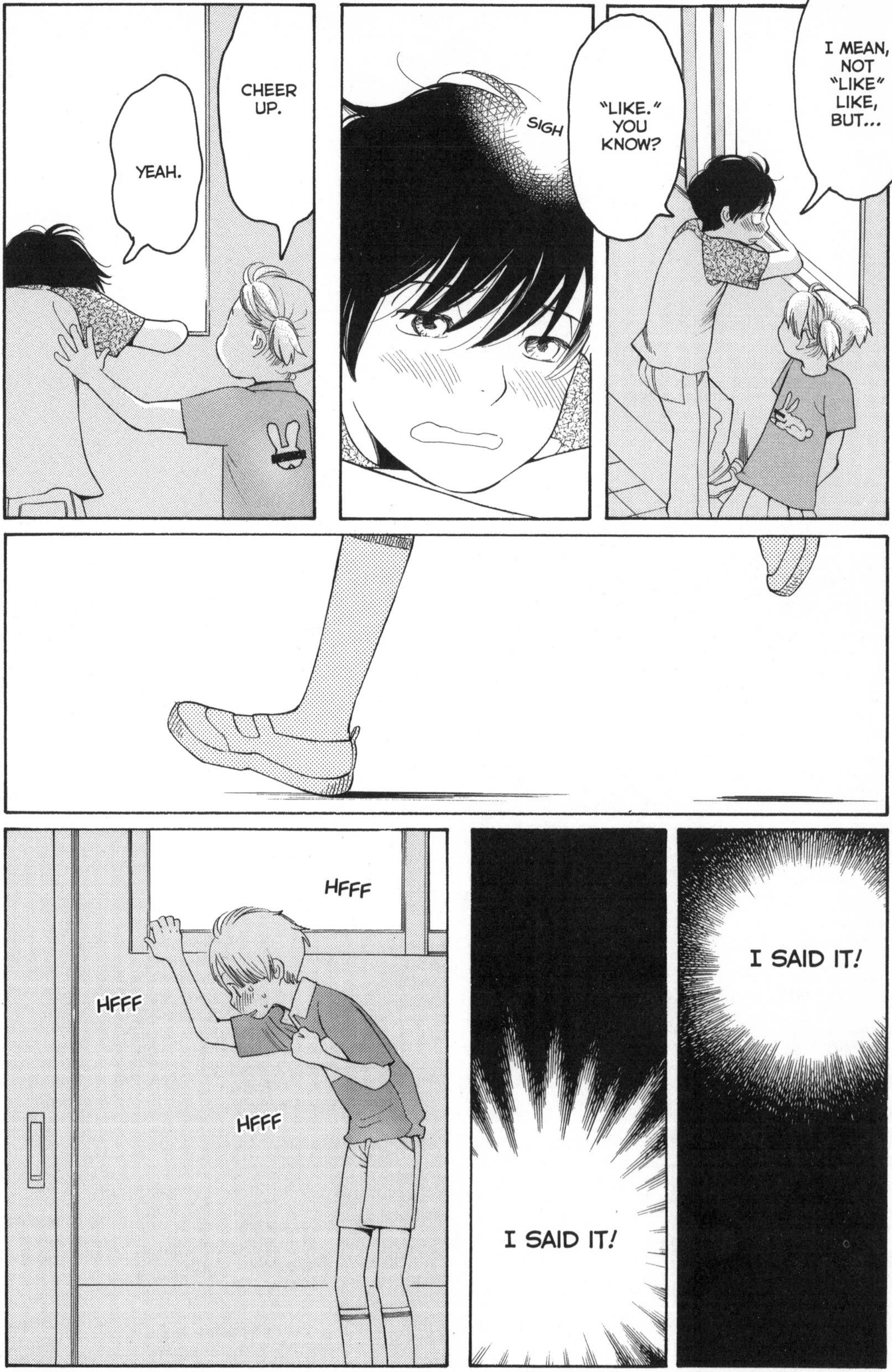
I MEAN, NOT "LIKE" LIKE, BUT...
"LIKE." YOU KNOW?
SIGH
CHEER UP.
YEAH.
I SAID IT!
I SAID IT!
HFFF
HFFF
HFFF

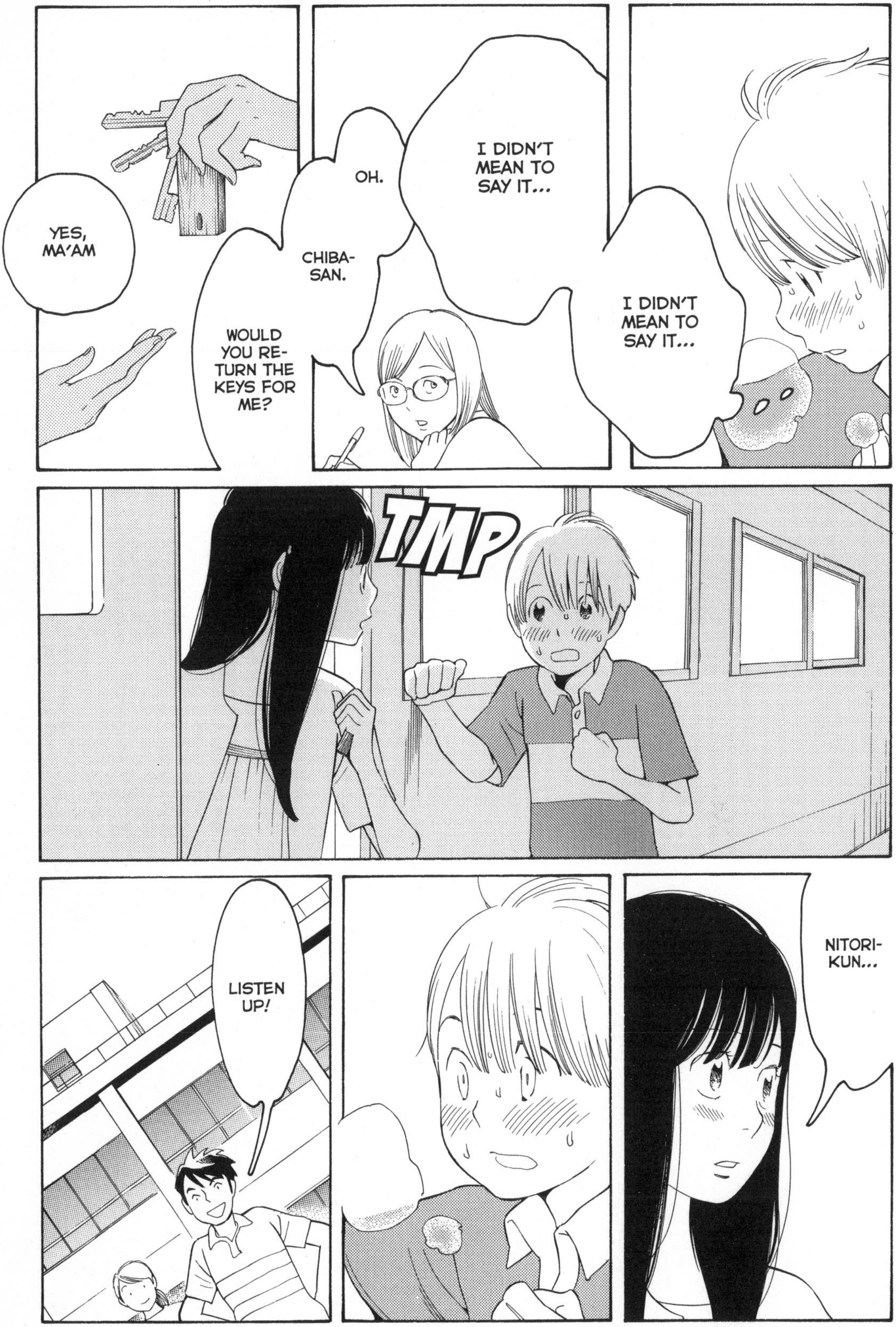

I DIDN'T MEAN TO SAY IT...
I DIDN'T MEAN TO SAY IT...
OH.
CHIBA-SAN.
WOULD YOU RE-TURN THE KEYS FOR ME?
YES, MA'AM
TMP
NITORI-KUN...
LISTEN UP!

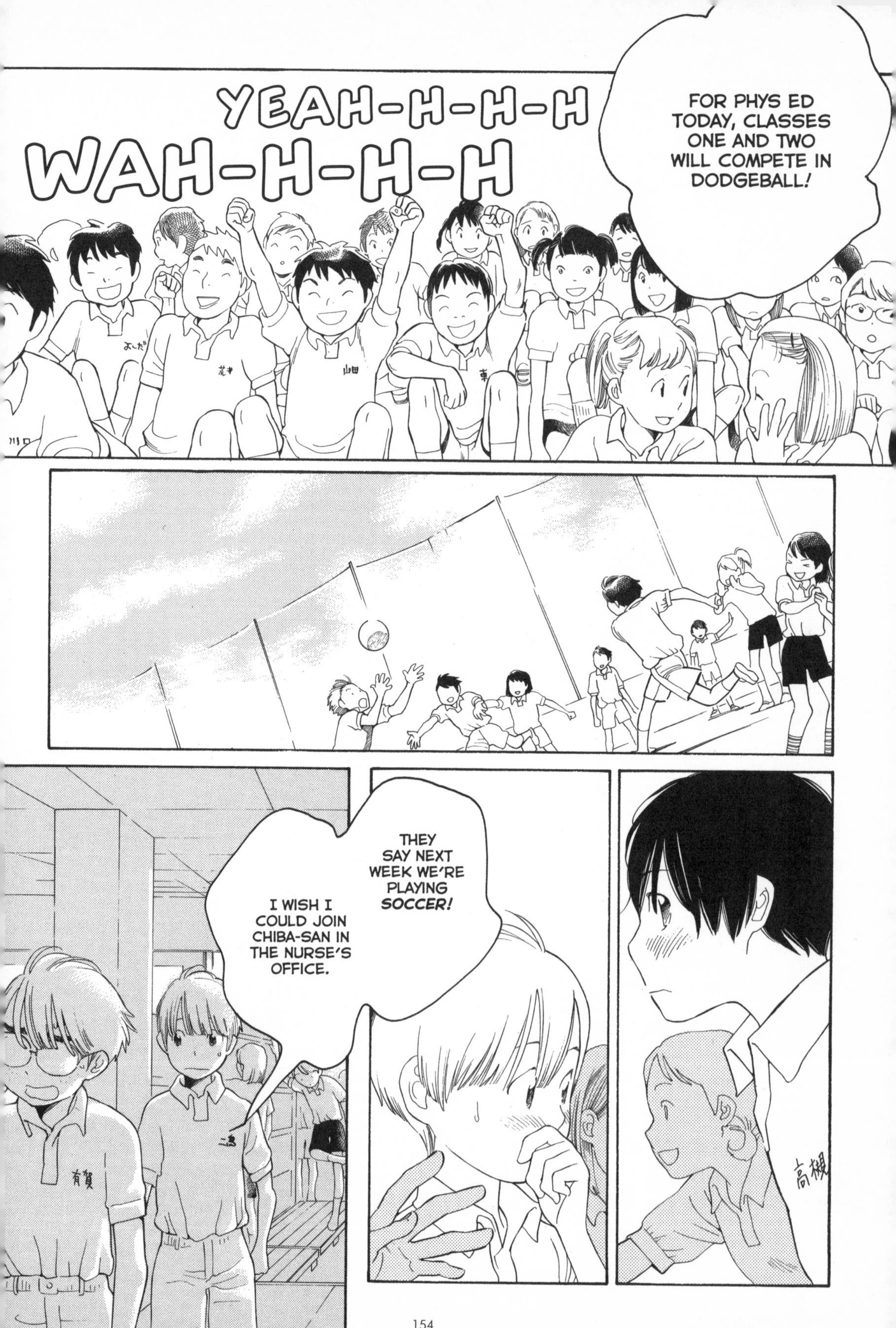

FOR PHYS ED TODAY, CLASSES ONE AND TWO WILL COMPETE IN DODGEBALL!
YEAH-H-H-H
WAH-H-H-H
THEY SAY NEXT WEEK WE'RE PLAYING *SOCCER!*
I WISH I COULD JOIN CHIBA-SAN IN THE NURSE'S OFFICE.

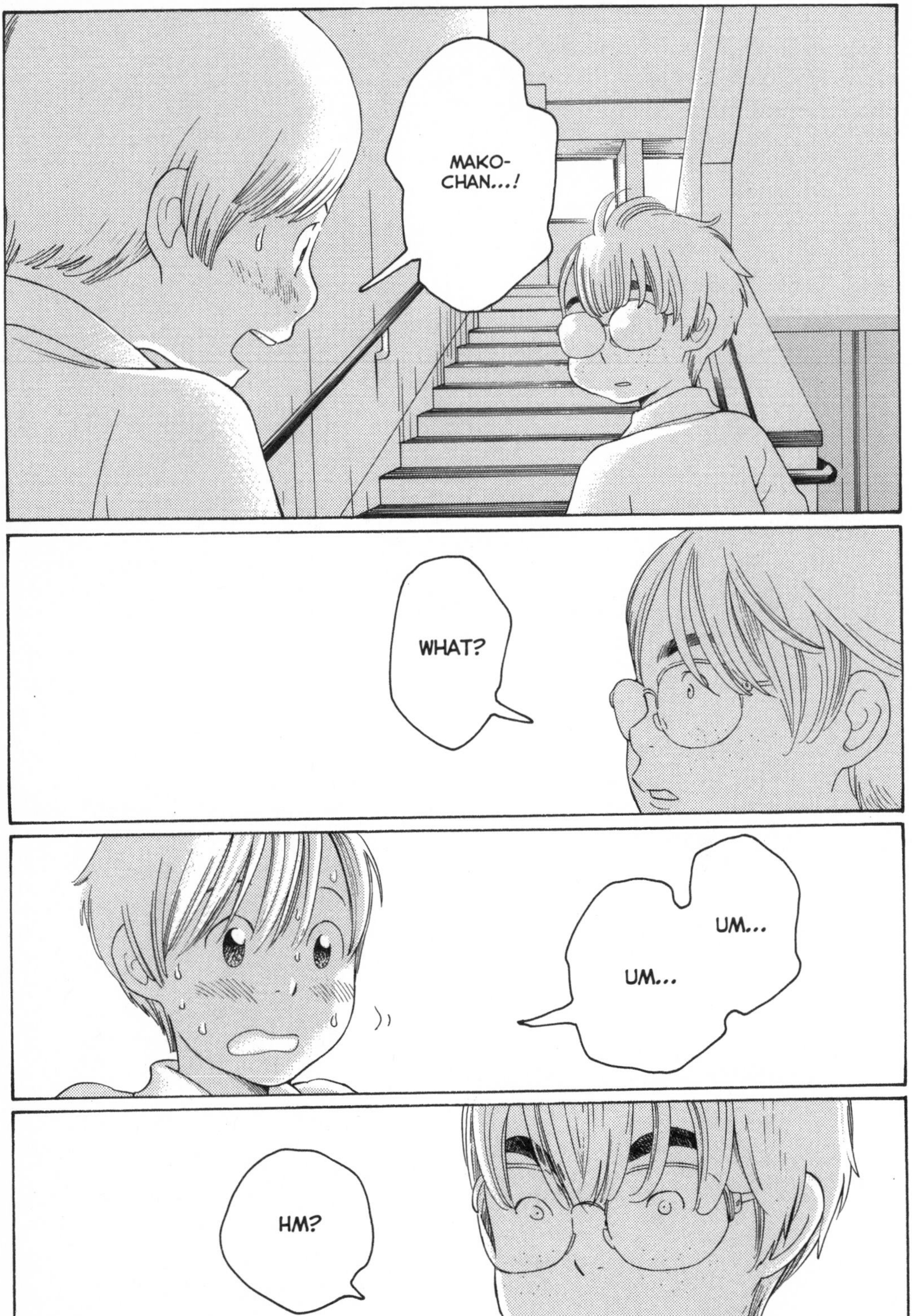
MAKO-CHAN...!
WHAT?
UM...
UM...
HM?

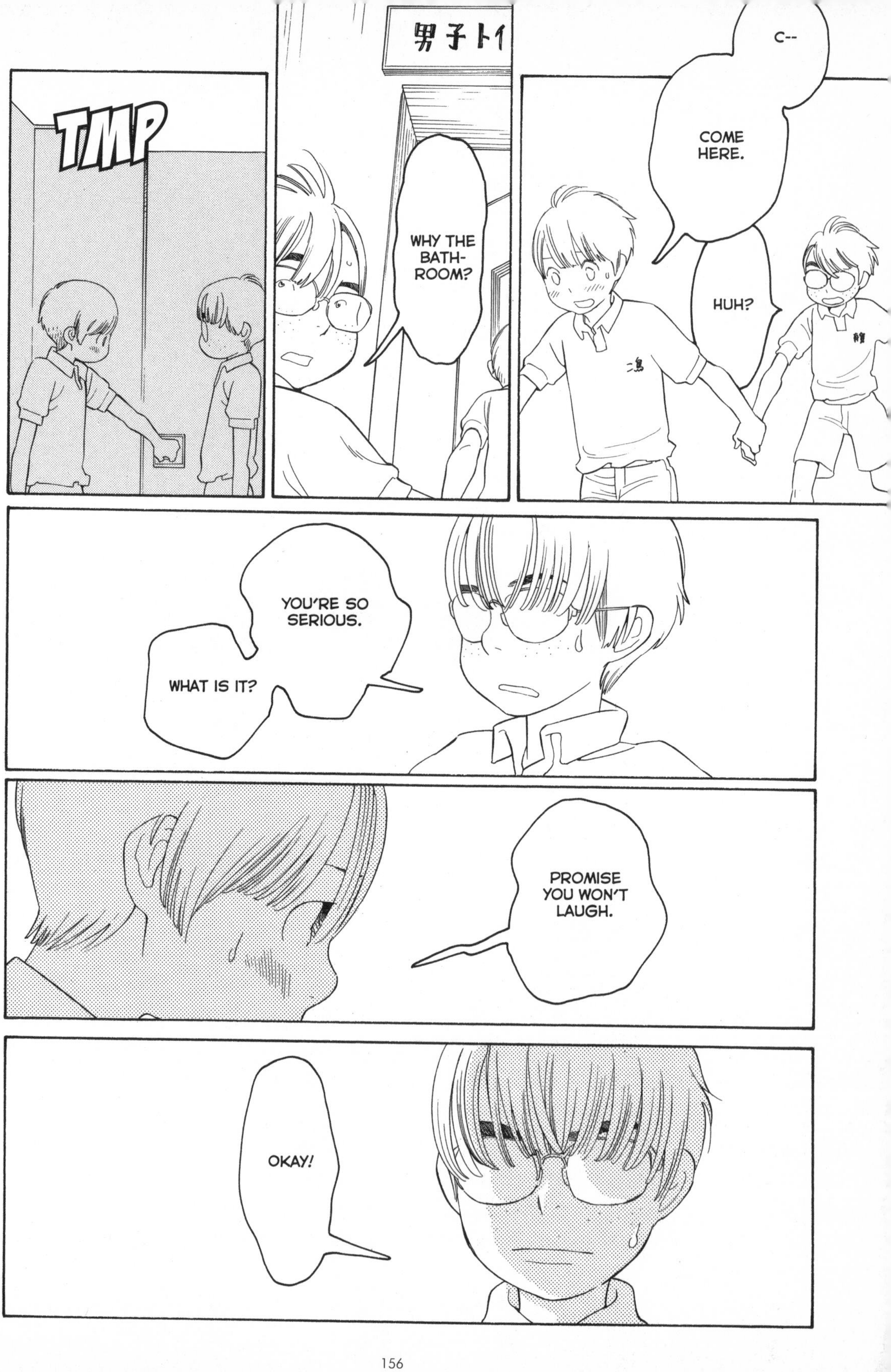
C--
COME HERE.
HUH?
男子トイ
WHY THE BATH-ROOM?
TMP
YOU'RE SO SERIOUS.
WHAT IS IT?
PROMISE YOU WON'T LAUGH.
OKAY!

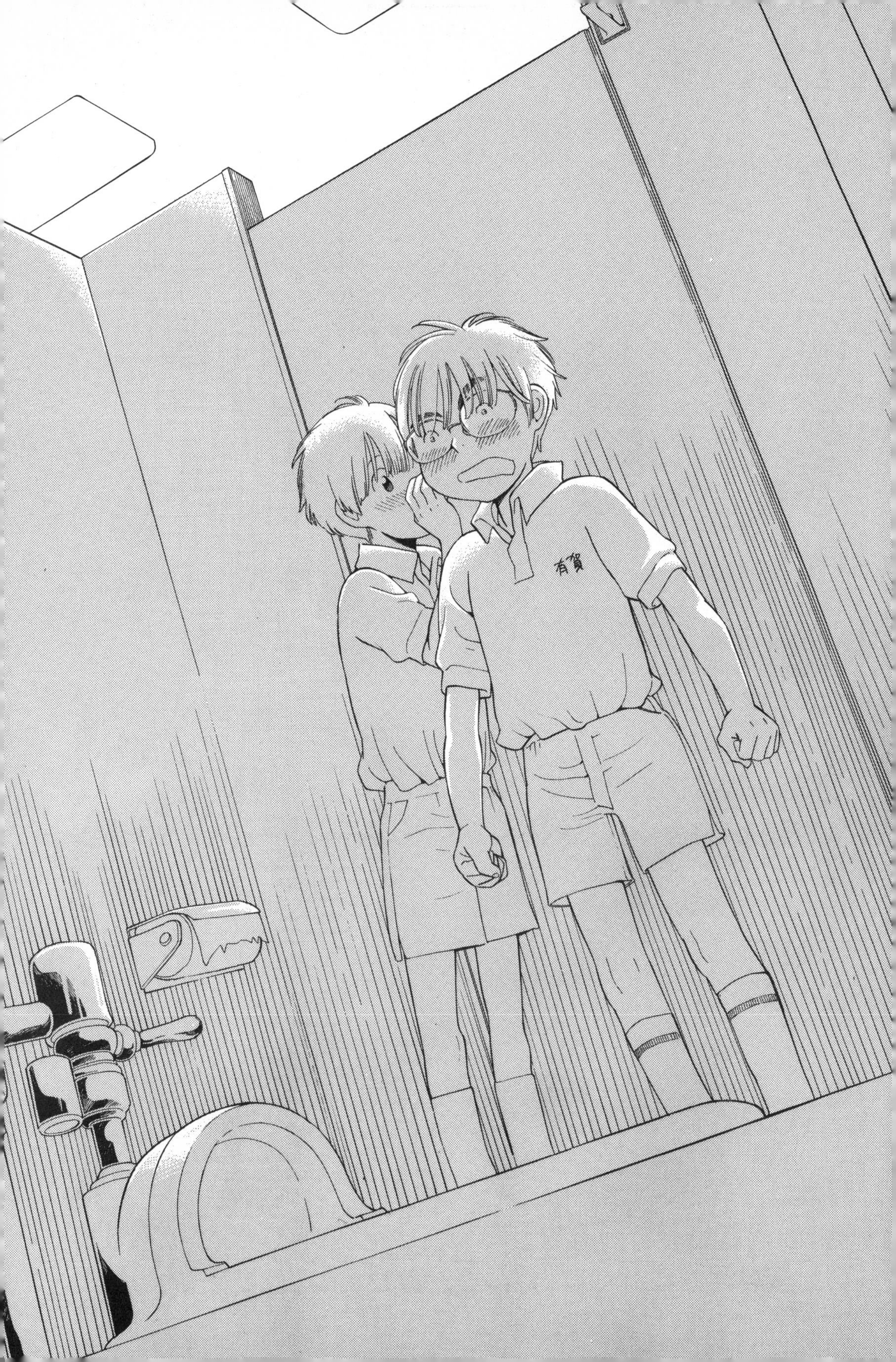
有賀

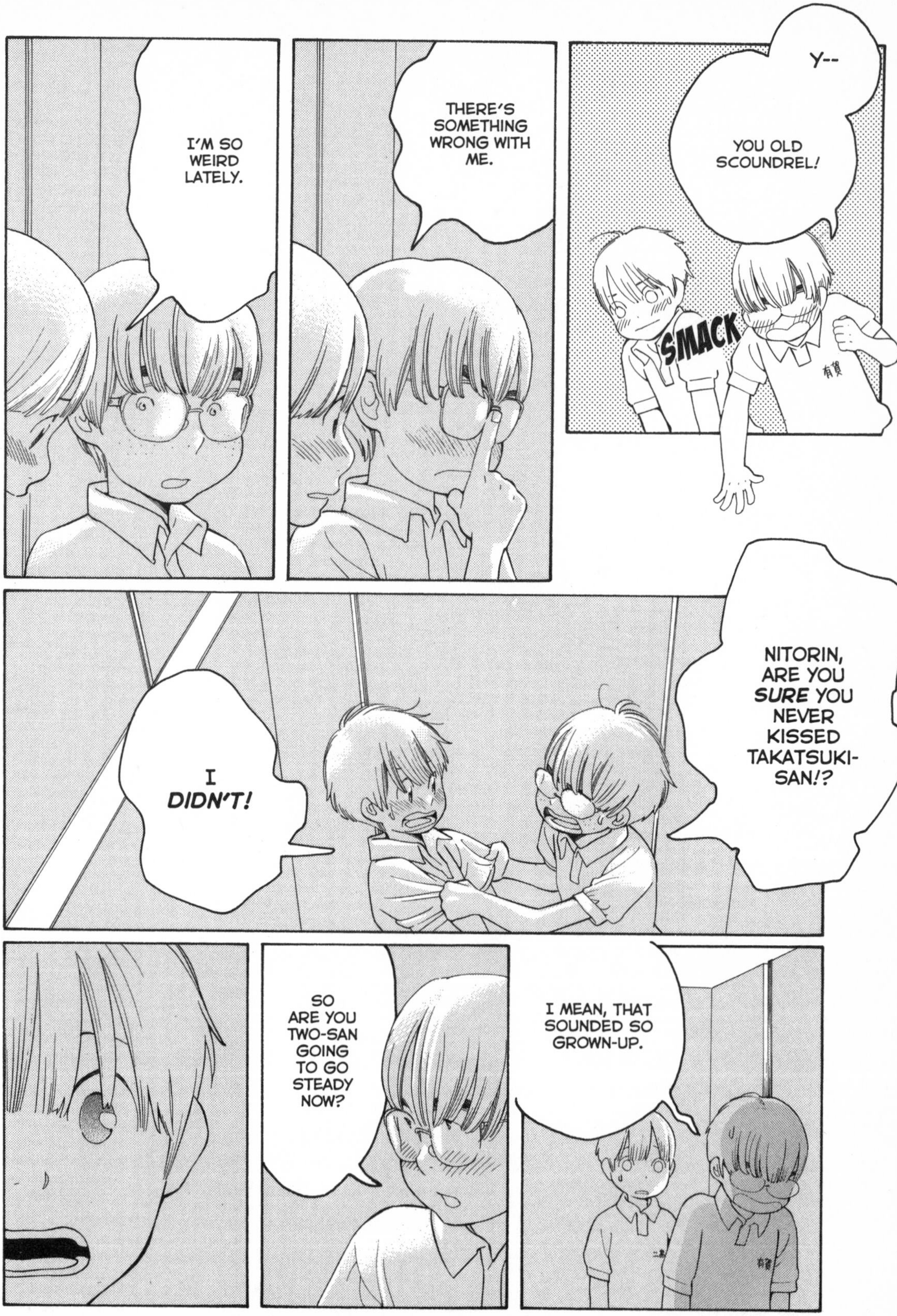
Y--
YOU OLD SCOUNDREL!
SMACK
THERE'S SOMETHING WRONG WITH ME.
I'M SO WEIRD LATELY.
NITORIN, ARE YOU *SURE* YOU NEVER KISSED TAKATSUKI-SAN!?
I *DIDN'T!*
I MEAN, THAT SOUNDED SO GROWN-UP.
SO ARE YOU TWO-SAN GOING TO GO STEADY NOW?

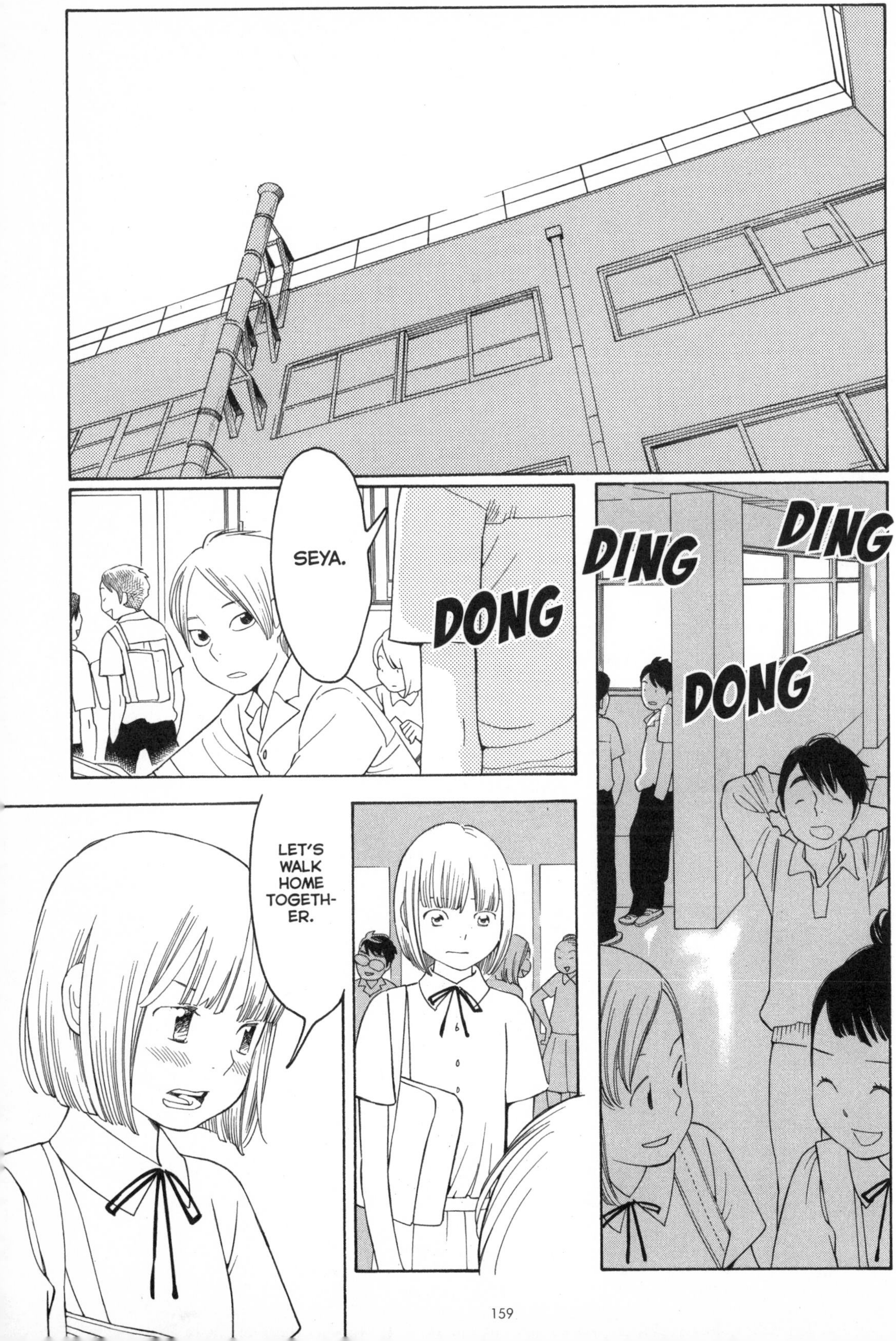
DING
DING
DONG
DONG
SEYA.
LET'S WALK HOME TOGETH-ER.

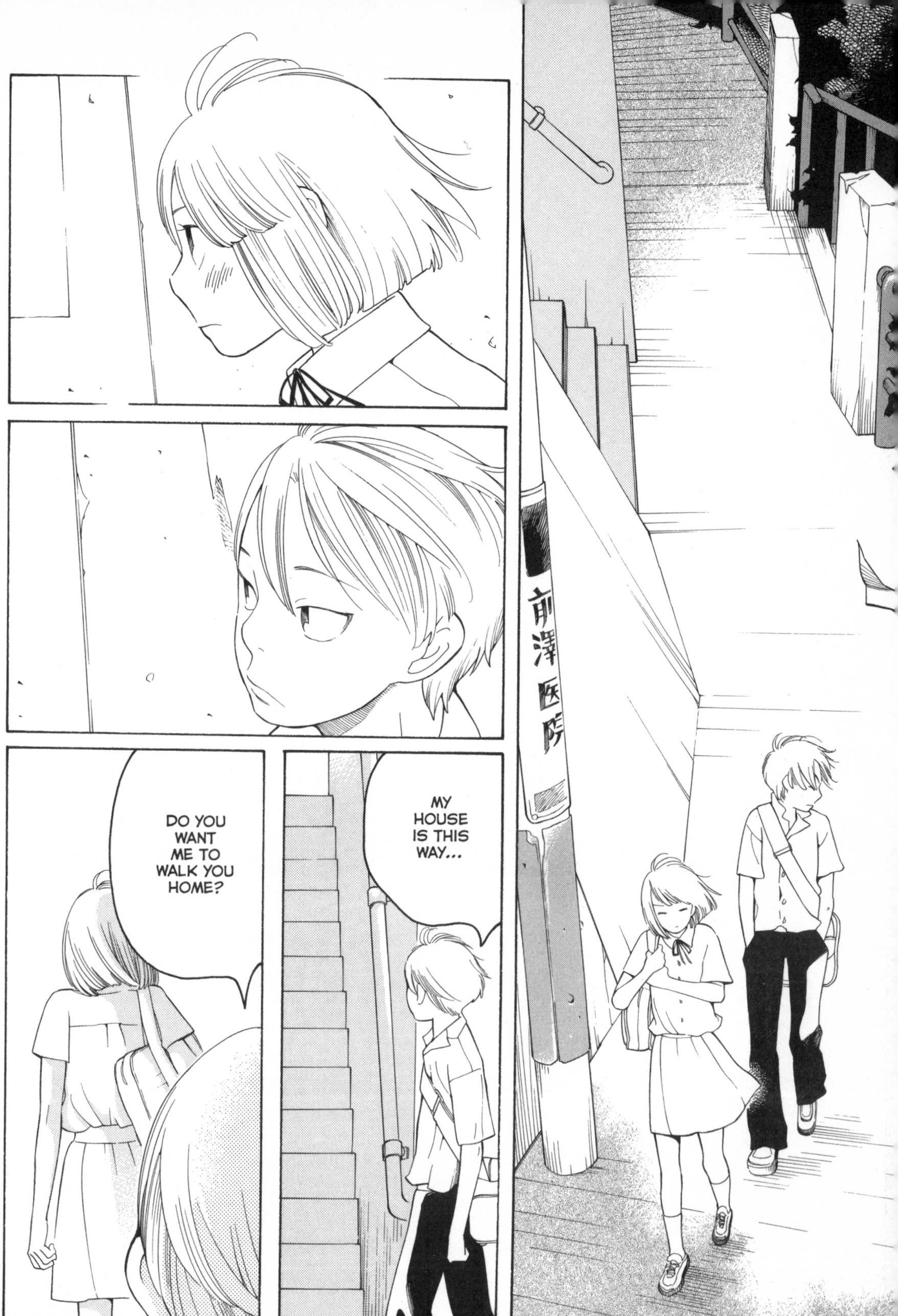
前澤医院
MY HOUSE IS THIS WAY...
DO YOU WANT ME TO WALK YOU HOME?

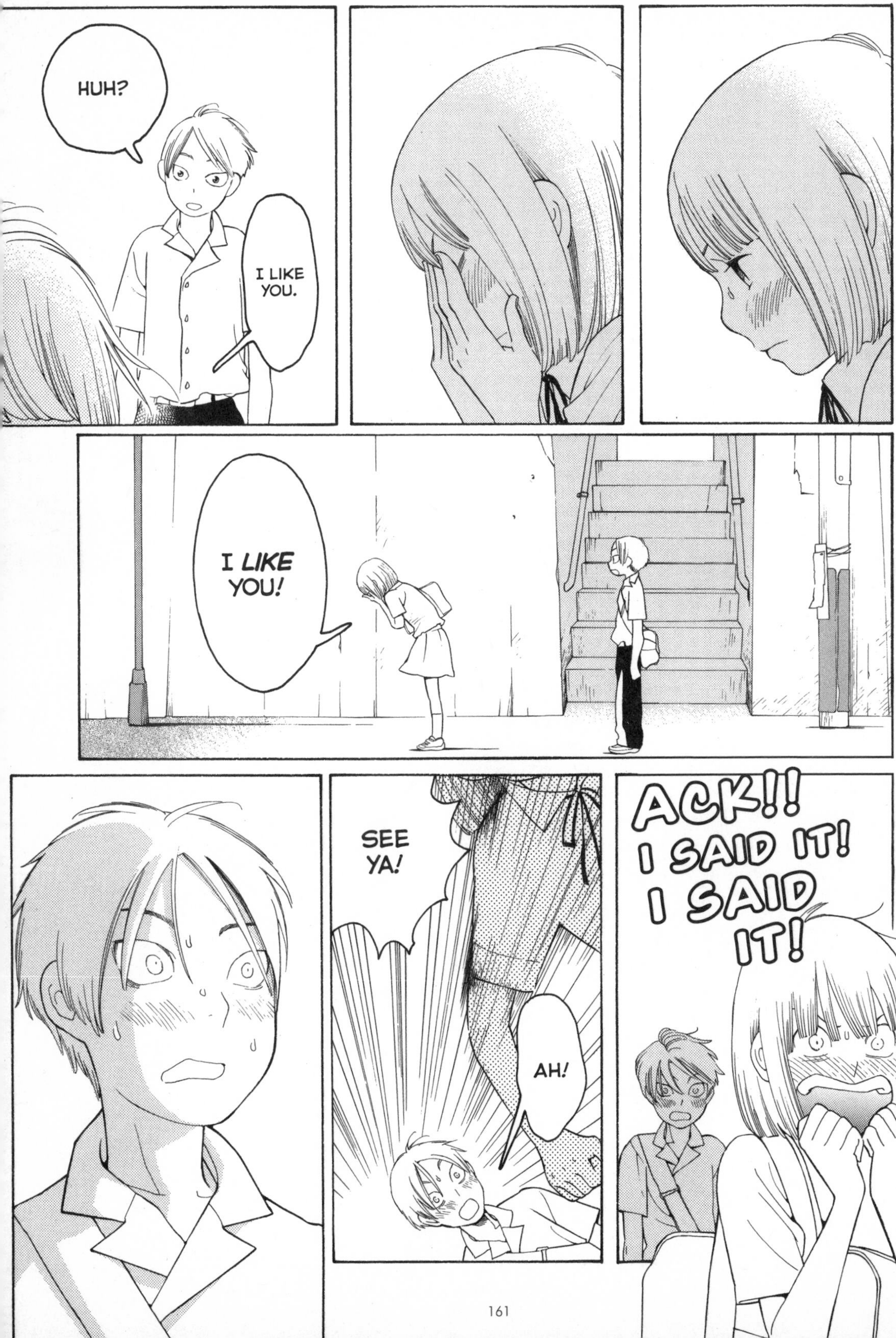
I LIKE YOU.
HUH?
I *LIKE* YOU!
ACK!! I SAID IT! I SAID IT!
SEE YA!
AH!

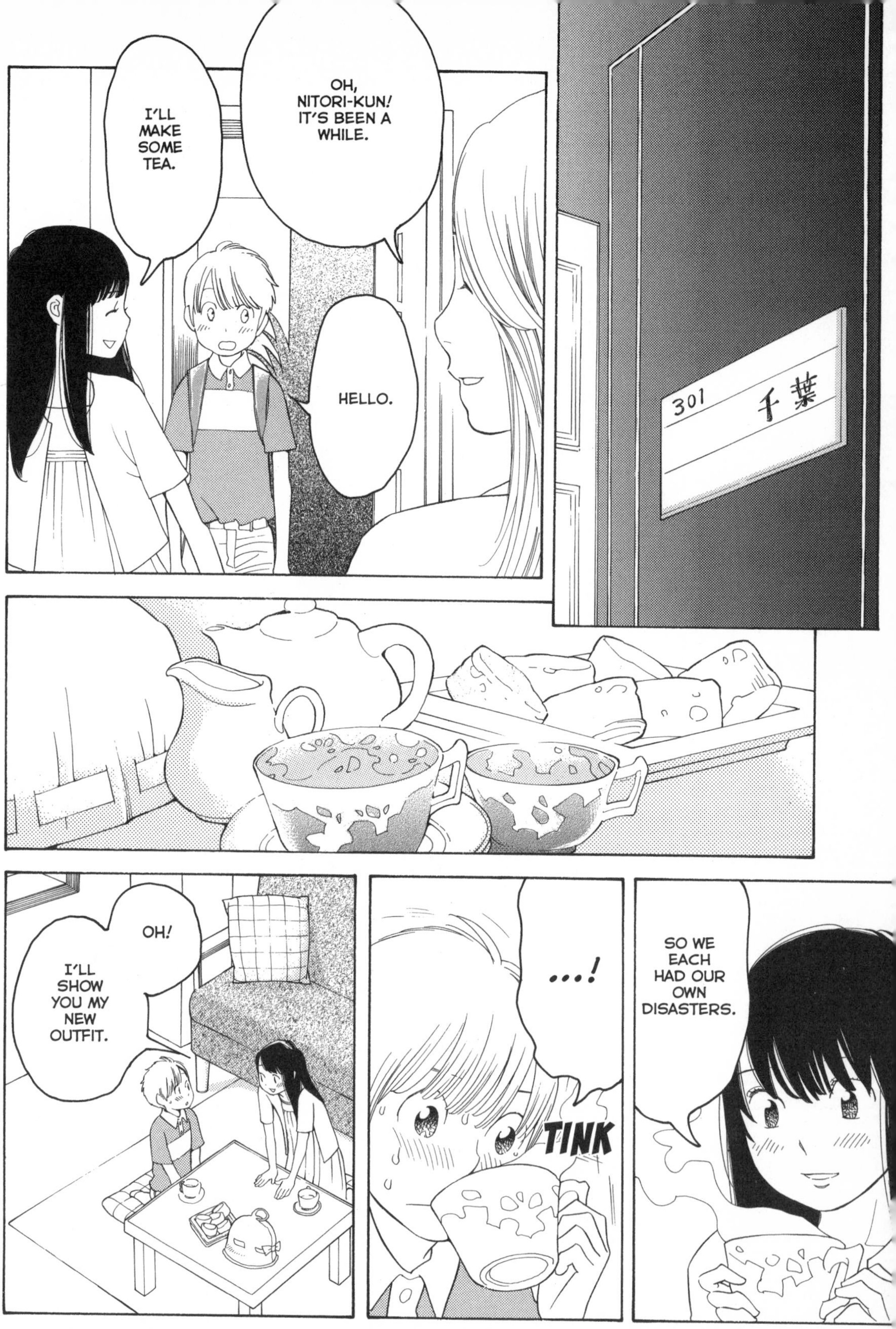
301 千葉
OH, NITORI-KUN! IT'S BEEN A WHILE.
HELLO.
I'LL MAKE SOME TEA.
SO WE EACH HAD OUR OWN DISASTERS.
...!
TINK
OH!
I'LL SHOW YOU MY NEW OUTFIT.

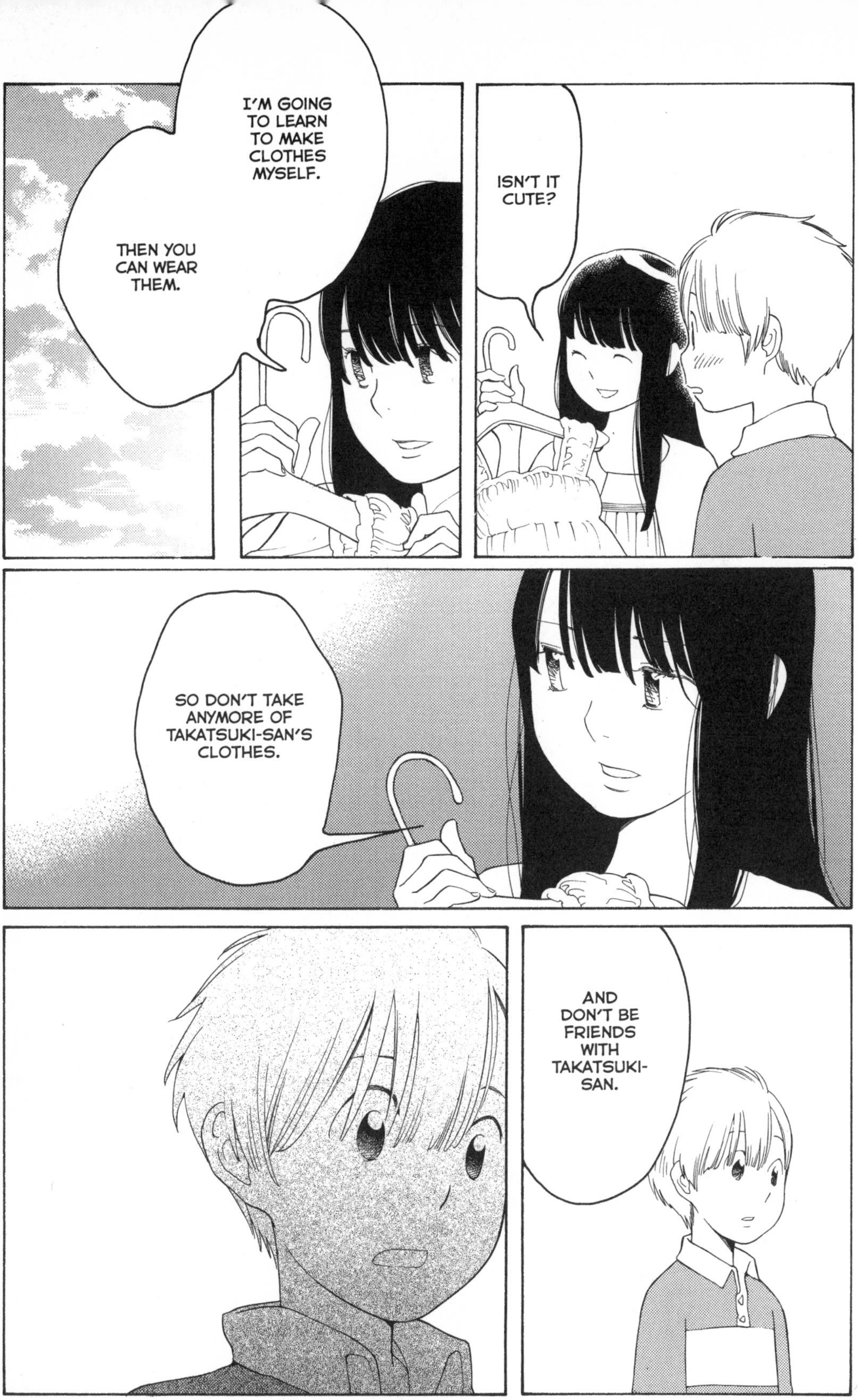
ISN'T IT CUTE?
I'M GOING TO LEARN TO MAKE CLOTHES MYSELF.
THEN YOU CAN WEAR THEM.
SO DON'T TAKE ANYMORE OF TAKATSUKI-SAN'S CLOTHES.
AND DON'T BE FRIENDS WITH TAKATSUKI-SAN.

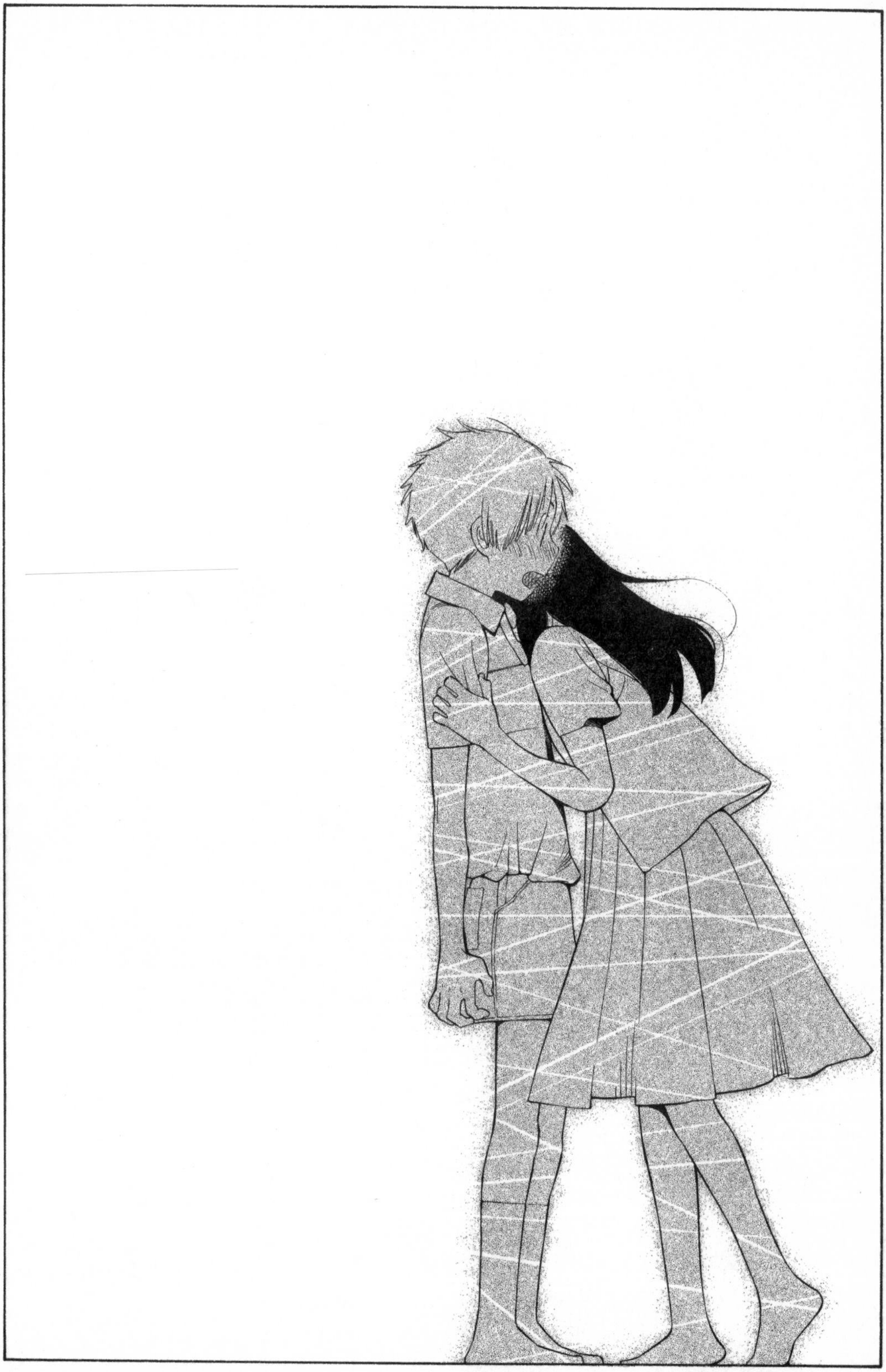

32

Cracks Reappear

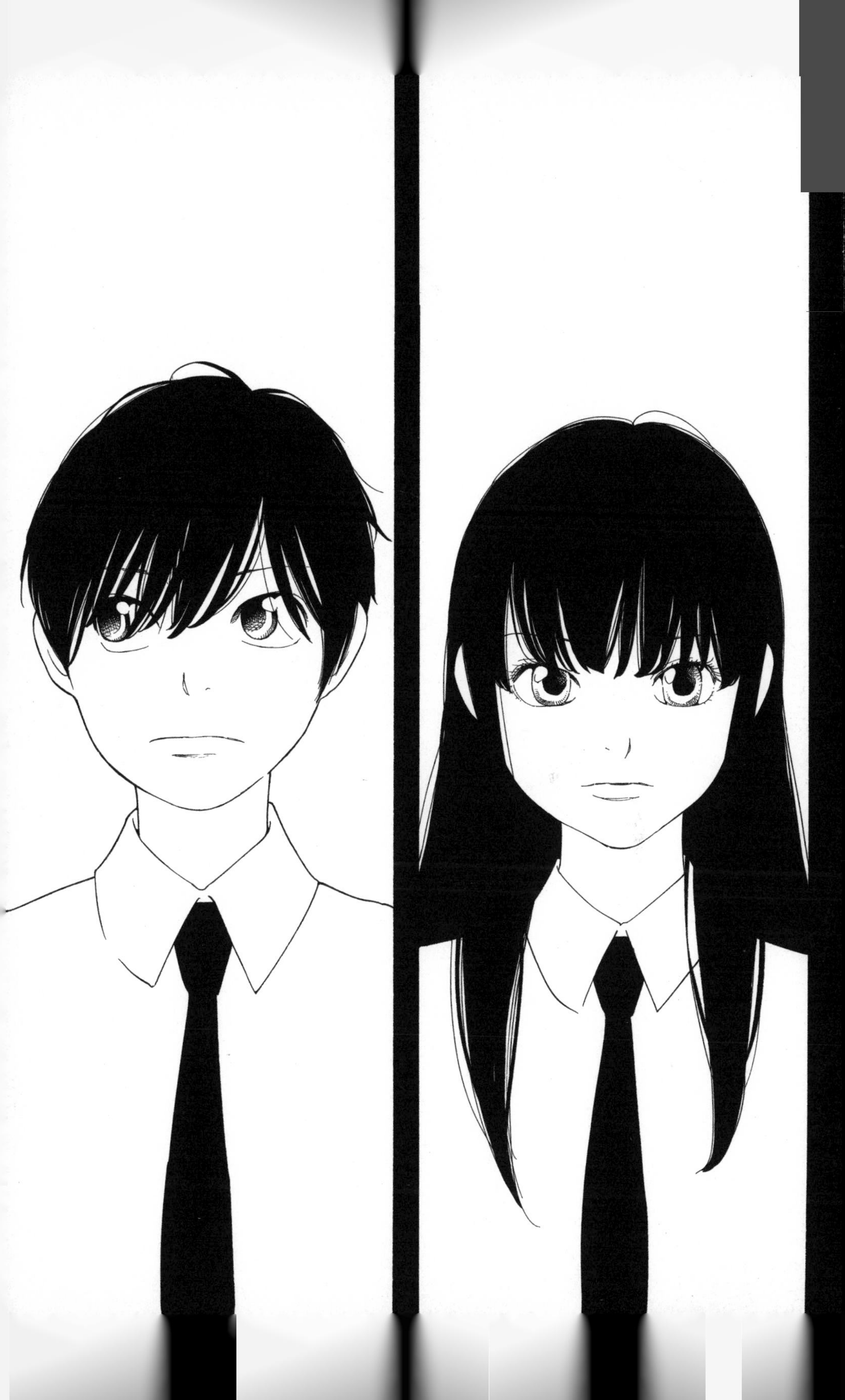

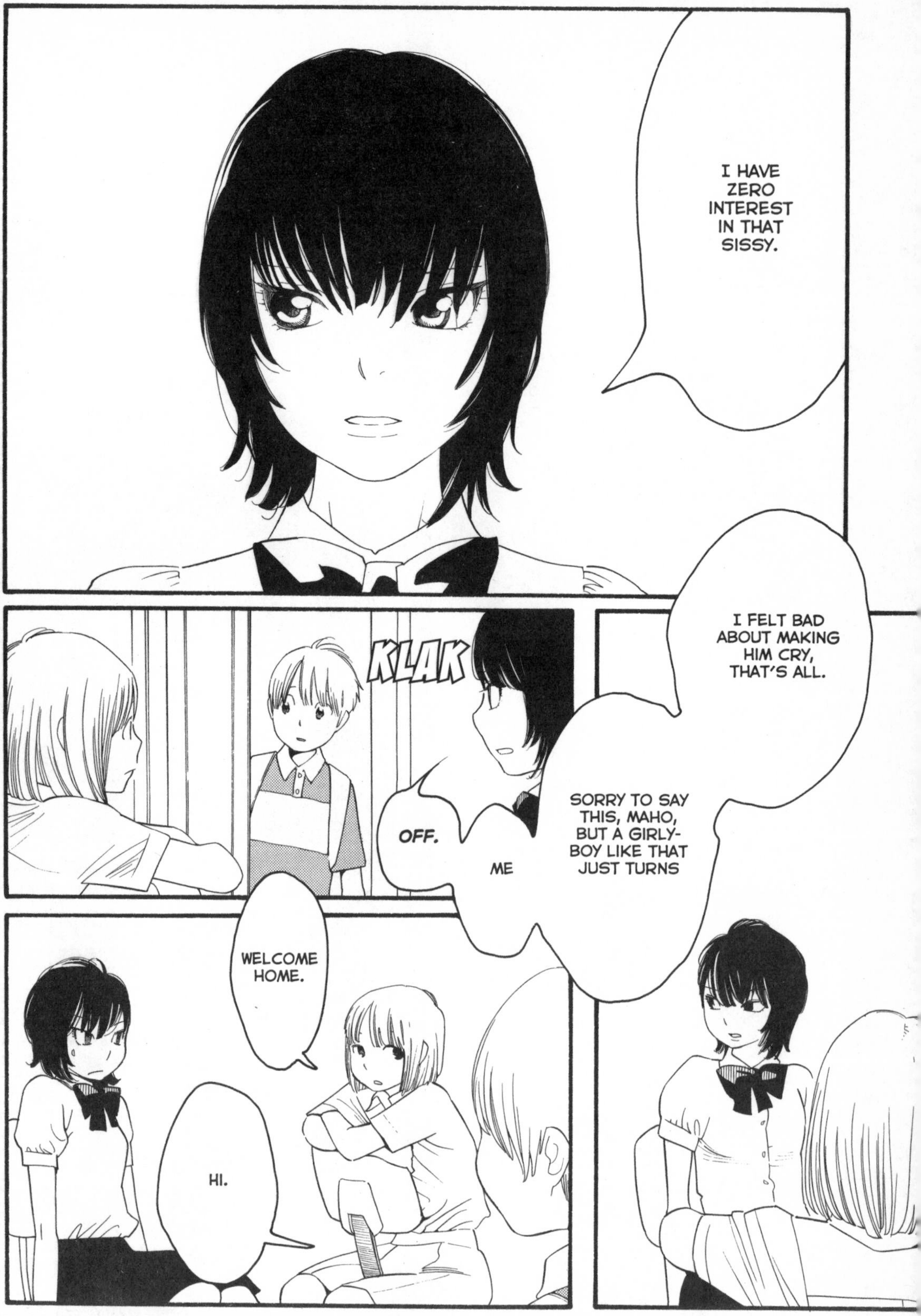
I HAVE ZERO INTEREST IN THAT SISSY.
I FELT BAD ABOUT MAKING HIM CRY, THAT'S ALL.
SORRY TO SAY THIS, MAHO, BUT A GIRLY-BOY LIKE THAT JUST TURNS
ME
OFF.
KLAK
WELCOME HOME.
HI.

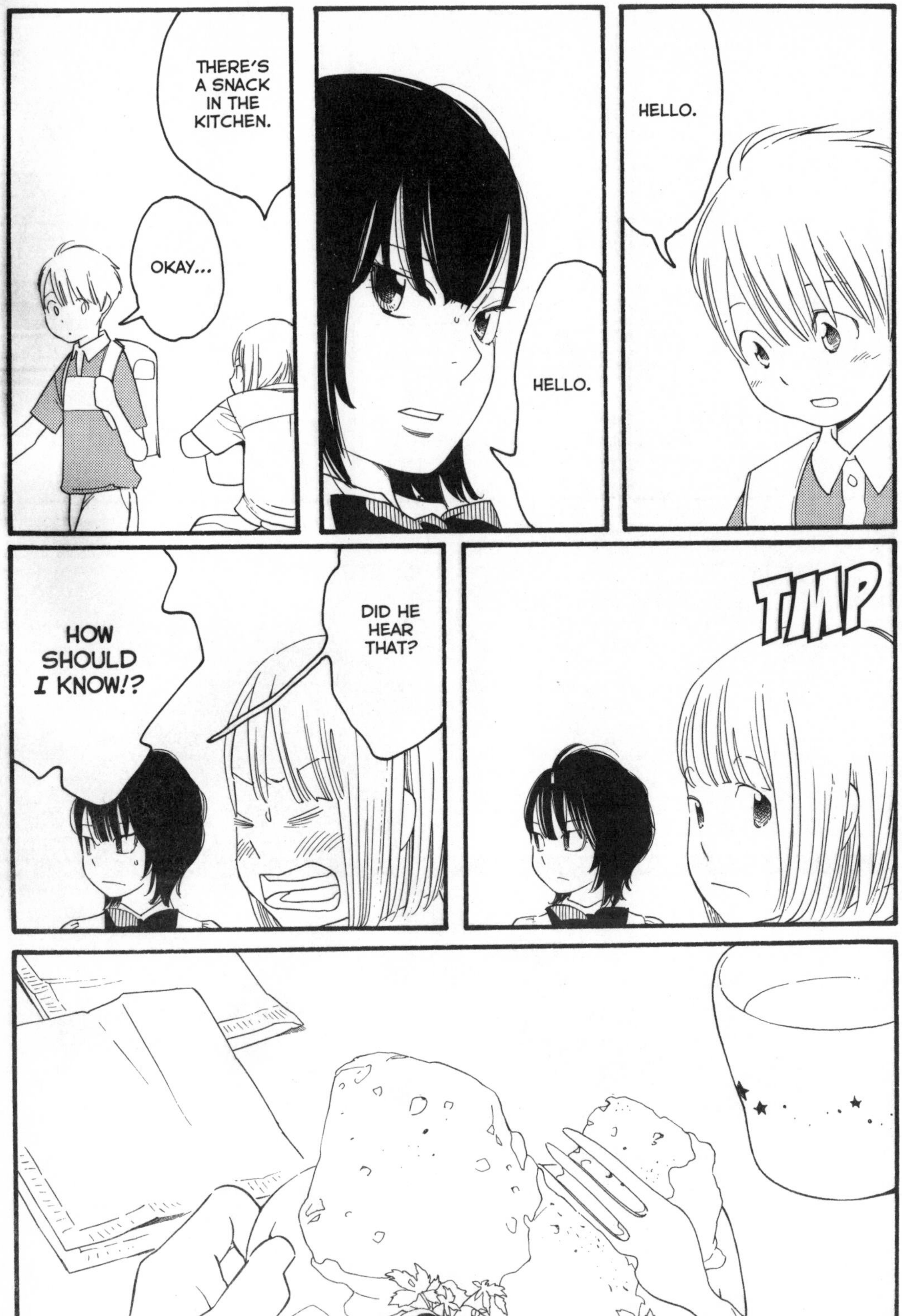
HELLO.
HELLO.
THERE'S A SNACK IN THE KITCHEN.
OKAY...
TMP
DID HE HEAR THAT?
HOW SHOULD I KNOW!?

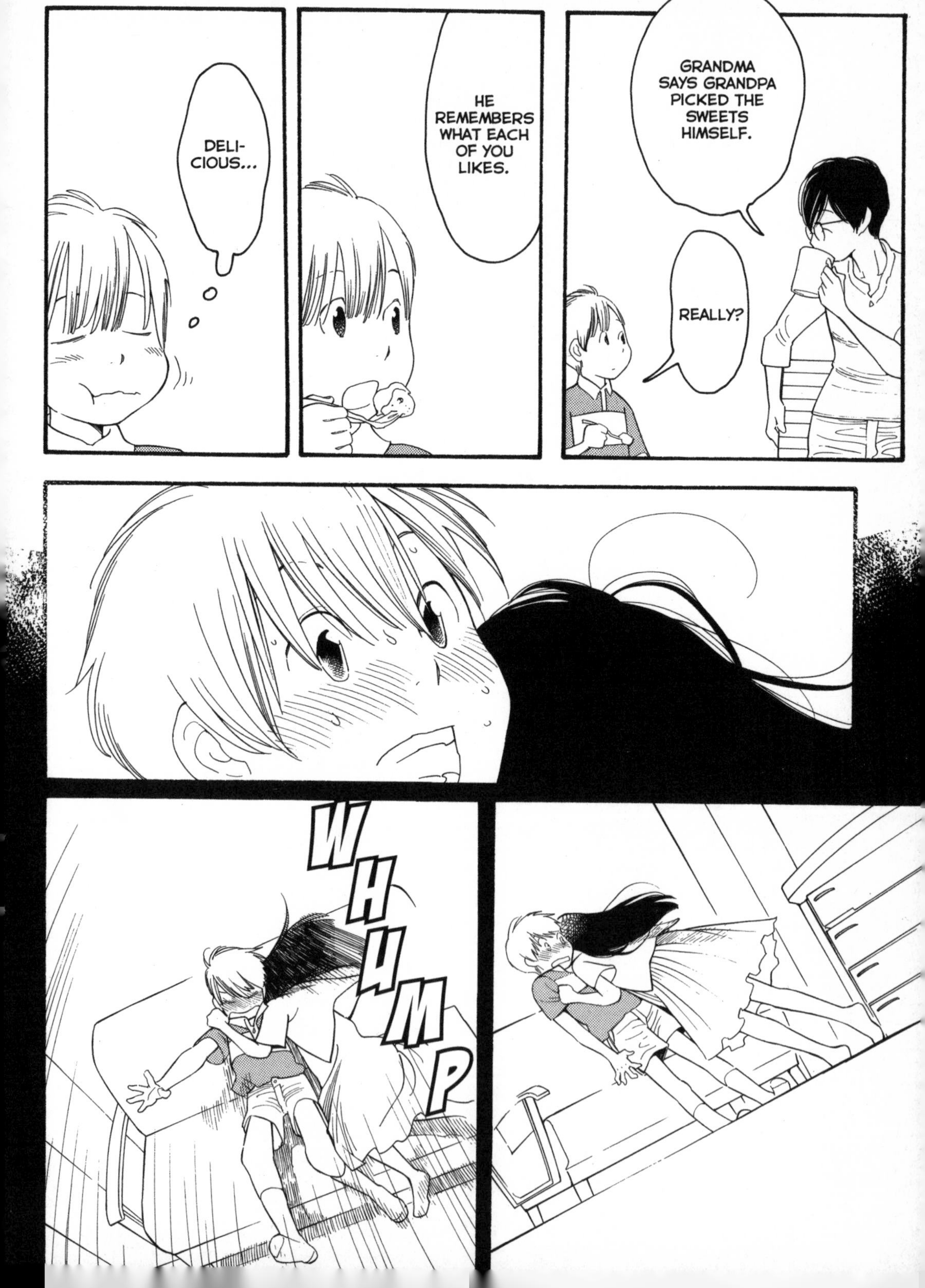
GRANDMA SAYS GRANDPA PICKED THE SWEETS HIMSELF.
REALLY?
HE REMEMBERS WHAT EACH OF YOU LIKES.
DELI-CIOUS...
WHUMP

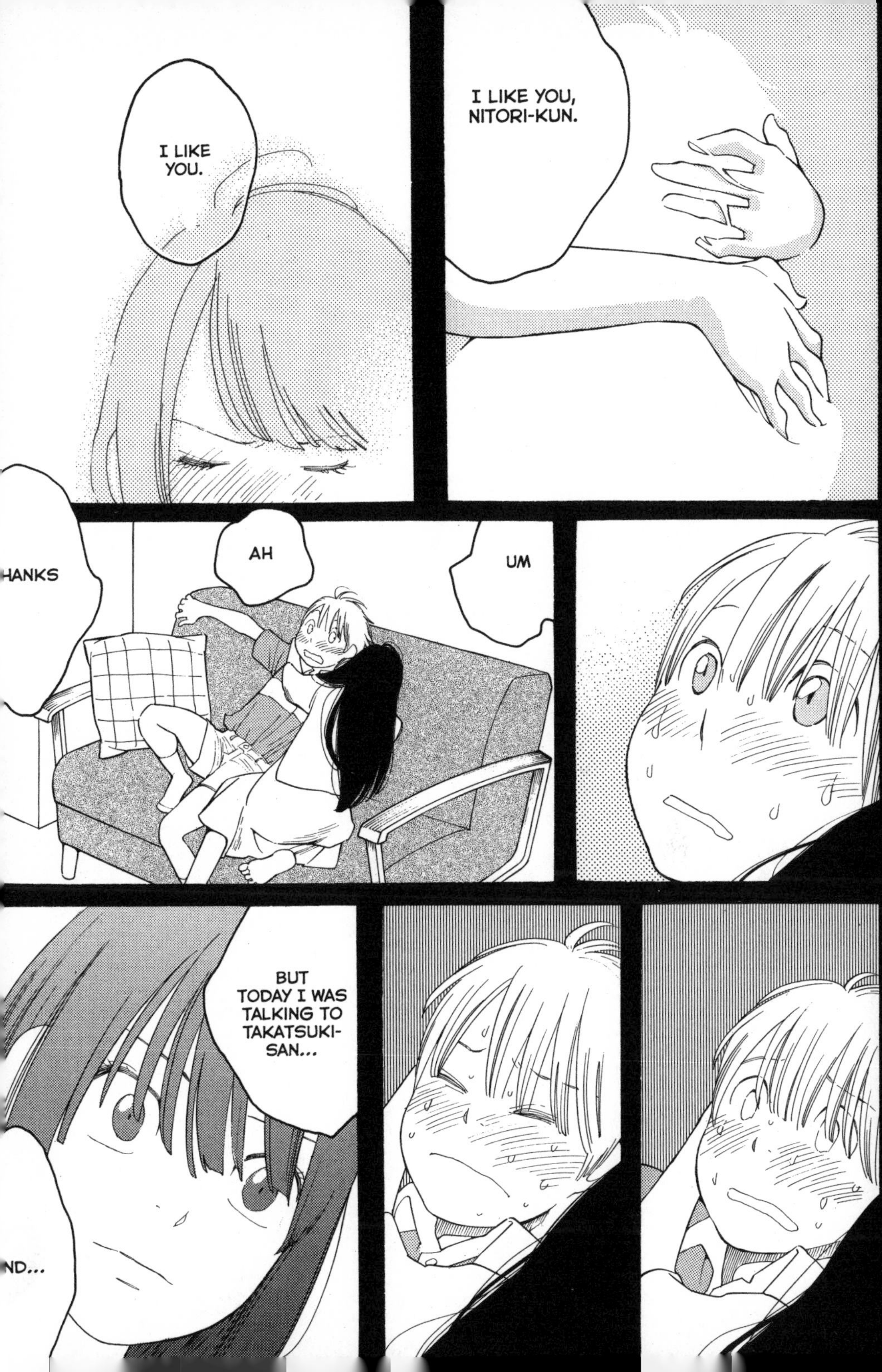
I LIKE YOU, NITORI-KUN.
I LIKE YOU.
UM
AH
HANKS
BUT TODAY I WAS TALKING TO TAKATSUKI-SAN...
ND...

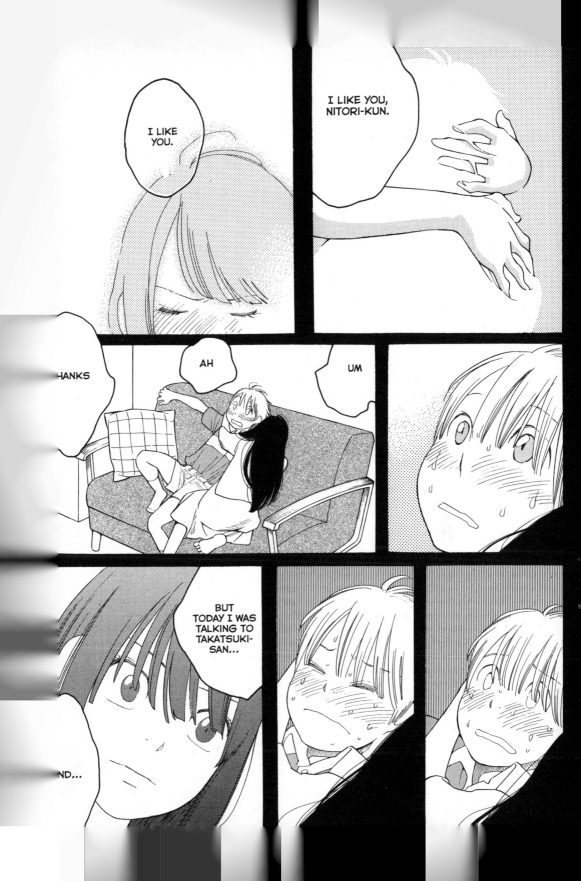

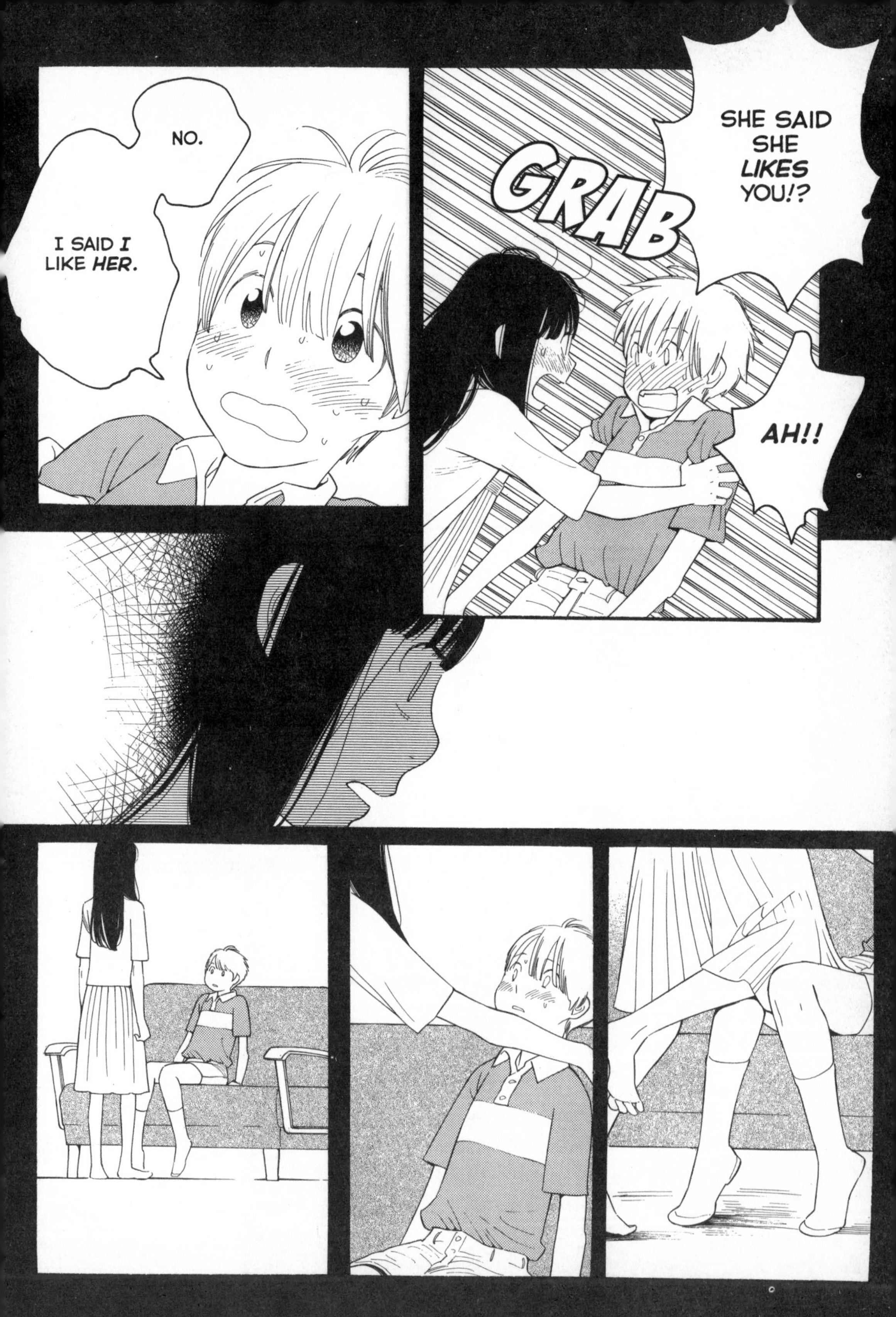
SHE SAID SHE LIKES YOU!?
GRAB
AH!!
NO.
I SAID I LIKE HER.

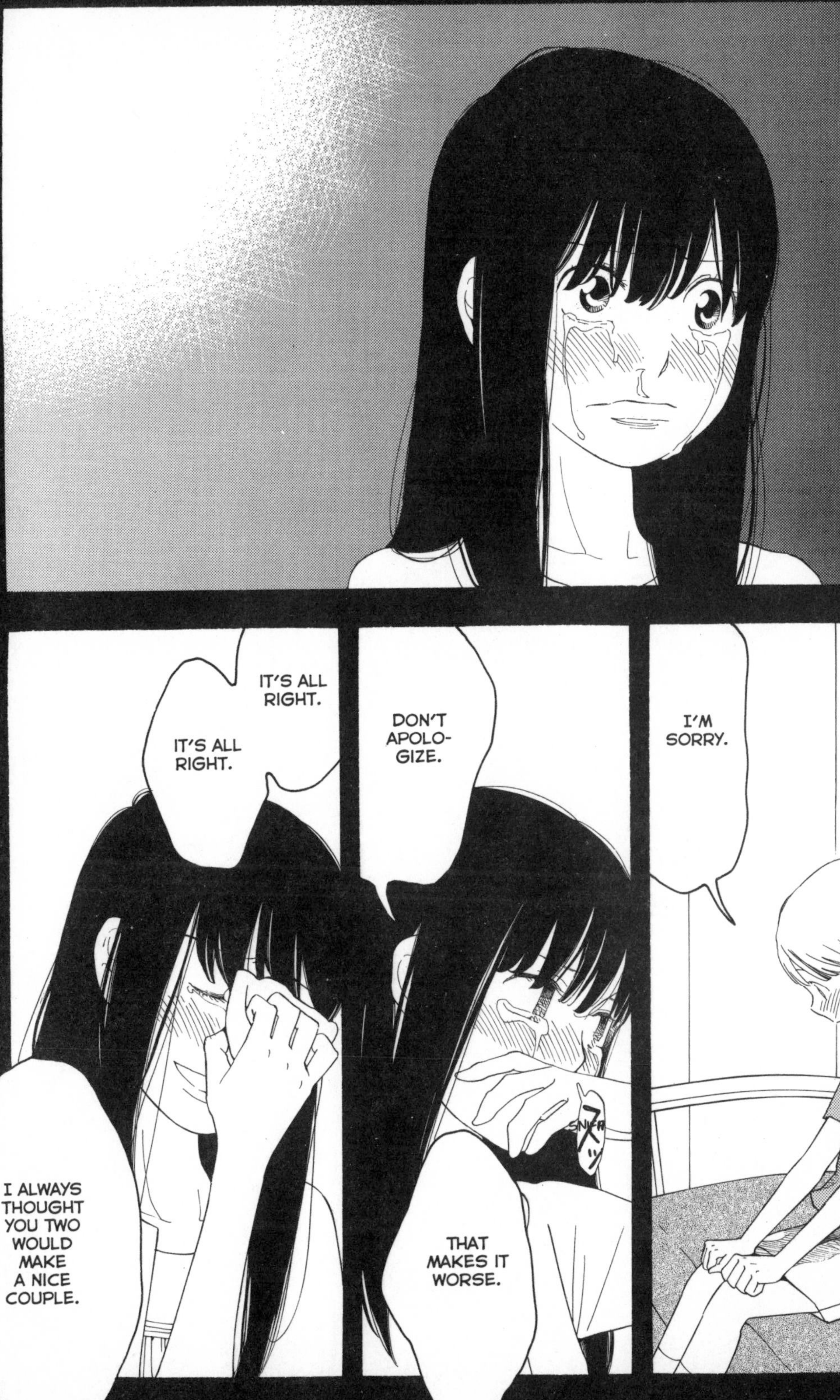
I'M SORRY.
DON'T APOLOGIZE.
SNIFF
THAT MAKES IT WORSE.
IT'S ALL RIGHT.
IT'S ALL RIGHT.
I ALWAYS THOUGHT YOU TWO WOULD MAKE A NICE COUPLE.

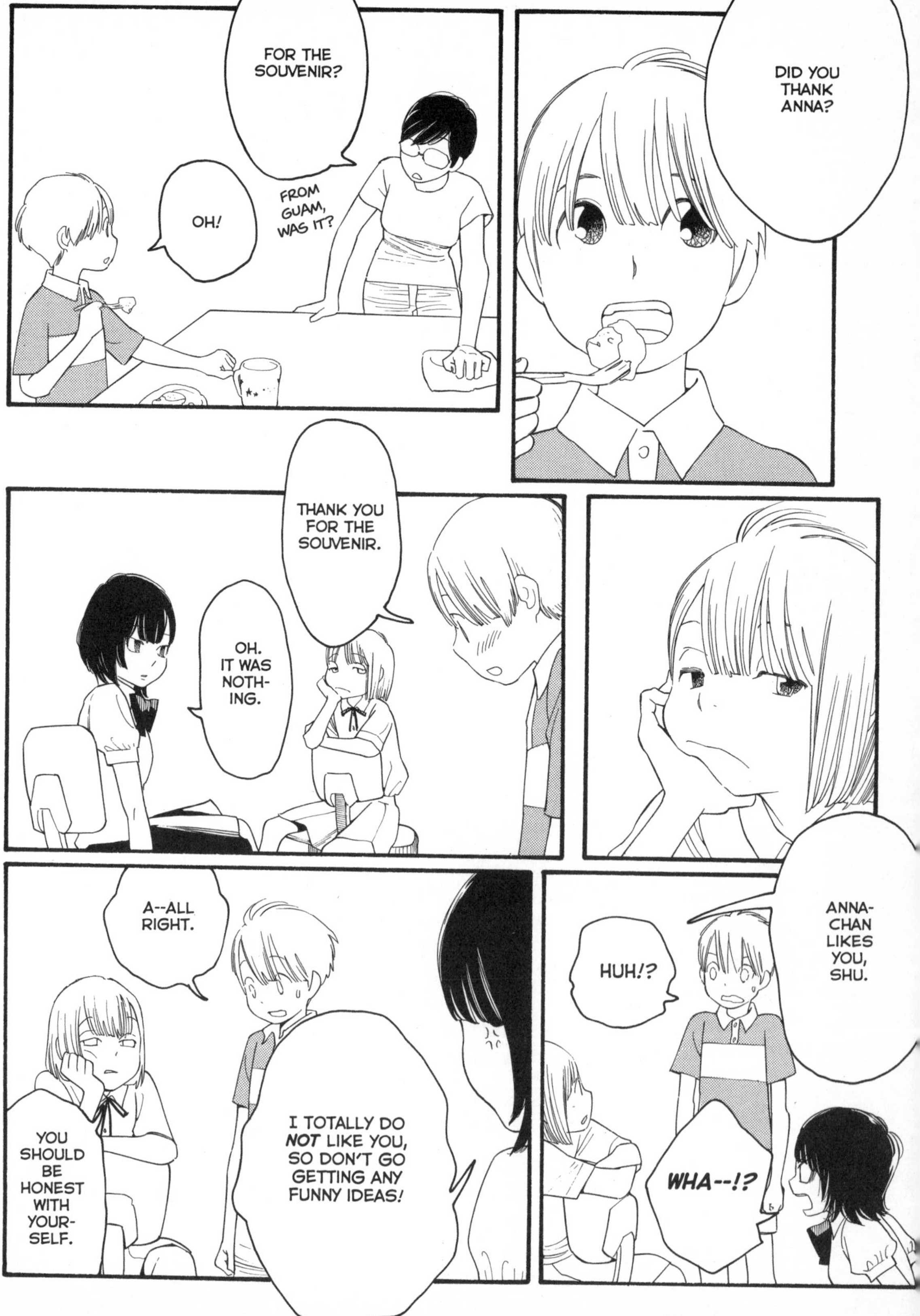
DID YOU THANK ANNA?
FOR THE SOUVENIR?
FROM GUAM, WAS IT?
OH!
THANK YOU FOR THE SOUVENIR.
OH. IT WAS NOTHING.
ANNA-CHAN LIKES YOU, SHU.
HUH!?
WHA--!?
I TOTALLY DO *NOT* LIKE YOU, SO DON'T GO GETTING ANY FUNNY IDEAS!
A--ALL RIGHT.
YOU SHOULD BE HONEST WITH YOURSELF.

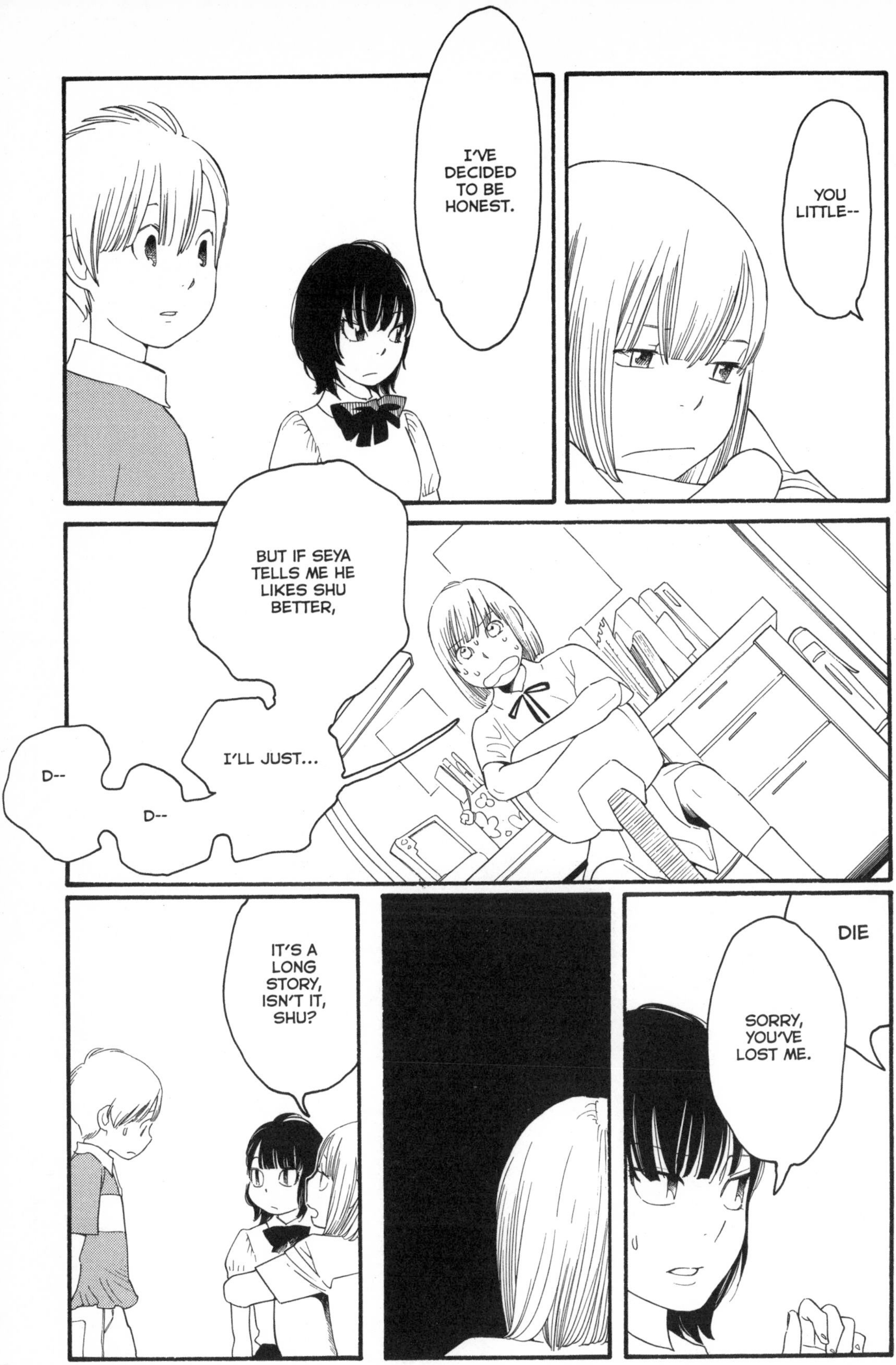
YOU LITTLE--
I'VE DECIDED TO BE HONEST.
BUT IF SEYA TELLS ME HE LIKES SHU BETTER,
I'LL JUST...
D--
D--
DIE
SORRY, YOU'VE LOST ME.
IT'S A LONG STORY, ISN'T IT, SHU?

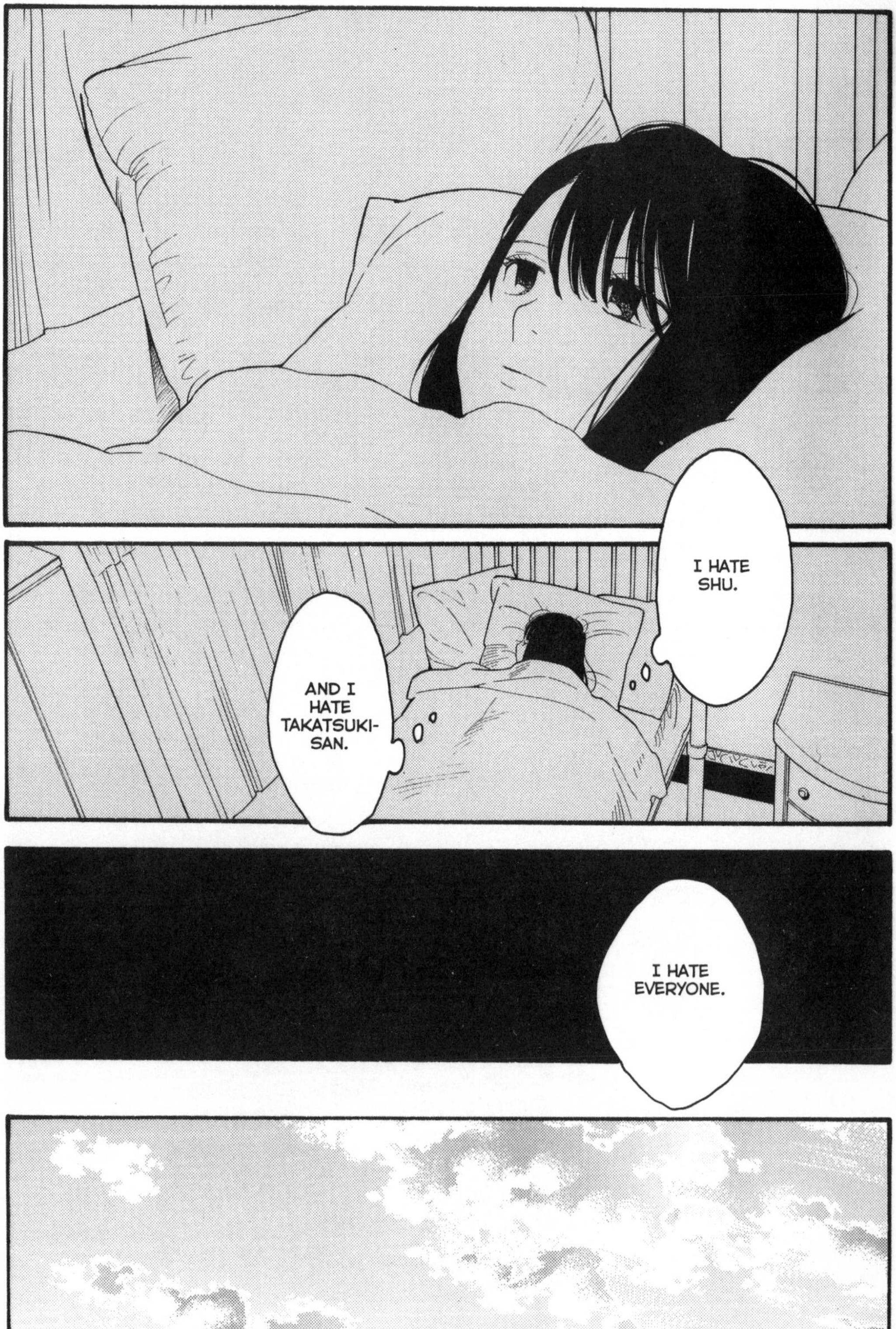
I HATE SHU.
AND I HATE TAKATSUKI-SAN.
I HATE EVERYONE.

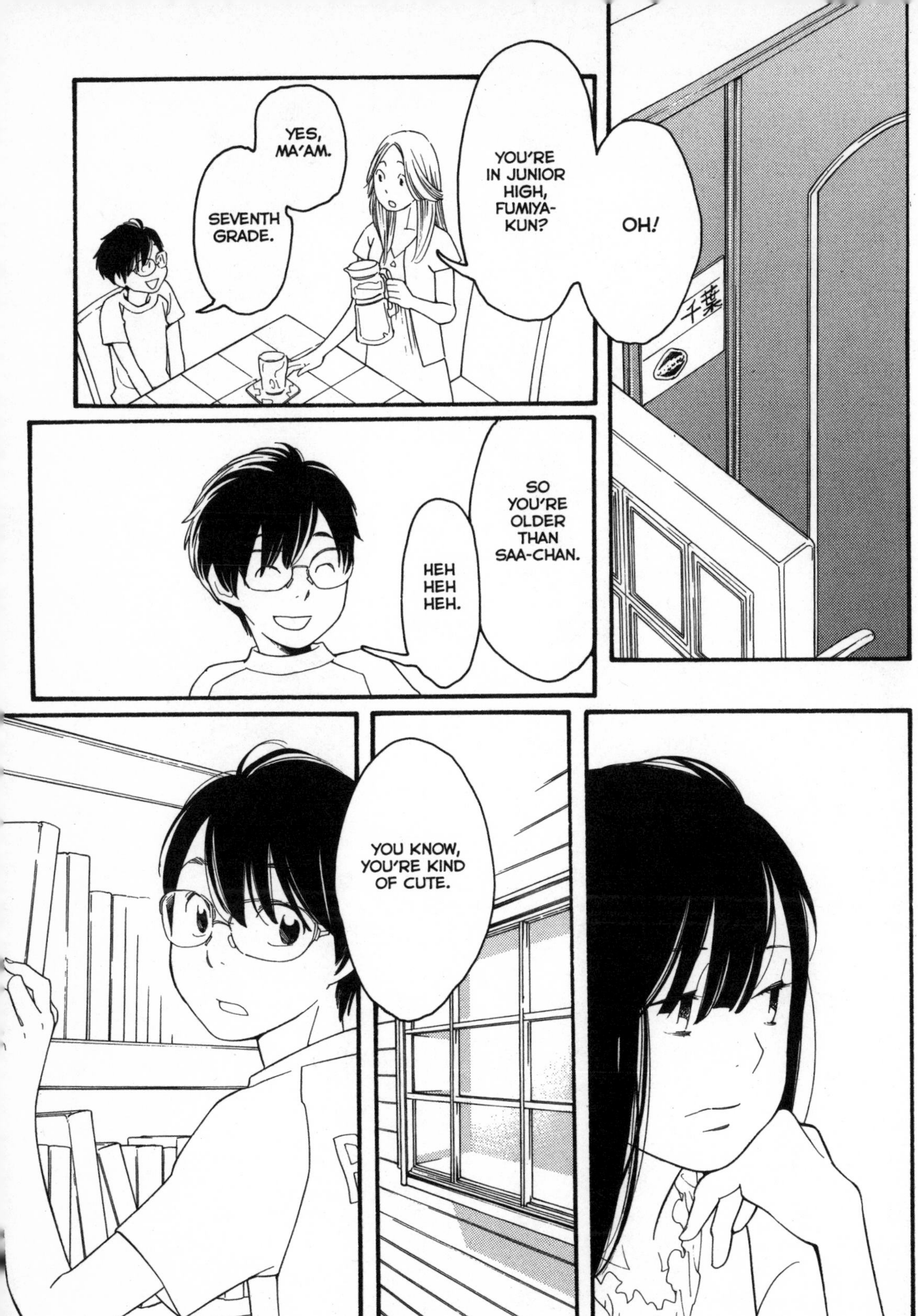
千葉
OH!
YOU'RE IN JUNIOR HIGH, FUMIYA-KUN?
YES, MA'AM.
SEVENTH GRADE.
SO YOU'RE OLDER THAN SAA-CHAN.
HEH HEH HEH.
YOU KNOW, YOU'RE KIND OF CUTE.

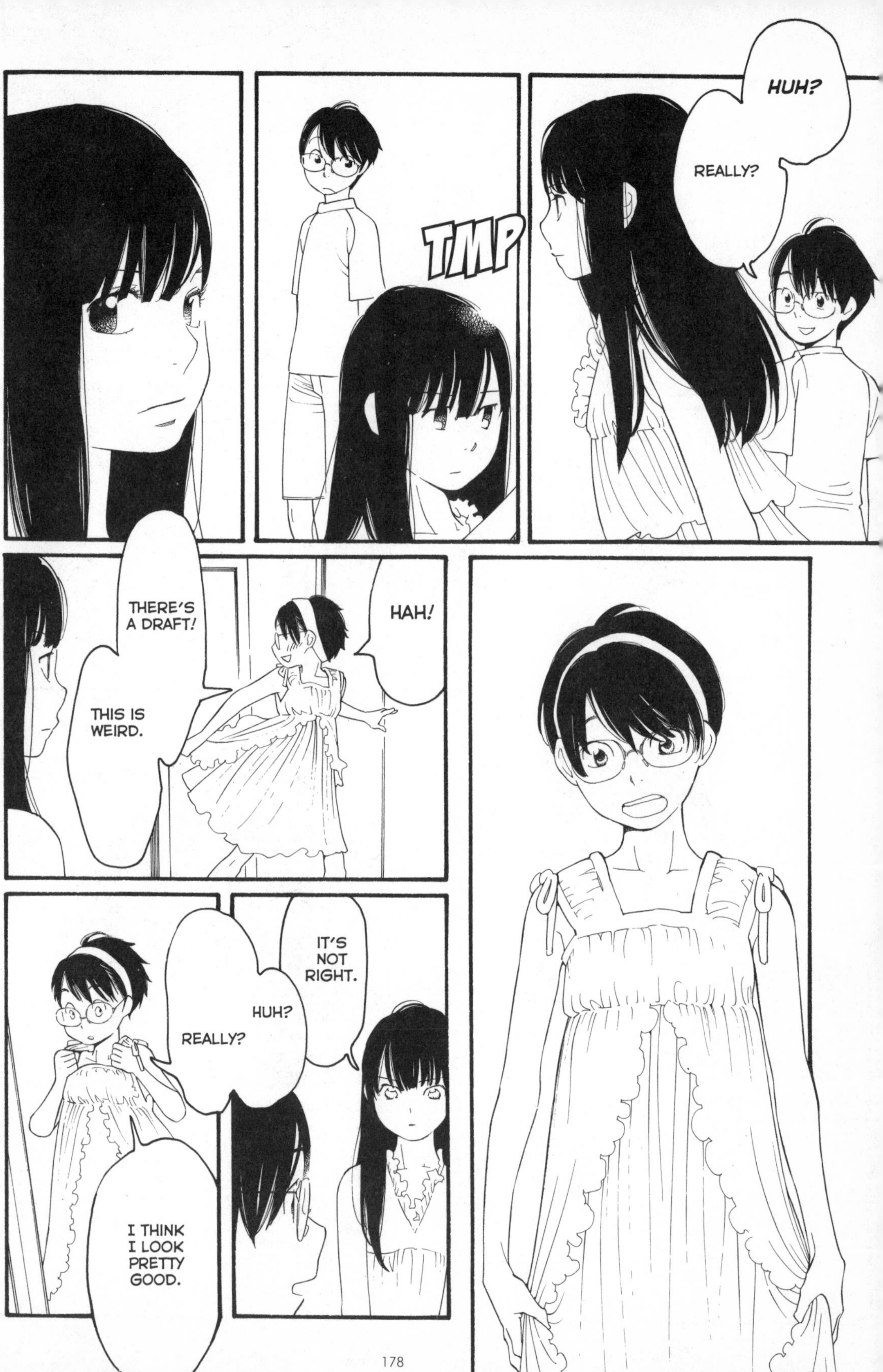
HUH?
REALLY?
TMP
HAH!
THERE'S A DRAFT!
THIS IS WEIRD.
IT'S NOT RIGHT.
HUH?
REALLY?
I THINK I LOOK PRETTY GOOD.

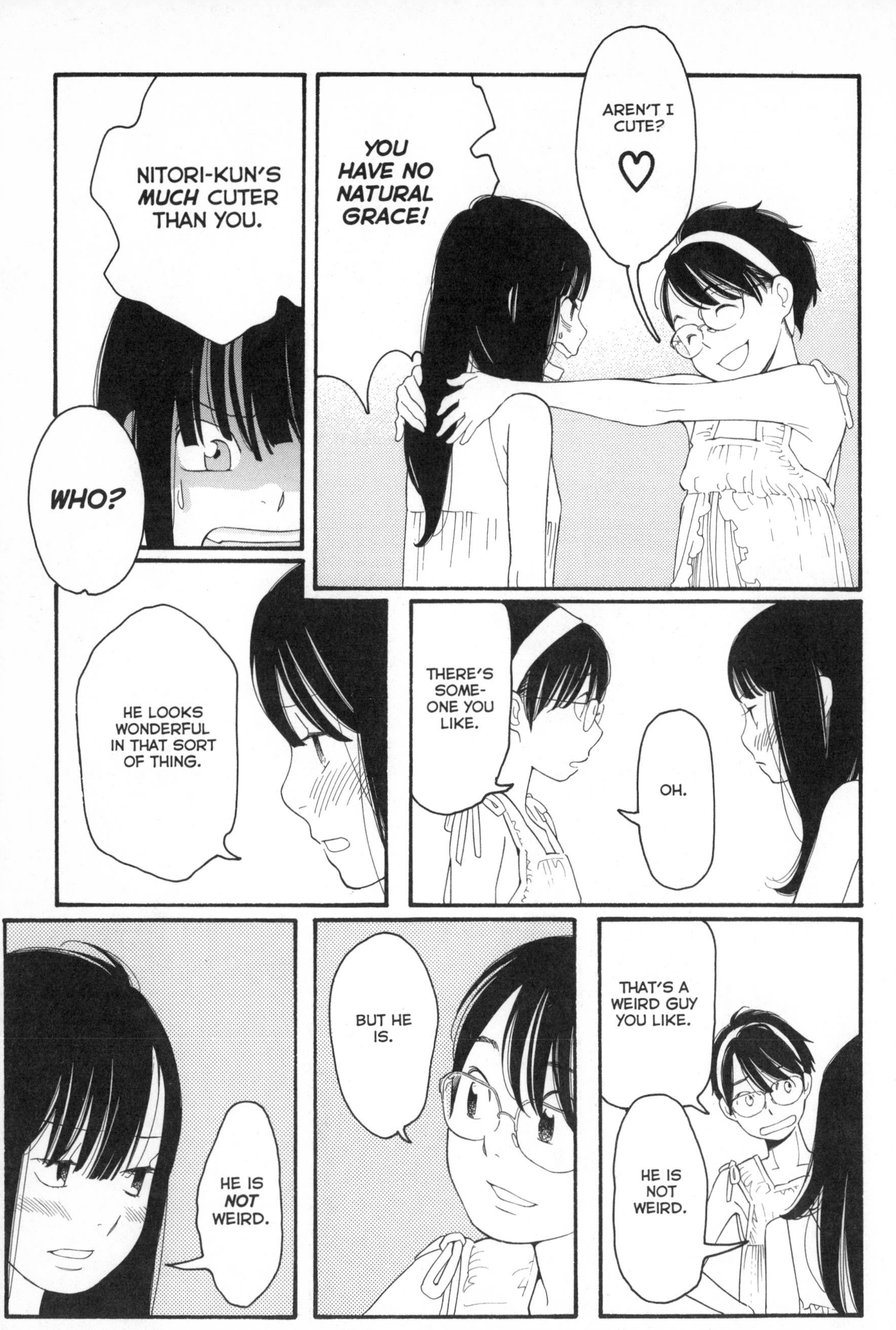
AREN'T I CUTE? ♥
YOU HAVE NO NATURAL GRACE!
NITORI-KUN'S *MUCH* CUTER THAN YOU.
WHO?
OH.
THERE'S SOME-ONE YOU LIKE.
HE LOOKS WONDERFUL IN THAT SORT OF THING.
THAT'S A WEIRD GUY YOU LIKE.
HE IS NOT WEIRD.
BUT HE IS.
HE IS *NOT* WEIRD.

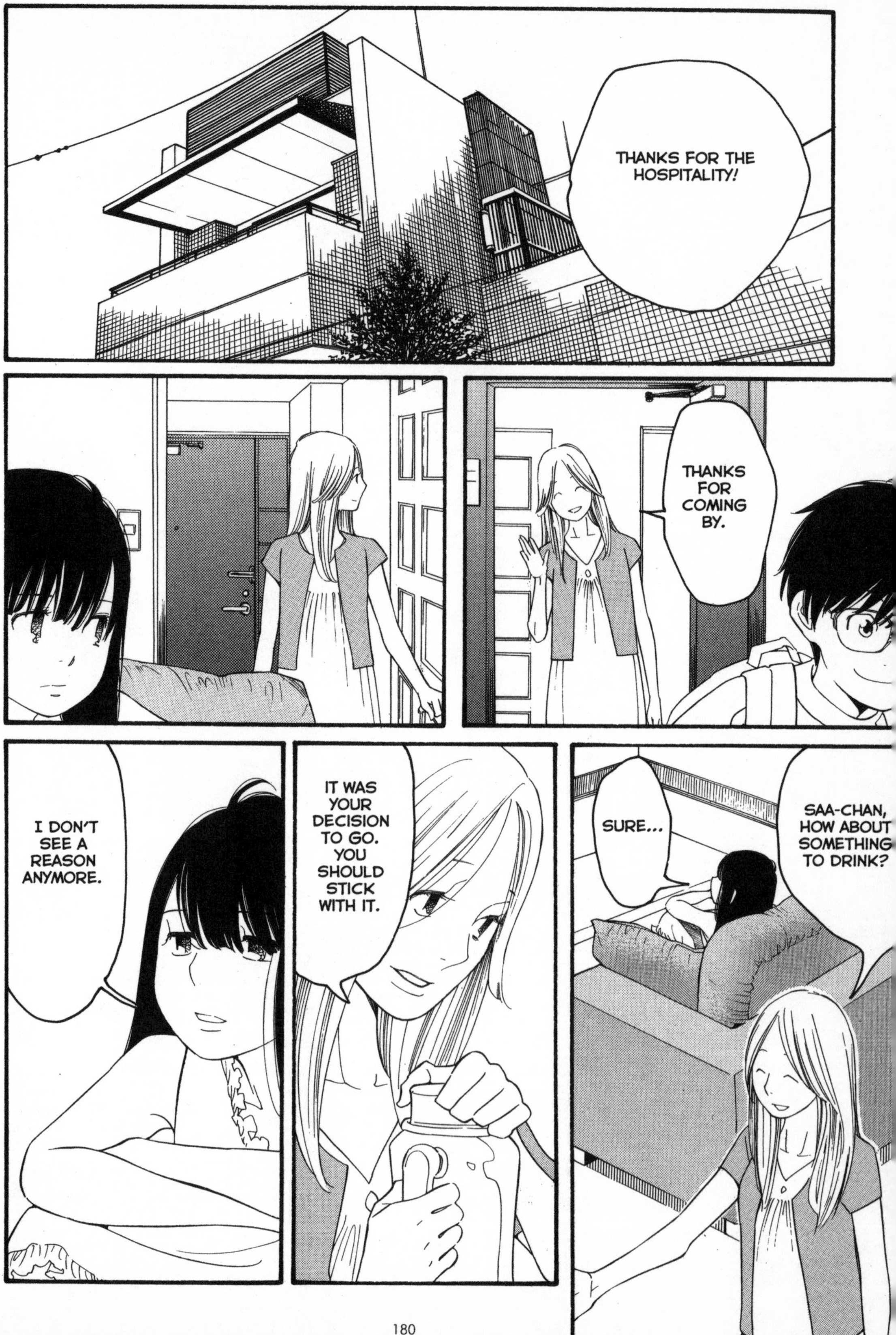
THANKS FOR THE HOSPITALITY!
THANKS FOR COMING BY.
SAA-CHAN, HOW ABOUT SOMETHING TO DRINK?
SURE...
IT WAS YOUR DECISION TO GO. YOU SHOULD STICK WITH IT.
I DON'T SEE A REASON ANYMORE.

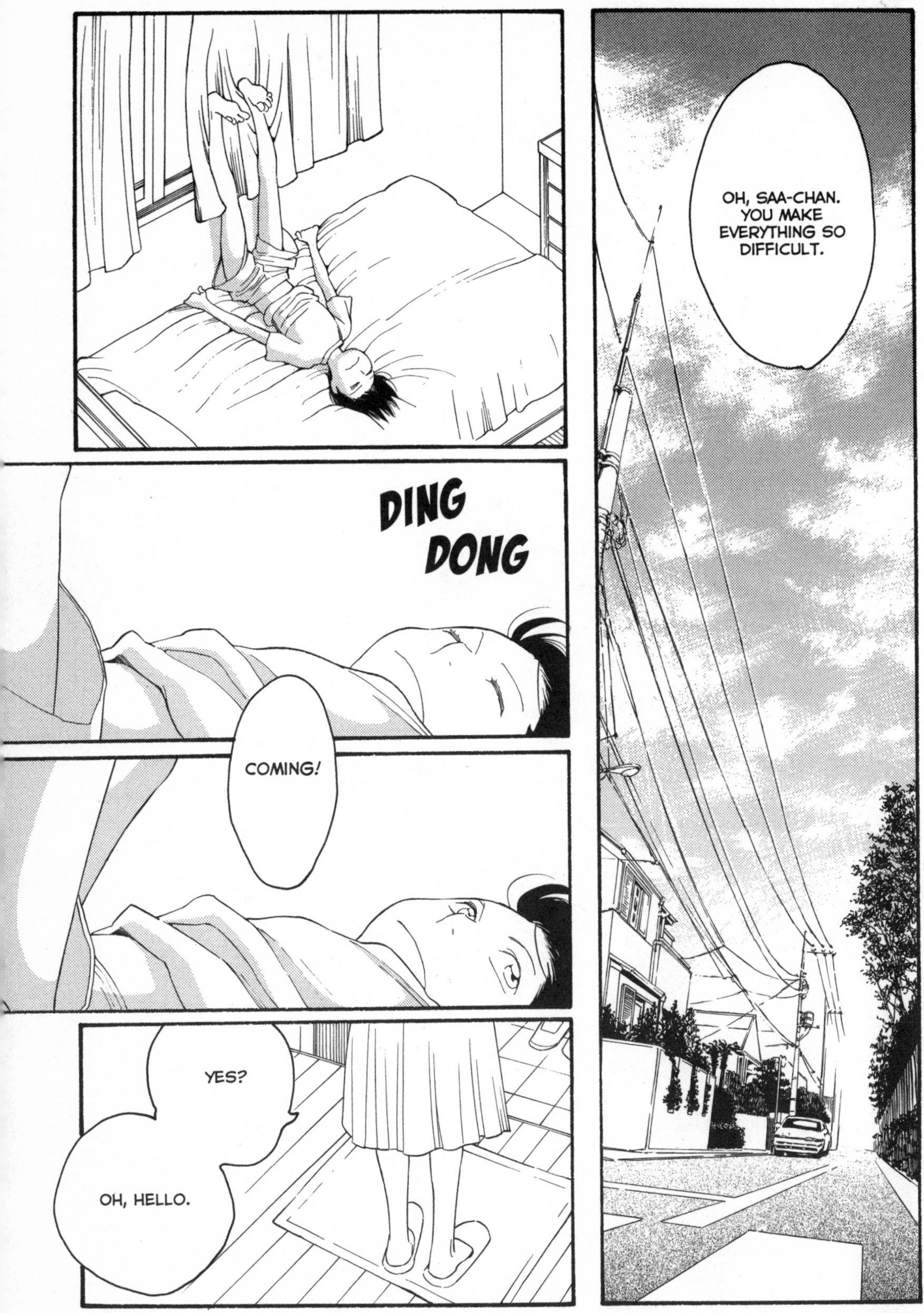
OH, SAA-CHAN. YOU MAKE EVERYTHING SO DIFFICULT.
DING DONG
COMING!
YES?
OH, HELLO.

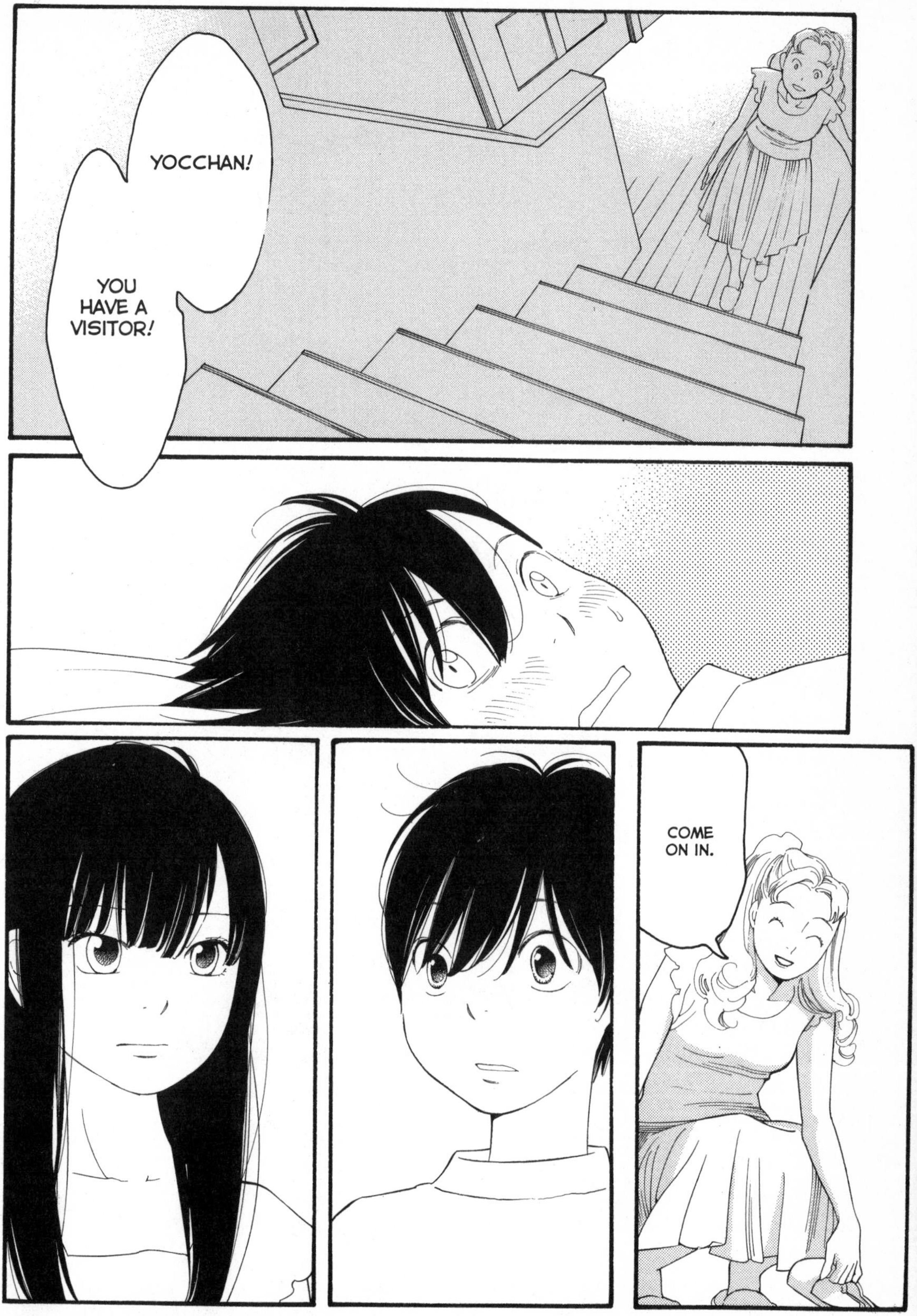
YOCCHAN!
YOU HAVE A VISITOR!
COME ON IN.

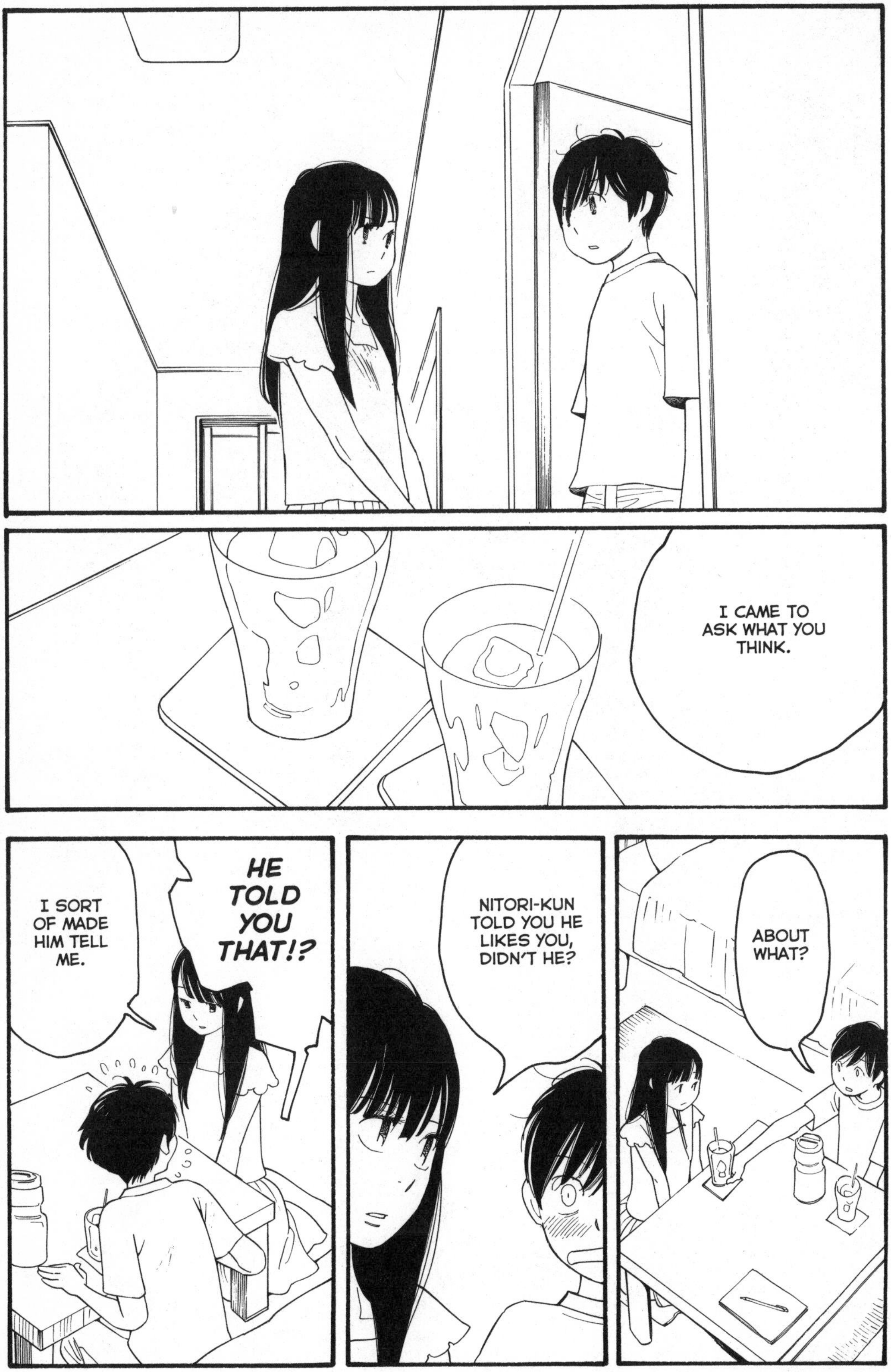
I CAME TO ASK WHAT YOU THINK.
ABOUT WHAT?
NITORI-KUN TOLD YOU HE LIKES YOU, DIDN'T HE?
HE TOLD YOU THAT!?
I SORT OF MADE HIM TELL ME.

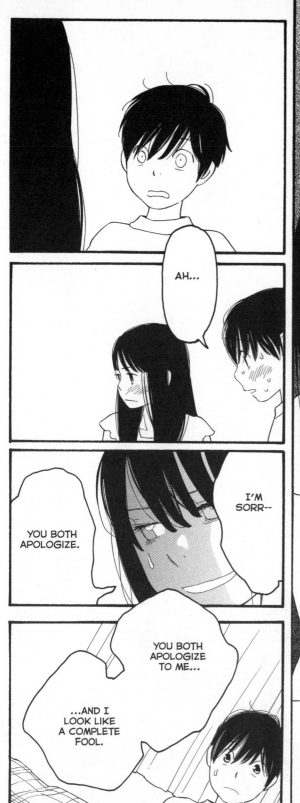

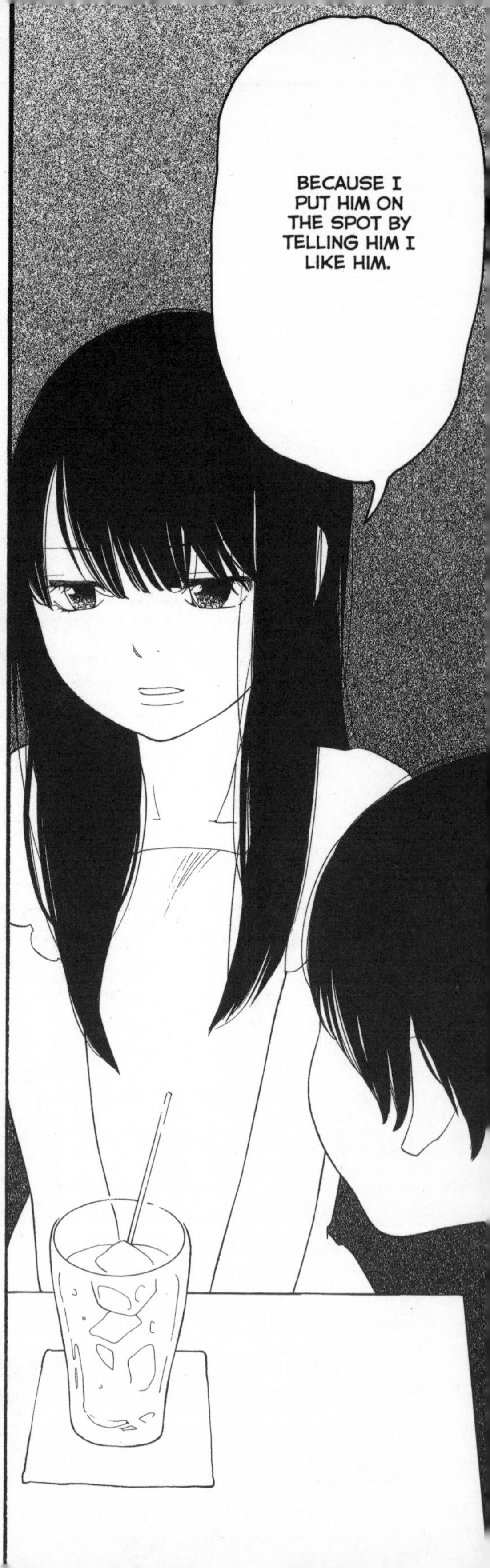
BECAUSE I PUT HIM ON THE SPOT BY TELLING HIM I LIKE HIM.
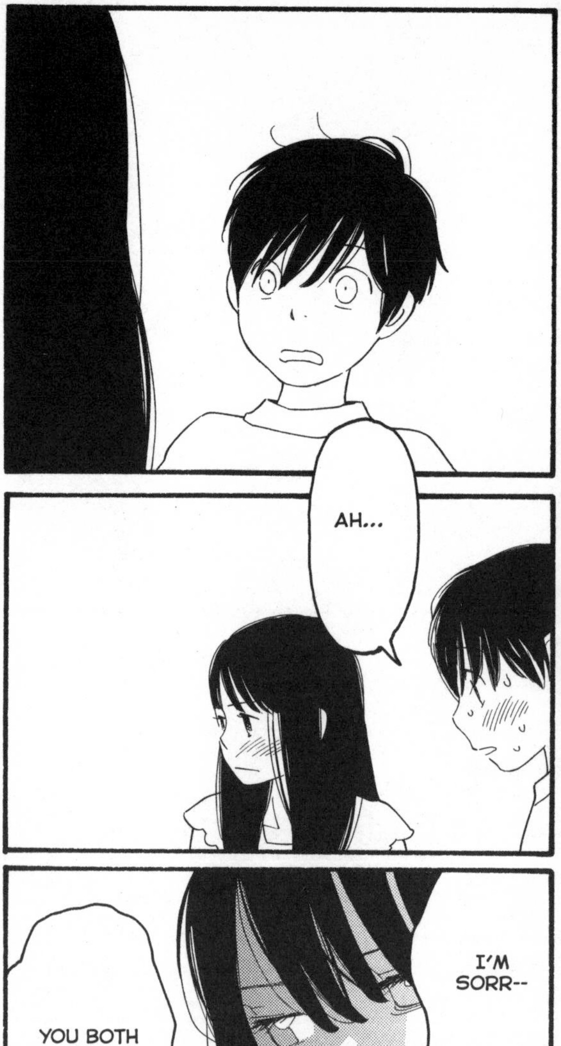
AH...
I'M SORR--
YOU BOTH APOLOGIZE.
YOU BOTH APOLOGIZE TO ME...
...AND I LOOK LIKE A COMPLETE FOOL.

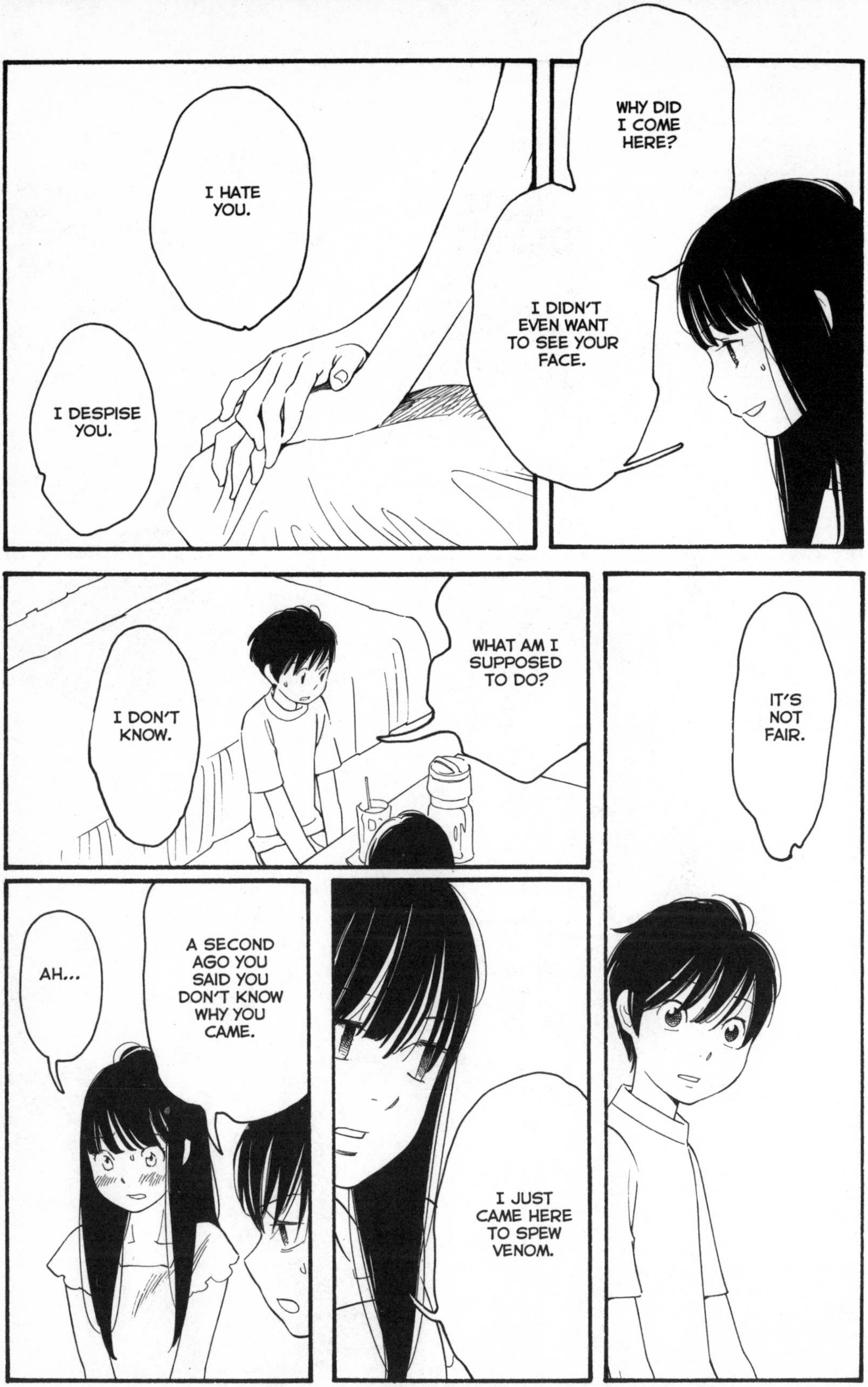
WHY DID I COME HERE?
I DIDN'T EVEN WANT TO SEE YOUR FACE.
I HATE YOU.
I DESPISE YOU.
IT'S NOT FAIR.
WHAT AM I SUPPOSED TO DO?
I DON'T KNOW.
I JUST CAME HERE TO SPEW VENOM.
A SECOND AGO YOU SAID YOU DON'T KNOW WHY YOU CAME.
AH...

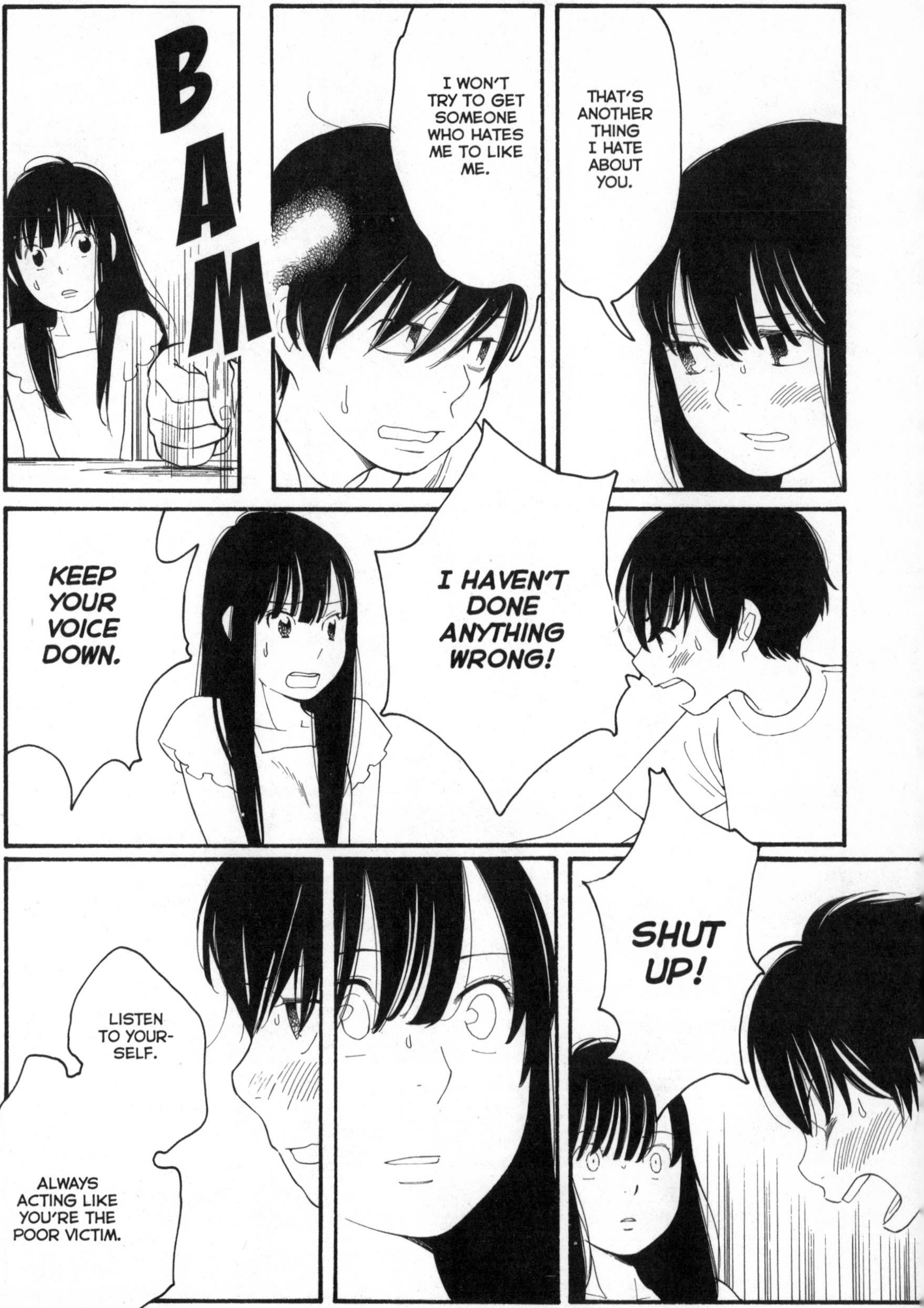
THAT'S ANOTHER THING I HATE ABOUT YOU.
I WON'T TRY TO GET SOMEONE WHO HATES ME TO LIKE ME.
BAM
I HAVEN'T DONE ANYTHING WRONG!
KEEP YOUR VOICE DOWN.
SHUT UP!
LISTEN TO YOUR-SELF.
ALWAYS ACTING LIKE YOU'RE THE POOR VICTIM.

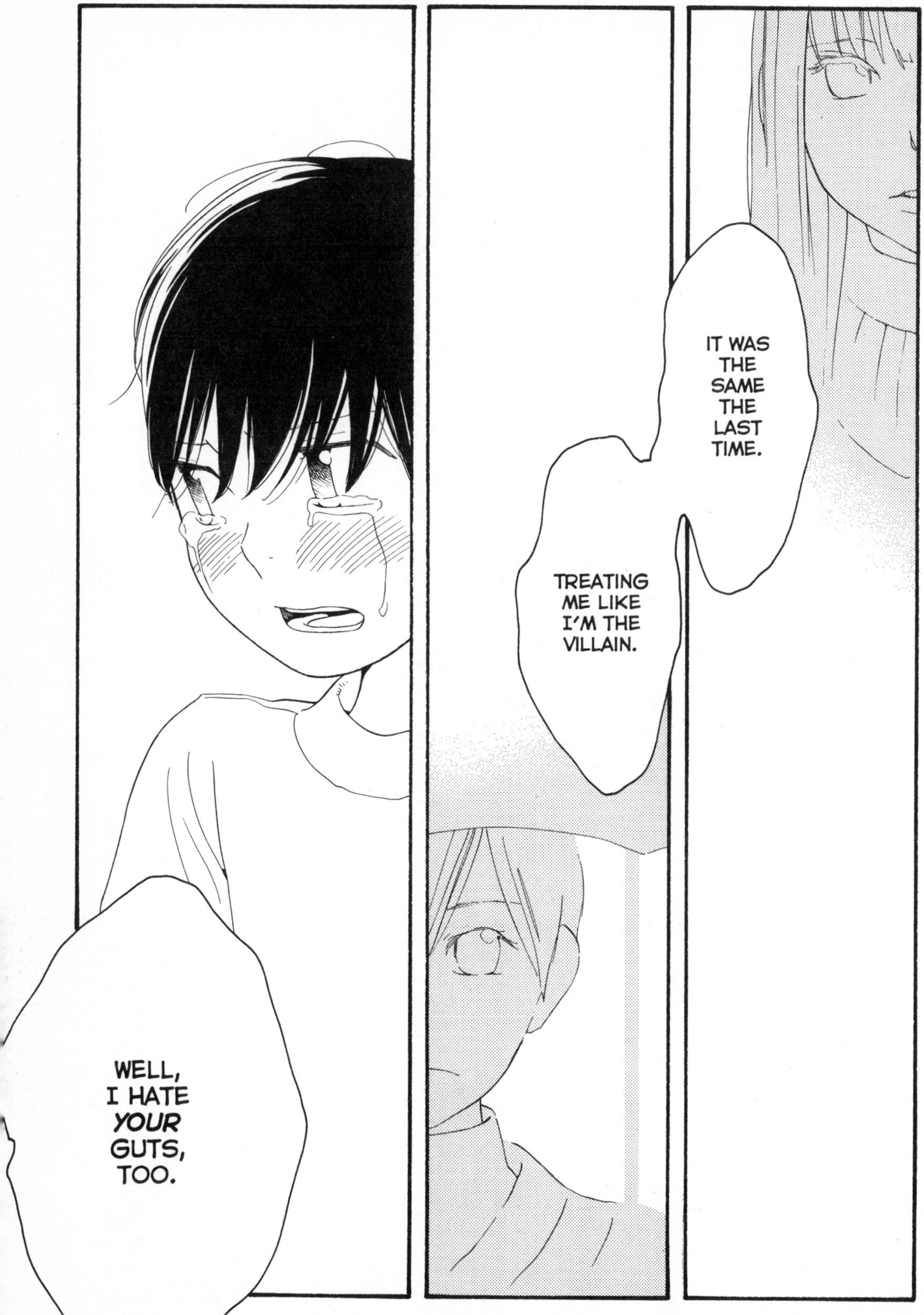
IT WAS THE SAME THE LAST TIME.
TREATING ME LIKE I'M THE VILLAIN.
WELL, I HATE *YOUR* GUTS, TOO.

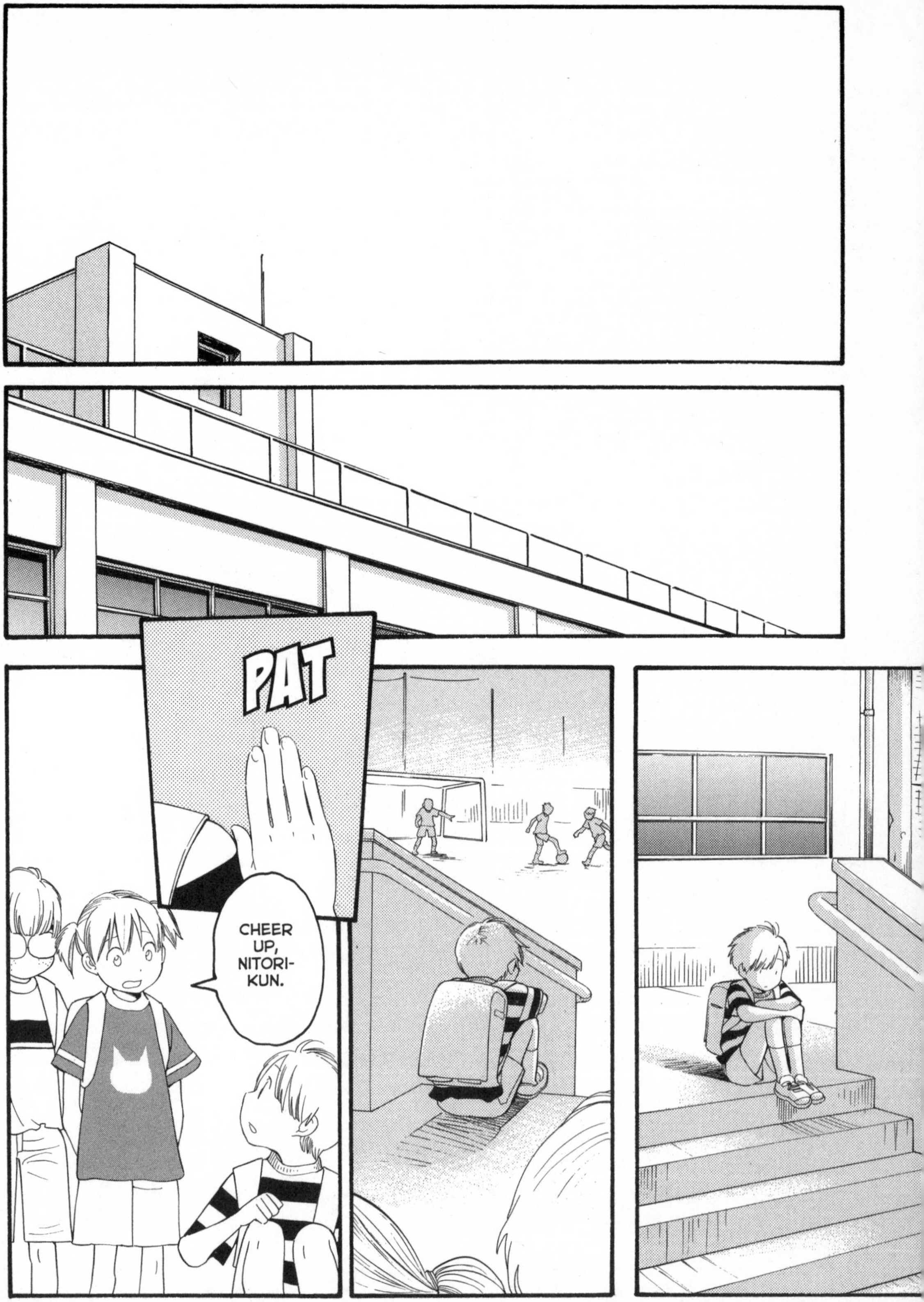
PAT
CHEER UP, NITORI-KUN.

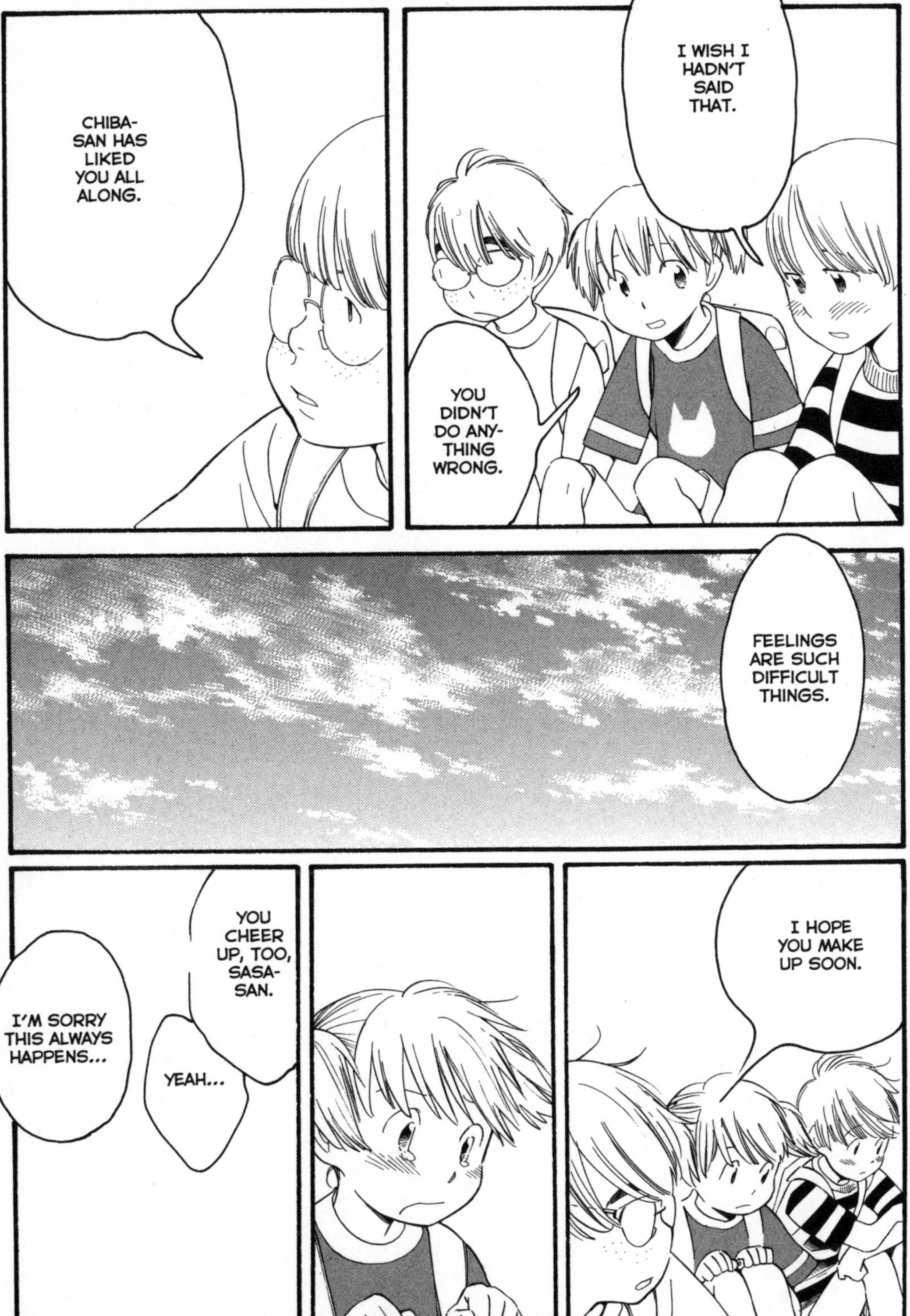
I WISH I HADN'T SAID THAT.
YOU DIDN'T DO ANY-THING WRONG.
CHIBA-SAN HAS LIKED YOU ALL ALONG.
FEELINGS ARE SUCH DIFFICULT THINGS.
I HOPE YOU MAKE UP SOON.
YOU CHEER UP, TOO, SASA-SAN.
YEAH...
I'M SORRY THIS ALWAYS HAPPENS...

WE DIDN'T MAKE UP.

BEFORE WE COULD MAKE UP...

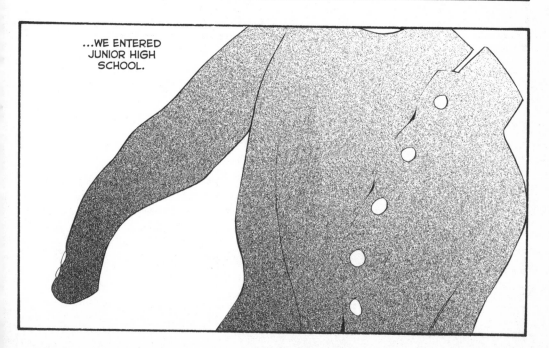

...WE ENTERED JUNIOR HIGH SCHOOL.

33

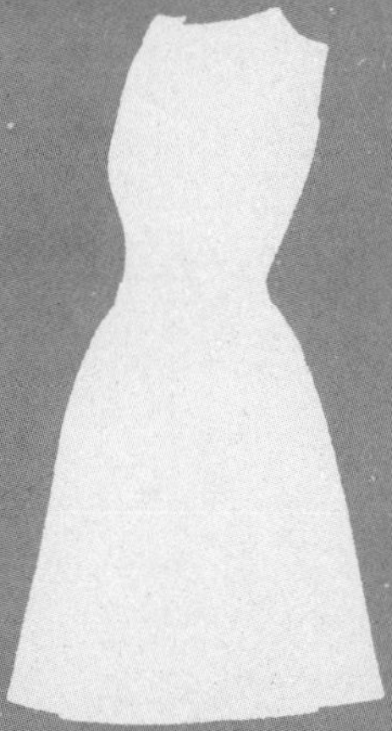

Ahh, Junior High

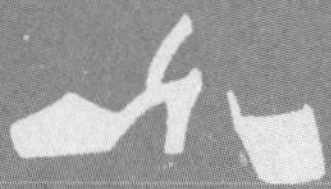

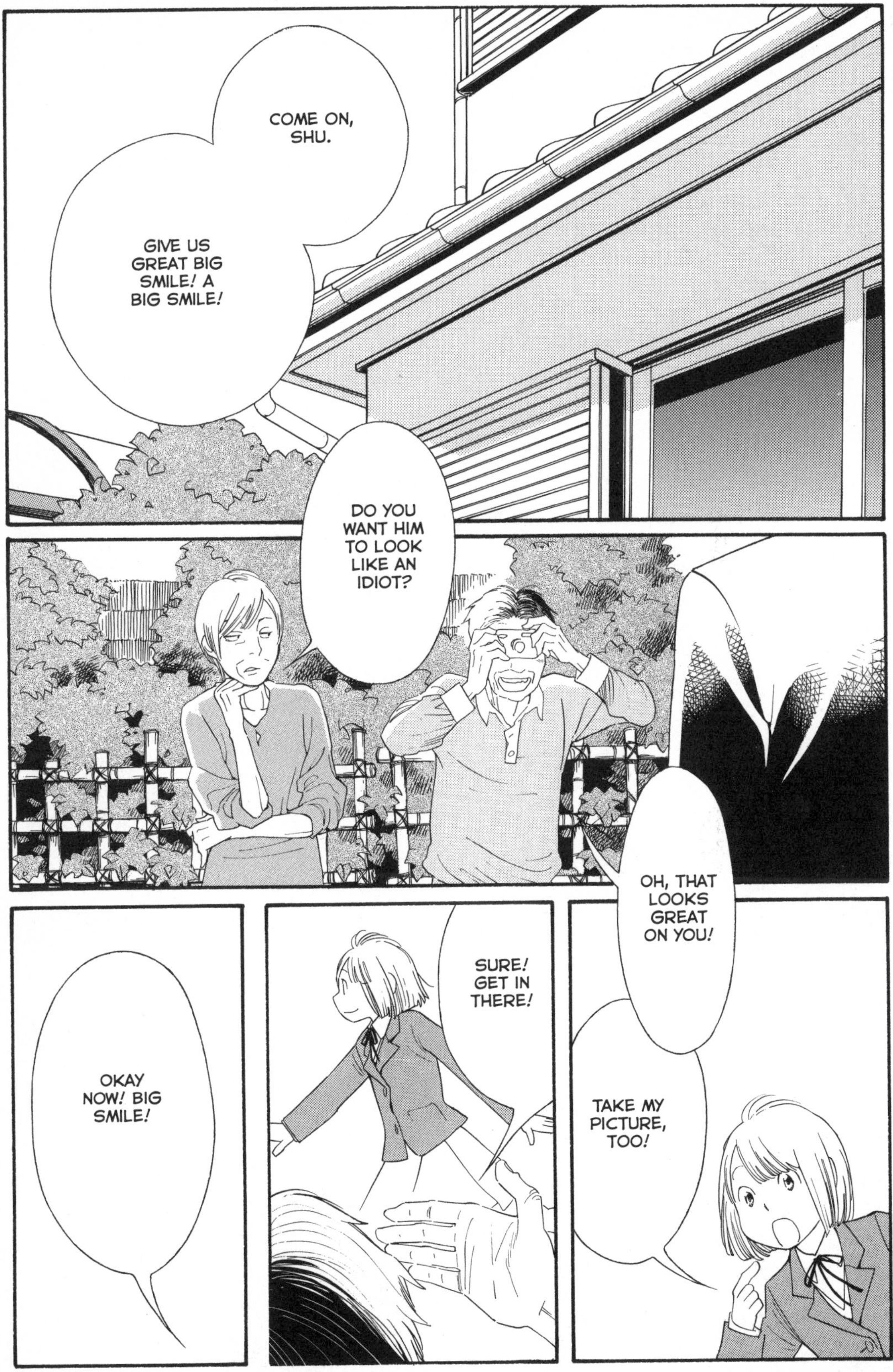
COME ON, SHU.
GIVE US GREAT BIG SMILE! A BIG SMILE!
DO YOU WANT HIM TO LOOK LIKE AN IDIOT?
OH, THAT LOOKS GREAT ON YOU!
TAKE MY PICTURE, TOO!
SURE! GET IN THERE!
OKAY NOW! BIG SMILE!

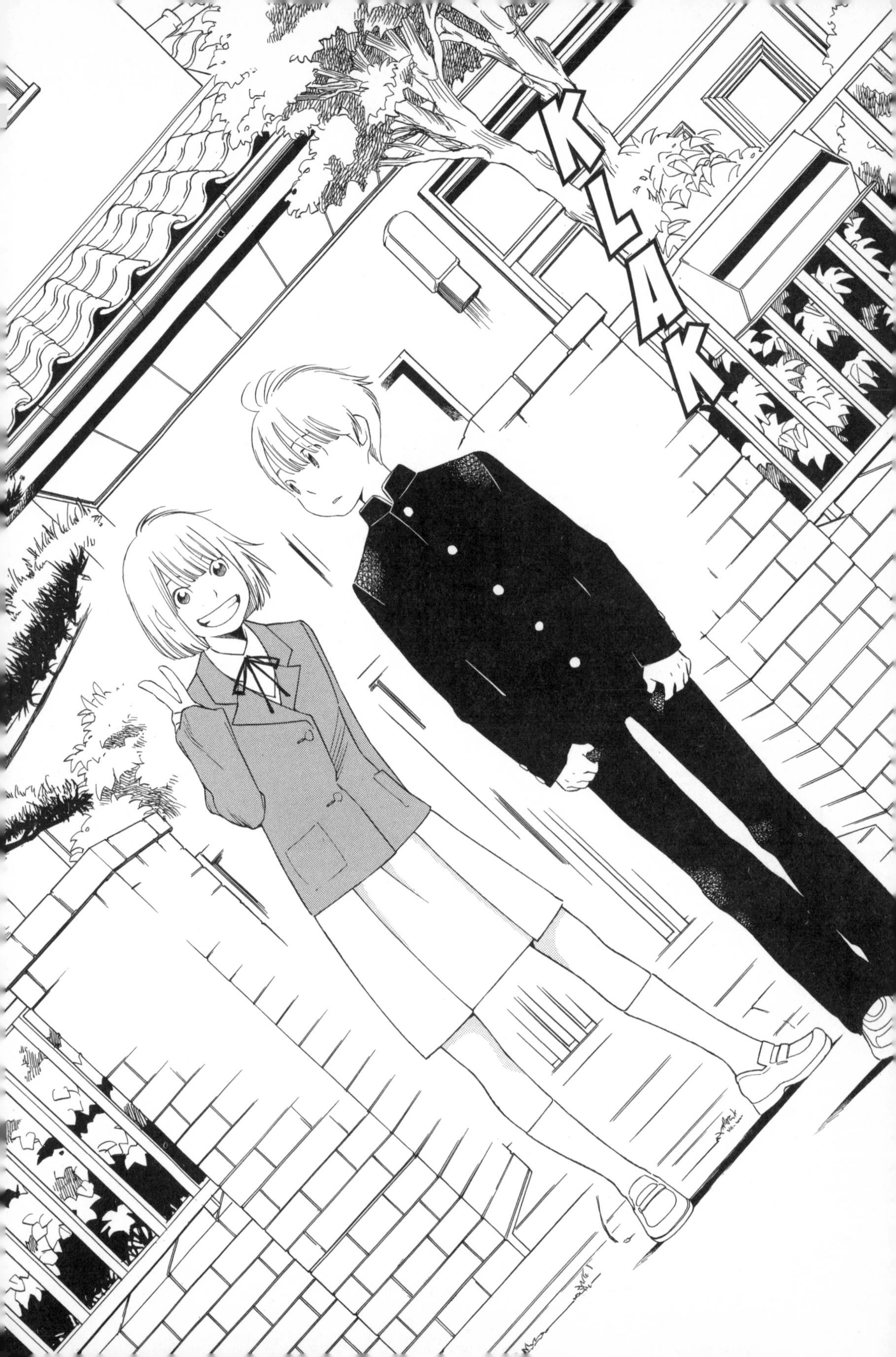
KLAK

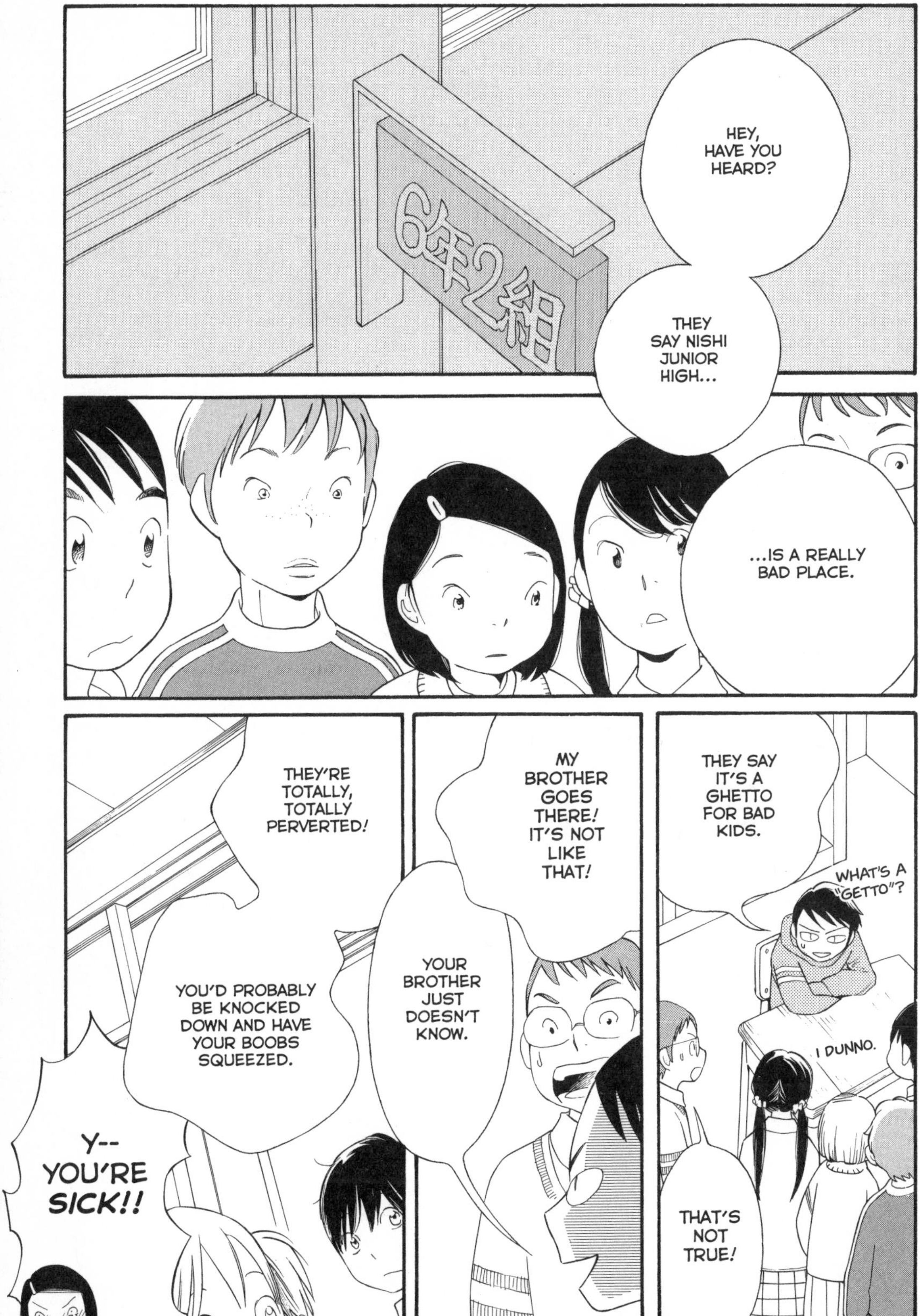
6年2組
HEY, HAVE YOU HEARD?
THEY SAY NISHI JUNIOR HIGH...
...IS A REALLY BAD PLACE.
THEY SAY IT'S A GHETTO FOR BAD KIDS.
WHAT'S A "GETTO"?
I DUNNO.
THAT'S NOT TRUE!
MY BROTHER GOES THERE! IT'S NOT LIKE THAT!
YOUR BROTHER JUST DOESN'T KNOW.
THEY'RE TOTALLY, TOTALLY PERVERTED!
YOU'D PROBABLY BE KNOCKED DOWN AND HAVE YOUR BOOBS SQUEEZED.
Y-- YOU'RE SICK!!

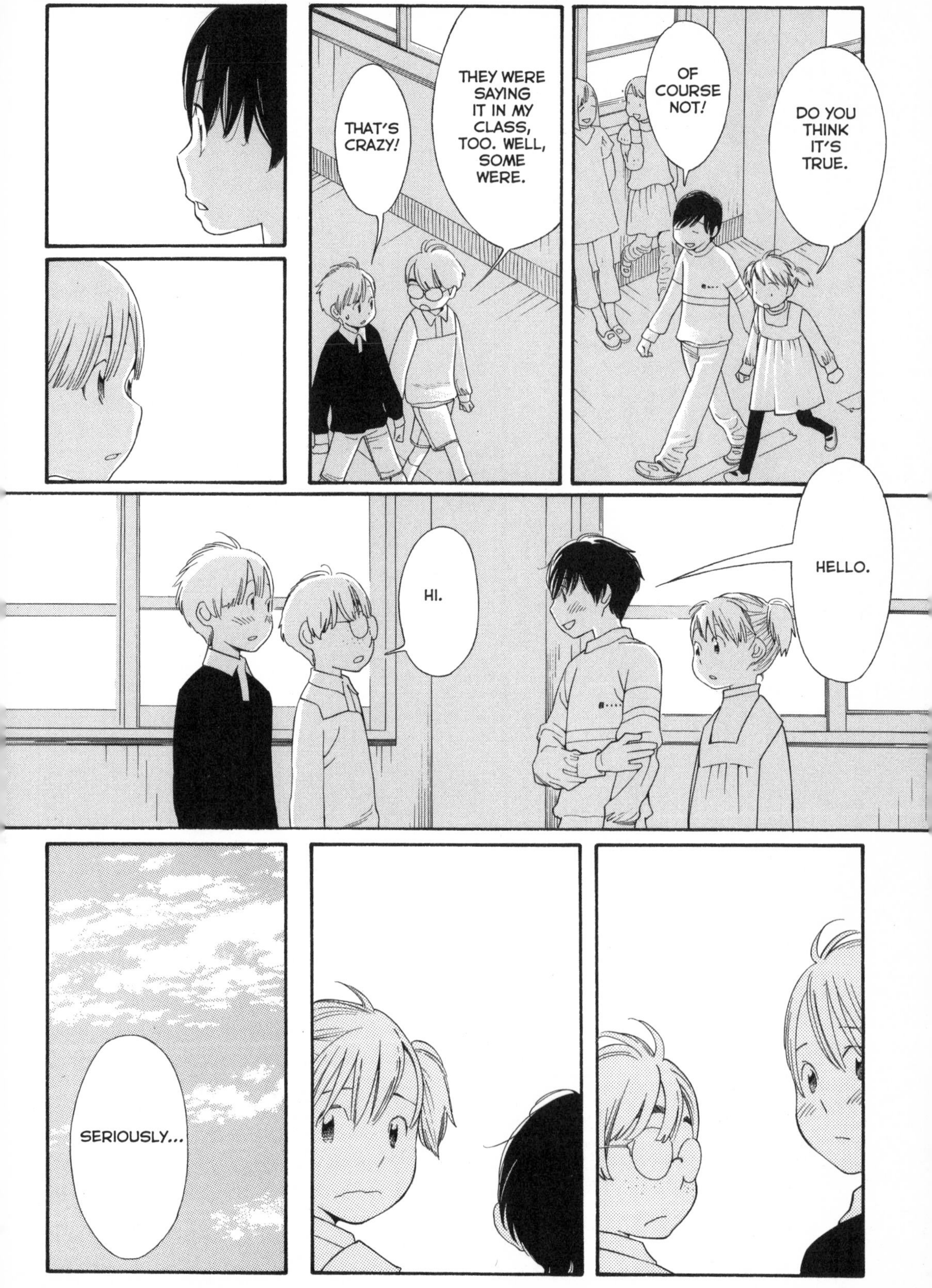
DO YOU THINK IT'S TRUE.
OF COURSE NOT!
THEY WERE SAYING IT IN MY CLASS, TOO. WELL, SOME WERE.
THAT'S CRAZY!
HELLO.
HI.
SERIOUSLY...

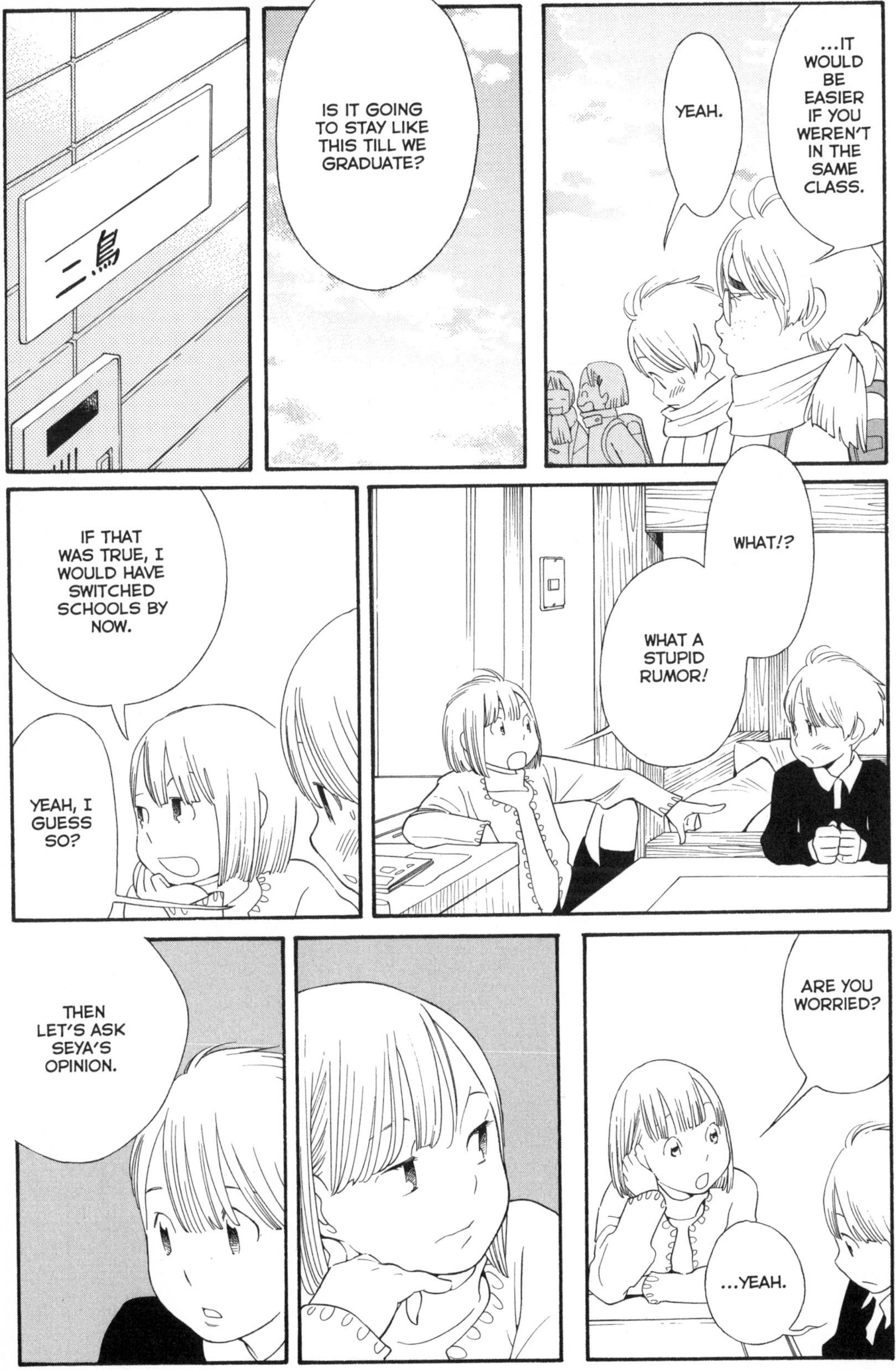
...IT WOULD BE EASIER IF YOU WEREN'T IN THE SAME CLASS.
YEAH.
IS IT GOING TO STAY LIKE THIS TILL WE GRADUATE?
二鳥
WHAT!?
WHAT A STUPID RUMOR!
IF THAT WAS TRUE, I WOULD HAVE SWITCHED SCHOOLS BY NOW.
YEAH, I GUESS SO?
ARE YOU WORRIED?
...YEAH.
THEN LET'S ASK SEYA'S OPINION.

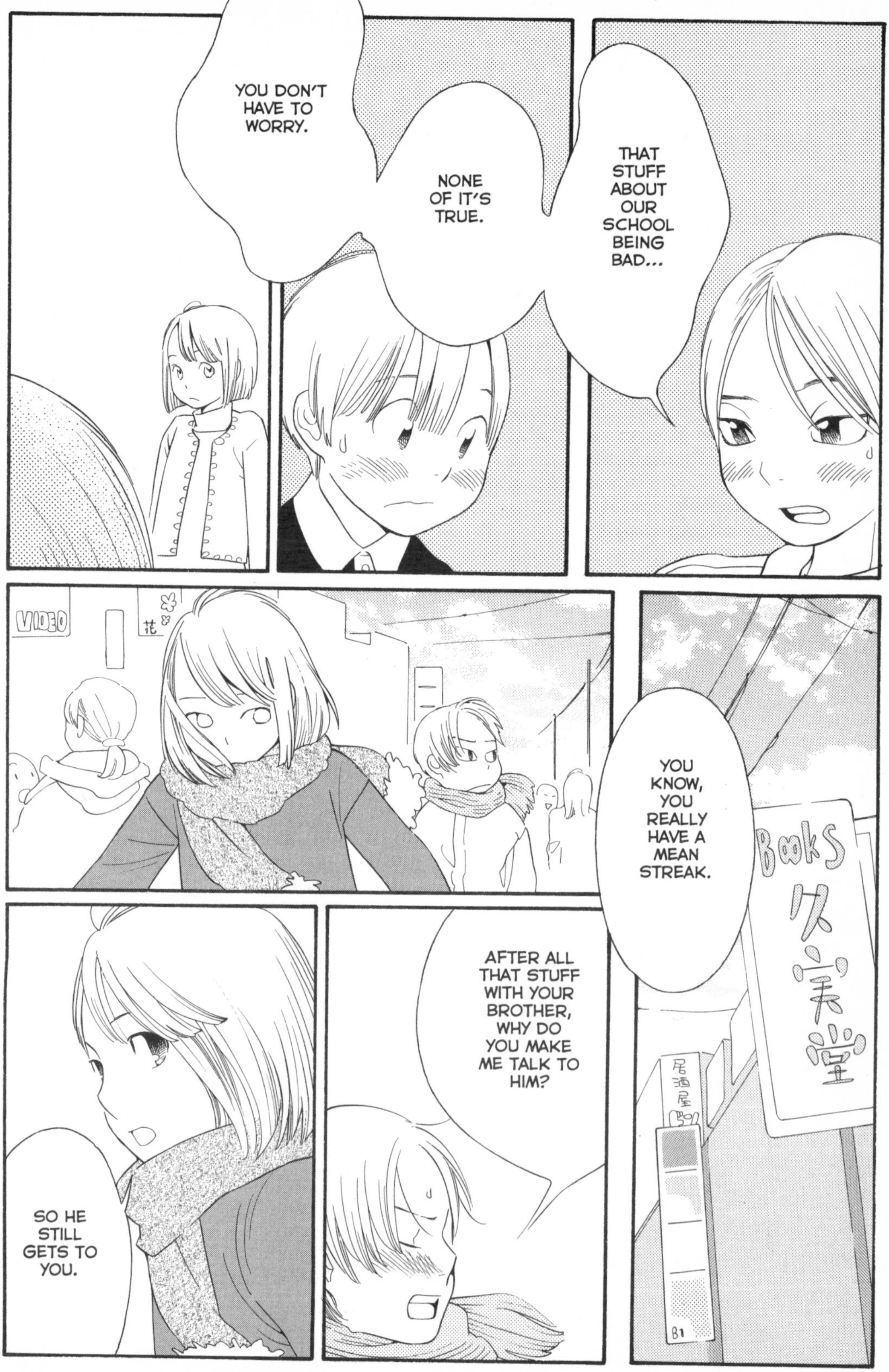
THAT STUFF ABOUT OUR SCHOOL BEING BAD...
NONE OF IT'S TRUE.
YOU DON'T HAVE TO WORRY.
YOU KNOW, YOU REALLY HAVE A MEAN STREAK.
Books
久実堂
居酒屋
B1
VIDEO
花
AFTER ALL THAT STUFF WITH YOUR BROTHER, WHY DO YOU MAKE ME TALK TO HIM?
SO HE STILL GETS TO YOU.

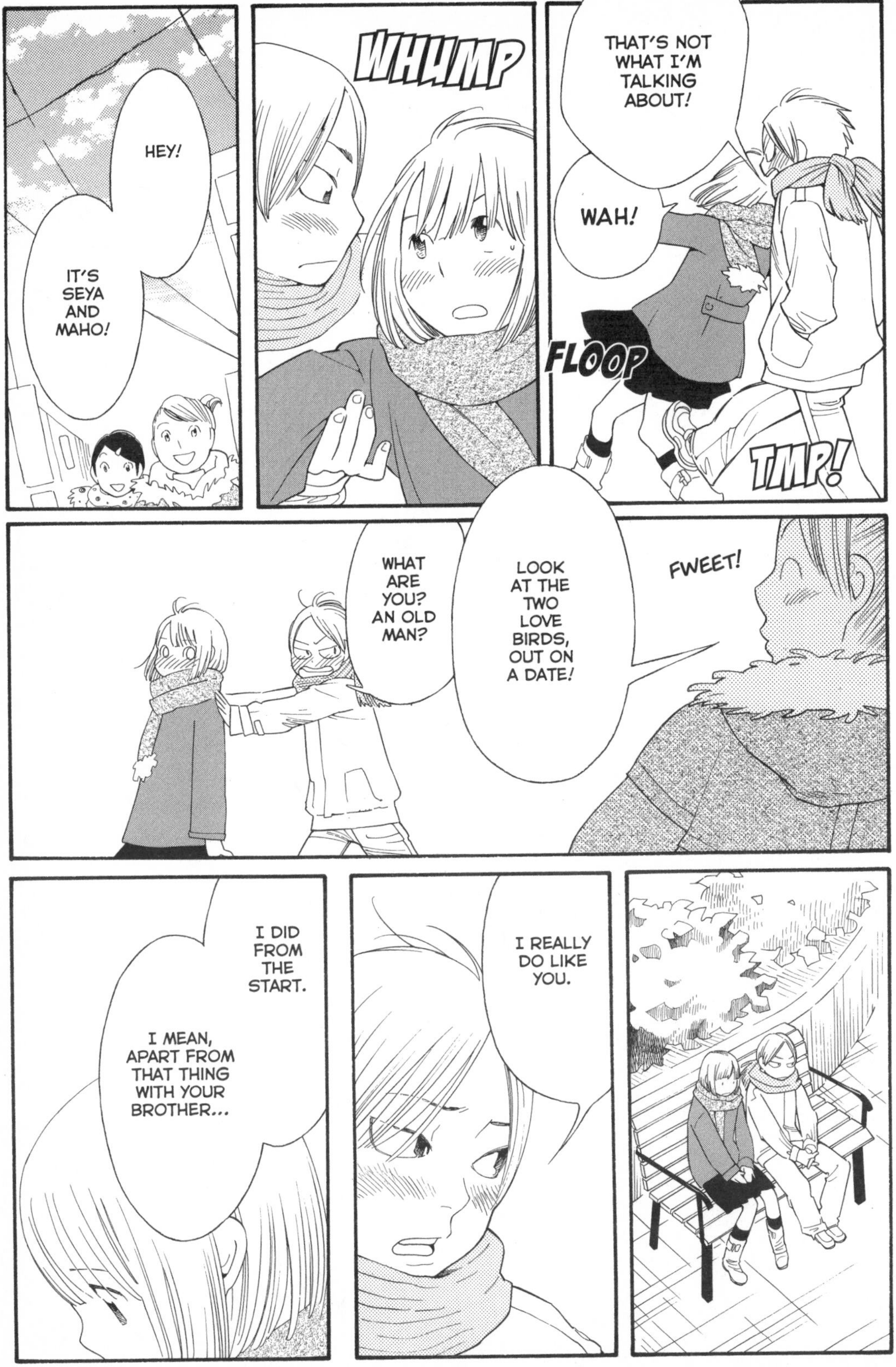
THAT'S NOT WHAT I'M TALKING ABOUT!
WAH!
FLOOP
TMP!
WHUMP
HEY!
IT'S SEYA AND MAHO!
FWEET!
LOOK AT THE TWO LOVE BIRDS, OUT ON A DATE!
WHAT ARE YOU? AN OLD MAN?
I REALLY DO LIKE YOU.
I DID FROM THE START.
I MEAN, APART FROM THAT THING WITH YOUR BROTHER...

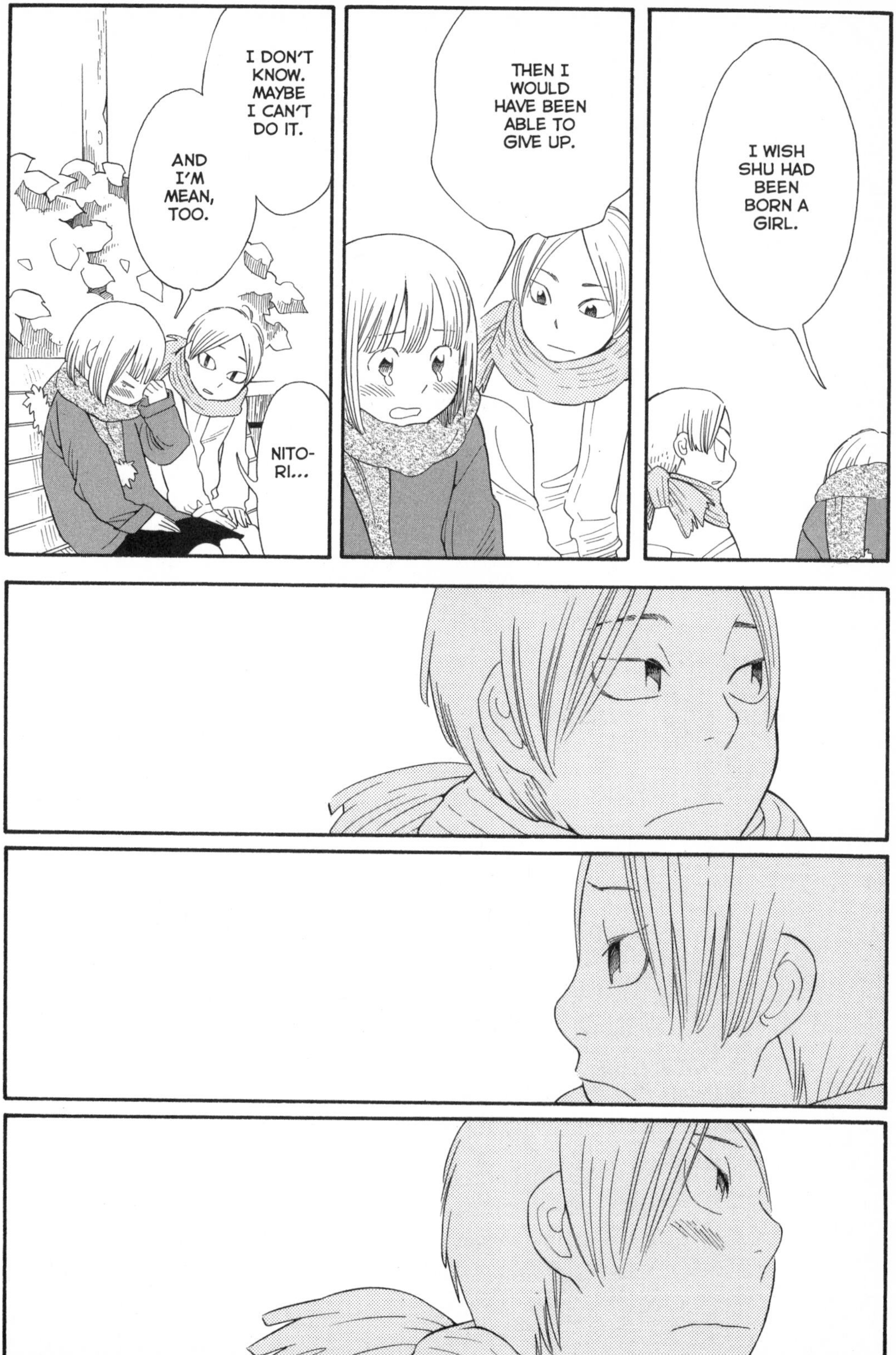
I WISH SHU HAD BEEN BORN A GIRL.
THEN I WOULD HAVE BEEN ABLE TO GIVE UP.
I DON'T KNOW. MAYBE I CAN'T DO IT.
AND I'M MEAN, TOO.
NITO-RI...

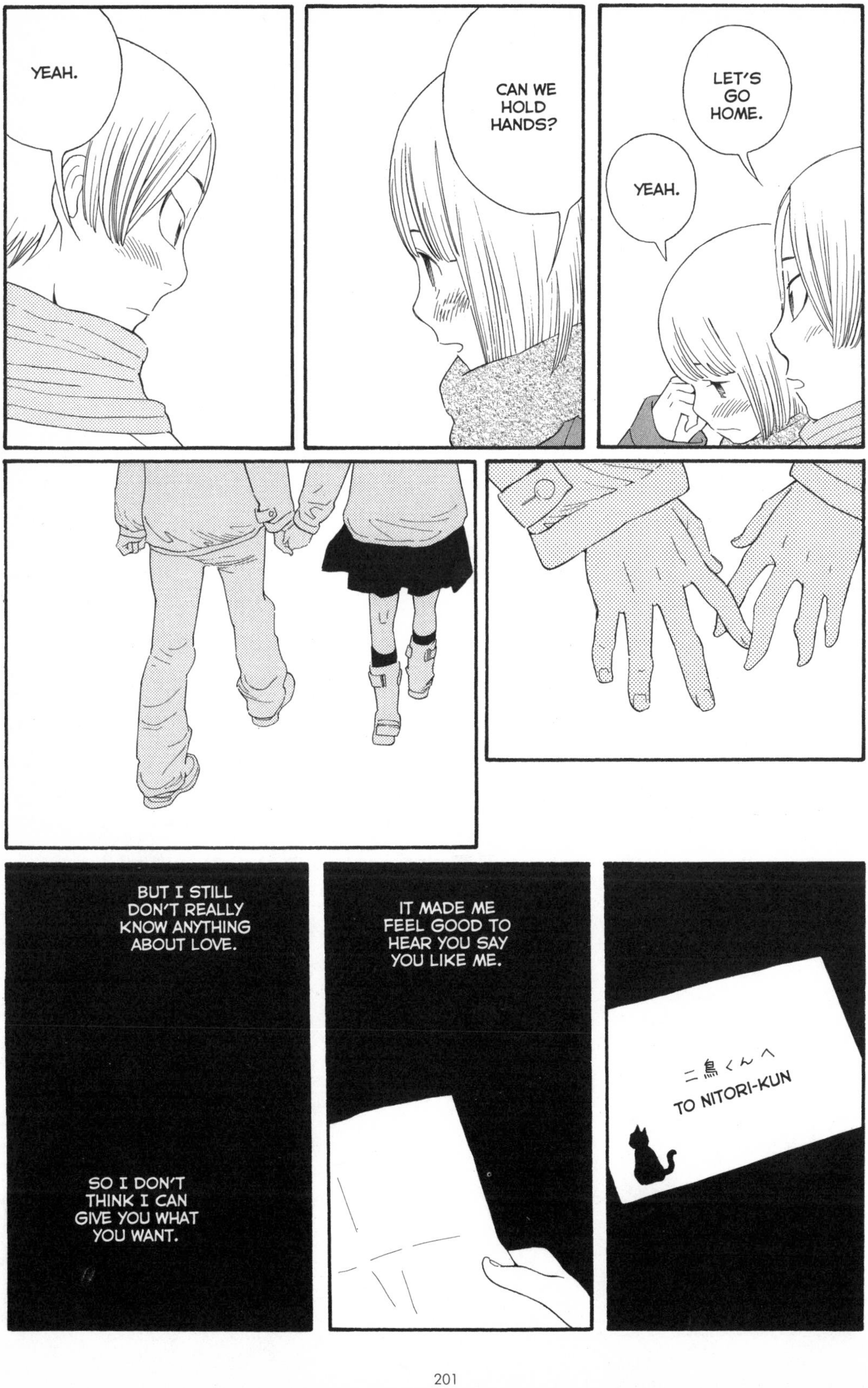
LET'S GO HOME.
YEAH.
CAN WE HOLD HANDS?
YEAH.
二鳥くんへ
TO NITORI-KUN
IT MADE ME FEEL GOOD TO HEAR YOU SAY YOU LIKE ME.
BUT I STILL DON'T REALLY KNOW ANYTHING ABOUT LOVE.
SO I DON'T THINK I CAN GIVE YOU WHAT YOU WANT.

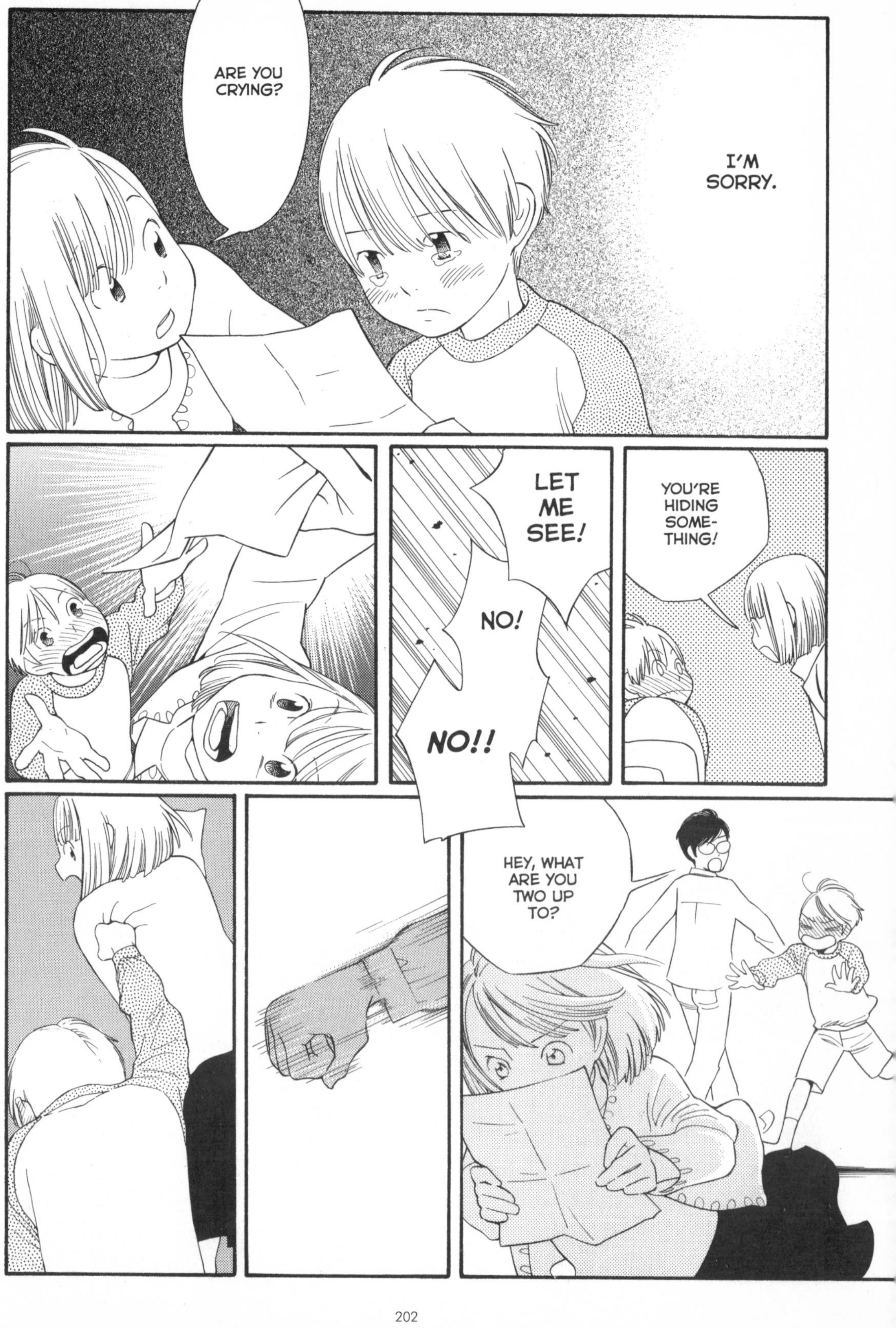
I'M
SORRY.
ARE YOU CRYING?
YOU'RE HIDING SOME-THING!
LET ME SEE!
NO!
NO!!
HEY, WHAT ARE YOU TWO UP TO?

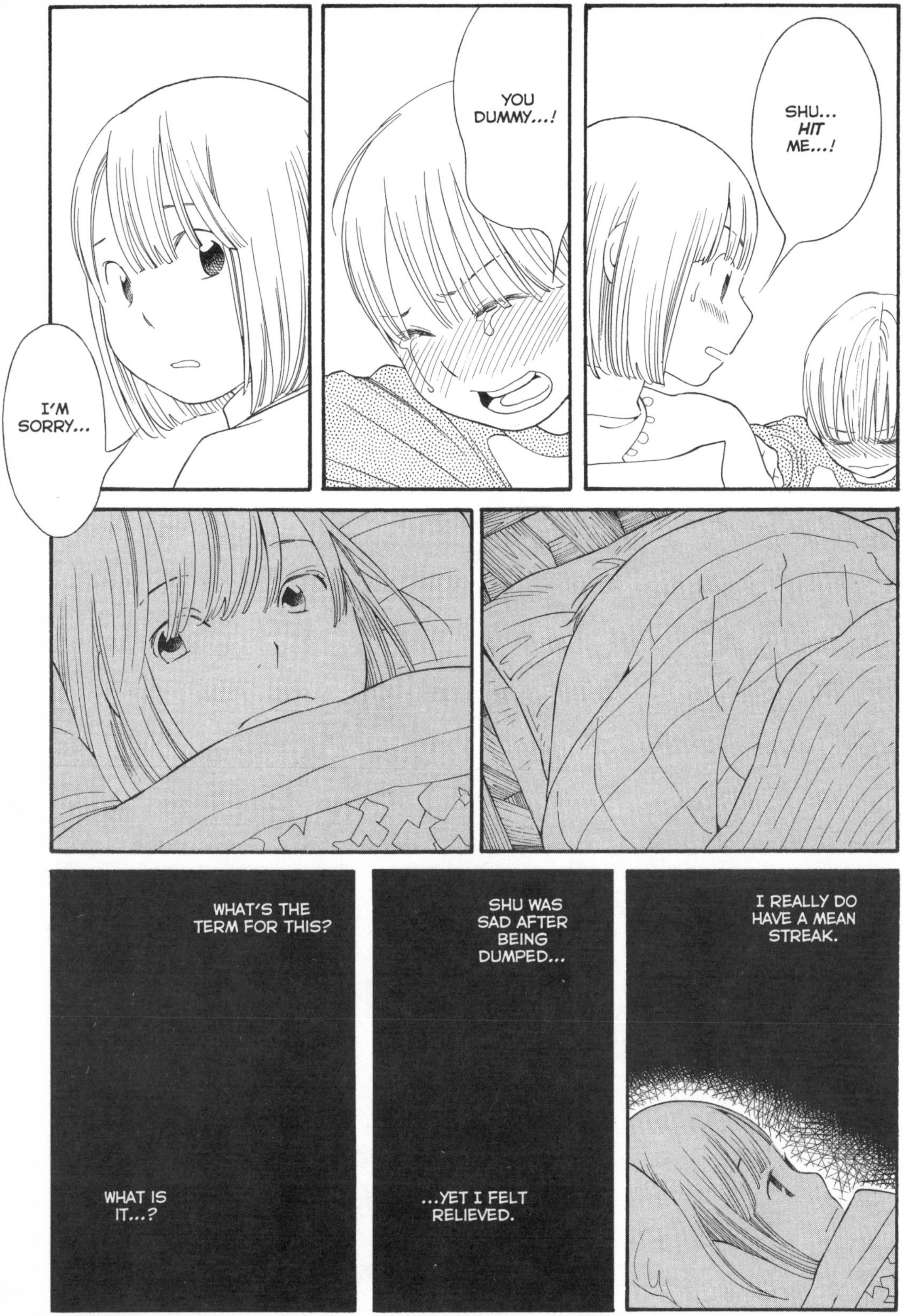
SHU... *HIT* ME...!
YOU DUMMY...!
I'M SORRY...
I REALLY DO HAVE A MEAN STREAK.
SHU WAS SAD AFTER BEING DUMPED...
...YET I FELT RELIEVED.
WHAT'S THE TERM FOR THIS?
WHAT IS IT...?

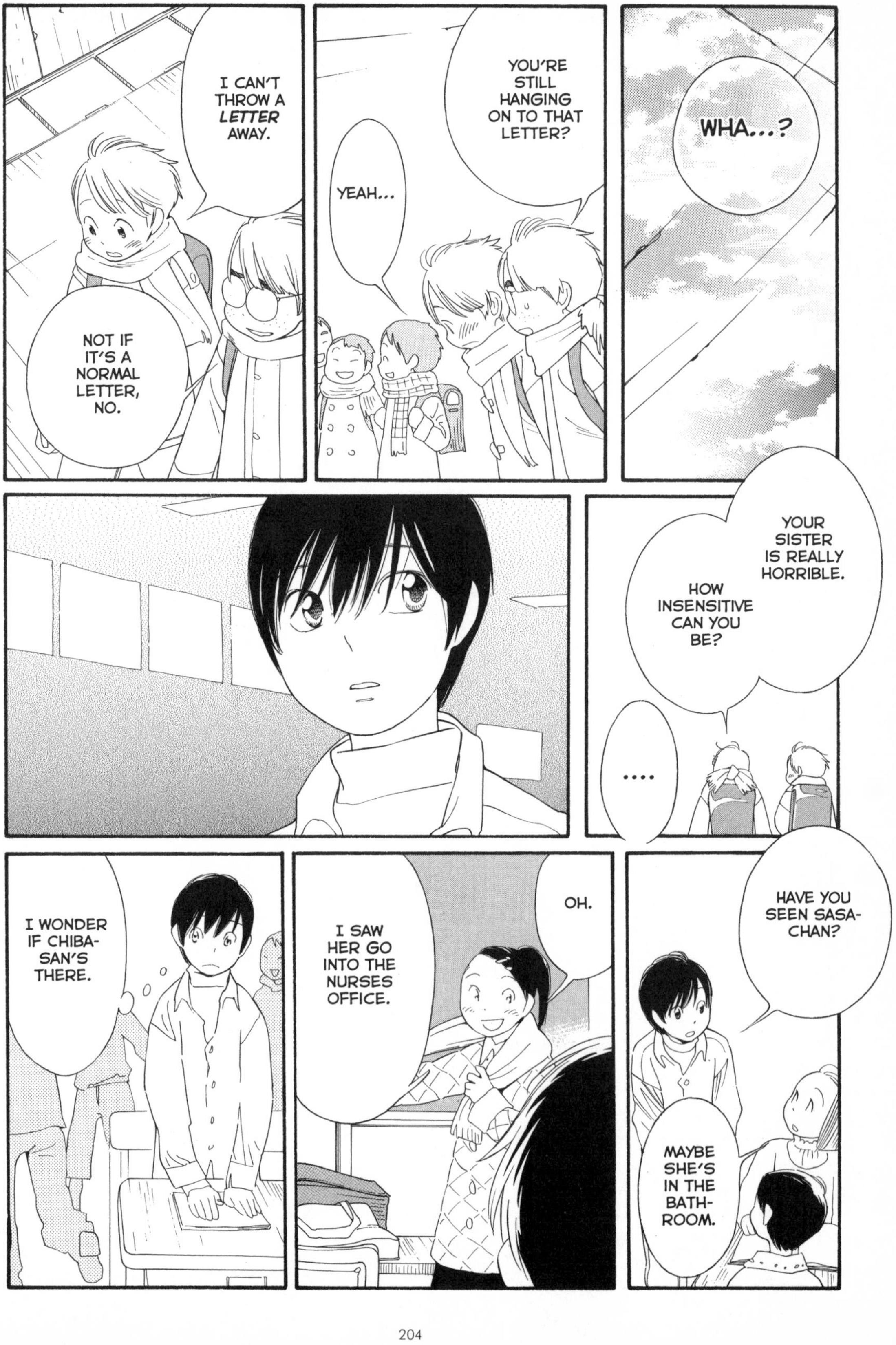
WHA...?
YOU'RE STILL HANGING ON TO THAT LETTER?
YEAH...
I CAN'T THROW A *LETTER* AWAY.
NOT IF IT'S A NORMAL LETTER, NO.
YOUR SISTER IS REALLY HORRIBLE.
HOW INSENSITIVE CAN YOU BE?
....
HAVE YOU SEEN SASA-CHAN?
MAYBE SHE'S IN THE BATHROOM.
OH.
I SAW HER GO INTO THE NURSES OFFICE.
I WONDER IF CHIBA-SAN'S THERE.

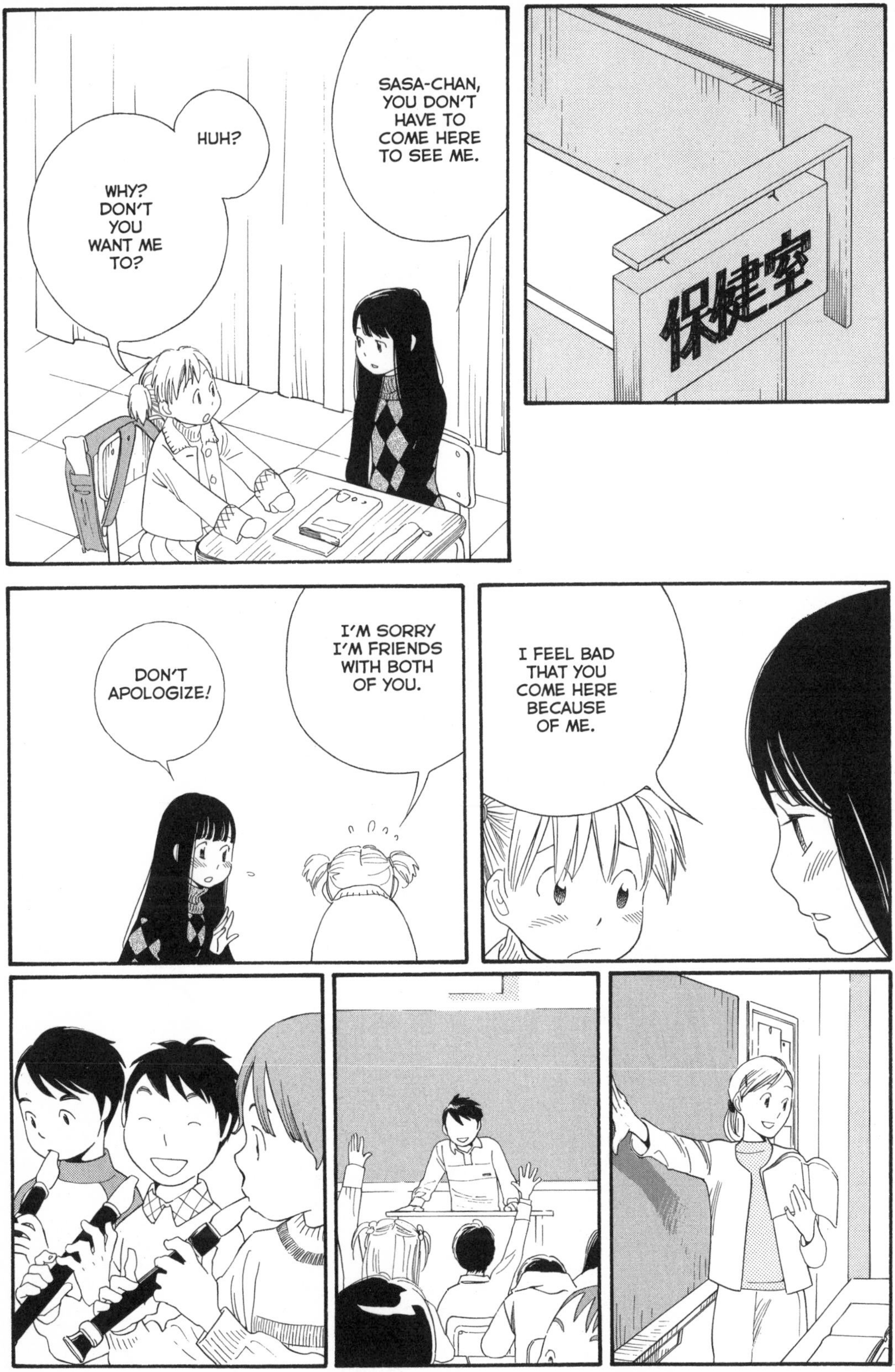
保健室
SASA-CHAN, YOU DON'T HAVE TO COME HERE TO SEE ME.
HUH?
WHY? DON'T YOU WANT ME TO?
I FEEL BAD THAT YOU COME HERE BECAUSE OF ME.
I'M SORRY I'M FRIENDS WITH BOTH OF YOU.
DON'T APOLOGIZE!

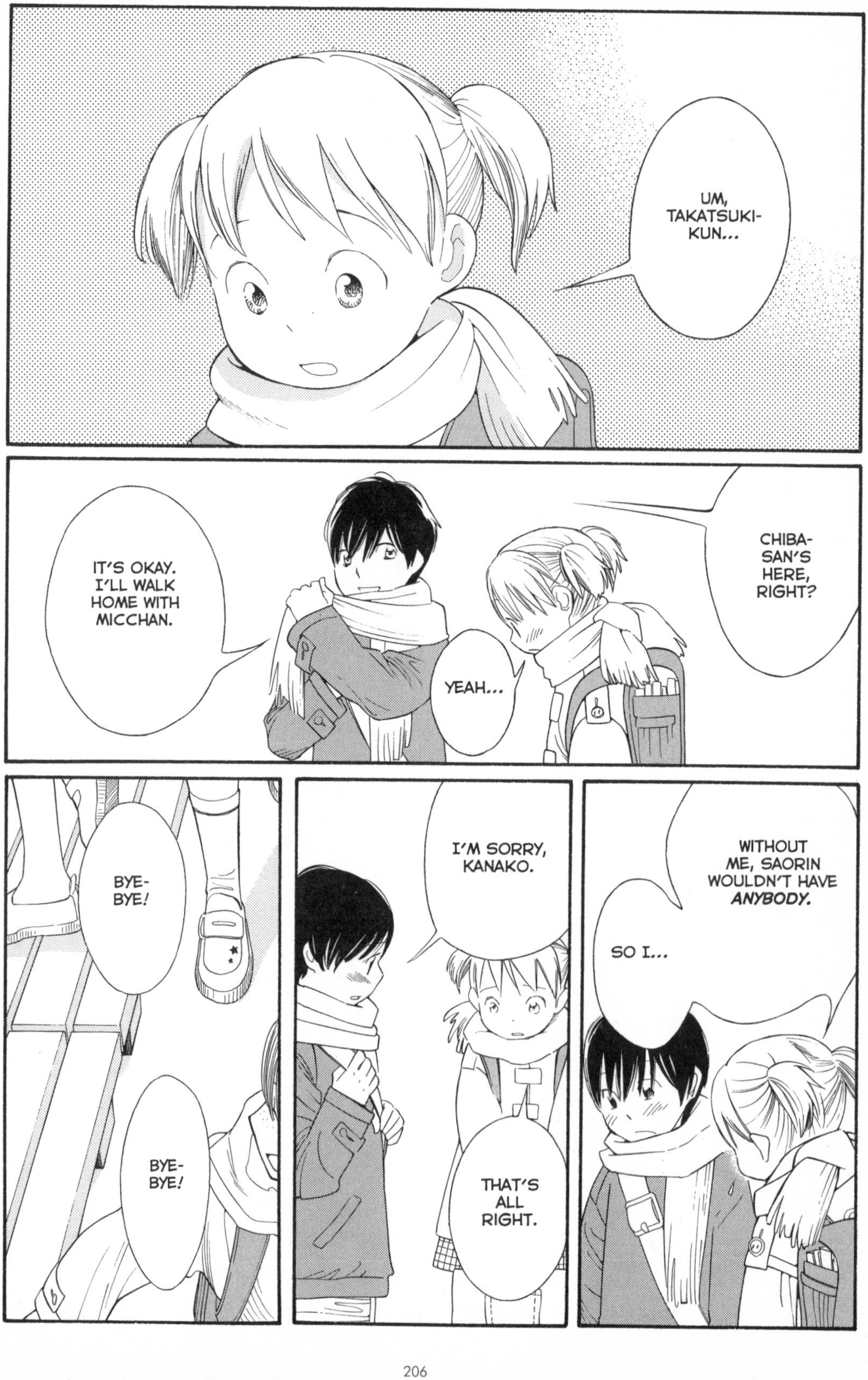
UM, TAKATSUKI-KUN...
CHIBA-SAN'S HERE, RIGHT?
YEAH...
IT'S OKAY. I'LL WALK HOME WITH MICCHAN.
WITHOUT ME, SAORIN WOULDN'T HAVE **ANYBODY.**
SO I...
I'M SORRY, KANAKO.
THAT'S ALL RIGHT.
BYE-BYE!
BYE-BYE!

I'VE GOT TO STOP RE-READING IT.

I HAVE TO PUT IT BEHIND ME.

F-- FARE- WELL...!

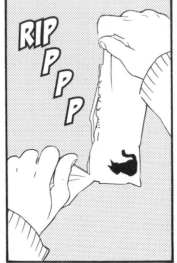

RIP
P
P
P

SKRNCH

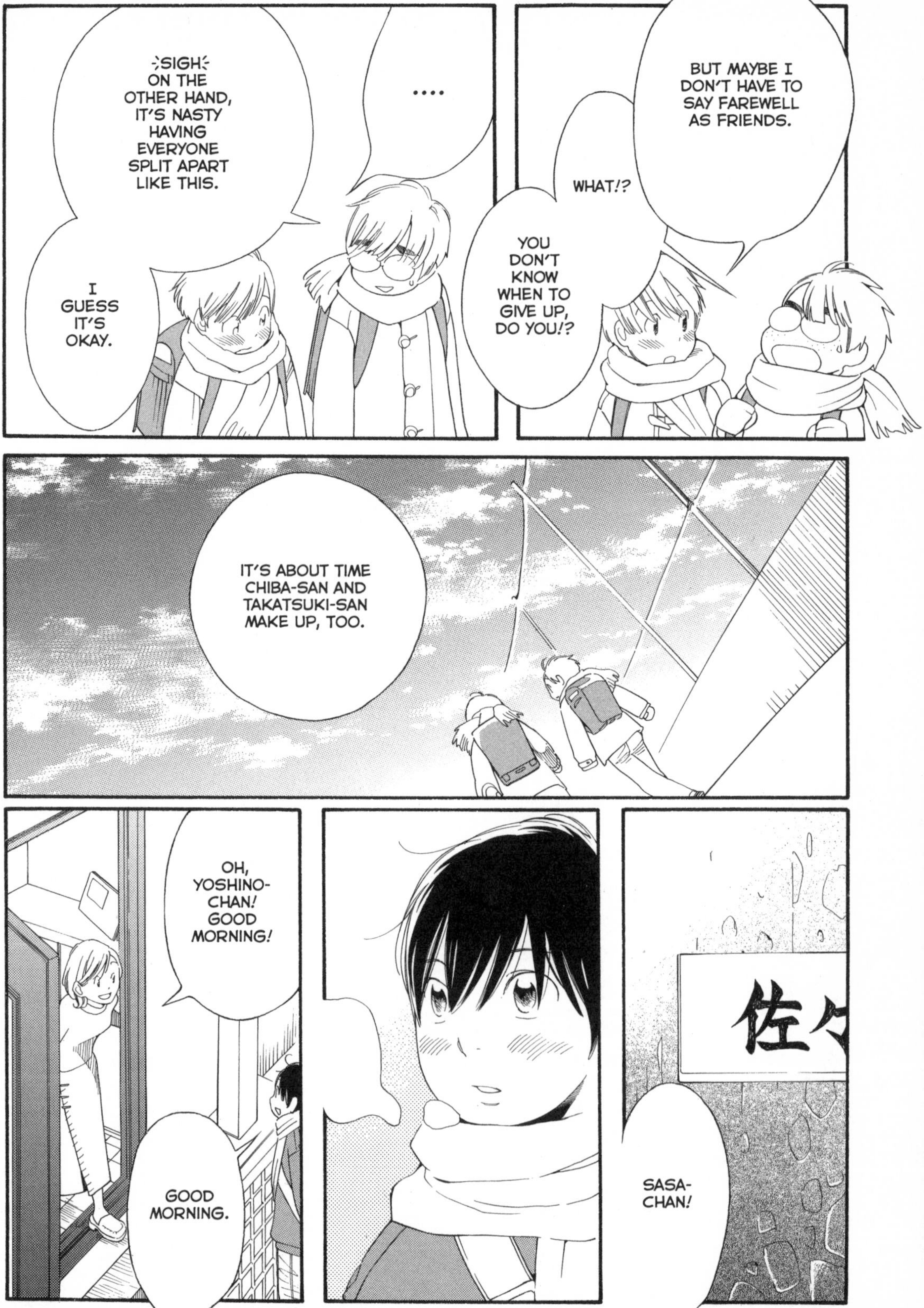
BUT MAYBE I DON'T HAVE TO SAY FAREWELL AS FRIENDS.
WHAT!?
YOU DON'T KNOW WHEN TO GIVE UP, DO YOU!?
....
-SIGH- ON THE OTHER HAND, IT'S NASTY HAVING EVERYONE SPLIT APART LIKE THIS.
I GUESS IT'S OKAY.
IT'S ABOUT TIME CHIBA-SAN AND TAKATSUKI-SAN MAKE UP, TOO.
佐々
SASA-CHAN!
OH, YOSHINO-CHAN! GOOD MORNING!
GOOD MORNING.

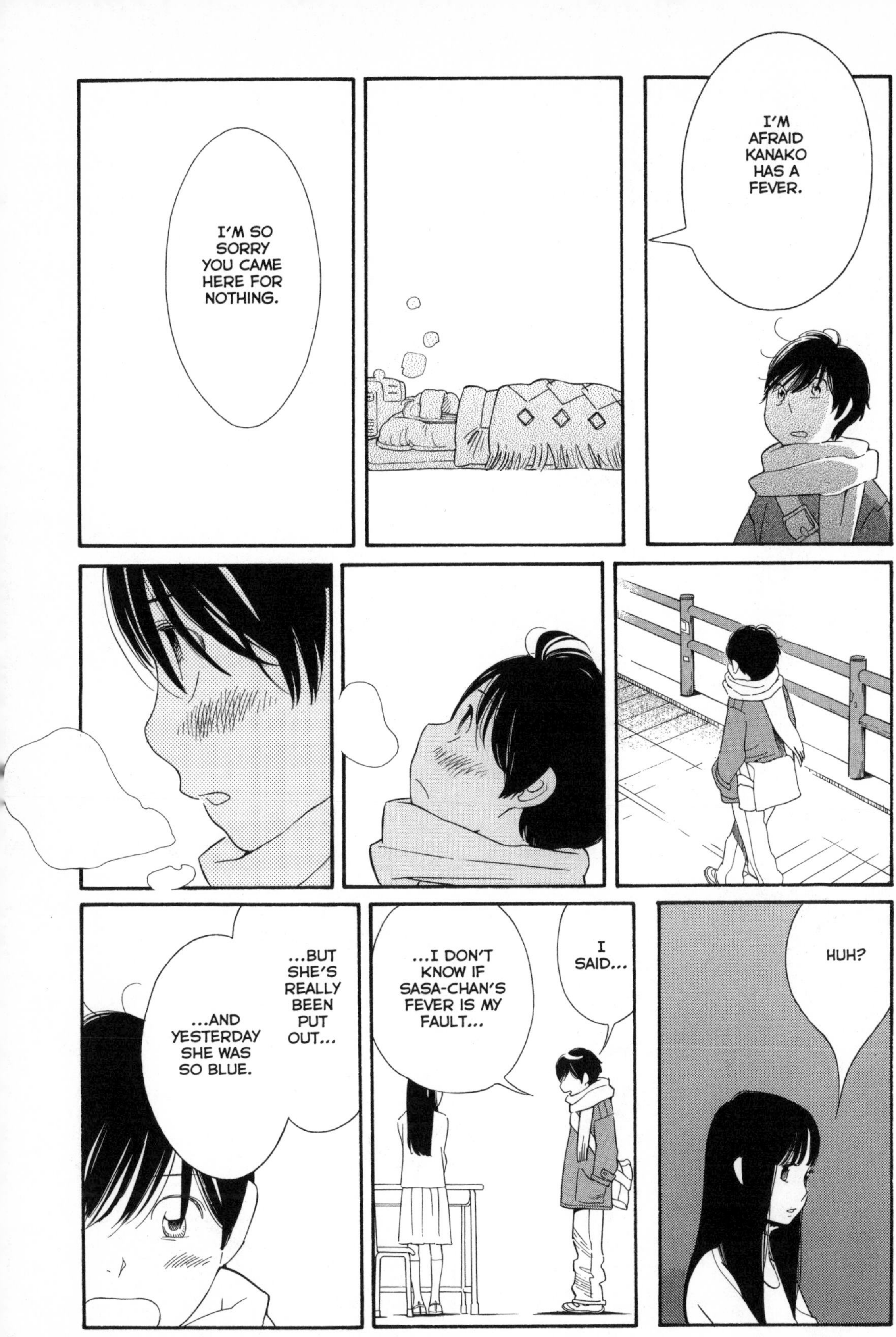
I'M AFRAID KANAKO HAS A FEVER.
I'M SO SORRY YOU CAME HERE FOR NOTHING.
HUH?
I SAID...
...I DON'T KNOW IF SASA-CHAN'S FEVER IS MY FAULT...
...BUT SHE'S REALLY BEEN PUT OUT...
...AND YESTERDAY SHE WAS SO BLUE.

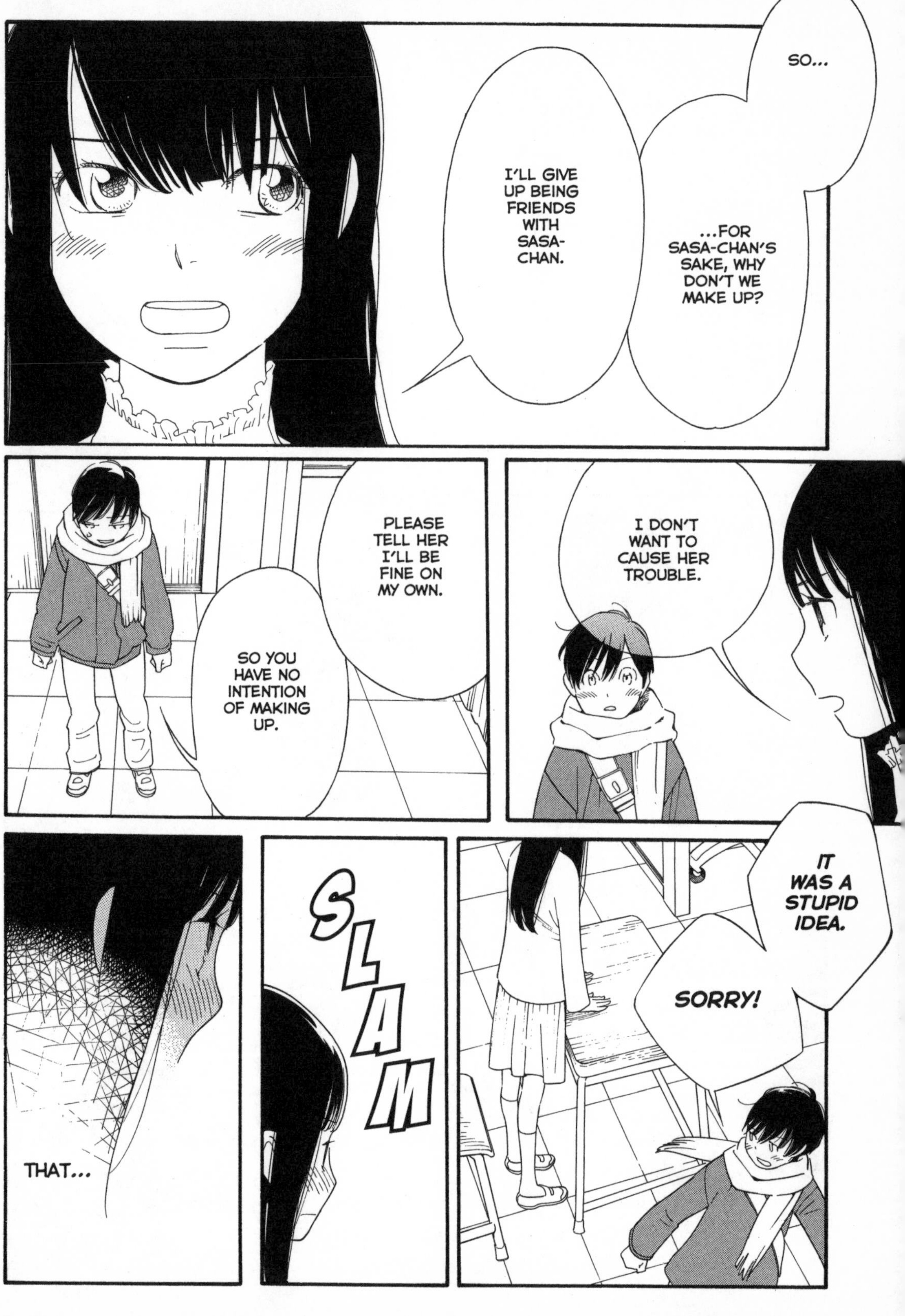
SO...
...FOR SASA-CHAN'S SAKE, WHY DON'T WE MAKE UP?
I'LL GIVE UP BEING FRIENDS WITH SASA-CHAN.
I DON'T WANT TO CAUSE HER TROUBLE.
PLEASE TELL HER I'LL BE FINE ON MY OWN.
SO YOU HAVE NO INTENTION OF MAKING UP.
IT WAS A STUPID IDEA.
SORRY!
SLAM
THAT...

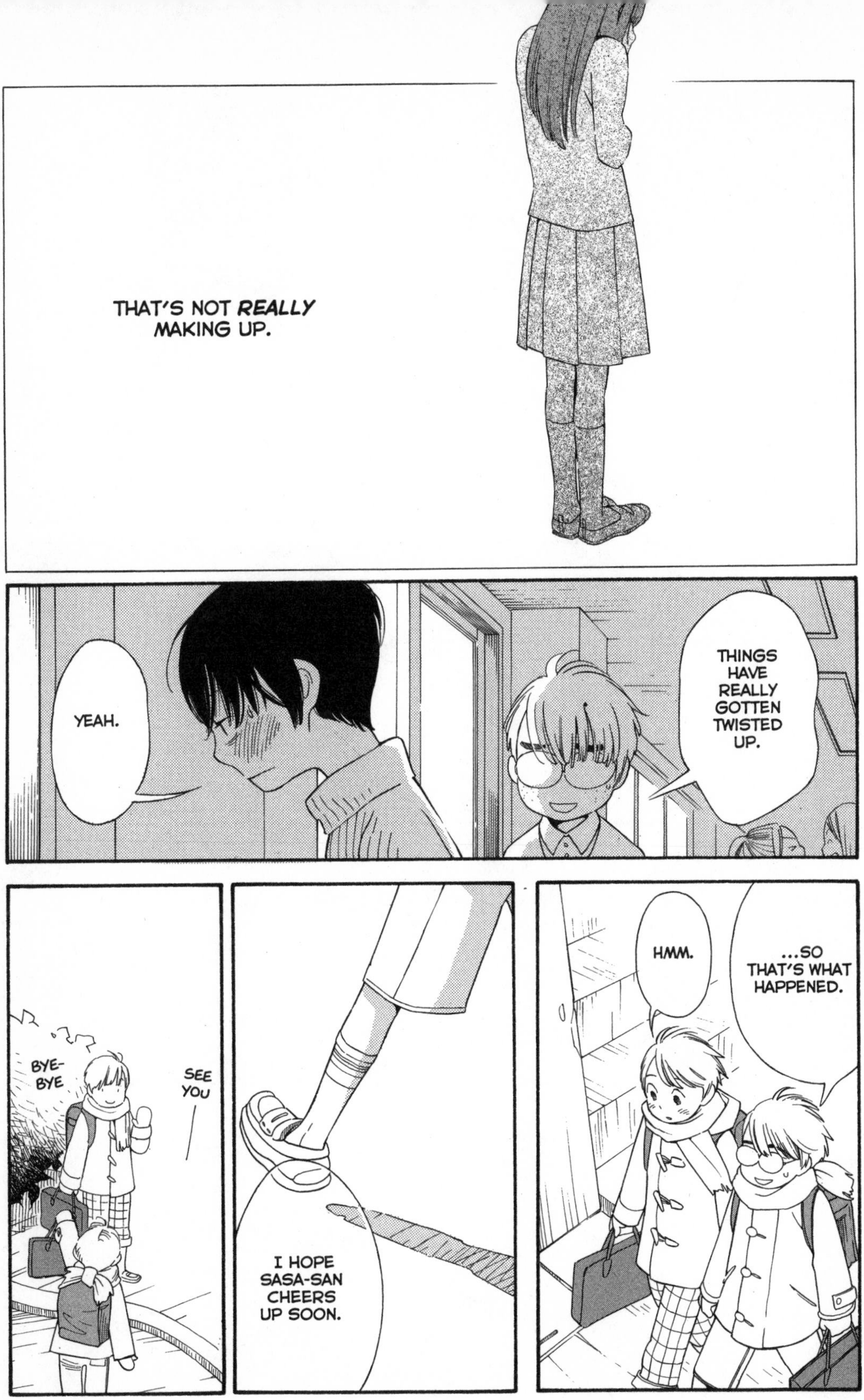
THAT'S NOT *REALLY* MAKING UP.
THINGS HAVE REALLY GOTTEN TWISTED UP.
YEAH.
...SO THAT'S WHAT HAPPENED.
HMM.
I HOPE SASA-SAN CHEERS UP SOON.
SEE YOU
BYE-BYE

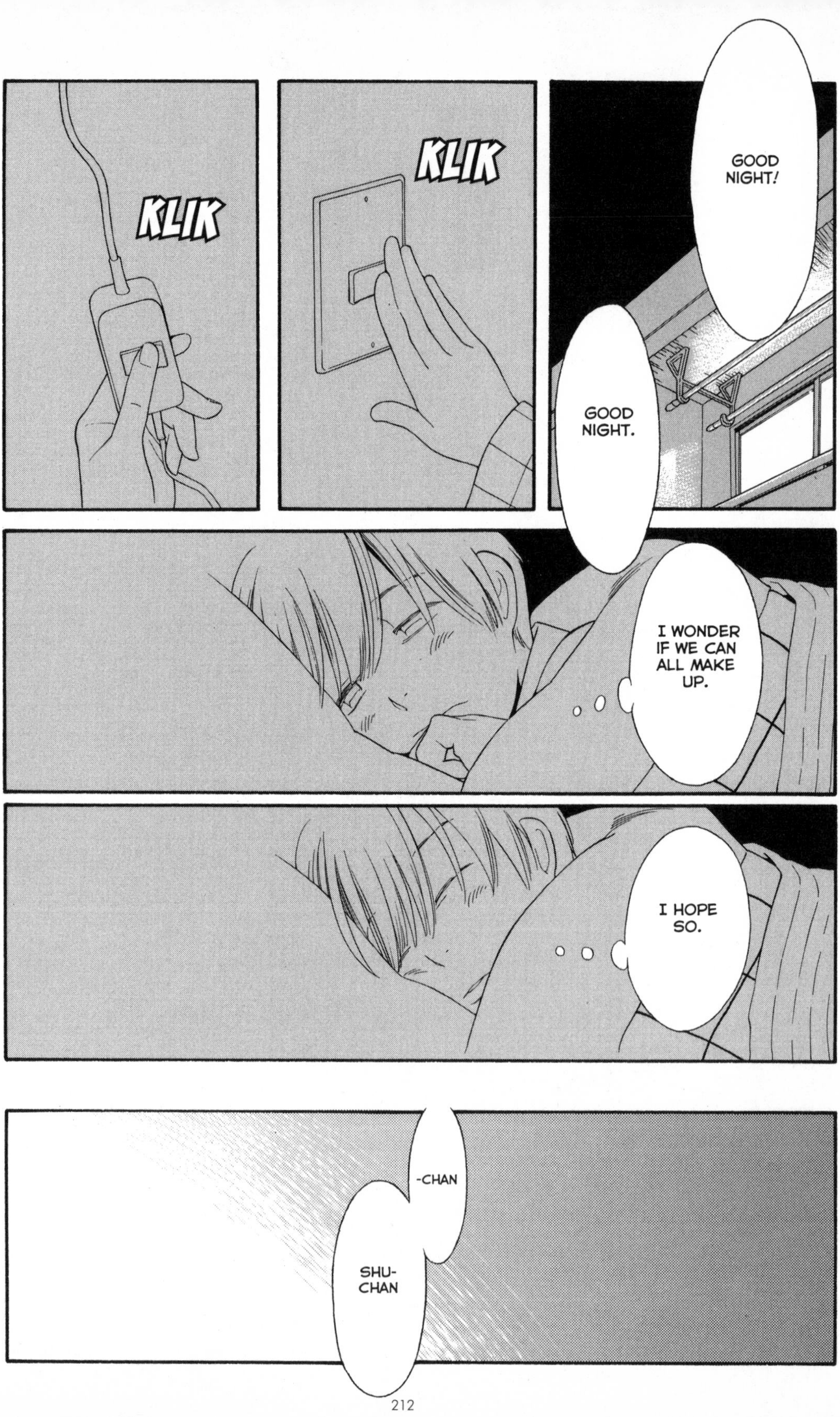
GOOD NIGHT!
GOOD NIGHT.
KLIK
KLIK
I WONDER IF WE CAN ALL MAKE UP.
I HOPE SO.
-CHAN
SHU-CHAN

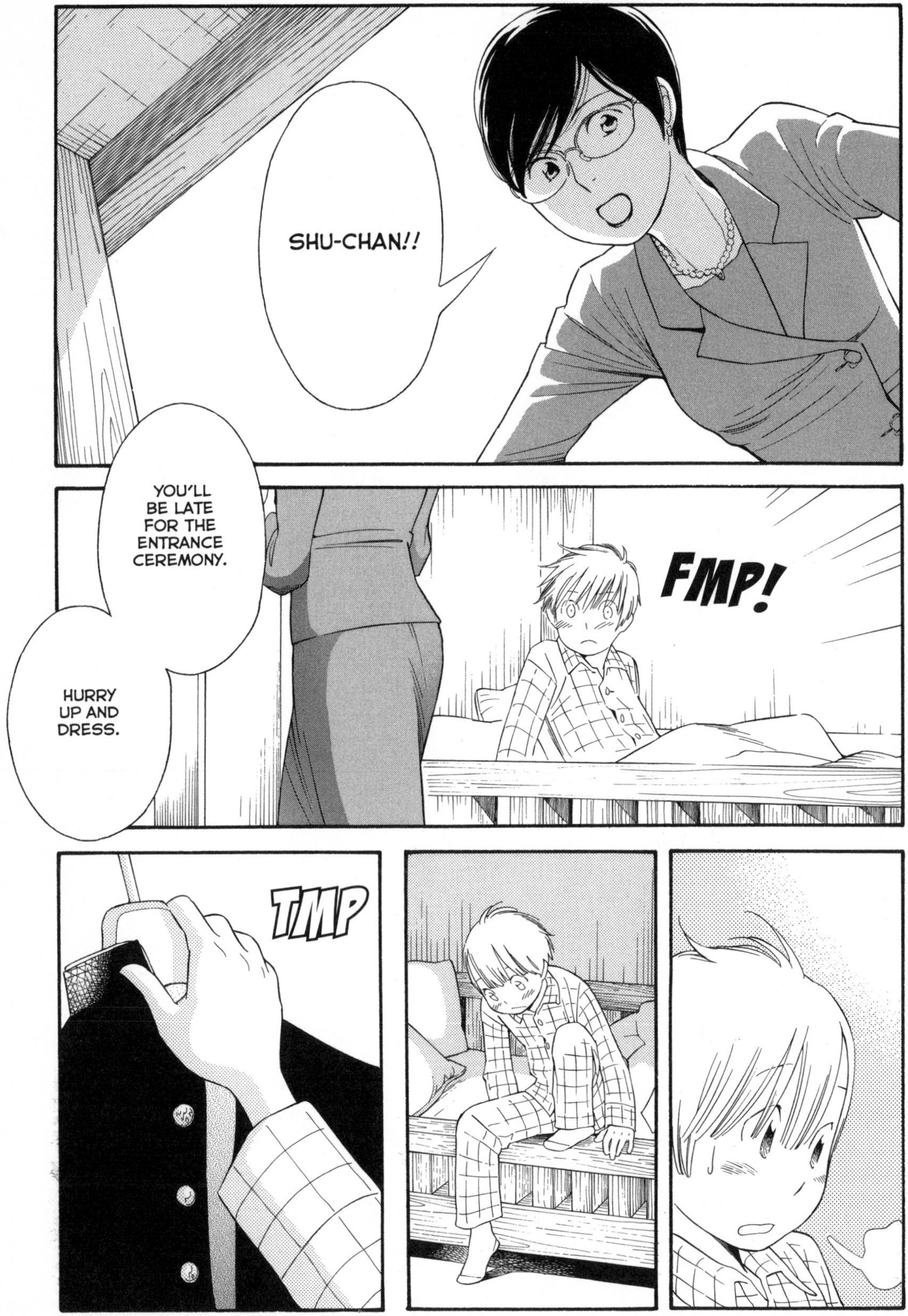
SHU-CHAN!!
FMP!
YOU'LL BE LATE FOR THE ENTRANCE CEREMONY.
HURRY UP AND DRESS.
TMP

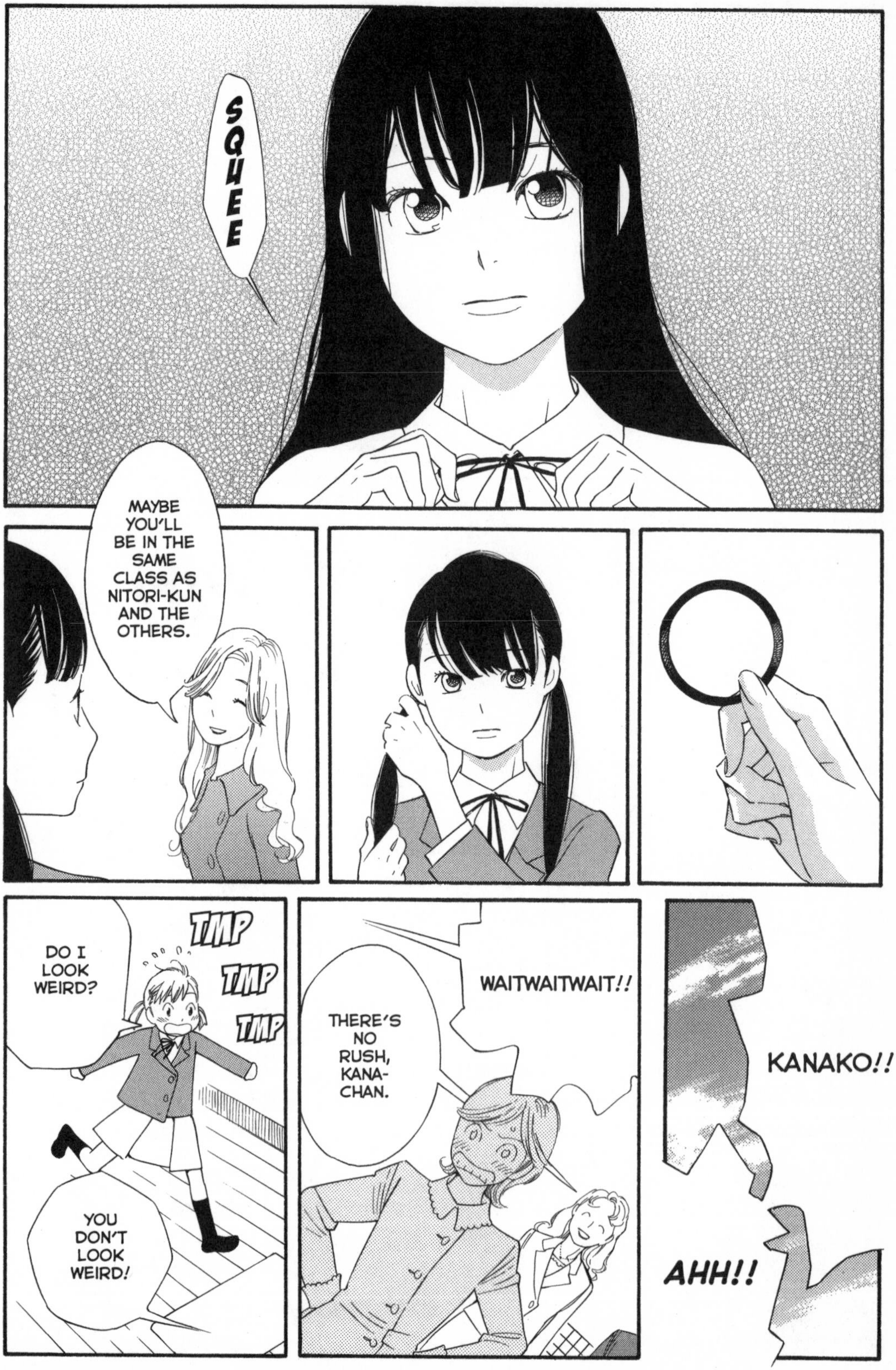

SQUEE
MAYBE YOU'LL BE IN THE SAME CLASS AS NITORI-KUN AND THE OTHERS.
KANAKO!!
AHH!!
WAITWAITWAIT!!
THERE'S NO RUSH, KANA-CHAN.
TMP
TMP
TMP
DO I LOOK WEIRD?
YOU DON'T LOOK WEIRD!

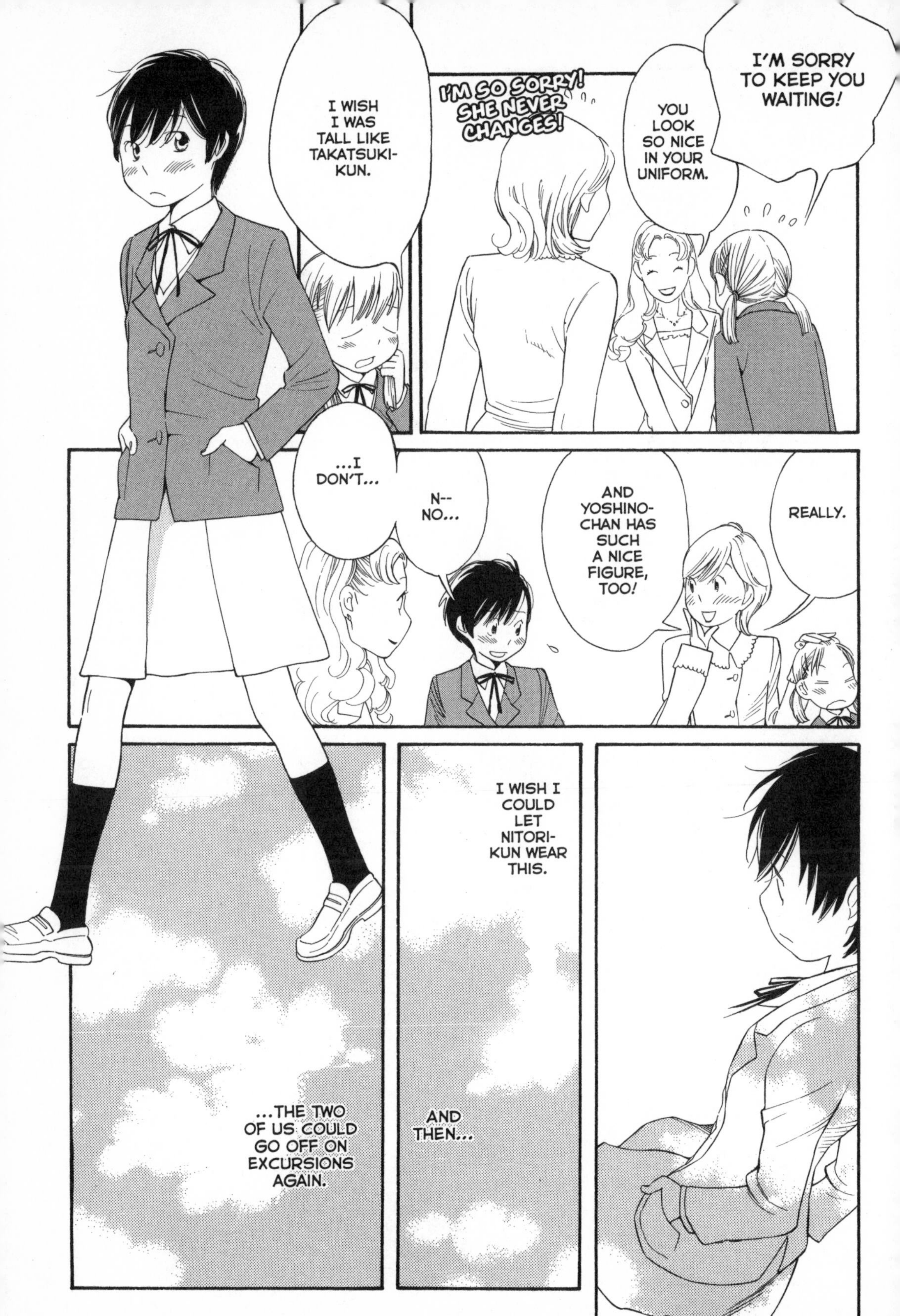
I'M SORRY TO KEEP YOU WAITING!
YOU LOOK SO NICE IN YOUR UNIFORM.
I'M SO SORRY! SHE NEVER CHANGES!
I WISH I WAS TALL LIKE TAKATSUKI-KUN.
REALLY.
AND YOSHINO-CHAN HAS SUCH A NICE FIGURE, TOO!
N-- NO...
...I DON'T...
I WISH I COULD LET NITORI-KUN WEAR THIS.
AND THEN...
...THE TWO OF US COULD GO OFF ON EXCURSIONS AGAIN.

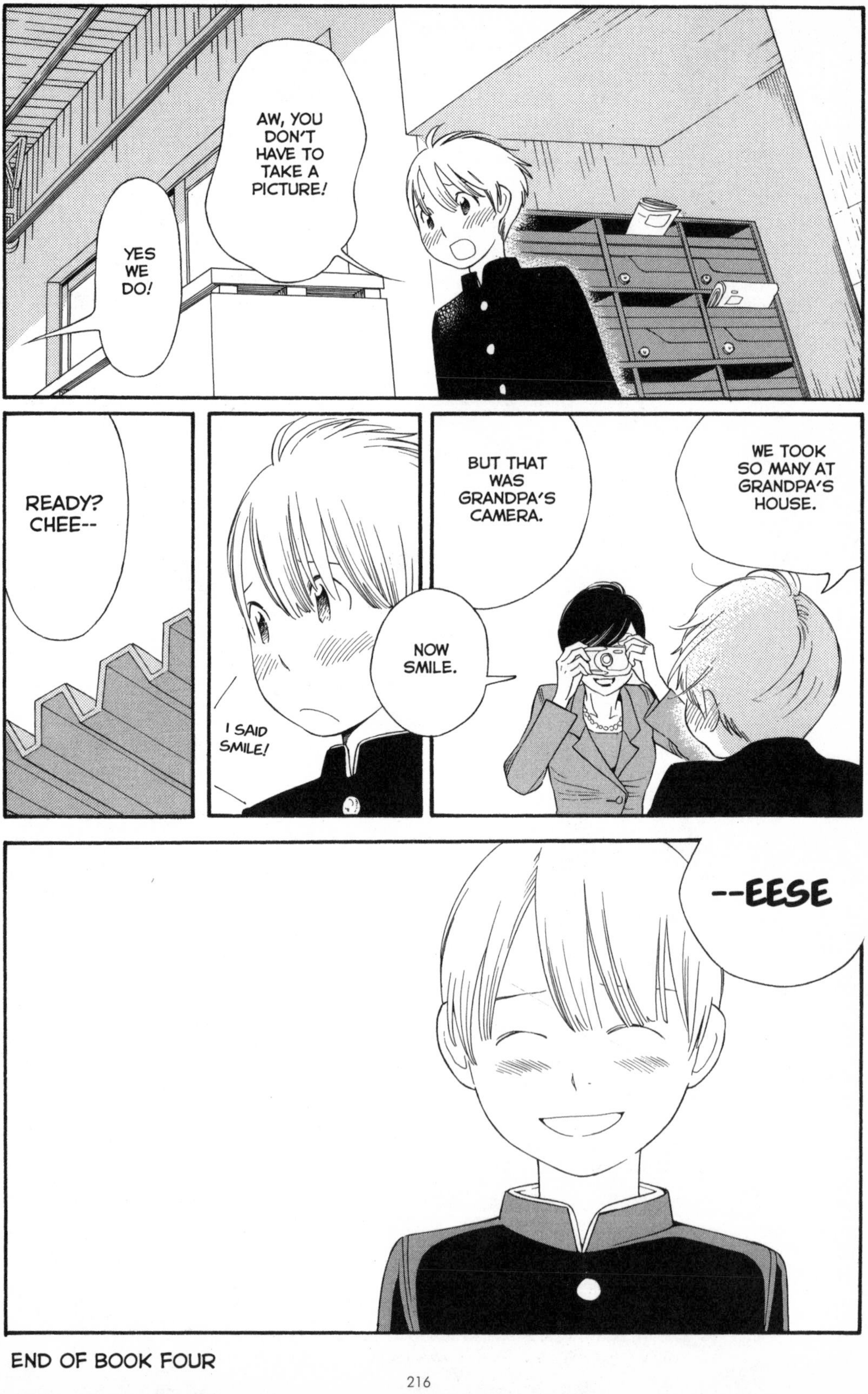
AW, YOU DON'T HAVE TO TAKE A PICTURE!
YES WE DO!
WE TOOK SO MANY AT GRANDPA'S HOUSE.
BUT THAT WAS GRANDPA'S CAMERA.
NOW SMILE.
I SAID SMILE!
READY? CHEE--
--EESE

END OF BOOK FOUR

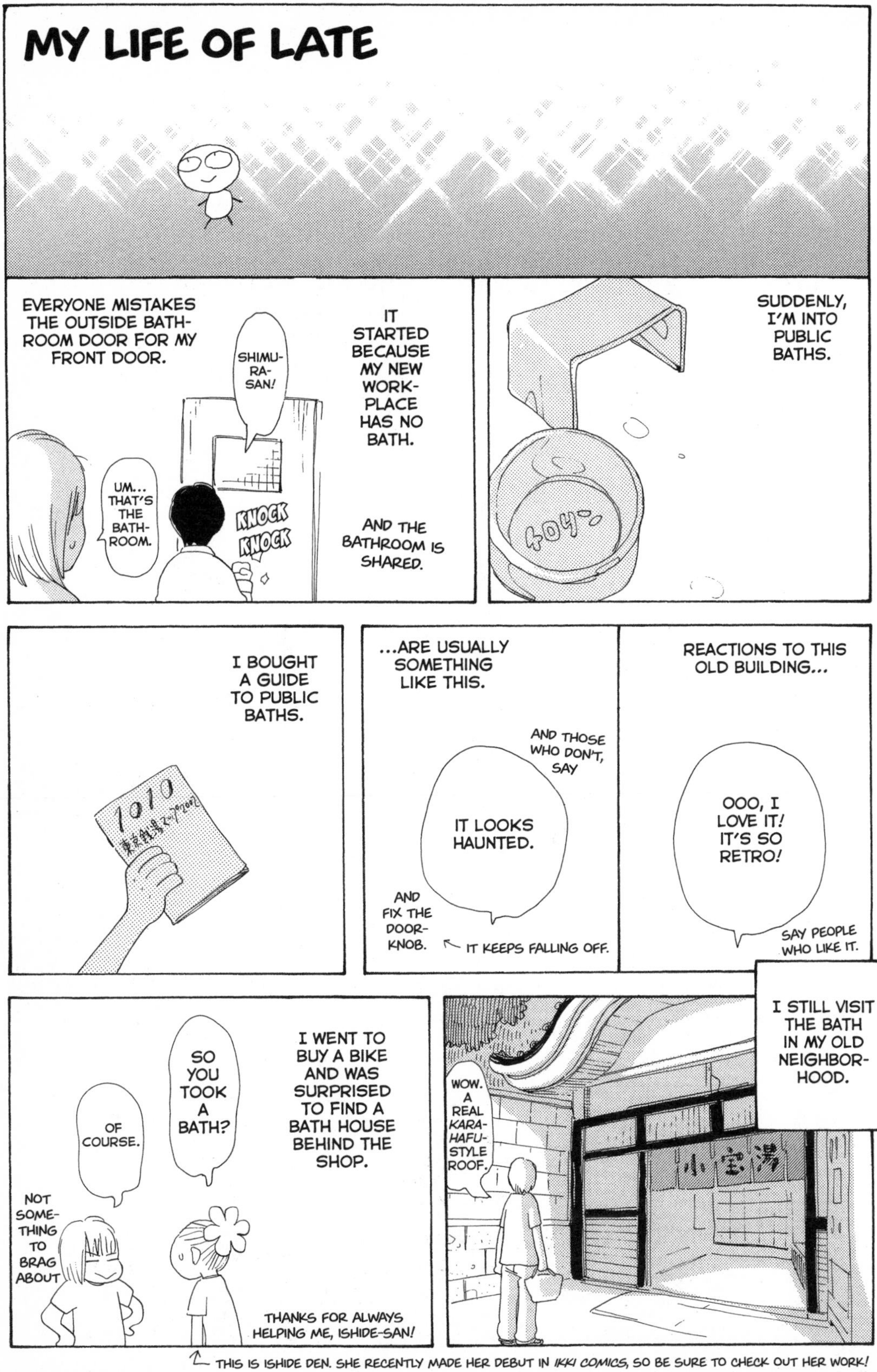
MY LIFE OF LATE
SUDDENLY, I'M INTO PUBLIC BATHS.
IT STARTED BECAUSE MY NEW WORKPLACE HAS NO BATH.
AND THE BATHROOM IS SHARED.
SHIMURA-SAN!
EVERYONE MISTAKES THE OUTSIDE BATHROOM DOOR FOR MY FRONT DOOR.
KNOCK KNOCK
UM... THAT'S THE BATHROOM.
REACTIONS TO THIS OLD BUILDING...
OOO, I LOVE IT! IT'S SO RETRO!
SAY PEOPLE WHO LIKE IT.
...ARE USUALLY SOMETHING LIKE THIS.
AND THOSE WHO DON'T, SAY
IT LOOKS HAUNTED.
AND FIX THE DOORKNOB.
IT KEEPS FALLING OFF.
I BOUGHT A GUIDE TO PUBLIC BATHS.
1010
I STILL VISIT THE BATH IN MY OLD NEIGHBORHOOD.
WOW. A REAL KARAHAFU-STYLE ROOF.
小宝湯
I WENT TO BUY A BIKE AND WAS SURPRISED TO FIND A BATH HOUSE BEHIND THE SHOP.
SO YOU TOOK A BATH?
OF COURSE.
NOT SOMETHING TO BRAG ABOUT
THANKS FOR ALWAYS HELPING ME, ISHIDE-SAN!

↖ THIS IS ISHIDE DEN. SHE RECENTLY MADE HER DEBUT IN *IKKI COMICS*, SO BE SURE TO CHECK OUT HER WORK!

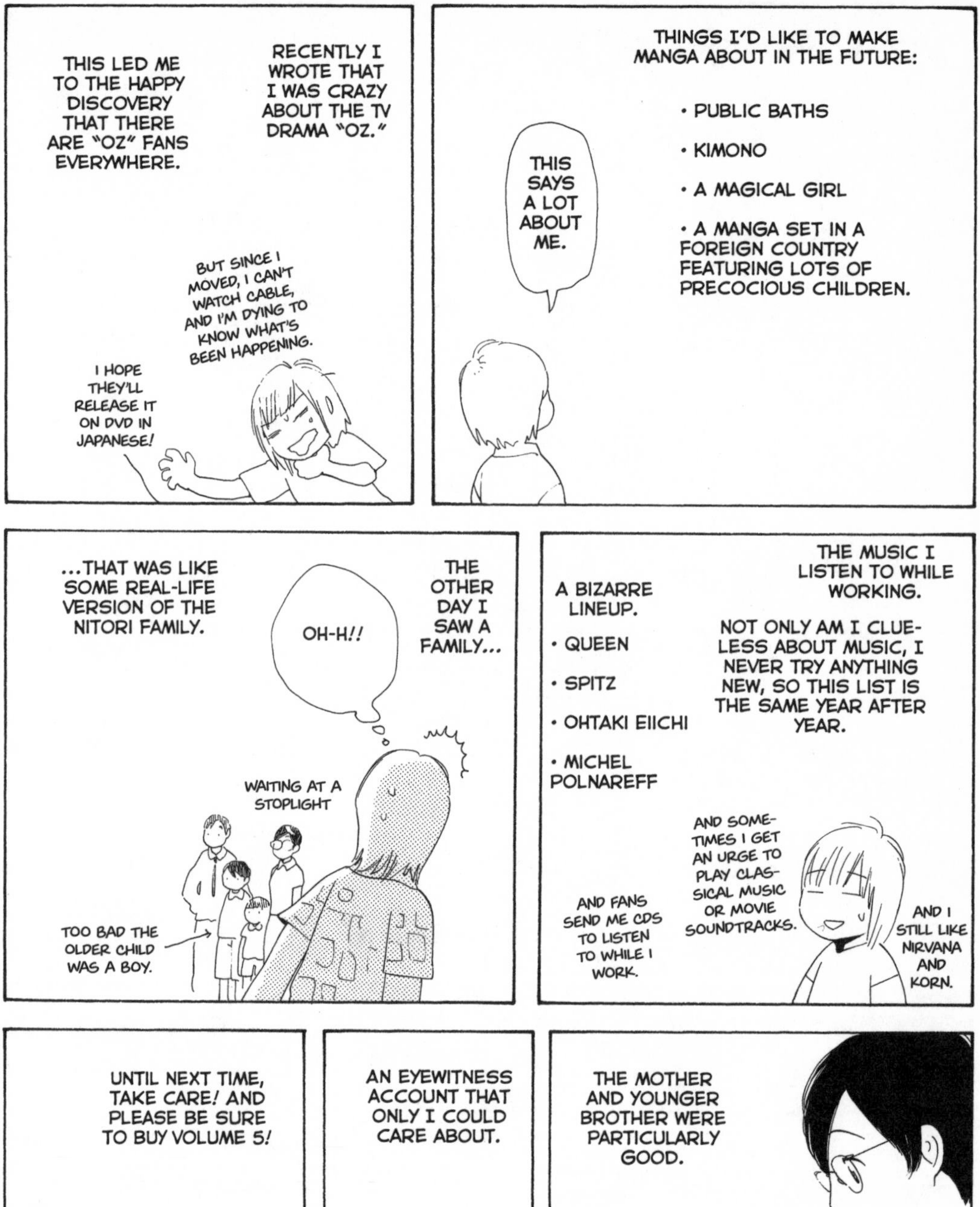
THINGS I'D LIKE TO MAKE MANGA ABOUT IN THE FUTURE:
• PUBLIC BATHS
• KIMONO
• A MAGICAL GIRL
• A MANGA SET IN A FOREIGN COUNTRY FEATURING LOTS OF PRECOCIOUS CHILDREN.
THIS SAYS A LOT ABOUT ME.
RECENTLY I WROTE THAT I WAS CRAZY ABOUT THE TV DRAMA "OZ."
THIS LED ME TO THE HAPPY DISCOVERY THAT THERE ARE "OZ" FANS EVERYWHERE.
BUT SINCE I MOVED, I CAN'T WATCH CABLE, AND I'M DYING TO KNOW WHAT'S BEEN HAPPENING.
I HOPE THEY'LL RELEASE IT ON DVD IN JAPANESE!
THE MUSIC I LISTEN TO WHILE WORKING.
A BIZARRE LINEUP.
• QUEEN
• SPITZ
• OHTAKI EIICHI
• MICHEL POLNAREFF
NOT ONLY AM I CLUELESS ABOUT MUSIC, I NEVER TRY ANYTHING NEW, SO THIS LIST IS THE SAME YEAR AFTER YEAR.
AND I STILL LIKE NIRVANA AND KORN.
AND SOMETIMES I GET AN URGE TO PLAY CLASSICAL MUSIC OR MOVIE SOUNDTRACKS.
AND FANS SEND ME CDS TO LISTEN TO WHILE I WORK.
THE OTHER DAY I SAW A FAMILY...
OH-H!!
...THAT WAS LIKE SOME REAL-LIFE VERSION OF THE NITORI FAMILY.
WAITING AT A STOPLIGHT
TOO BAD THE OLDER CHILD WAS A BOY.
THE MOTHER AND YOUNGER BROTHER WERE PARTICULARLY GOOD.
ARE YOU HOT?
HIS PERFECT BOWL CUT WAS TOO CUTE.
YEAH...
AN EYEWITNESS ACCOUNT THAT ONLY I COULD CARE ABOUT.
THAT WAS AWESOME.
UNTIL NEXT TIME, TAKE CARE! AND PLEASE BE SURE TO BUY VOLUME 5!
THE JUNIOR HIGH YEARS BEGIN! THERE ARE NEW CHARACTERS, TOO. MAKING MANGA EVERYDAY IS SO MUCH FUN.

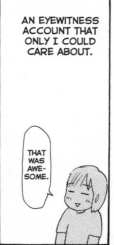

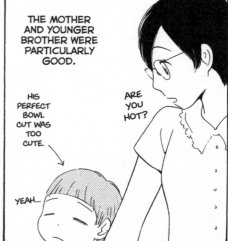

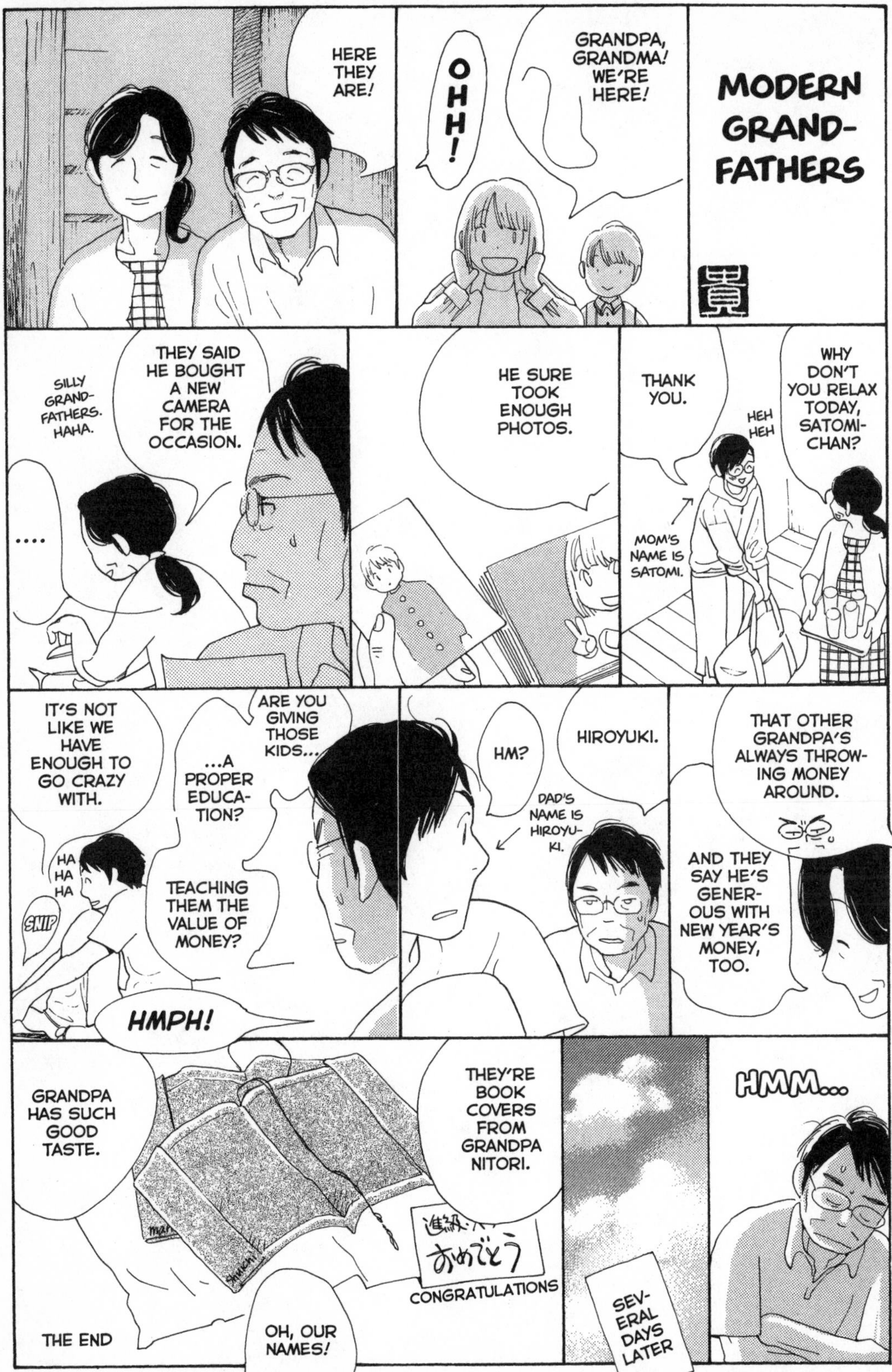
MODERN GRAND-FATHERS
GRANDPA, GRANDMA! WE'RE HERE!
OHH!
HERE THEY ARE!
WHY DON'T YOU RELAX TODAY, SATOMI-CHAN?
HEH HEH
THANK YOU.
MOM'S NAME IS SATOMI.
HE SURE TOOK ENOUGH PHOTOS.
THEY SAID HE BOUGHT A NEW CAMERA FOR THE OCCASION.
SILLY GRAND-FATHERS. HAHA.
....
THAT OTHER GRANDPA'S ALWAYS THROWING MONEY AROUND.
AND THEY SAY HE'S GENEROUS WITH NEW YEAR'S MONEY, TOO.
HIROYUKI.
HM?
DAD'S NAME IS HIROYUKI.
ARE YOU GIVING THOSE KIDS...
...A PROPER EDUCATION?
TEACHING THEM THE VALUE OF MONEY?
IT'S NOT LIKE WE HAVE ENOUGH TO GO CRAZY WITH.
HA HA HA
SNIP
HMPH!
HMM...
SEV-ERAL DAYS LATER
THEY'RE BOOK COVERS FROM GRANDPA NITORI.
進級
おめでとう
CONGRATULATIONS
GRANDPA HAS SUCH GOOD TASTE.
OH, OUR NAMES!
THE END

STOP!

THE MANGA IN THIS BOOK IS "UNFLIPPED." MEANING PAGES RUN BACK-TO-FRONT AND PANELS START AT THE TOP-RIGHT AND END ON THE BOTTOM-LEFT. TURN THIS PAGE AND YOU'LL BE AT THE END OF THE STORY. FLIP THE BOOK AROUND FOR A MUCH MORE SATISFYING READING EXPERIENCE.

PRONUNCIATION
GUIDE

VOWELS

a   as in "f<u>a</u>ther"

i   as in "spaghett<u>i</u>"

u   as in "p<u>u</u>t"

e   as in "th<u>e</u>m"

o   as in "p<u>o</u>le"

"Long" vowels are usually indicated by a macron ("ō"), circumflex ("ô") or diaeresis ("ö"), although sometimes the vowel is simply repeated. In personal names, a long "o" is sometimes represented as "oh." In cases where one vowel is followed immediately by a different vowel, but is not in the same syllable, they are often separated by a dash or apostrophe to indicate the end of one syllable and beginning of another. Here are common pairs of vowels that sound to the English-speaker's ear like one syllable (and thus are not separated):

ai   as in "m<u>y</u>"

ei   as in "r<u>ay</u>"

oi   as in "t<u>oy</u>"

ao   as in "c<u>ow</u>"

CONSONANTS *that require clarification*

g   as in "get" (never as in "age")

s   as in "soft" (never like "rise")

t   as in "tale" (never like "d")

ch   as in "church"

ACCENTS

Most English words have "accented" and "un-accented" syllables. This is generally not the case in Japanese, which is more "flat." When English speakers encounter a new word, they tend to accent the first syllable if it has two syllables, the second if it has three, and after that they wing it. If you can't resist accenting a syllable in a Japanese word, accent the first and you'll be fine.

HONORIFICS
GUIDE

This translation retains certain Japanese honorifics which (hopefully) will help the reader to better grasp the atmosphere and, more importantly, the relative relationships of the characters to each other. Here's a simple glossary of the honorofics you'll find.

-san: The best-known and most common honorific, it is, in most cases, neutrally polite and applicable to both sexes and between people of differing ages. Some women or girls can be very intimate, yet never stop addressing each other as -san. In school or in the workplace, -san is more commonly used in addressing girls and women. When in doubt, surname + san will get you through most situations.

-kun: A form of address used most commonly in speaking to younger boys or men, but which can also be used in speaking to younger girls or women. Some bosses will address all their subordinates as -kun, regardless of the subordinate's gender. As a rule, it is never used to address someone older, even if that person is "junior" to the speaker within the school or workplace. School teachers are generally expected to address girls as -san and boys as -kun, though some male teachers will gruffly call a pupil by his or her surname, with no honorific.

-chan: An affectionate, diminutive form of -san. It is commonly used among family members for both sexes, and for girls among close friends. When it is used in speaking to or of a boy or man among friends, it is usually because it has become part of a nickname. Despite all the rules of who should address whom in what manner, when it comes to nicknames (which are very common in Japan), anything goes.

sensei: This is both a title and an honorific, used to address a teacher or any accomplished scholar, writer, or artist. It can be applied with equal validity to your aerobics teacher and a Nobel Prize Laureate.

Note that given names are generally used only by family members or fairly close acquaintances or friends. For the most part, Japanese call each other by their surnames. In particular, boys in the same grade are likely to call each other by surnames, without any honorific, or by nicknames. Girls are more likely to err on the side of politeness. Calling someone with whom you are not intimate by his or her given name is considered presumptuous and can be seen as rude.

The honorifics I've introduced should not be taken at face value in every case. Japanese will sometimes use them in inappropriate situations, either consciously (with irony or malice) or unconsciously (because they have misread the nature of a relationship). Honorifics can also be omitted as a show of contempt. (Addressing someone older than yourself without using an honorific is akin to a slap in the face.)

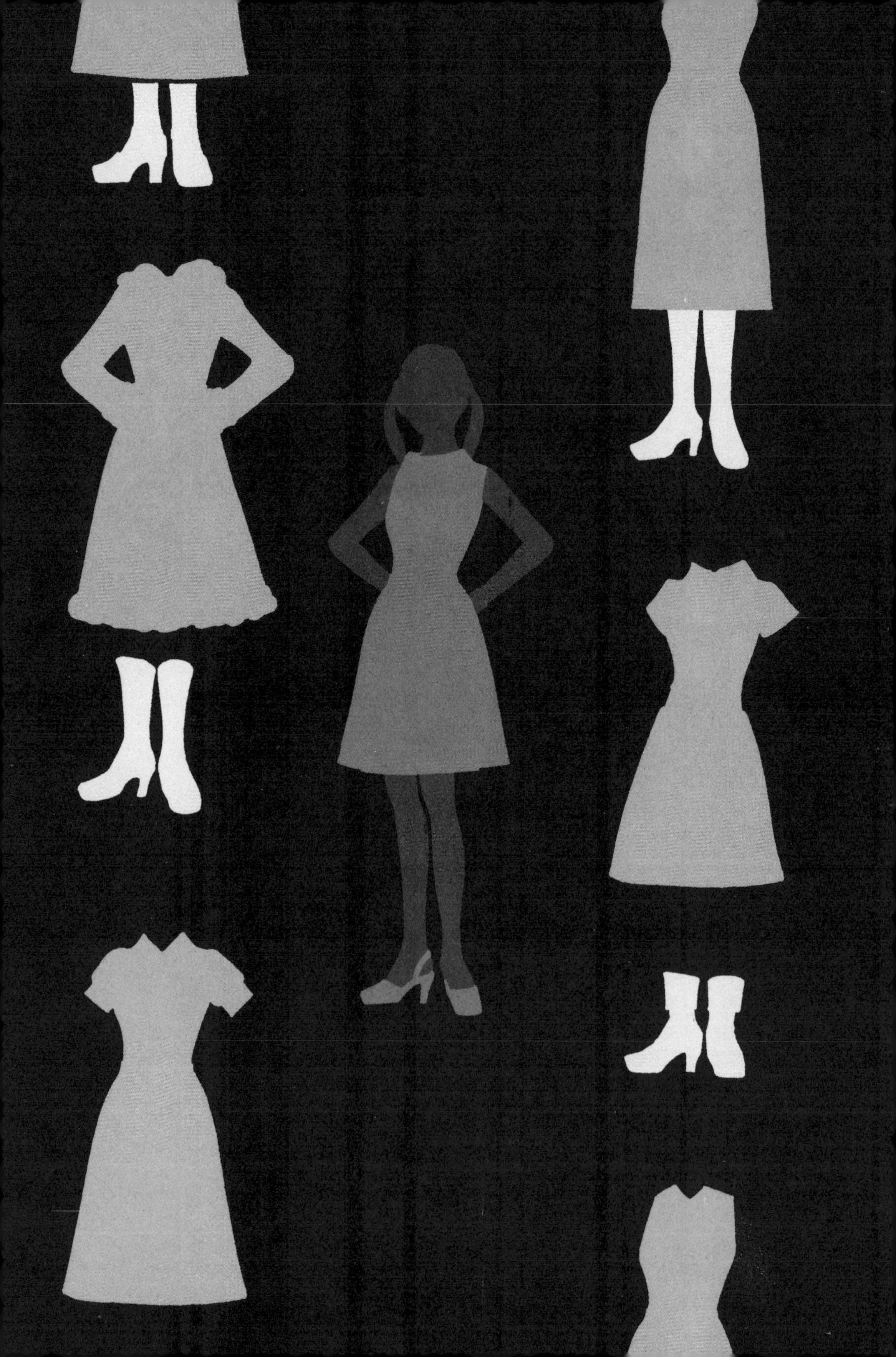